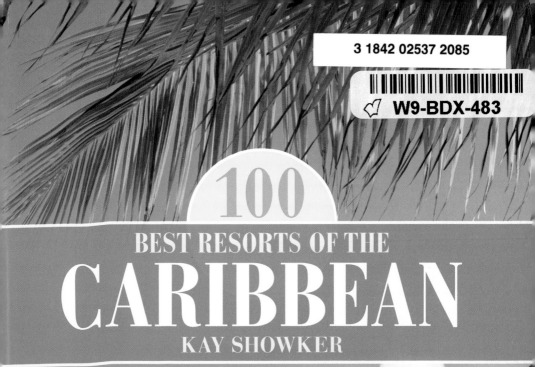

100
BEST RESORTS OF THE
CARIBBEAN
KAY SHOWKER

NINTH EDITION

gpp
travel
Globe Pequot Press
Guilford, Connecticut

The prices, rates, and hours listed in this guidebook were confirmed at press time, but we do not guarantee them. Rather, we recommend that you contact the resort to obtain current information before traveling.

To buy books in quantity for corporate use
or incentives, call **(800) 962-0973**
or e-mail **premiums@GlobePequot.com.**

Editor: Amy Lyons
Project Editor: Heather Santiago
Layout: Joanna Beyer
Text Design: Sheryl Kober
Map: Stefanie Ward © Morris Book Publishing, LLC

ISSN 1546-5799
ISBN 978-0-7627-7152-3

Printed in the United States of America
10 9 8 7 6 5 4 3 2 1

CONTENTS

Contents

Contents

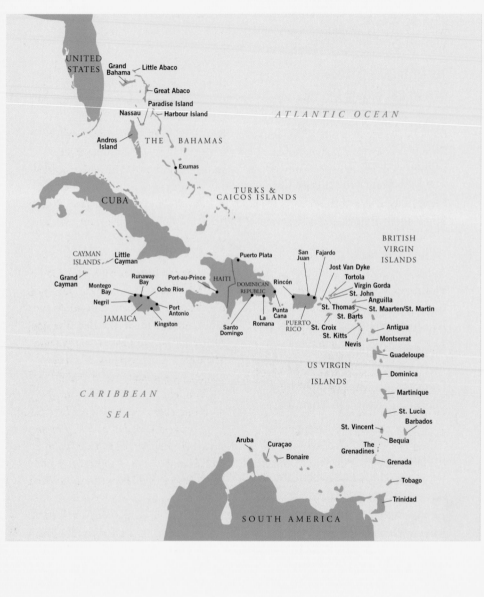

INTRODUCTION

Ask any ten Caribbean cognoscente to name the best or even their favorite resort in the Caribbean and you will probably get ten different answers. You will certainly start an argument.

In the 30 years or so that I've been writing about the Caribbean, the questions I'm asked most often are "What's your favorite place?" and "What's the best place to stay?" It is not surprising, since the choice of a hotel is usually a traveler's first concern. But the best resort, like beauty, is in the eye of the beholder. And resorts, like people, differ. Not every resort suits everyone's needs and style.

Any of us can recognize high quality and good service. We all appreciate good architectural design and interior decor. But to be the best, a hotel or resort must have that "something special" that is almost impossible to define and strikes each of us differently.

Then, too, there was a time when the choices in the Caribbean were clearer, because good resorts were few. But now, after three decades of steady building throughout the region, the number has more than doubled (the Caribbean Hotel Association's reference guide lists over 2,500 entries). The choice is more difficult, but, happily, the selection is more interesting.

Consider, too, that these hotels, inns, and resorts are spread over nearly 40 separate islands, or island groups, and you will see that the task is daunting. *100 Best Resorts of the Caribbean* is meant to make the choice easier. Most people do not want or need the standard long list of hotels with only short descriptions that appear in most Caribbean guidebooks; they prefer some selectivity, and selectivity is precisely the aim of this book.

Because standards vary so much from island to island, it is difficult to set up arbitrary rules or criteria to apply across the board. What passes as the best in Trinidad may be only acceptable in Anguilla. What has some travelers turned on in St. Barts would be turned down in Jamaica. A great deal also has to do with an island's tradition—British, French, Dutch, Spanish—and the kind of tourists it attracts.

The Caribbean best are recognized by the same attention to detail and quality of service, food, care, comfort, and facilities that distinguish the best hotels and resorts around the world. But in judging the Caribbean, you have to be generous. There are many problems in trying to operate a top-quality resort in the Tropics. This, coupled with the region's high operating costs, means that the best tend to be equated with the most expensive.

Yet it would have been a mistake to include only the most expensive resorts. The selection would have been easy, but you don't need me to tell you which are the 100 most expensive hotels in the Caribbean. Any good travel agent can tell you that. What's more, being expensive is no guarantee of being the best—or even good—and there are some real dogs out there. Rather, consideration was given to ambience, historic setting, management style, uniqueness, and other elements that make some resorts the best for other than traditional reasons.

What impresses me, even after all these years, is the enormous variety the Caribbean offers. I wanted this book to reflect that variety and to represent a broad range of establishments: large and small, beachside and hillside, modest and deluxe, homey and elegant. I made a conscious effort to provide diversity, choosing the resorts I considered the best in each category. The selections run the gamut from rustic retreats to private island hideaways to large, full-service layouts. They range in their degree of luxury from minimal to extravagant, from back-to-nature Maho Bay Camp on St. John, US Virgin Islands, at one end and posh Cap Juluca on Anguilla at the other.

What is a Resort?

But first, what is a resort? Because my selection covers such a broad range, you may wonder how I define *resort,* and you will certainly want to know the criteria I used.

Webster's defines *resort* as a place providing recreation and entertainment, especially to vacationers. *Roget's Thesaurus* and *Rodale's The Synonym Finder* list *hotel, inn, club, lodge, spa, watering place, and camp* as synonyms. This book includes places fitting all these appellations, along with *haven, hideaway,* and *retreat.*

But let me make it simple. I define resort as "a place to go for a vacation." It is a broad definition, but it reflects a reality—namely, that vacationers are an extremely diverse group whose ideas of a vacation differ as much as their interests, needs, and expectations. What is paradise for one person might be hell for another.

For some people the ideal resort is a pleasure palace by the sea—the more luxurious, the more pampering, the more exclusive, the better. For others it is the exact opposite. They willingly trade creature comforts to be close to nature with as few man-made intrusions as possible.

Then there are the honeymooners, golfers, divers, birders, hikers; those who want action; those who want serenity; others who care about cuisine; those who take family vacations; those who want to be directly on the beach; others who want a vacation in the mountains; those who select a resort by the variety of sports and recreation available; those who care little about activities. All of these people will find resorts in this guide to suit them.

Criteria

So what were my criteria? To be the best a resort needs a combination of factors: location, setting, layout, service, appearance, ambience, dining experience, sports facilities, management, and staff. But then it must have something beyond these—the intangibles, that *je ne sais quoi.*

Maybe it's warmth, maybe it's style. It is a certain quality, a feeling that is hard to define but that you know instinctively when you find it. When I described my dilemma to a fellow writer, he replied instantly, "Yes, I know what you mean. Would you want to spend a week there?"

"That's it," I replied. "That's it."

Would you want to spend a week there? And perhaps more important, at the end of the week, do you long to return? Every entry in this book was put to that test. There were other tests, too. Does the resort live up to the goals it designed for itself? Does it fulfill its role—whatever the style, price, category—better than any other?

Another important criterion: The resort had to have been in business for at least one year. Most of those included here have been around much longer than a year; they have stood the test of time. Some that opened in the last year or so, and hold promise of being among the best are listed in the "On the Horizon" section at the end of the book.

Certainly some testing was influenced by my personal likes and dislikes. When I go to the Caribbean, I want to know I'm in the Caribbean. I want to feast on its beauty as well as its bounty, to feel the balmy air and hear the sea. My ideal resort takes advantage of its location; it lets the trade winds cool the air and blow away the sand flies. Its rooms and restaurants are open to the sea, with breezy balconies and splendid views. Architecture is to me as important as ambience—the two work together to make a place special. Good architectural design fits its environment and helps create the ambience. I also care a great deal about the Caribbean's heritage—natural, historical, cultural—and have more to say about this later in the Green Leaf Awards section.

I like places that make me feel good as soon as my taxi pulls up to the front door. I like places that look as though they are expecting you, from an alert doorman to a friendly check-in desk to a bellhop who tells me everything I need to know about my room and points out the features of the hotel that I am likely to need soon after my arrival. I appreciate one who takes the time to find the luggage rack and place my suitcase on it, and checks the ice bucket or water in the fridge to ensure that I can have a cool drink of water after my long trip.

Little things mean a lot: good reading lights, firm mattresses, efficient bathrooms with a place for toiletries, fresh flowers, lit footpaths or flashlights to light the way. I like omnipresent but unobtrusive managers, and I want to shake hands with the person minding the store.

Although I let my experience guide me, I sought the opinions and advice of many others—travel agents and other writers who specialize in the Caribbean, hoteliers with long Caribbean experience, friends who live in the Caribbean, and dozens of vacationers I met along the way. They were particularly helpful in highlighting the features that had made their visit to a particular resort memorable. But in the end the choices are mine. So, too, are the comments and criticism.

The Goal

My principal objective in the resort profiles was to define a resort's personality and stress the elements that make it different and distinctive from other resorts to enable you to identify with those best suited for you. But defining a resort's personality is not an exact science. Sometimes it is the history of the structure that helped shape the resort's character, sometimes the owner or manager whose imprint is indelible, sometimes the setting, the staff, the ambience, or a specific feature—or all of the above.

In the beginning I thought finding 100 different ways to describe 100 different resorts would be the hardest part about writing this book. Instead, I found that the resorts have such distinctive personalities, the descriptions almost wrote themselves. In a way the ease of writing about them further confirmed my choices.

Small Versus Large

Those who know the Caribbean well will not be surprised to learn that out of the total 100 resorts in this book, more than half have fewer than 50 rooms, and 41 have fewer than 30 rooms. Less than a fourth are large resorts with a hundred or more rooms. This was not a deliberate decision. In fact, I had not even analyzed the numbers until after I had written all the entries.

There's no mystery about the results. Big resorts are better known because they have the muscle to market and promote themselves, but small ones of fewer than 50 rooms are more typical of the Caribbean and are its strength, providing a more authentic Caribbean experience.

Small hotels have a personality— that's what makes them worthy of attention—while large ones tend to be homogenized. Let me quickly add, however, that the large resorts included here run counter to the norm; they, too, have strong character.

The size of a hotel makes a difference in the type of Caribbean holiday you have. Large hotels have a greater array of activities and facilities, a busier atmosphere, and more round-the-clock staff and services than a small hotel, where the atmosphere is usually quiet and very relaxed.

At the smallest ones you get more personal care and attention from the manager, who is often the owner, and from the staff, who will call you by name and learn your preferences from the first day of your visit. Usually you feel as though you are a guest in a friend's home or at a weekend house party. The service may not be as polished as at large resorts, but it is warm and genuine.

Commitment

The Caribbean is full of wonderful stories about people with a dream. Owning a small hotel in the Caribbean is a fantasy that's right up there in popularity with buying a boat and sailing around the world. So irrepressible is the idea that many, many people have done it and continue to do it. Most give up after a few years when they learn how difficult it is to run a really good hotel in the Caribbean. The innkeepers in this book are people who made it; invariably, they reflect the high degree of personal commitment it takes to succeed.

Amenities

Many small hotels, including some of the most expensive, do not have air-conditioning, television, or phones in the rooms. Not having a phone is a blessing to some people, an inconvenience to others. The Calabash in Grenada has the ideal solution: All guest rooms have telephones—along with a printed note that says, "The phone will be removed if you find it a nuisance." On the other hand, many hotels have recognized the inevitable and have installed wireless Internet access and accept the use of cell phones with specific restrictions as to where and when they can be used. Not all cell phones work on all islands, however.

As for air-conditioning, you may be surprised (I was amazed) to discover how many resorts don't have it—and don't need it. Ceiling fans and natural breezes do a better job. Generally, the absence of air-conditioning in a good hotel says the structure was built to be architecturally sensitive to its setting.

In the past Caribbean hoteliers believed they could not attract guests, particularly Americans, if they did not have air-conditioning. But during the oil crises of the 1970s, when skyrocketing fuel bills almost put them out of business, many returned to Mother Nature out of necessity. The response from guests was so positive that more followed suit and frequently went to solar power—a trend that has picked up momentum with the recent escalating cost of oil and concern over protecting the fragile Caribbean environment.

Architects with Caribbean experience have long since abandoned square concrete-block hotels in favor of styles that suit the natural environment, stressing open-air dining, louvered windows and doors, shaded terraces, and tile and terra-cotta floors. What a joy!

Paradise isn't Perfect

Even the best resorts aren't perfect. Where I feel it's warranted, I point out weaknesses. And you may notice that I save my toughest judgment for the posh corners of paradise, where prices unhappily have risen to heights as heavenly as the pleasures. To me, expensive resorts have a greater responsibility to deliver what they promise than those that keep rates low and don't try to be fancy. Higher rates, however, are usually justified as the degree of luxury increases, because almost everything is imported, and catering to Americans—a demanding lot—is costly. Nonetheless, people who seek luxury still want their money's worth.

Maintenance in the Tropics, government taxes, and service charges also drive up costs. High labor costs and restrictive policies—often more politically than economically motivated, because hotels are usually the island's largest employers—are contributing factors, too. Which brings me to the matter of service.

Service

The Caribbean offers service at a stroll. Swift, at-the-snap-of-a-finger, professional service is unusual. If that's your yardstick for judging service, you'll be disappointed even in the best of the best places. If you require this kind of service to be happy, the Caribbean is the wrong place for you.

Caring, cheerful, and thoughtful service from a friendly staff, not speed or polish, are the criteria on which to make a judgment here. Turn off your motor, leave your watch at home, relax. This is not a cop-out or apology for service in the Caribbean. Rather, it is said to help you enjoy your vacation by knowing the parameters within which Caribbean resorts operate.

Careers in service industries are only now getting the respect they deserve from people who, having passed from colonialism to independence, traditionally equated such work with servitude. Fortunately, this attitude is fading as islanders have come to recognize their need for tourism and as local ownership of hotels has broadened. Professionalism, too, is increasing as training and opportunities grow and the hospitality profession, as it matures, offers meaningful advancement to young people.

Cuisine

The time has come for travelers and travel writers to stop saying, "You can't get a good meal in the Caribbean." It simply isn't true. I've enjoyed wonderful meals from the Bahamas to Trinidad. It's neither difficult, nor impossible; too many restaurants and hotels have demonstrated otherwise.

In judging a resort I gave cuisine a great deal of attention. Some places have brought a quality and creativity to their cuisine not associated with the Caribbean in the past. Many have young, imaginative chefs who are turning out great dishes. Now, too, culinary competitions islandwide and regionwide are regular events and have stimulated participants to be creative and innovative.

Trouble in Paradise

Idyllic places today must be more than pretty to get our attention and gain

our loyalty. They must be reasonably efficient, if not always convenient, and secure. Trouble in paradise is troubling whenever it rears its ugly head, but with the exception of a few islands—ironically, those that have the most tourists—crime is less of a problem at hotels in the Caribbean than in any major city in the United States.

We who live by security systems and double-bolted doors have forgotten what it's like not to worry about security. But imagine! There are still Caribbean islands where people don't lock their doors. And there are still resorts where you aren't given a room key because they don't have them—or need them.

Crawling Critters

Welcome to the Tropics. If this is your first visit, I have some explaining to do. If you have been to Florida or the Mississippi Delta, you already know about bugs and other creatures that thrive in warm, humid climates. Ninety-nine percent are harmless. "I saw a roach 2 inches long," I've heard visitors new to the Tropics say. And I reply, "Yes, I see them often."

This is true even at the best Caribbean resorts. Recently, at one of the very finest, most expensive resorts in this book, I opened a drawer, and there it was—a huge water bug flat on its back, dead.

You'll also see geckos or chameleons and, after the first shock, you'll grow fond of them, like pets. They are wonderfully interesting to watch; some have great color, too.

At certain times of the year, mosquitoes can be fierce, particularly after a rain. I know; they love me. I never go anywhere without insect repellent. Most good hotels provide a can of repellent in their guest rooms and usually have a can on hand at the bar. People with allergies may have a problem using repellents and should consult their doctors. Needless to say, in air-conditioned places you are less likely to be bothered. It's the best reason I know for air-conditioning.

How the Book is Organized

100 Best Resorts of the Caribbean is organized alphabetically by island or island group. Each island or island group starts with an island profile intended as no more than a quick introduction. I have made the assumption that you have been to the Caribbean before or have other guidebooks by me or other writers with the nitty-gritty details for planning a vacation. Within each island or island group, the resorts are also listed alphabetically.

At the end of each resort's entry, you will find an information block providing standard information on the resort usually not included in the text, such as where to make reservations or how much local tax or service charges are levied. Other information, such as room amenities like television and air-conditioning or sports facilities, such as tennis courts and water-sports equipment, is also listed for quick reference. If, however, a resort is known for a particular sport like golf or diving, more information on its special features is provided in the text.

Seasons & Symbols

There is absolutely no uniformity in designating the beginning and ending of high season and low season in the Caribbean. The dates differ from island to island and hotel to hotel. Unless specified to the contrary, the definitions throughout this book are those used generally in the region: High season is the winter months from mid-December to mid-April; low season is comprised of the balance of the year when hotel rates are reduced by 30 percent or more. More and more resorts are adding a third season, known as the shoulder season (mid-Apr to late May and/or Sept to Oct), when rates are also reduced substantially.

Rates peak during holiday periods, particularly during Christmas and New Year's and in February, when most resorts require a one-week or longer stay. When your priority is a winter vacation, paradise can be pricey, but you can often save a bundle by shifting slightly from March to mid-April or by going in November instead of December. And do not overlook packages. Even the fanciest resorts have them, particularly in the shoulder and low seasons. They usually represent meaningful savings and have additional bonus features.

Rates found at the end of each resort indicate the resort's price range rather than the rates for each different type of accommodation. All rates are subject to change, and if the past is prologue, they will change. Consult the resort or its US reservations or a travel agent who can get the most current information. Prices are quoted in US dollars unless indicated otherwise.

The symbols used are as follows:

EP   (European Plan): Room only, no meals.

CP   (Continental Plan): Room with continental breakfast.

FAB   (Full American Breakfast): Room with full American breakfast.

MAP   (Modified American Plan): Room with breakfast and dinner.

AP   (American Plan): Room with three meals daily.

FAP   (Full American Plan): Room with three meals; full American breakfast daily.

ALL-INCLUSIVE:

The rate includes accommodations, all meals, on-premises sports and entertainment, drinks, tax, and service.

You should know that many resorts call themselves all-inclusive or say they have all-inclusive packages when in fact they do not. The hotel's brochure spells out what is and is not included. It is important to read the fine print.

Facilities

Almost any of the resorts in this book can arrange those sports not available at their property and island tours or boat trips to nearby islands. Most have tennis and beachside sports, but it is important when you compare prices to factor in these additional costs when the use of facilities is not included in room rates.

Dress Code

Specific guidelines are given under each resort, as the code does vary, but generally throughout the Caribbean, dress during the day and evening is casual and informal. This, however, does not mean sloppy, tacky, or tasteless.

West Indians are often quite offended by the way some tourists dress. Hotel owners are also. They ask that beachwear be kept for the beach. Many resorts require a jacket for dinner in the winter season, but only a very few still require ties for men. Some of the smallest, least pretentious hotels have the strictest dress codes for evening.

Children

More and more couples are vacationing with their children. Most Caribbean resorts welcome children, but a few do not, or they limit the age or the time period. The policy is spelled out for every resort in this book. Those that welcome families often have special rates for children; some have special meals and supervised activities. All that take children can arrange babysitters, although some resorts request that you notify them in advance.

Meetings

Almost all resorts now take meetings, but some small ones are likely to take them only at certain times of the year. Alternatively, you can book the entire hotel—not a bad idea for small groups.

Stargazing

Since I have already selected 100 resorts out of the 2,500 plus hotels in the Caribbean, you may wonder why I added stars. I wonder, too, because it could cause me nothing but grief—from readers who will tell me I overrated this or that resort, and from hoteliers who will think I've underrated them. I agonized over each one, but I don't claim that I always got it right.

The distinctions are as follows:

★ ★ ★ ★ ★

A league of their own. Not only do they stand out as the best on their island, but they stand up to each other as well.

★ ★ ★ ★

Close to the top but not quite in a league all their own.

★ ★ ★

All-around good but not quite in the top league.

★ ★

All-around good but on a modest scale.

★

Small, very modest.

N/S/T

A few resorts were not given stars because they are (N) too new to be judged, (S) too specialized to be classified in the usual manner, or (T) in transition under new owners or management.

Green Leaf Awards ✎

Protecting the environment is not a fad but a concern day in and day out. In no place in the world is this more essential than the Caribbean. The natural environment is this area's number one asset and protecting it must be its number one priority. The need is as great, if not greater, for the people who live there as for visitors. Without it, they have nothing.

More and more people are becoming aware of their role as travelers, and many (myself included) want to support those who demonstrate an environmental awareness and are making an effort to protect this heritage through their daily actions.

In researching this book I created an environmental profile that I asked every resort to complete; their participation was entirely voluntary. To my knowledge it was the first time a guidebook had made such an attempt in any part of the world. My purpose was not to serve as critic, because there are some recently-created, internationally-recognized standards by which to judge, nor do I consider myself an expert, only a concerned citizen. Rather, I wanted to survey this group in particular to learn if the 100 that are the best at operating their resorts treat their environment with the same care they give their guests. I awarded Green Leaves to those who demonstrate an ongoing concern through their conservation policies and practices.

I was surprised and pleased by the results. Of the 100 resorts, 75 responded. Environmental awareness and conservation among these hotels is at a much higher level than I had realized. I welcome your suggestions for future editions.

Author's Postscript

I want to assure readers that there was no charge for a hotel to be in this guide—a practice not uncommon for books of this kind, particularly in Europe and Asia. Nor did I incur any obligation whatsoever in the course of researching the resorts and making my selections.

The choices are entirely my own. I sought opinions often and listened to advice. I tried to cast myself into the mold of the people for whom a resort was designed. But in the end the process was subjective. I don't claim to be all-knowing; nor do I expect everyone to agree with all my selections. However, I can say without hesitation that there is no resort in this book I wouldn't be happy to return to many times. Indeed, I believe that sentiment is the most valuable criterion a writer can use.

From time to time the Caribbean region experiences hurricanes and tropical storms that can cause damage. If there has been a hurricane or storm recently in the area you plan to travel to, you should phone ahead or consult the resort's website to make sure that the resort you'd like to visit is open and that any storm damage has been repaired.

The prices and rates listed in this guidebook were confirmed at press time, but under no circumstances are they guaranteed. We recommend that you contact establishments before traveling to obtain current information.

ANGUILLA

Sea, sand, and serenity—these are the assets of this tranquil hideaway in the northeastern corner of the Caribbean. Anguilla (pronounced Ann-GWEE-la), 5 miles north of St. Martin, is a dry, low-lying coral island that receives only 35 inches of rainfall per year.

What Anguilla lacks in mountains and tropical foliage, it makes up for in powdery white beaches, which you can have almost to yourself, and fantastically clear aqua and cobalt-blue waters that have attracted yachtsmen for decades and fishermen for centuries. More recently the spectacular waters have been luring snorkelers and scuba divers to the large reefs that lie off Anguilla's coast.

Yet until it burst on the scene in the 1980s with some superdeluxe resorts, Anguilla was the best-kept secret in the Caribbean. Since then trendsetters have been flocking to this little-known spot to learn what all the fuss is about. A beachcomber's island at heart, Anguilla even now is so laid-back that you might need to practice doing nothing to enjoy its tranquillity. Over the years the island has gained an array of good restaurants, shops, and tourist facilities—all low-key—and it even has a budding artist colony. Yet, the island only got its first golf course in 2006 and still has no casinos or shopping arcades, and all but a few small cruise ships pass it by. If you want a change of pace, though, Anguilla is only a 20-minute ferry ride from the casinos and duty-free shopping of St. Martin.

Traditionally among the region's most skilled boatmen and fishermen, the Anguillans supply the markets and restaurants of St. Martin with much of their fish. The Anguillans also make boats, including an unusual racing vessel that gets tested during Anguilla's annual Race Week in August. Sleek yachts and humble fishing boats are available to take you to nearby atolls for a picnic and a day of snorkeling.

For a destination whose total number of guest rooms is less than that of a large hotel, Anguilla has a surprising range of accommodations, from guest houses to posh hotels.

Information

Anguilla Tourist Information, (877) 4-ANGUILLA or (914) 287-2400; Fax: (914) 287-2404; www.anguilla-vacation.com; e-mail: mwturnstyle@aol.com

ALTAMER

Shoal Bay West, Anguilla, B.W.I.

The story of Altamer reads like a dream. More than a decade ago, an American couple, Michael and Rebecca Eggleton (he, an international banker; she, a CPA) were vacationing on Anguilla when they decided to buy some property and build a beach house. Their 6 acres abut crescent-shaped Shoal Bay West, a secluded beach on the western end of Anguilla with views of St. Martin in the distance across the Caribbean Sea.

They envisioned a reasonably modest home, but by the time they decided to build, the government had enacted laws requiring all beachfront property to be operated as a hotel or villa available for rent to visitors.

Near their property were the futuristic, snow-white villas of Covecastles, designed by well-known architect Myron Goldfinger with interiors by his wife, June. The Eggletons wanted their villa to be consistent with the nearby architecture, but unique in its design. With Goldfinger as the architect, they planned Altamer—a beach house like no other.

Rebecca Eggleton and June Goldfinger set off on several worldwide odysseys to find artists, furniture makers, and artisans to duplicate historical items for use in the decor and to arrange for such extravagances as handmade $10,000 Murano glass light fixtures for the living room. For the African Sapphire villa, Altamer commissioned artisans in South Africa to create a chandelier designed by June Goldfinger that has over half-million beads, all made by hand.

The resulting collections are stunning. Throughout, the furnishings combine stylish modern pieces with fine antiques and rare art from around the world, with an emphasis on Turkey, Russia, Africa, Brazil, and Italy. To say that these beach houses are over the top might be an understatement. Now comprised of three large, ultramodern villas, all rooms have floor-to-ceiling windows facing the blue Caribbean waters.

In Russian Amethyst, the first villa, the eye is greeted with a fantasy-like opulence, with oversize rattan furniture awash in a sea of multihued plush cushions—pink, periwinkle, and purple—arranged in conversation groupings. Vases of floral bouquets are everywhere.

On the first floor of the main villa are the Great Room with a soaring 21-foot ceiling, sitting areas, a formal dining room with a custom-designed table for twelve, views of the beach from the large sliding glass doors and windows, and a state-of-the-art professional gourmet kitchen where the villa's chef turns out his fabulous creations. Forget calories.

Behind the elongated oval glass dining table is a large three-part painting, *Cloud Triptych*, by Jan Aronson. It is the perfect complement to the ceiling, which seems to touch the sky. There is a second Aronson painting in the room and a priceless antique Russian chest to keep board games of all kinds. Here, too, is a magnificent gilded candelabra—a little something that Rebecca and June picked up in Russia. It's 18-karat gold on bronze and was formerly owned by one of the czars. Whew!

There are no rugs or carpets, simply a spotlessly clean tile floor. When asked why, the senior butler is quick to reply, "After all, it's a beach house."

Outside this first floor is the swimming pool, which runs almost the length of the building. The second floor, with full views of St. Martin and the Caribbean, has a triangle-shaped game room with a wet bar, pool table, and home theater with flat-screen television and a DVD player. Guest rooms One and Two, also with full sea views, are on this level, each with a marble bathroom with a Jacuzzi tub and separate shower. Extending out toward the sea and accessible only from this level is a 50-foot-long skywalk, allowing guests to lounge, dine, bird-watch, or catch the sunrise at the water's edge.

On the third level is the grand master bedroom, which more than lives up to its name. Measuring 26 feet by 26 feet, it has a 19-foot ceiling, a curved balcony, and bar above, and three large skylights for natural lighting. A king-size bed swathed in fine Italian linens has a television at its foot. In the marble bathroom are long twin vanities, a Jacuzzi for two, separate walk-in shower, and a wall-mounted television. Directly off the bedroom is a huge private balcony with extensive views. Guest rooms Four and Five with high ceilings and skylights are also on this level.

The fourth-floor balcony over the master bedroom has a sitting area and can be converted into an office with a computer with high-speed Internet access, printer, scanner, and fax. The balcony also has a stainless steel and marble wet bar.

A caveat: The other bedrooms, while comfortable, cannot compare to the master bedroom. Those planning to take the villa with friends might want to draw straws to decide who gets the master bedroom first, and then rotate (the butlers will switch the clothing). Near the entrance to the villa in a separate building is a guest room that can accommodate two additional persons. It also houses a fitness center for this villa.

Two more villas, each slightly larger than the first villa, were added in 2003 and 2004. Brazilian Emerald, which takes Brazilian culture as its decor inspiration, has 5 bedrooms and 7 baths; while the third villa, African Sapphire, is filled throughout with museum-quality art and artifacts from Africa, each more interesting and unusual than the last, and has 8 bedrooms and 9 baths. Each villa has a fitness room, a private pool, and hot tub.

Altamer's Conference Centre, designed and state-of-the-art equipped, provides video conferencing, high-speed Internet access, videotaping facilities, starfish speakers, computer projector and screen, VCR, DVD, desktop computers, facsimile, copier, and resort sound system. The main room, measuring 800 square feet, has boardroom seating for up to 30 around the custom-built teak board table or seating for 80 people theater style. There are two small breakout rooms used for a four-person meeting or as private office space. The centre can provide a conference coordinator, IT coordinator, and secretarial services.

The staff of 10 for each villa includes 4 butlers, a resident manager, concierge, 2 housekeepers, and 2 gardeners. A chef and assistant are available for an additional charge. Head of villa operations and general manager, Carl Irish, is a Montserrat native and natural people-person, who will probably meet you at the airport on arrival. Most of the other staff members are Anguillan; 5 of whom have been with the resort since it opened.

From the island's main road, the turnoff to Altamer is onto a paved road marked by an Altamer sign and leads to the resort's small gatehouse. Because guests fill out in advance a guest preference form, which includes credit card information as well as menu choices, arrival is like being welcomed into the home of a rich uncle. There are no formalities, save for the entire staff being on hand to greet you.

You are offered iced towels and drinks. Depending on the time of arrival, you will probably sit down for a "snack" on the terrace. By the time you get to your bedroom, your suitcases will have been unpacked and your clothes neatly folded in drawers or placed on hangers in the closet.

Evenings are spent watching movies from the extensive DVD library, or lazing in the Great Room listening to CDs from a collection that numbers in the hundreds. The remote that controls music throughout each villa can be operated from anywhere in it. The refrigerator in the kitchen is yours to raid at any hour, and the chef thoughtfully leaves a sweet and some late-night snacks in plain view.

When the time comes to leave, Carl and his staff make it easier by packing your gear while you have breakfast or take a last swim.

Most people cannot imagine the experience Altamer offers. Call it contemporary sybaritism with no detail overlooked, no amenity too small, and no need too great. Service is impeccable. You soon discover that you rarely have to ask for anything. The butlers not only anticipate every need, they seem to read your mind.

The sheer elegance and grandeur of Altamer can be overwhelming, but it will appeal to those who crave barefoot elegance in superb surroundings with extreme comfort and excellent service—provided, of course, they can afford it.

ALTAMER ★ ★ ★ ★ ★

Box 3001, Shoal Bay West, Anguilla, B.W.I.; or 6800 SW 40th St., Box 333, Miami, FL 33155
Phone: (264) 498-4000, (888) 652-6888; Fax: (264) 498-4010; e-mail: info@altamer.com; www.altamer.com
Owners: Michael and Rebecca Eggleton
General Manager: Carl Irish
Open: Year-round
US Reservations: (888) 652-6888, rings to Anguilla office for reservations
Deposit: 50 percent to secure reservation; 60 days balance
Minimum Stay: None
Arrival/Departure: Altamer meets guests at airport and arranges taxi. (Note: Anguilla hotels cannot provide their own transportation for guests due to taxi regulations.)
Distance from Airport: 8 miles; 20 minutes by taxi
Accommodations: 3 villas accommodating 40 people (2 villas with 5 bedrooms and 7 baths with Jacuzzi tubs and separate showers; 2 bedrooms available in separate quarters; and 1 villa with 8 bedrooms and 9 baths)
Amenities: Air-conditioning, ceiling fans; professional kitchen; high-speed Internet connection; flat-screen television with DVD player, state-of-the-art digital sound system with 30,000 song titles; safe; butler and maid service 7 a.m.–10 p.m.; hot tub; game room with custom-built pool table; marble bathrooms with Jacuzzi bathtubs; wet bars on multiple levels; wheelchair accessible; elevators in each villa
Fitness Facilities/Spa Services: Fitness center in each villa; massage and spa services on request
Sports: Beach, swimming pool; 2 tennis courts; snorkeling, deep-sea fishing, sailing, diving arranged; each villa has a fitness center, tennis court with pavilion, 45-foot swimming pool, and hot tub.
Electricity: 110 volts
Dress Code: Casual
Children: All ages
Meetings: Conference table seating for 20, 30 in total. Theater-style configuration increases capacity to 70 to 80 depending on setup.
Day Visitors: None
Handicapped Facilities: Yes
Packages: Weddings; corporate
Rates: Per day, All-Inclusive. *High Season* (Dec–Apr): weekly $42,350–$48,400. *Low Season:* $30,250–$36,300. For holidays, Christmas/New Year's, inquire.
Service Charge: 10 percent
Government Tax: 10 percent

ANACAONA BOUTIQUE HOTEL

Mead's Bay, Anguilla, B.W.I.

Soothing to your mind and gentle on your pocketbook, this small ridgetop resort refutes the ill-founded image that Anguilla is a hideaway only for the filthy rich. Only a short slope—200 yards, maybe—from powdery sands, Anacaona Boutique Hotel gives you fabulous Mead's Bay beach but at a third of the cost of Malliouhana, the pricey preserve of celebrities and moguls that anchors the beach's eastern end.

In late 2010, after being purchased by Robin and Sue Ricketts, established hoteliers with a long association with Anguilla, Anacaona (formerly La Sirena Hotel) was given a major face-lift, refurbished, and upgraded.

Designed by a Swiss architect, Anacaona combines Mediterranean tradition with Caribbean touches: white stucco walls and arches, peaked ceilings, weathered red tile roofs, and generous balconies trimmed with white latticework.

The resort offers two types of accommodations in two locations: Hotel rooms in the main buildings and villas near the shore, about a minute walk to the beach. At the top of the rise is the main hotel, an attractive complex of 2- and 3-story buildings housing the restaurants, bar, lounge, a boutique, small spa, Internet cafe, and most accommodations. Guests here take a 3-minute walk along a path to the same fine beach—hardly an inconvenience.

Allamanda House's main buildings have guest rooms on three floors, each with a balcony overlooking the gardens and the large swimming pool. Rooms have terra-cotta tile floors and tiled bathrooms, and are comfortably furnished in minimalist white with colorful pillows and throws, and fresh flowers. All rooms have balcony or patio, air-conditioning, ceiling fan, and cable television, along with Frette linens and duvets, mini-fridge, iPod docking station, laptop-size in-room safe, complimentary Wi-Fi, Melita-Java-pod coffeemaker, phone, hairdryer, and locally crafted bathroom amenities.

On the second floor in the Allamanda House, standard rooms are furnished with queen bed and bathroom with shower. Superior rooms, on the ground, second or third floor have king-size bed or two double beds and bathroom with large shower. Junior suites enjoy ocean views and are furnished with king-size bed and pullout sofa, a living room area, and kitchenette. The most desirable double rooms are on the top-floor, and have high ceilings and the best views. Even more desirable are the junior suites, 2 on the top floor of the main building and 2 in a building in the gardens.

Stone pathways through the gardens lead to the 4 comfortable, modest villa suites and the mile-long beach. Three villa suites have 2 bedrooms with 2 baths, and one has 3 bedrooms, each with a bath and a separate entrance. The villa suites have lounges, fully equipped kitchens, some with private patio and others with screened lanais, cable television, telephone, barbecue equipment, daily maid service, and their own freshwater pool. As with the hotel guest rooms, the villa suites are furnished with Frette linens, mini-fridge, iPod docking station, laptop size in-room safe, complimentary Wi-Fi, Melita-Java-pod coffeemaker, hairdryer, and locally crafted bathroom amenities. The villa suites are particularly well suited for families.

The Fire Fly Restuarant and Bar, overlooking the main pool, serves breakfast, lunch, and dinner, offering Caribbean-Eurasian fusion cuisine as well as traditional Anguillian specialties. Meal Plans are available. Monday night entertainment brings dinner theater with the Sunshine Theatre Company and dancing to a local string band. Thursday night features a West Indian buffet and a performance by the Mayoumba Folkloric Group followed by dancing to a local band. The resort has spa services at its Massage Center.

Anacaona is well suited for families. Up to two children under 12 may stay free in a junior suite with up to two paying adults in the same room. One child under the age of 12 stays free in the superior room when accompanied by a paying adult.

Anacaona may not have the panache of its ritzy neighbors, but many people would probably find its casual and comfortable digs far more suitable for a relaxed beachside vacation. Its low-key, friendly atmosphere is well suited to singles who want a quiet vacation, young couples, and families with children who are happy building sand castles on the beach and can go without a daily fix of television or Nintendo.

ANACAONA BOUTIQUE HOTEL

★ ★ ★

Mead's Bay, Anguilla, B.W.I.

Phone: (264) 497-6827; **Fax:** (264) 497-6829; **e-mail:** info@anacaonahotel .com; www.anacaonahotel.com

Owners: Ricketts & Associates (Anguilla) Ltd.

General Manager: Delroy Lake

Open: Year-round, expect Sept to mid-Oct

Reservations: Direct to hotel (877) 647-4736

Deposit: 3 nights within 48 hours of making a reservation; 10-night or longer bookings require 6 nights deposit. Refunds made only when written notice received by hotel no later than 30 days (winter and festive season) or 21 days (summer) prior to scheduled arrival. Other conditions may apply at certain times.

Minimum Stay: 7 nights during Christmas/New Year's

Arrival/Departure: Transfer arranged upon request for fee

Distance from Airport: (Wallblake Airport) 9 miles; taxi one-way, $26

Distance from Main Town: 9 miles; taxi one-way, $26

Accommodations: 27 rooms with balcony or patio in 3-story main building (16 doubles with queen-, king-, or 2 full-size beds; 4 singles with queen); 4 junior suites (with king and queen sleeper sofa); and 6 villas with 15 bedrooms, each with 2 queens or 1 king

Amenities: Air-conditioning, ceiling fans; telephone; bath with shower only, hair dryer, basket of toiletries; minibar, safe; cable television; massage center

Sports: 2 freshwater swimming pools; free snorkeling gear; bicycles $18 per day plus $10 per day delivery charge; tennis, boating, fishing, snorkeling, diving arranged.

Electricity: 110 volts

Dress Code: Informal

Children: All ages; cribs; babysitters; up to two children under 12 stay free in junior suite with two adults; one child with one adult in standard and superior room.

Meetings: No

Day Visitors: Inquire

Handicapped Facilities: No

Packages: 4-night getaway; 7-night romance; solo; others

Rates: Per room, daily, EP. *High Season* (mid-Dec–Apr 8): $250–$375 (rooms); $410–$475 (junior, 1 bedroom suites); $450–$565 (villas). *Low Season:* $150–$180 (rooms); $220 (junior, 1 bedroom suites); $260–$310 (villa suites). Check out specials and Loyalty program on its website; 15 percent added to meal plans.

Service Charge: 10 percent

Government Tax: 10 percent

CAP JULUCA

Maunday's Bay, Anguilla, B.W.I.

Cap Juluca could win any contest for being the most beautiful resort in the Caribbean, if not the world. It is sensual, romantic, and glamorous. Situated on 179 acres at Maunday's Bay, on Anguilla's leeward shores, with St. Martin in the distance, Cap Juluca is a villa resort stretching for a mile along the curve of a magnificent beach.

The posh resort is comprised of superdeluxe villas in Moorish style, complete with arches, domes, turrets, and keyhole doorways in a fairyland of colors. The blue skies, azure sea, magenta bougainvillea, and green gardens seem all the more intense against the snow-white villas. Cap Juluca is fittingly named for the Arawak god of the rainbow.

In April 2008, Cap Juluca was acquired by Cap Juluca Properties Ltd.,

an investor syndicate and newly formed Anguillian company. The company spent $28 million on renovations and new guest amenities. The new owner's group is headed by travel industry executive Adam M. Aron, and includes Manfredi Lefebvre, chairman of Silversea Cruises, and the Government of Anguilla, which has 20 percent ownership in Cap Juluca Properties Ltd.

The resort's guest rooms are situated in 2-story "hotel" villas and pool villas with up to 5 bedrooms, and come in a bewildering variety: from a bedroom with shower to a large villa with a private pool. The sumptuous interiors vary, but they all have Italian tile floors and louvered doors of Brazilian walnut. Generally, those east of the main pool have built-in banquettes of white masonry with colorful cushions and pillows that give the interior a clean, sophisticated look. Moroccan artifacts and design elements inspired by colorful Moorish motifs are set against pure white walls, conveying the impression of a palace in Tangier.

The recent renovations added 40-inch televisions and DVD players, new beds and bedding from Morocco, and custom-made rugs to all guest rooms, while 21 rooms got new doors and new furniture. Other improvements included the widening of the beach and landscaping with more trees, plants, and flowers that added more color to the property. The huge, luxurious bathrooms found in some suites are second to none. They feature a king's ransom of Italian marble and mirrors along with an oversize bathtub, double sinks, a separate shower, and a bidet. Some even have a double bathtub with headrests and a private solarium.

You can sink into the mile of soft, deep white sand at your doorstep, or loll about the large freshwater pool. A continental breakfast served in your room or on your terrace or patio is part of the luxury at Cap Juluca. You can also have breakfast and lunch at Blue (formerly Georges), a beachside restaurant under an onion-shaped dome by the central pool pavilion. Roving beach waiters offer chilled towels, complimentary mineral water and sorbet, and drinks on request.

The eastern end of the beach is anchored by Pimm's, the main restaurant, featuring innovative "Eurobbean" fusion cuisine. Named for a refreshing drink popular with the British in the days of the raj, Pimm's has an enchanting setting directly by the sea, looking

across the sweep of Cap Juluca by the bay Lunch and dinner menus have seafood selections based on the island's supply of fresh fish, along with chicken, lamb, veal, and beef specialties, and too many yummy desserts—but all prepared with a light touch. Next to Pimm's is Spice (formerly Kemia) featuring a Pan-Asian menu. Blue serves Mediterranean cuisine tinged with Caribbean flavors and lighter fare at lunch, and offers beachfront dining with tables and chairs set right in the sand. Two special nights are held weekly—a seafood beach buffet on Friday and a grand marché on Monday after the manager's cocktail party. Should you care to leave your villa or haven by the pool, Cap Juluca has 3 Omni-turf tennis courts (2 lighted) and a pro shop. The use of Sunfish, snorkeling gear, windsurfers, and Hobie Cats is included in the rate. Excursions farther afield are available on Cap Juluca's 2 boats. The resort has an herb garden and self-guided walking trails that lead to a lagoon behind the resort—a popular bird-watching location. The garden supplies fresh herbs for the chef and is a novelty for guests.

There is not much entertainment at Cap Juluca. Several evenings feature dancing at Georges. The main building also has a library and boutique and reception area, where you check in while you sip a welcome drink. To the east side of the building is an expanded fitness center with cardio equipment and four spa treatment rooms. Cardi, an Anguillan and a cricket player who played professionally in England, is available as a personal trainer. A well-trained staff of professionals offers many Asian and other trendy specialty treatments. Treatments can also be given in one's room. Pilates or yoga and beach fitness session with Cardi are available almost daily.

Cap Juluca has been designed as a secluded, stylish retreat for sophisticated travelers and is meant to have a mystique of exotic, erotic luxury about it.

CAP JULUCA ★ ★ ★ ★ ★

PO Box 240, Maunday's Bay, Anguilla, B.W.I.
Phone: (264) 497-6666; **Fax:** (264) 497-6617; **e-mail:** capjuluca@capjuluca .com; www.capjuluca.com
Owner: Cap Juluca Holdings, Ltd.
General Manager: Gary Thulander
Open: Year-round except Sept and Oct
US Reservations: Cap Juluca, (888) 8-JULUCA (858-5822), (866) 458-5822, (305) 466-0916
Deposit: 3 nights; 30 days cancellation
Minimum Stay: 7 nights during Christmas/New Year's
Arrival/Departure: Guests met at airport in Anguilla by hotel representative; complimentary transfer service in packages. On request, transfers can be arranged from St. Maarten airport on the shared Sea Shuttle for $75 per person one-way when booked through Cap Juluca (or private boat charter service for $425, one way for up to four people plus $25 one-way for each additional person. Departure tax per person, $20
Distance from Airport: (Clayton J. Lloyd International Airport) 5 miles; taxi one-way, $25; via ferry from St. Martin, 4 miles, $24; taxi from the ferry terminal in Anguilla to hotel, $25
Distance from the Valley: 5 miles; taxi one-way, $25

Accommodations: 58 rooms and junior suites and 7 suites in hotel villas and 6 pool villas; with terraces or patios; all have king-size beds; some suites have extra queen-size daybed
Amenities: Air-conditioning, ceiling fans; refrigerator with free water during stay; telephone; some baths with tub, some with solarium and double tub, some with shower only; hair dryer, deluxe toiletries, bathrobe and slippers; nightly turndown service, room service as requested; kitchen in villas
Fitness Facilities/Spa Services: Fitness center; in-room treatments upon request
Sports: Freshwater swimming pool, 6 villa pools; tennis, Sunfish, Hobie Cats, snorkeling gear, waterskiing free; scuba, fishing, golf arranged for charge
Electricity: 110/220 volts
Dress Code: Casual by day; casually elegant in evening; no jacket or tie required
Children: All ages, but advance inquiry requested for those under 3; cribs; baby-sitters; supervised children's program several times a year
Meetings: Up to 40 people
Day Visitors: No
Handicapped Facilities: No
Packages: Romantic Retreat; weekend getaway; weddings; and others
Rates: Per room, daily, CP. *High Season* (Jan 3–Apr 15): $995–$3,485. *Low Season* (Apr 15–May 31 and Nov 1– mid-Dec): $595–$1,985. *Low Season:* $495–$1,585. One-bedroom/private pool suites and 3- and 5-bedroom villas priced separately; inquire.
Service Charge: 10 percent
Government Tax: 10 percent

CUISINART GOLF RESORT & SPA

Rendezvous Bay, Anguilla, B.W.I.

A resort for the 21st century, Cuisin-Art is a hideaway for baby boomers who want it all—large comfortable rooms with the latest electronic gadgets, huge marble bathrooms, a beautiful beach, a vanishing-edge swimming pool, gourmet cuisine by a celebrated chef, a hydroponic farm (no pollution, no pesticides), a full-service spa for pampering, with a fitness center and par course for just enough exercise not to feel guilty. What else could you ask for?

Set on the beautiful white sands of Rendezvous Bay on Anguilla's southern coast with views of St. Martin across the Caribbean Sea, the stylish resort's lavishness makes it clear that no costs were spared, no shortcuts taken.

The resort is approached by a drive along a flower-bordered boulevard that leads to the grand entrance of the blue-domed main building with the reception and concierge desks, three boutiques, a video library, a game room with a billiards table, a bar, a lounge, and restaurants. Everywhere the whitewashed walls are ablaze with vivid, decorative paintings by Italian artists, establishing one of CuisinArt's dual goals—art patronage. And you thought it was named for a kitchen appliance!

(I will let you in on a little secret. Many people seem puzzled by the name CuisinArt. The quick explanation: The resort's owner, Leandro Rizzuto, owns Conair, the parent company of Le Cuisinart.)

The resort is set around tropical gardens centered by a large swimming pool from which a series of small pools and waterfalls drop to the beach. To each side are large whitewashed villas of Mediterranean-inspired architecture. Flower-filled courtyards at each entrance are framed by an archway with a wooden door that adds an accent and stairs whose art deco brick glass is integrated into the white stucco walls.

All 10 villas are directly on the beach; each has 8 spacious units. The first and second floors have junior suites while the top floor has one-bedroom and luxury junior suites with patios or terraces that convert to two-bedroom suites. The verandas are large enough for a table with 2 chairs and 2 chaise lounges. All have cable television with 47 channels, telephone, and high-speed Internet connection. Large bathrooms are set in soft-toned Italian marble and have double sinks, deep oval tubs, and a separate shower. Luxury junior suites and one-bedroom suites also have a private solarium for sunning.

The 3-story main building has 11 accommodations: 9 luxury rooms and 2 spectacular penthouses. Of the latter, one is a 4,300-square-foot, 3-bedroom suite, the other a 7,600-square-foot, 2-bedroom suite. Each has a living room, a fully equipped kitchen (with Cuisinart appliances), and wraparound terraces with expansive views. Two additional guest rooms are available for penthouse guests.

The spacious accommodations—double the size of most hotel rooms—are furnished in a comfortably elegant style with fine rattan and wood furniture imported from Mexico.

Six Villas by CuisinArt, at the eastern end of the property, were added recently and offer luxury with privacy, only steps away from all resort facilities. Each villa has its own entry courtyard graced with a fountain and garden splendor. The villas have a lovely living and dining area, full kitchen, master suite with its own solarium, plus a courtyard guest suite—all with the latest technology and creature comforts. The 3 three-bedroom beachfront villas have an expansive outdoor patio with private pool and sea views and provide the ambience of a grand beach house. These accommodations are also available as 1-bedroom units. The 3 five-bedroom garden villas, each with a private pool, are ideal for families or a group of friends

CuisinArt has four venues for dining. Santorini, the resort's gourmet restaurant, offers a creative menu of contemporary cuisine infused with the flamboyant flavors and spices of the Caribbean. Santorini also has a Chef's Table, where executive chef Daniel LeGuenan presents a weekly 6-course dinner with wine pairings from the resort's new 3,600-bottle cellar; hands-on cooking classes are offered twice a week for lunch. Cafe Mediterraneo, overlooking the pool, serves seafood, grilled items, pizza, and salads of fresh home-grown vegetables. Bring money: Prices here are on a par with those of top eateries in New York.

The third venue is a Lobby Bar and Lounge where small plates, sandwiches, and pizzas are served, accompanied by live music several nights during the week. The latest dining venue, The Beach Bar and Grill, is for those who can't tear themselves away from the beach. Lunch menus offer "snacking skewers" of beef, lobster, and local fish, served with hydroponic salad and vegetable chips. In the evening, light casual fare of local selections are served under the stars.

The Hydroponic "farm" (which looked like a greenhouse to me), grows much of the vegetables, edible flowers, and herbs used by the resort in its restaurants and by the spa to create some of its organic lotions and oils.

CuisinArt has three lighted tennis courts, a boccie court next to the swimming pool, a championship croquet field, and a 1-mile par course with exercise stations. Nonmotorized water sports are complimentary for guests.

The resort's full-service Venus spa and fitness center recently got a $10-million-dollar expansion and was tripled its size. It now has a total of 16 treatment rooms including couples and VIP suites, a thalassotherapy pool, a yoga/Pilates studio, a fitness center with Technogym equipment, and more. The therapy pool with built-in lounges and hydrotherapy jets enables guests to soak in warm nutrient and mineral-enriched saltwater. The trained staff offers massages, seaweed wraps, reflexology, aromatherapy, hot stone therapy, sea salt scrubs, and an array of other treatments. CuisinArt's gardens, created by landscape designer and horticulturalist Caryl Clement as an oasis within Anquilla's dry environment, showcase more than 150 species of trees, fragrant flowers, and exotic plants.

In summer of 2011, Cuisinart's owner was the successful bidder to acquire Anguilla's only golf course, an 18-hole championship layout designed by Greg Norman. Future plans have not yet been announced, but presumably, in time, it will become one of the resort's amenities. Stay tuned.

CUISINART GOLF RESORT & SPA
★ ★ ★ ★

PO Box 2000, Rendezvous Bay, Anguilla, B.W.I
Phone: (264) 498-2000; **Fax:** (264) 498-2010; **e-mail:** reservations@cuisin art.ai; www.cuisinartresort.com
Owner: Leandro Rizzuto
General Manager: Stephane Zaharia
Open: Year-round except Sept–mid-Oct
US Reservations: (800) 943-3210
Deposit: 3 nights; 30 days cancellation
Minimum Stay: 10 nights during Christmas/New Year's
Arrival/Departure: VIP meet/greet service at St. Maarten Airport; guests met at Anguilla airport and Blowing Point ferry terminal by hotel representative
Distance from Airport: (Wallblake Airport) 6 miles (20-minute drive): taxi one-way, $26; via ferry from Marigot, St. Martin, to Blowing Point Ferry terminal, (25 minutes), $15. Boat shuttle from St. Maarten Airport to Blowing Point Ferry Terminal (20 minutes) $55 per person. Taxi from Blowing Point to resort, $18.
Distance from the Valley: 4 miles; taxi one-way, $26
Accommodations: 93 rooms and suites, all with terraces; 6 villas (3 three-bedroom; 3 five-bedroom
Amenities: Air-conditioning, ceiling fans; mini-bar; telephone, high-speed Internet; bath with tub and separate shower, hair dryer, deluxe toiletries, bathrobe; nightly turndown service, room service; concierge

Fitness Facilities/Spa Services: Full-service spa, fitness center, scheduled classes, 1-mile par course, hair salon, Jacuzzi

Sports: Freshwater swimming pool; three lighted tennis courts, pro and clinics; boccie court; championship croquet field; snorkeling, windsurfing, sailing; golf arranged

Electricity: 110/220 volts

Dress Code: Casual by day; casually elegant in evening; no jacket or tie required

Meetings: Up to 50 people

Children: All ages; supervised children's program during holiday periods only

Day Visitors: Welcomed at spa and restaurants

Handicapped Facilities: No

Packages: Year-round

Rates: Per room, daily, CP. *Winter* (Jan 3–Apr7): $815–$5,300. *Spring* (Apr 8–28): $545–$3,600. *Summer* (May–Nov 21) $440–$3,200. *Holiday* (mid-Dec–Jan 3): $1,325–$8,300. (Note: Holiday rates require a 10-night minimum stay.)

Service Charge: 10 percent

Government Tax: 10 percent plus marketing levy: $1 per adult, 12 years and older, per night

MALLIOUHANA

Mead's Bay, Anguilla, B.W.I.

Located on Anguilla's northwestern coast on a 25-acre bluff overlooking two spectacular beaches, Malliouhana (the Arawak Indian name for Anguilla) is a sybaritic fantasy in Mediterranean design set in a garden of Eden.

Almost from the day it opened in 1984, the resort won rave reviews for its extraordinary interiors, style, refinement, gourmet cuisine, and attention to detail. It raised deluxe to a lofty new level that few have equaled.

Before creating Malliouhana, British industrialist and well-traveled bon vivant Leon Roydon and his late wife, Lyane, had dreamed of building a Caribbean resort with the standards to which they were accustomed in Europe. Like most people, the Roydons fell in love with Anguilla when they visited it for the first time in 1980.

There are no signs pointing the way to Malliouhana. A driveway passes through landscaped gardens exploding with color and shaded by stately palms to a cluster of white stucco buildings with arched galleries and red tile roofs that look more like palatial Mediterranean hilltop mansions than a hotel.

From the elegant lobby you step through a series of tall, cool white arches that rise to cathedral ceilings of warm Brazilian walnut. They lead to terraced gardens and high-ceilinged, breeze-filled lounges with light terra-cotta tile floors and upholstered rattan furniture.

All Malliouhana's accommodations feature huge bedrooms with king-size beds; they are located in wings of the main building and other buildings on the cliff and in villas with 1-bedroom suites and 2 double rooms directly on the beach. Junior suites have large bedrooms and dressing rooms; 1-bedroom and 2-bedroom suites have separate bedrooms, living-dining rooms, and covered patios. Guest rooms have marbled and mirrored bathrooms almost as large as

the bedrooms, and terraces overlooking Anguilla's peacock-blue waters.

Exquisitely designed tropical furniture of the highest-quality rush and bamboo and rich Brazilian mahogany louvered doors and windows with solid-brass fittings contrast with the stark white bedcovers, tile floors, and walls adorned with subdued Asian prints and vibrant Haitian paintings.

The resort has a mile of powder-fine beach on one side and a small, intimate cove, accessible only from the hotel (or by boat), on the other. There are 4 Laykold tennis courts (lighted), a water-sports center and fitness center. The hotel's launch is available for trips to nearby islets and reefs for snorkeling and picnics and for excursions to St. Martin.

The evening's highlight is dining on haute cuisine in the casually elegant terrace restaurant overlooking the sea.

At the resort's top-rated restaurant, Michel Rostang at Malliouhana, its award-winning chef, Frederic Cougnon, continues the tradition of cuisine developed for Malliouhana by the late Jo Rostang of La Bonne Auberge—a two-star Michelin restaurant on the French Riviera. At the same time and in close collaboration with the famous son, Michel Rostang, he has created menus that pair classic French with Caribbean and Mediterranean influences, changed seasonally. For those who prefer a casual day, the resort has another pool and poolside cafe, Le Bistro, by the beach. The second floor of the cafe has a large room for meetings; it can be converted into a disco.

Malliouhana has two new culinary treats offered weekly: A festive Anguilla

Night at Le Bistro on Thursday with music by Dumpa and Company, Anguillla's best known local combo, and a 6-course Chef's Tasting Menu at Michel Rostang at Malliouhana on Monday and paired with superb wines from the resort's celebrated 25,000-bottle "Le Cave" wine cellar. Price: $125 per person. A third innovation is a daily prix fixe lunch menu. It is priced at $85 per person; $45 per child under 10 years old.

If you had any doubt that times have changed, Malliouhana's children's facilities are proof positive. For the increasing number of guests traveling with their children and grandchildren, the posh hideaway offers the Children's Place, a well-equipped beachfront playground with its own pirate ship beached on the sand, a paddling pool, and two Playworld Systems areas: one for ages 2 through 5, the other for ages 5 through 12. The playground is supervised daily from 9 a.m. to 5:30 p.m. and is free for guests.

The resort's 15,000-square-foot spa offers massage, skin and hair care, and body treatments that use island herbs, spices, flowers, and fruits creatively.

Roydon clearly understands the needs of his discerning guests. A staff-to-guest ratio of more than 2 to 1 and the high level of service by the resort's staff of 200 Anguillans, more than half of whom have been with the resort since it opened, ensure that those needs are met in a gracious atmosphere.

From the time it opened, Malliouhana has attracted celebrities, movie stars, and a loyal following of well-heeled, sophisticated travelers. Leon Roydon and his son Nigel manage the hotel with meticulous care. One of them is on hand to greet guests on arrival and to say farewell at the end of their stay. At other times, however, the managers keep their distance, believing that people come to Malliouhana for privacy.

In May 2011, Malliouhana announced that it would be closed until November 2011, however, at press time, the resort is in negotiations to be sold. If so, it likely will not reopen until late 2012.

MALLIOUHANA ★ ★ ★ ★ ★

PO Box 173, Mead's Bay, Anguilla, B.W.I.

Phone: (800) 835-0796, (264) 497-6111; **Fax:** (264) 497-6011; **e-mail:** malliouhana@anguillanet.com; www .malliouhana.com

Owner: Leon Roydon

General Manager: Nigel Roydon

Open: Year-round except Sept–Oct; for 2011, May 22–mid-Nov

US Reservations: Direct to hotel, (800) 835-0796

Deposit: 3 nights; 30 days cancellation

Minimum Stay: 7 nights, Dec–Mar

Arrival/Departure: Transfers not available

Distance from Airport: 8 miles from Wallblake Airport and Blowing Point Ferry terminal; taxi one-way, $20

Distance from Main Town: 9 miles; taxi one-way, $20

Accommodations: 55 rooms (including 34 double rooms, 6 junior suites, 7 one-bedroom suites, 3 Jacuzzi suites, 1 pool suite, and 2 two-bedroom suites)

Amenities: Air-conditioning, ceiling fans (also in bathrooms); telephone;

stocked minibars; ample closet space; bathroom vanities with makeup lights, deep tub, shower stall, bidet, plush towels, bathrobes, hair dryer, toiletries; room service until 10:30 p.m.; beauty salon; designer boutique, sundries shop; cable television in television room and library; some televisions and VCRs available for rent

Fitness Facilities/Spa Services: Fitness center and full-service spa; personal trainer

Sports: 3 freshwater pools and large heated Jacuzzi; snorkeling; 4 tennis courts (lighted); fishing gear, water-skiing, windsurfing, Sunfish, Lasers, Prindle catamarans; deep-sea fishing, diving arranged for fee

Electricity: 110 volts

Dress Code: Casual but chic sportswear by day; casually elegant in evening

Children: All ages; babysitters available; children's pool and playground

Meetings: Small groups on request

Day Visitors: No

Handicapped Facilities: No

Packages: Romance (honeymoon, anniversary); Jun 1–Aug 31, packages of 4 or more nights and Spa, 5 nights (Apr–mid-Dec); Family & Friends, 5 nights (May–mid-Nov)

Rates: Single or double, daily, EP. *High Season* (mid-Dec–Mar 31): $720–$3,340. *Shoulder Season* (Apr 1–Apr 30 and Nov 19–mid-Dec): $465–$2,015. *Low Season* (May 1–Aug 31 and Nov 1–19): $345–$1,465. Surcharge for Christmas holiday period.

Service Charge: 10 percent

Government Tax: 10 percent

ANTIGUA

Shaped somewhat like a maple leaf, Antigua has protruding fingers that provide its coastline with sheltered bays, natural harbors, and extra miles of beautiful beaches—one for every day of the year, the Antiguans say—fringed by coral reefs. These assets have made Antigua one of the most popular beach and water-sports centers in the Caribbean. As a bonus, low humidity and year-round trade winds create the ideal climate for tennis, golf, horseback riding, and a variety of other sports and sightseeing.

Antigua (pronounced Ann-TEE-ga) is the largest of the Leeward Islands. Located east of Puerto Rico, between the US Virgin Islands and the French and Dutch West Indies, Antigua is a transportation hub of the region and the home of LIAT (Leeward Islands Air Transport), the regional carrier of several Eastern Caribbean states.

After English settlers from St. Kitts established a colony near Old Town on the southern coast in 1632, Antigua remained a British possession until 1981, when full independence was achieved. Today the island's British heritage and historic character are most evident at English Harbour, once the headquarters of the British navy, where the buildings of the old wharf (now known as Nelson's Dockyard) have been restored to house shops, inns, restaurants, and museums.

St. John's, the capital and once a sleepy West Indian village, has become a popular tourist mecca. Charming historic buildings of West Indian architecture house attractive boutiques and restaurants.

This relaxed and quietly sophisticated island has a few large resorts and casinos, but most of Antigua's hotels are small and operated by their owners—a feature that helps give the island a less commercial atmosphere than some other Caribbean destinations.

Information

Antigua and Barbuda Department of Tourism, 305 E. 47th St., Ste. 6A, New York, NY 10017; (212) 541-4117, (888) 268-4227; Fax: (646) 215-6008; www.antigua-barbuda.org

CARLISLE BAY

St. Mary's, Antigua

Set on a secluded beach on the south coast of Antigua, with a backdrop of rolling hills, Carlisle Bay by well-known British hotelier Gordon Campbell Gray, brings urban chic to the Tropics—and his first Caribbean venture.

Upon arrival at Carlisle Bay, you will cross a short bridge over a small pond into the Pavilion, a large, high-ceilinged, open reception area with contemporary sofas in white and dark wood tables and chairs set against pickled gray walls. To the right of the Pavilion entrance is the reception desk, of an Asian design. At the opposite end is the Pavilion Bar, where light snacks are served, and beyond, the swimming pool. At the center is a large round table with vases of orchids and coffee table books. Dominating the room at the entrance and in the Pavilion are huge, 7-foot-high, dark wood Indonesian planters—all very dramatic.

Off the lobby and overlooking the large swimming pool is East, the resort's gourmet dinner restaurant, serving Asian fusion cuisine. Guests enter through a pair of massive, carved Indonesian wooden doors flanked by a glass wall. On the floor of maple, stained dark to boat finish, are dark wood tables and tomato pink, slipcovered chairs, enhancing East's exotic look.

Indigo on the Beach is an open-to-the-breezes beachfront bar and restaurant serving three meals with an accent on grills, fresh seafood, and salads. The restaurant's decor repeats the gray pickled wood on the floor, dark wood Caribbean chairs with gray-striped cushions, and dark wood tables with polished Indigo blue tops—hence the name.

The pretty, free-form swimming pool, tiled in dark green and gray mosaic, is surrounded by natural hardwood lounge chairs shaded by white umbrellas. A new treat for individual couples only is dinner on the jetty, a 5-course menu custom designed with the chef, for $140 per person.

There are two sets of guest rooms, some directly on the beach in the buildings of the former hotel situated here, and now renovated from top to bottom; others set back a few steps from the beach in large, 3-story villas in landscaped gardens, all with private terrace or balcony facing the sea. The resort takes advantage of the two sets of accommodations by designating the first group directly on the beach as "family suites" intended for guests with children; while the 3-story villas are designed for couples and individuals who probably fit the "urban sophisticate" profile for whom the resort was designed.

All accommodations are spacious suites—from junior to 3-bedroom—in a cool contemporary style designed by London interior designer Mary Fox Linton, using four subdued color schemes—lavender, sunset, aqua, and gray-blue—and accented by straight-line dark wood furniture with white Frette bed linens and textured silk curtains of Thai silk from Jim Thompson. The suites are equipped with CD and DVD players, satellite television, and minibar. Fiber optic reading lights on each side of the king-size bed, high-speed wireless Internet access, an espresso machine, and exotic toiletries are among the suites' unusual amenities. The large bathroom has a separate shower, bathtub, and toilet—all in glass and stainless steel fixtures giving the room a rather severe, masculine look.

The suites' wardrobe doors are covered in specially commissioned black-and-white photographs of Antiguan plant life by Jason Taylor. The outdoor terraces are furnished with wide, dark wood daybeds, a gray rattan table and chairs covered in silver-gray cotton, and more of the 7-foot-high Indonesian planters that greet visitors at the entrance and in the Pavilion.

The 3-bedroom Carlisle Suites are designed to accommodate six guests maximum and have 2 king-bedded rooms and 1 twin-bedded room. No discounts are offered for reduced occupancy.

In addition to family-friendly accommodations, the resort welcomes children with Cool Kids Club, a purpose-built, professional staff facility catering to children from 6 months to 12 years old. The air-conditioned center with a shaded terrace is equipped with jungle gym, sandpit, paddling pool, and 4 mini tennis courts and is open daily. There is no charge for children 3 years and older. For babies and toddlers and for evening babysitter, the rate is $15 per hour plus service and tax.

Children are split into age groups: 6 months through 3 years, activities include finger painting, water play, treasure hunts, and beach games; 4 through 6 years, activities include art projects, song and dance, junior tennis, and swimming; 7 through 12 years, activities include outdoor sports, indoor activities, and 2 excursions per week (there is a charge for off-site visits).

Teenagers, age 13 to 19, have their own program, Crush, during the summer months and other school vacation times. It gives them their own room to cool-out and offers various sports and other exclusive activities.

Blue, the spa, gym, and wellness center in a glass-walled pavilion near the tennis courts, has 6 treatment rooms including a couples' room. It offers a wide range of health and beauty treatments using pure and natural products. It also has a beauty salon offering exclusive Natura Bisse treatments from Spain. A menu of treatments is available on the resort's website.

The state-of-the-art gymnasium, with 360-degree views over the beach and hills, has a relaxing lounge, separate men's and women's plunge pools and saunas, Pilates area, and a juice bar. Yoga is offered in an open-sided pavilion in the gardens.

Carlisle Bay has 9 tennis courts with Har-Tru surfaces; 2 are lighted for night play. Water sports include snorkeling, dinghy and catamaran sailing, windsurfing, and diving with a qualified dive instructor. Kite-surfing, deep-sea fishing, and scuba diving are available, but no motorized water sports. The casual Jetty Bar is on the beach by the water-sports center.

The glass-fronted library, with a collection ranging from great works to great beach reads, has 2 computer desks with flat-screen iMac computers, free Wi-Fi, and Internet access, and an unusual feature: Lucite and glass bookshelves that are backlit and slowly change color. Another glass-sided facility, the Carlisle Room, overlooks the tennis courts and is used for meetings or private dining. It comfortably seats 30 dining guests in chairs with hyacinth blue slipcovers. The air-conditioned Screening Room has 45 Italian-designed blue leather chairs. Current films and old favorites are screened every evening, and children's movies are offered during the day.

CARLISLE BAY ★ ★ ★ ★

Old Road, St. Mary's, Antigua, W.I.
Phone: (268) 484-0000; **Fax:** (268) 484-0001; **USA Toll free:** (866) 502-2855; **e-mail:** info@carlisle-bay.com; www.carlisle-bay.com
Owner: Campbell Gray Hotels
General Manager: Jonathan Reynolds
Open: Year-round except Sept to mid-Oct
US Reservations: Direct to hotel
Deposit: Full payment in advance
Minimum Stay: 10 nights, Christmas/New Year's
Arrival/Departure: No private hotel transfer service due to local regulations; however, airport meet/assist service available
Distance from Airport: 30 minutes from International Airport; taxi $48 for up to four passengers
Distance from St. John's: 30 minutes; 20 minutes from English Harbour
Accommodations: 82 suites (27 beach; 48 ocean; 4 three-bedroom Carlisle suites)
Amenities: King-size or twin beds, Frette bed linens; air-conditioning, ceiling fan; Natura Bissé toiletries; direct-dialing phone, free Wi-Fi, DVD and

CD player, Internet access, flat-screen TV, satellite television; cell phone for rent; minibar; espresso machine; safe; 24-hour room service; terrace or balcony with double daybed

Fitness Facilities/Spa Services: Spa with 6 treatment rooms; separate men's and women's plunge pools and saunas; gym, yoga and Pilates area; personal trainer; juice bar

Sports: Freshwater swimming pool; 9 tennis courts, 2 floodlit; snorkeling, sailing, windsurfing, hiking, diving, kite-surfing, deep-sea fishing, and scuba diving available; no motorized water sports

Electricity: 110 volts

Dress Code: Smart casual

Children: All ages; professionally staffed kids club

Meetings: Up to 45 people in Carlisle Room; 45-seat screening room

Day Visitors: Restaurants, with reservations

Handicapped Facilities: No

Packages: Spa, tennis, yoga, couples, celebration/honeymoon; 4 and 7 nights

Rates: Per room, double, FAP and afternoon tea. *High Season* (mid-Dec–late Apr): $920–$1,675; Carlisle suite $2,750–$4,150. *Low Season:* $635–$970; Carlisle suite $1,875–$2,175. Third person and meal plans available.

Service Charge: 10 percent

Government Tax: 10.5 percent

CURTAIN BLUFF

St. John's, Antigua, W.I.

Ideally located on a secluded promontory on Antigua's southern coast, with Atlantic surf washing the beach on one side and the tranquil Caribbean lapping the shore on the other, Curtain Bluff is an exclusive enclave of tropical splendor spread across 20 beachfront acres against a backdrop of verdant hills.

The time-tested resort has been called Antigua's blue-chip address for conservative travelers by some and a tropical paradise with a country club ambience by others, but perhaps the best description was offered by the guest who said, "This is a place where you fall in love with your wife all over again." Not a bad vote of confidence for a resort that set a new standard for the Caribbean when it opened in 1961, watched a host of competiters blossom—and wither like dandelions—and is still going strong.

Whatever Curtain Bluff is, for sure reflects its creator, the late Howard Hulford. A legend in his own time, he was called by many the best hotelier in the Caribbean. Gruff, opinionated, love-me-if-you-dare, Hulford was as famous for his silver mustache as he was for his manner. He and his fine staff made sure his standard of excellence was maintained at Curtain Bluff for half a century. As a result, the resort continues to be booked a year in advance, primarily by repeat visitors.

Curtain Bluff operates as an all-inclusive resort. Included in the price are all meals, afternoon tea, and table wine; most sports; top-quality alcoholic beverages, all motorized and nonmotorized water sports, including scuba diving, deep-sea fishing; and even postage stamps. Room service is available for all meals, and bar service is provided at no extra charge—an unusual amenity for an all-inclusive resort.

Accommodations include seafront double rooms with sitting areas as well as 1- and 2-bedroom suites in 2-story, low-rise buildings, all with terraces and dreamy views. The tastefully appointed rooms have tile floors and wicker furniture dressed in pastels. The 2-bedroom, 2-level suites offer a breeze-cooled patio with a hammock just waiting to be used; the second bedroom can be rented as a separate accommodation.

The most luxurious: Deluxe suites perched in stair-step fashion near the top of the bluff. Each unit has a bedroom larger than most New York apartments, with great reading lights mounted by the headboard, a spacious living room that opens directly onto a large terrace with spectacular views, 5 ceiling fans, and a well-equipped marbled bathroom with separate tubs and showers. The counters, with double sinks, are topped with gorgeous, unusual green or blue variegated marble. One of the newest buildings has 18 marvelous junior suites, of which 7 are connecting pairs and accommodate families. Another group of 22 junior suites, each with 750 square feet, have 9 pairs connecting. Above the two floors of junior suites are 2 extravagant suites, Grace Bay and Morris Bay, comprising the entire third floor.

Your introduction to Curtain Bluff begins at the central building, surrounded by a riot of flowers and gardens. At the reception and concierge desk, you will be greeted by the amiable Wendy Eardley, the resort's very efficient assistant manager who seems to have the answer to your every need. Beyond is a small patio, shaded by a large tamarind tree, and the dining terrace. To one side is a boutique and the Sugar Mill Bar, the gathering spot for predinner drinks and hors d'oeuvres. Both the dining terrace and bar are open to the view and have stairs that lead down to the gardens and the beachside rooms.

Daytime activities are centered on the calm, palm-fringed Caribbean beach, which offers the Beach Club, where informal lunches are served; the Wednesday barbecue buffet is a beach party with steel band music. You'll find umbrellas, changing rooms, showers, and water-sports equipment. Here, too, is the large swimming pool in a pretty grove overlooking the beach.

Tennis is one of Curtain Bluff's main attractions. It has 4 all-weather championship courts (lighted), a squash court, viewing stands, a resident pro, and a pro shop. Beyond the tennis courts is an air-conditioned fitness center with a full line of exercise equipment and an outdoor area where aerobic, Pilates, and yoga sessions are held with a professional trainer six times weekly.

Meals are served in the main restaurant, tea on the Bar Terrace. The kitchen at Curtain Bluff is directed by Christophe Blatz, the former sous-chef, following the retirement of chef Reudi Portmann, who had been with Curtain Bluff for 37 years. Blatz, like Portmann, keeps his menus limited, changing them daily to maximize the use of fresh products.

Lunches are light, but dinners are a real treat with your choice of hot and cold soups, appetizers, salads, 6 different entrees, and too many yummy desserts each night. The wine cellar, with approximately 25,000 bottles of the finest vintages, was Hulford's pride, second only to his fabulous gardens. Curtain Bluff also offers Monday "Barefoot on the Beach" dinners with live music as diners enjoy the catch of the day. Chef Blatz conducts cooking classes, teaching guests his personal style of fusing French flavors with Caribbean cuisine and having them cook some of Curtain Bluff's favorite recipes. Classes cost $70 and include lunch and wine from Curtain Bluff's wine cellar.

Curtain Bluff has kept up with changing times. Now, all bedrooms have air-conditioning and wireless Internet access. But it's the spa with its fabulous location that tops the list of amenities. Perched on the bluff at the south end of the property with wide-angle views of the Caribbean and the island of Montserrat in the distance, the Spa at Curtain Bluff has 5 treatment rooms: 4 single and 1 for couples—each has its own private balcony. Open-air walkways and waterfalls enhance the setting, while a relaxation room, a 10-person hot tub, and a veranda provide ideal spots to relax and enjoy the spa's freshly brewed lemongrass tea made from herbs grown in the resort's garden. Fruit and vegetable snacks developed by spa director, Gilly Shillingford, and Curtain Bluff's chef, are served after treatments. Among the spa's signature treatments are a caviar-and-champagne massage when one's body is saturated with special oils and champagne poured over it; a soothing wrap of water lily, green tea, and chamomile; and an antiaging with

Myoxy caviar mask. The spa also offers treatments for children that parents can observe. The spa uses Pevonia products and is open daily from 10 a.m. to 7 p.m. A list of treatment and prices is available on the resort's website.

Curtain Bluff is not for everyone, but it does not try to be. The ambience may seem a little old-fashioned to some, but it appeals to Curtain Bluff's loyal patrons, who are now in their third generation and who enjoy dressing for dinner and dancing under the stars to music updated for the young and young-at-heart with jazz, rock, reggae, and calypso.

CURTAIN BLUFF ★ ★ ★ ★ ★
PO Box 288, Old Road, St. John's, Antigua, W.I.
Phone: (268) 462-8400, (888) 289-9898, (212) 289-8888; Fax: (268) 462-8409; www.curtainbluff.com; curtainbluff@curtainbluff.com
Owner: The Hulford family
Managing Director: Rob Sherman
General Manager: Calvert A. Roberts
Open: Nov 1–late Aug
US Reservations: Direct to hotel or Karen Bull, (800) 259-8017
Deposit: 3 nights; 30 days cancellation except mid-Dec–Jan 1, for which payment must be received before Nov 1
Minimum Stay: 10 nights during Christmas
Arrival/Departure: Hotel transfers not available due to local taxi regulations
Distance from Airport: 16 miles (35 minutes); taxi one-way, $50
Distance from St. John's: 13 miles; taxi one-way, $30

Accommodations: 72 rooms and suites, all with terraces. All accommodations have either a king or 2 twin beds.
Amenities: Ceiling fans; telephones (suites have them in bath); wall safes; bath with tub and shower, bathrobes, umbrella, miniature flashlight, hair dryers available; fresh flowers daily; full room service; suites have minibars; no television (television room); room service for food during meal times, for bar 10 a.m.–11 p.m.; in-room wire Internet connection, free Wi-Fi.
Fitness Facilities/Spa Services: See text
Sports: Tennis; squash; croquet; putting green; Hobie cats, snorkeling, waterskiing, windsurfing; diving for certified divers only; deep-sea fishing; swimming pool; hiking trips in nearby hills; area offers some of the best birding locations in Antigua
Electricity: 110 volts
Dress Code: Casual by day; cover-up required in dining room; long pants for gentlemen (jacket and tie optional) required after 7 p.m. in public areas
Children: All ages, except February, when only those 12 years and older welcome; cribs; babysitters
Meetings: Up to 20 people
Day Visitors: No
Handicapped Facilities: Limited
Rates: Per room double, daily, All-Inclusive. *High Season* (mid-Dec–mid-Apr): $1,095–$2,250. *Low Season* (mid-May-Jul 23): $715–$1,150. Single-room rate $100 less than double-room rate.
Service Charge: 10 percent
Government Tax: 10.5 percent

GALLEY BAY RESORT & SPA

St. John's, Antigua, W.I.

By the time you have made the long drive from the airport, through St. John's, and down the narrow country road to Galley Bay, you may be having second thoughts. But press on. It's worth it.

Galley Bay (not to be confused with Galleon Beach on the eastern side of Antigua) has one of the prettiest away-from-it-all settings in the Caribbean. Tucked away on the western coast on 40 tropical acres—some landscaped, some natural—the resort is bordered on one side by ½ mile of uninterrupted white-sand beach and, on the other, by a lagoon and bird sanctuary, banded by green hills.

After a hurricane all but leveled the resort in 1995, it was completely rebuilt by its new owners whose group has other hotels in Antigua and other Caribbean islands. The rebuilding modernized and upgraded Galley Bay without changing its essential character. The beautiful entryway with a land bridge spanning the lagoon is downright elegant. Galley Bay offers three types of accommodations: beachfront rooms, suites directly on the beach, and thatched-roof huts called Gauguin Cottages, resting under shade trees by the lagoon, a stone's throw from the sea. The beachfront rooms, in 2-unit cottages with patios, have terra-cotta floors, rush rugs, and a fresh look with rattan furniture covered with attractive prints and louvered windows that catch the breezes.

Deluxe rooms are about a third larger and have huge marble bathrooms with a long, wide counter over two sinks and a big shower. There is a walk-in closet and enough hangers for a year's stay.

All have air-conditioning, ceiling fans, telephone, television, coffeemakers, and minifridges stocked with soft drinks and beer. Another beachfront group of 16 more luxurious one-bedroom suites are located on the south side of the beach. Premium suites, 32 most recently added on the north side are the most luxurious of all, with mahogany furniture and 400-thread-count sheets, as well as flat-screen, wall-mounted television, iPod docking stations, DVD players, and wireless Internet access. The oversized baths have his and hers showers and soaking tubs for two.

The Gauguin Cottages are much more comfortable than you might expect upon first sight. They are two rooms whose masonry walls are covered with white stucco and wooden strips and topped with thatched roofs made to look like huts; they are connected by a thatch-covered breezeway-patio. One "hut" is a spacious bedroom with a sitting area; the other has a bath/dressing room where you will find extra-plush towels and toiletries. The upgraded Gauguin Cottages have private splash pools. Except for their style and location, they vary little from the other accommodations. But they do have a sort of South Sea islands feeling—if you use your imagination.

Recently added are 6 cabanas, near the main restaurant, which have bath and shower, air-conditioning, safe, phone, and 2 chairs. The charge for use is $25, which is donated to charity.

The resort has a hard-surface tennis court, racquets, and balls; bicycles; a rough track around the lagoon for walking and jogging; a shaded Ping-Pong table in its own thatched hut; a new croquet lawn; and a small, air-conditioned exercise pavilion beside the lagoon. Indulge, a small spa with 2 elevated massage decks, overlooks the lagoon and bird sanctuary and 2 pods for massages—one for couples. The spa uses Pevonia Botanica products; a spa menu is available.

Galley Bay has a splendid beach but be aware that in the winter months the sea is often rough with swells, which is why the swimming pool was such a welcome addition. Equipment for snorkeling, windsurfing, and sailing is provided.

Another of Galley Bay's distinctive features is its open-air beachside bar, which sits under a high pyramid of weathered wood and plaited palms. Next door, the open-air lounge, furnished with traditional planter's chairs and comfortable sofas, is the gathering place for most activities— daytime chats, afternoon tea, and lots of doing nothing. By evening cocktail time, when folks have gotten dressed a bit fancier, there's something of a house-party atmosphere for after-dinner socializing and dancing.

The Seagrape, the open-sided dining room, bordered by an attractive boardwalk of weathered wood, is the venue for all meals and offers full menus and table service—in other words, no buffets, a feature that distinguishes Galley Bay from most all-inclusive resorts. Menus change daily and offer an imaginative selection. Dine by candlelight with the sea lapping at the shore and the stars twinkling overhead—it's as romantic a setting as you will find in the Caribbean. The service is outstanding. There is piano music most nights; live entertainment, featured three or four evenings a week, might be a calypso singer, a combo, or a steel band.

The Gauguin, a second, rustic restaurant at the far end of the beach, serves grilled food for lunch and dinner. Here some tables by the sea are under their own separate thatched roof, giving them an intimate, romantic feeling. A third small restaurant, Ismay's, surrounded by tropical gardens, is used as a special occasion venue with a charge of $35 per person.

Galley Bay, a member of the Elite Island Resorts group, is a comfortable, laid-back, informal retreat. Most guests in winter are British and European; in summer more are American. It has the advantage of seeming to be on a remote island when, in fact, it is only about 15 or 20 minutes by car (which you will need) from town and nightlife. That should be ideal for active urbanites who are attracted to a relaxed lifestyle but unaccustomed to vegging out and might get restless.

GALLEY BAY RESORT & SPA ★ ★ ★ ★

Box 305, Five Islands, St. John's, Antigua, W.I.

Phone: (268) 462-0302; **Fax:** (268) 462-4551; **e-mail:** galleybay@candw.ag; www.galleybarresort.com
Owners: Rob Barrett and James Lane
General Manager: James Lane, Jr.
Resident Manager: Cedric Henry
Open: Year-round
US Reservations: (866)237-1644, (954) 949-2142; reservations@galleybayresort .com
Deposit: 3 nights; 14 days cancellation; for arrivals during Feb, reservations and complete payment must be received no later than 45 days prior to arrival. Cancellations from Nov to Mar will result in a 7-night penalty fee.
Minimum Stay: 5 nights; 7 nights mid-Dec–Jan 1.
Arrival/Departure: Transfer service not provided
Distance from Airport: (Bird Airport) 8 miles; taxi one-way, $26
Distance from St. John's: 4 miles; taxi one-way, $18
Accommodations: 98 rooms and suites with patios (including 10 superior and 29 deluxe beachfront rooms; 48 beachfront suites; 13 thatched cottages) with king-size beds and 13 with splash pools
Amenities: Ceiling fans, air-conditioning; flat-screen television; bath with shower (some premium with large tubs and his and hers showers); bathrobe, safe, radio, hair dryer, deluxe basket of toiletries; stocked minifridge, coffeemaker; iPod docks; DVD player. Open-air library with free Wi-Fi
Fitness Facilities/Spa Services: Air-conditioned room with exercise equipment; spa with various moderately priced treatments, facial; hair salon
Sports: Tennis, sailing, snorkeling, windsurfing, kayaking, bicycling equipment included; diving, golf arranged (clubs provided; transfer $22 one way); pool; Ping-Pong; croquet lawn; jogging track; bird sanctuary
Electricity: 110 volts
Dress Code: Casual by day; after 7 p.m. long pants or stylish jeans, collared shirt, shoes; no shorts or T-shirts in bar and restaurant areas
Children: None under 16 years of age
Meetings: Small facility for day meetings
Day Visitors: Yes, day pass for 10:30 a.m. to 6 p.m. including lunch and drinks, $140 plus 20.5 percent service charge and tax.
Handicapped Facilities: No
Packages: All-inclusive
Rates: 2 people, per room, daily, All-Inclusive. *High Season* (mid-Dec–mid-Apr): $990–$1,175. *Low Season:* $880–$1,045. For single, deduct $100 per day.
Service Charge: Included
Government Tax: Included

HERMITAGE BAY

St. John's, Antigua, W.I.

Hidden in a secluded cove on Antigua's west coast, Hermitage Bay is set between tropical clad hills and a beautiful beach. The property is the essence of understated luxury. Comprised of 25 individual cottages built in dark tropical hardwoods that blend into the natural landscape, the cottage suites combine a contemporary minimalist style in decor with echoes of Antigua's colonial past—and all with panoramic views of the Caribbean Sea and neighboring islands in the distance.

The luxury begins at check-in when you are greeted by a guest services attendant who checks you in, while you enjoy a cool drink. The all-suite boutique resort offers 5 Beachfront Cottage Suites (900 square feet); 3 more located directly behind them near the main infinity-edge, freshwater swimming pool. These units have a terraced veranda with a daybed and an air-conditioned bedroom and sitting area.

The 14 Hillside Pool suites (1,100 square feet) and 3 Premium Hillside Pool suites are set against hillside in terraced gardens, each with a wraparound, open-air deck with a lounge area, a daybed, a dining area, and a private infinity-edge plunge pool and grand views of the Caribbean Sea. They have an air-conditioned bedroom with a king bed, large bathtubs, and a separate outdoor garden shower. Dressed in minimalist, contemporary decor, all units have flat-screen television, a DVD player, an iPod docking station, Wi-Fi, an in-room safe, and a minibar.

The restaurant and bar overlooking the beach serves international cuisine with a Caribbean flair. Dining menus are a la carte and include breakfast, lunch, afternoon tea, hors d'oeuvres at cocktail time, and dinner, as well as a selection of house wines and most beverages. A full wine list and deluxe brands are available at an extra charge. Non-motorized water-sports equipment is available on the beach—along with staff for instruction—and is included in the all-inclusive price.

The resort's full-service spa is housed in its own villa with 2 treatment rooms. Treatments are based on the Dorissima color rituals with each of the 7 colors corresponding with the Chakra systems of the body. Your treatment room will be bathed in the color light meant to reflect the ritual: red for empowerment, yellow for confidence, green for balance, etc. Spa treatments are an additional charge. There is a boutique.

Designed for couples, the resort nods to the family market from July 1 to August 31, when it welcomes children 8 and older in the beach suites. Make no mistake, Hermitage Bay is a secluded, hard-to-find hideaway for those seeking peace and tranquility.

Care was made to preserve the natural setting and to keep in harmony with it. The resort has a gray-water system to conserve water and has its own organic farm. It contributes to the local economy by obtaining herbs, jams, and fresh provisions from local farmers.

HERMITAGE BAY ★ ★ ★ ☙
PO Box 60, St. John's, Antigua, West Indies

Phone: (268) 562-5500; **Fax:** (268) 562-5505; **e-mail:** info@hermitagebay .com; www.hermitagebay.com
Owners: Andrew Thesen and Alex Michelin
General Manager: Rachel Browne
Open: Year-round
US Reservations: Direct to hotel
Deposit: 3 nights; 21 days cancellation
Minimum Stay: 7 nights during Christmas/New Year's
Arrival/Departure: Transfer airport service provided for 3 nights or longer stay
Distance from Airport: 35 minutes from airport
Distance from St. John's: About 7 miles; 20 minute drive from St. John's
Accommodations: 25 detached cottages (with king-size beds) with wraparound verandas
Amenities: Air-conditioning, ceiling fan; bath with oversize tubs; a separate outdoor garden shower (hillside); hair dryer, bathrobes, deluxe toiletries, safe; flat screen television, tea/coffeemaker, DVD player; iPod dock; Wi-Fi connection; mini-bar; iron and ironing board; turn down service; buggy shuttle for hillside suites; charge for room service.
Fitness Facilities/Spa Services: See text
Sports: Freshwater swimming pool, kayaks, windsurfing, snorkeling, Sunfish, Hobie Cat, scuba diving, deep-sea fishing, golf arranged for fee
Electricity: 110 volts; each suite has one 220v outlet
Dress Code: Casual by day; slightly more dressy for evening; no jacket or tie required
Children: None under 12 years old, except for July and Aug when children

8 and over are accepted. One child may share suite with two adults.
Day Visitors: No
Handicapped Facilities: No
Packages: Honeymoon
Rates: Per suite, double, daily, **All-Inclusive.** *High Season* (Dec 21–Mar 31): $1,200–$1,975. *Shoulder Season* (Apr 30–May 31; Nov 5–Dec 20): $970–$1,360. *Low Season* (June 1–Sept 5): $920–$1,170. Single deduct $150 per night.
Service Charge: 10 percent
Government Tax: 10.5 percent

JUMBY BAY
Antigua, W.I.

Less than a mile off the northern coast of Antigua is the ultimate private-island resort, Jumby Bay. Situated on a 300-acre dot of land scalloped with pearly beaches, the exclusive 88-acre resort was created in 1983, and the name, Long Island, was changed to Jumby Bay. After a series of owners, the resort was sold in 2002 back to the island's 14 homeowners who engaged Rosewood Hotels & Resorts of Dallas to manage the property and Jumby was given a multimillion-dollar refurbishment . But then, in June 2008, the resort closed for almost 18 months to undergo another multimillion dollar development that brought major changes including a large second pool and a pool grill, a full service spa, a redesigned Veranda Terrace restaurant and bar, upgrading 12 suites, and rebuilding 28 guest rooms.

Jumby Bay offers quietly luxurious accommodations, facilities, and amenities, as fine as can be found in the Caribbean, for one all-inclusive price. That means all meals, cocktails and wine with meals, afternoon tea, cocktail beverages in your room, all sports and recreational facilities on the property, transfers, and even postage stamps. At the airport in Antigua, you are met by a Jumby Bay representative and whisked off to the nearby Beachcomber dock, where the Jumby Bay high-speed catamaran is waiting.

Jumby Bay has 3 groups of accommodations, all near, but not directly on, the beach. Semi-rondavel villas, each with 2 suites, are set along paved paths leading from the main beach to a 200-year-old plantation house, the centerpiece. These 12 accommodations were updated in the most recent renovations. More rooms and suites are located on the north side of the arrival beach. All accommodations have outdoor/indoor showers; some have an outdoor tub as well. The beautifully appointed rooms, all with sitting areas, have custom-designed furniture, most with four-poster, king-size beds with pillows and bedcovers in understated quality fabrics. Another 6 super deluxe villas set alongside Pond Bay, are the most luxurious of the lot. Each villa has 2 spacious suites and a veranda facing the sea and share a swimming pool.

On the south side of the island are the Harbor Bay and Harbor Beach villas—1 three-bedroom villa and 10 huge two-bedroom suites with large living rooms and kitchens; 3 suites have infinite-edge swimming pools. Also, 6 of the large, private estates, ranging from three to six bedrooms, are available for rent.

Each cluster of villas is different, but all resort accommodations have walls of louvered doors and windows of Brazilian walnut, adding a rich accent to the decor and providing cross ventilation. High, beamed ceilings create a sense of space and airiness. Bathrooms are unusually large. Bicycles are standing outside the doors, and you'll find a hammock, too.

The beautifully restored Estate House, with its red tile roof, white-washed arches, and delightful garden courtyard, is reminiscent of a Mediterranean palazzo. The courtyard opens onto a pretty indoor-outdoor dining terrace used for dinner. Courtyard steps lead to a second-floor lounge with a cozy bar, library, and television.

The large, flower-bedecked Verandah Terrace and Bar near the entry dock and main beach is the center of daytime activity. Doubled in size, a show kitchen was added in the redesign. Breakfast, lunch, afternoon tea, and, from mid-December to April 31, dinner, are served on its open-air terraces—and shared with a host of bananaquits and hummingbirds. Early dining for children is available. Private dining at a Chef's Table for up to eight guests can enjoy with exclusive use of the Verandah Kitchen along with a personal chef and a personal sommelier.

Next to the beach pavilion are 3 Laykold tennis courts (lighted); a full-time pro is available. Beyond is a large freshwater lap pool, bordered by white canvas "chalets" with attractive chaise lounges providing shade and privacy. The Beach Hut serves as the sports center. If you feel less ambitious, you can take up residence on a lounge chair beneath a thatched umbrella by the 1,800-foot white-sand beach.

Among the most important of the new additions are the Pool Grille, a third dining option overlooking a large, infinite edge swimming pool and the sea. The Pool Grille serves breakfast and a light lunch and opens seven days per week. Dinner is available from December through April.

Even more anticipated was SENSE®, a Rosewood spa added in 2010, the resort's first stand-alone spa. The open-air, ocean-front facility has vaulted ceilings, polished marble counters, teak cabinetry, and travertine tile floors. Each of the 5 treatment suites, including one for couples, has individual showers and terraces overlooking the Caribbean. Bose surround-sound system provides the soothing background music for the full array of spa treatments.

Jumby Bay maintains an impressive nursery to grow an enormous variety of tropical plants. Except for the flower-festooned resort grounds and lush gardens of the private mansions, the island is covered with dry woods; nature trails and biking paths meander past sumptuous villas and lead to beaches. One path goes to Pasture Bay, where the endangered hawksbill turtle comes to lay her eggs from May to November. Under a watch by WIDECAST (Wide Caribbean Sea Turtle Conservation Network), Jumby Bay hosts marine biology students studying the endangered species

during the nesting season. The program celebrated its 25th anniversary in 2011. Guests can sign up for "turtle watches" to see the turtles nest.

Another recent addition is Rosebud Camp Jumby for 3 to 12 year olds. Three different pavilions offer a host of possibilities for outdoor fun and creative expression, such as "Little Chefs" and "Discover Science," and more. Also new, the camp has teamed up with the Jumby Bay Hawksbill Project to create a kid's turtle adoption program to foster conservation among its youngest guests. Kids may adopt one of four resident turtles and are provided monthly updates on their status. Kids may also sign up for "turtle watch" from June to November to play an active role in the conservation effort. Jumby Bay, with its gracious informality and aura of well-being, is made for honeymooners and romantics, but it appeals equally to those who simply want to get away from it all in spacious, sophisticated surroundings.

JUMBY BAY ★ ★ ★ ★
Box 243, Jumby Bay Island, Antigua, W.I.
Phone: (268) 462-6000, -6002, -6003; **Fax:** (268) 462-6020; **e-mail:** jumbygs@candw.ag; www.jumbybayresort.com
Management: Rosewood Hotel & Resorts
Managing Director: Andrew Hedley
Open: Year-round
US Reservations: Direct to hotel, (800) 237-3237; (888) ROSEWOOD (767-3966)
Deposit: 3 nights; 30 days cancellation
Minimum Stay: 10 nights during Christmas/New Year's

Arrival/Departure: Transfer service $60 adults, per person, round-trip; $30 per child 2 to 12. Those arriving by private plane, inquire

Distance from Airport: Less than 1 mile (5-minute ride) to ferry dock; 10-minute boat ride to Jumby Bay dock; Jumby Bay operates its own scheduled water shuttle between resort and Beachcomber dock in Antigua

Distance from St. John's: 7 miles (15 minutes) from Beachcomber dock in Antigua; taxi one-way, $26

Accommodations: 40 rooms and suites (with king-size beds; 2 queens in second bedroom when booked as 2-bedroom unit) all renovated or rebuilt. Eleven two-bedroom suites in Harbor Bay and Harbor Beach villas; 6 private villas with 3 to 6 bedrooms

Amenities: Air-conditioning, ceiling fans; hair dryer, deluxe toiletries, bathrobes, plush towels changed twice daily; wall safe; umbrellas, walking sticks; cable television, coffeemakers, mini-bar, telephones, DVD and CD player; bicycle; iron/ironing board; ice service daily; golf carts for guests in villas; 24-hour concierge; room service 7 a.m.–10 p.m. for $10 minimum surcharge plus costs of food; complimentary Internet/Wi-Fi; nightly movies

Fitness Facilities/Spa Services: Fitness center; fully service spa (see text)

Sports: Freshwater swimming pool, putting green, croquet court, 3 tennis courts, windsurfing, snorkeling, Sunfish, hiking trails, bicycles included; scuba diving, deep-sea fishing, golf in Antigua arranged for fee

Electricity: 110 volts

Dress Code: Casual by day; slightly more formal for evening; no jacket or tie required

Children: All ages. Rosebud Camp Jumby for ages 3 to 12 (see text)

Meetings: Pond Bay House or entire island can be rented

Day Visitors: No

Handicapped Facilities: Most facilities accessible

Packages: Honeymoon, wedding

Rates: Per room, double, daily, All-Inclusive. *High Season* (Jan 7-Apr 15): $1,495–$3,350. *Shoulder Season* (mid-Apr–May 31; Nov 1–mid-Dec): $1295–$2,700. *Low Season:* $995–$1,975. Two-bedroom, inquire. Children under 2 years old free; 2 to 12 years old, sharing, $150 per night holiday/winter, $75 in spring/summer.

Service Charge: 10 percent

Government Tax: 10.5 percent

LIGHTHOUSE BAY

Low Bay, Barbuda, W.I.

On an island you may not know, with a tiny luxury resort you probably know even less about, there is a leading candidate for the best-kept-secret-in-the-Caribbean.

Lighthouse Bay on Barbuda, the sister island of Antigua 26 miles south, is not actually a new hotel. Rather this 9-suite paradise seems to have been hiding its light (house, that is) under its remoteness. Opened in 2007 by Barbuda native Mike Branker, along with Don Dillon and Patrick Kerrigan, on the site of Branker's grandparents' one-time beach house, Lighthouse Bay has taken exclusivity and seclusion to new heights. Situated on its own private stretch of a narrow 17-mile strip of untouched pink sands, washed by gin-clear Caribbean waters out front and the blue-green serenity of Codrington

Lagoon at its back, privacy is all but guaranteed. The resort is accessible only via boat across the lagoon from Codrington town or by helicopter. Normally, a 15-minute helicopter ride from Antigua's international airport will drop you directly at Lighthouse Bay.

The 9 well-appointed, air-conditioned accommodations are comprised of 4 junior suites (375 square feet), 4 master suites (790 square feet), and 1 grand suite (950 square feet). They are set around a kidney-shaped pool only steps from the pink sand beach and Caribbean sea. The master and grand suites each boast a large terrace, the ideal perch for watching the world go by.

Inside, under a high ceiling with mahogany wood beams that provides an open, airy feeling; the nicely decorated suites have travertine tile throughout; the marble-lined bathroom is fitted with blue bahia granite counters topped with double sinks and a glass-brick, walk-in shower.

Despite the remote location, guests can feel plugged in as every suite has a flat-screen satellite television, an iPod dock/alarm clock, CD/DVD player, and complimentary international telephone calls. The resort also has laptops, iPods, and iPads for guests' use during their stay. Free Wi-Fi Internet connection is available in all guest rooms and throughout the resort. Free laundry service is also available. The all-inclusive resort provides each suite with a mini-fridge stocked with sodas, juices, water, and beer, and an espresso machine for coffee at your liking.

The junior suites are furnished with either a queen-size or 2 double beds, the master suites have a queen bed and an expansive living room, dining room, and terrace. The grand suite has a king-size bed with a large living room. Its spacious private terrace has an outdoor shower and Jacuzzi tub, and direct beach access from your bedside. In addition to its own helipad, the resort has its own electrical supply and desalination plant.

Cafe Lagoon, the resort's the open-air, beachside restaurant, serves break-fast, lunch, and dinner, or you can dine in your suite. Daily menus by Chef Lennox Cadogan offer a variety of freshly baked breads, homemade pastas, organic vegetables, herbs from the resort's garden, and locally caught seafood, including famous Barbuda lobster, which Chef Lennox is an expert in preparing the

Lighthouse Bay Way. He will also create menus to your liking.

When the spirit (or spirits) move you to action, swimming, snorkeling, kayaking, and tennis and basketball on the resort's new courts, are complimentary. Sailing, horseback riding on the beach, diving, fishing, and spa services can be arranged for an additional charge, as can a boat ride in the lagoon. At the north end of the lagoon is one of the world's largest sanctuaries for the Magnificent Frigatebird, where you can observe them at very close range—an experience not to be missed.

Honeymooners in search of an idyllic hideaway need look no further. Weddings are a Lighthouse Bay specialty, with a full-service planner on-site. For the wedding, family reunion, corporate retreat, or special occasion, rent the entire resort and this corner of paradise will be yours.

Down the beach a bit, there are 38 home sites for sale to private owners, ranging in size from 1 to 15 acres and costing $2 to $15 million for the land alone. I don't think you need to worry about a crowded beach anytime soon.

LIGHTHOUSE BAY ★ ★ ★
Low Bay, Barbuda; Antigua and Barbuda, West Indies
Phone: (646) 688-2903; **e-mail:** info@ lighthousebaybarbuda.com; www.light housebayresort.com
Owners: Mike Branker, Don Dillon, and Patrick Kerrigan
General Manager: Terrence Linton
Open: Closed Sept and Oct
US Reservations: Toll-free (888) 214-8552; (877) 818-9213

Deposit: 50 percent at time of confirmation to guarantee reservation. Cancellation 90 days premium season, 30 days high season, 15 days shoulder.
Minimum Stay: 3 nights in high season, 10 nights for premium season
Arrival/Departure: Resort can arrange; prices per person unless noted otherwise: Caribbean Helicopters from Antigua Airport (ANU) direct to resort, $1,600. Helicopter carries 6 minimum-size passengers with hand bags. S.A.G. (St. Vincent and the Grenadines Airlines) scheduled flight to Codrington, Barbuda, $93.70 round-trip, followed by boat-ride across the lagoon. Chartered plane, $800; Barbuda Express Ferry, $40.
Distance from Airport: From Antigua, 25-minute plane ride; from Codrington town, 10-minute boat ride
Distance from Capital: 1 mile plus, across Codrington lagoon from Codrington town
Accommodations: 9 suites (4 junior, 4 master, 1 grand suite); queen-size bed or 2 double beds in junior and master suites; king-size bed in grand suite as well as terrace with outdoor shower and Jacuzzi
Amenities: Air-conditioning, ceiling fan, flat-screen satellite television, iPod dock/alarm clock, CD/DVD player, complimentary international telephone calls; laptop, iPod, or iPad for use during stay; free Wi-Fi throughout resort; marble bathroom with granite counters, double sinks, and walk-in shower; free laundry service; espresso machine, mini-fridge with sodas, juices, water, beer
Fitness Facilities/Spa Services: Spa services available on request for fee.
Sports: Swimming pool, beach, snorkeling, kayaking, tennis, basketball complimentary. Sailing, horseback riding on beach, diving, fishing arranged for fee.
Electricity: 110 volts
Dress Code: Casual
Children: All ages
Meetings: With rental of entire resort
Day Visitors: Yes
Handicapped Facilities: Limited but not advised due to difficulty of access
Packages: Wedding, Getaway, family; see website
Rates: Per room, per night, single or double, *Premium Season* (Dec 18–Jan 9): $1,799–$2,999. *High Season* (Jan 10–Mar 27): $1,499–$2,499. *Shoulder/ Low* (Mar 28–Aug 31; Nov–mid-Dec): $1,299–$2,499. Rates include 3 meals, all beverages, activities, and amenities. For 3 to 6 nights, one-way and for longer than 6, round-trip helicopter transfer from Antigua included.
Service Charge: 20.5 percent
Government Tax: 20.5 percent

ARUBA

Aruba was little more than a sleepy sandbar in the 1950s before the gracious Arubans began to develop their tourism industry. Now they have created one of the most popular, fun-loving playgrounds in the Tropics. And they never stop: This Dutch island is booming with new resorts, marinas, smart boutiques, and more.

Fifteen miles off the Venezuelan coast, this dry, low-lying island in the Netherlands Antilles has surprisingly diverse landscapes and natural attractions for an island only 20 miles long. Similar to the American Southwest, with rocky desert terrain and less than 20 inches of annual rainfall, the island has two totally different faces.

On the southern coast tranquil beaches, sophisticated resorts, and glittering casinos line Palm Beach, a beautiful 5-mile band of sand where most of the hotels are located. In sharp contrast, the rugged northern shore reveals moonscape terrain with pounding surf, shifting sand dunes, caves with prehistoric drawings, and strange gigantic rock formations sculpted by the strong winds. The countryside is dotted with tiny farm villages of Dutch colonial architecture. They're surrounded by cactus fields, which turn overnight from a lifeless gray to flowering green following a good rain, and the distinctive ever-present divi-divi tree. The outback can be fun to visit on horseback or by jeep safari with a naturalist guide.

Aruba is ringed by coral reefs, making snorkeling and diving popular; the deep-sea fishing is good, too. But the strong winds that shape the divi-divi trees and keep the island cool have made Aruba one of the leading windsurfing and kiteboarding locations in the Caribbean. In June an annual international windsurfing competition is held at Eagle Beach, where winds can exceed 25 knots.

In the capital of Oranjestad, a redesigned town center and shopping plaza showcase Aruba's Dutch colonial past. The Aruba Historical Museum, housed in Fort Zoutman, and William III Towers, one of the island's oldest landmarks, reveal its ancient past. The museum and other examples of historical preservation reflect Aruba's increased emphasis on its cultural and historical heritage.

Information

Aruba Tourist Authority, 100 Plaza Dr., First floor, Secaucus, NJ 07094; (800) TO-ARUBA, (201) 558-1110; Fax: (201) 558-4767; www.aruba.com

HYATT REGENCY ARUBA

Palm Beach, Aruba

Located on Palm Beach, along 12 beautiful beachfront acres on Aruba's southwestern coast, the Hyatt Regency Aruba proves that you can have your cake and eat it, too. In other words, with good design it is possible to have a large, full-service resort and still retain the warmth and grace of a small hotel.

Opened in 1990, the hotel recently completed a $20 million, two-year "extreme makeover," as the hotel terms it, that retained the hotel's handsome Spanish-mission-inspired architecture while creating a sophisticated, contemporary look throughout the interiors, gardens, and facilities.

The Hyatt Regency Aruba consists of a 9-story tower flanked by two wings of 4 and 5 stories that overlook the hotel's centerpiece: a landscaped, multilevel pool and lagoon. It starts as a waterfall by the open-air lobby, flows into a series of interconnected pools in flower-filled gardens, and leads to a wide, white-sand beach. You can slip quietly into the pool at one end and splash down a 2-story winding water slide at the other, or swim up to the bar on yet another side.

In the public areas the new decor of the lobby and lounges have been enhanced by a light and airy look with white marble floors, white muslin curtains, and contemporary white sofas against brown wicker furniture and dark wooden floors.

By the Ruinas del Mar restaurant, a rock wall, which seems to float in the lagoon near the center of the gardens, is built of a native limestone called Aruba rock, quarried on the island's northern coast. Here, the design plays on Aruba's gold-mining days at the turn of the century. Mock ruins, special carvings, textured and tinted concrete, and weather-beaten rocks in the gardens and around the pool create the look of the old mines still found in several locations on the island.

All guest rooms have water or garden views, and most have balconies. Their contemporary decor combines avocado and olive green with soft orange and brown, plus a signature orchid in each room. The newest additions are plasma television, Hyatt's signature Grand Bed™ (1 king or 2 queens), and high-speed Internet. The renovated bathrooms have granite countertops, marble floors, rainshower heads, and Moen fixtures throughout. Hyatt is particularly proud of its "Respire by Hyatt," hypoallergenic rooms designed to provide a comfortable sleeping environment, especially for allergy sufferers. These rooms undergo an additional six-step process to reduce airborne particles and potential irritants and to install state-of-the-art air purification system and treatment of all fabrics and surfaces in the room.

Located on the ninth floor, The Regency Club—Hyatt's executive rooms enhanced with more luxurious amenities—was also redesigned and refurbished. It has a private concierge and a lounge where complimentary continental breakfast and evening cocktails and tasty hors d'oeuvres are served daily. There are 4 specialty suites ranging in size from 1,150 to 2,500 square feet and with 1 to 4 bedrooms, large living rooms with cathedral ceilings, stocked wet bars, and guest baths, as well as rooftop terraces with wraparound views of Palm Beach and the Caribbean.

Low-key compared to other large Aruban resorts, the Hyatt has as many services and facilities as its flashier neighbors, if not more. The Ruinas del Mar, an indoor-outdoor restaurant, offers a breakfast buffet and nightly dinner and especially popular Sunday champagne brunch. Nearby is Cafe Piccolo, a small Italian cafe specializing in regional cuisine, particularly northern Italian dishes and pizza hot from a large brick oven, and Cafe Japengo, a seafood and sushi restaurant. The casual Palms, a beachfront grill with an exhibition kitchen and an outdoor terrace, has been redesigned as a Latin bistro offering creative local and Caribbean cuisine and specializing in seafood.

The poolside Balashi Bar, a swim-up or walk-up bar adjacent to the swimming pool, serves sandwiches and salads during the day. Footprints Beach Grill offers "barefoot dining" right on the beach, under a thatched roof beside tiki torches. Pampered in Paradise is the ultimate tropical private dining with the sea at your feet, tiki torches on the sand, and a private butler to serve a 4-course meal and to see to your every need. Menus are available on the resort's website, as are reservations.

In the evening you can take in a sunset cruise, a comedy show, or the disco.

Especially popular at sunset with a daily specialty drink is Piets Pier Bar by the ocean. The recently expanded Casino Copacabana has a nightly live musical show and offers introductory clinics on casino games. The Alfresco Lobby Bar overlooking the pools, an open-air lounge and bar adjacent to the lobby, redesigned in a South-Beach-meets-the-Caribbean fashion with canopied daybeds and colorful lighting, offers live musical entertainment nightly and salsa demonstrations on Thursday.

The resort offers a full service dive and water-sports facility operated by Red Sail Sports, including dive programs for the disabled with instructors certified by the Handicapped Scuba Association, and special-interest dives such as a PADI underwater naturalist course. It can arrange golf, deep-sea fishing, sailing, and other sporting excursions. The Stillwater Spa offers a wide range of body and beauty treatments and state-of-the-art exercise equipment, a sauna and steam room, massage rooms, men's and women's locker rooms, and showers. Pool and beach aerobics and other activities are offered daily. Hyatt's arrival/departure lounge has lockers and showers, allowing early-arriving or late-departing guests full access to hotel facilities.

While you are checking out the gym, you can check the kids into Camp Hyatt, a program of supervised day and evening activities for children ages 3 to 12, available daily year-round. Camp Hyatt facilities include a children's outdoor playground, arts and crafts, and more than a hundred different types of games and toys. Activities, led by professional counselors, include nature walks,

Papiamento lessons, swimming lessons, and more. Prices are $45 from 9 a.m. to 3 p.m. ($20 for additional siblings); $35 in the evening from 6 to 10 p.m. Prices are reduced by $5 each sequential day and the fifth day is free. Casual and friendly, the Hyatt Regency Aruba has a certain glamour and attracts a wide range of guests, mostly from the United States and Latin America. It appeals to couples, families with children, and water-sports enthusiasts.

HYATT REGENCY ARUBA
★ ★ ★ ★

J. E. Irausquin Boulevard #85, Palm Beach, Aruba
Phone: (297) 586-1234; **Fax:** (297) 586-1682; www.aruba.hyatt.com
Owner: Aruba Beachfront Resorts
General Manager: Fred Hoffmann
Open: Year-round
US Reservations: Hyatt Worldwide, (800) 55-HYATT
Deposit: Varies, depending on season; 14 days cancellation, except 60 days for Christmas
Minimum Stay: 10 nights during Christmas
Arrival/Departure: No transfer service
Distance from Airport: 7 miles; taxi one-way, $20
Distance from Oranjestad: 4½ miles; taxi one-way, $8
Accommodations: 360 guest rooms and suites with queen- or king-size beds, most with terrace; Regency Club floor (29 rooms)
Amenities: Air-conditioning, ceiling fans; bath with tub and shower, basket of toiletries, hair dryer; makeup mirror;

telephones, dataport; minibar; coffeemaker; iron and ironing board; safe; plasma television with CNN and other cable services, clock, radio, Wi-Fi ($10 per day; $35 per week); nightly turn-down service on request, 24-hour room service; floor of nonsmoking rooms; concierge; business services; quality boutiques; hair salon. Regency Club: Club lounge; continental breakfast, evening cocktails and hors d'oeuvres; concierge; upgraded amenities and linens
Fitness Facilities/Spa Services: Full-service health club and spa (see text)
Sports: 3-level pool with waterfalls and slide; wide white-sand beach; 2 free tennis courts (lighted); biking; water sports; dive resort and specialty courses; PADI certification for fee; luxury glass-bottom catamaran; deep-sea fishing arranged; 18-hole golf course 2 miles from resort
Electricity: 110 volts
Children: All ages; cribs, high chairs; babysitters; Camp Hyatt for ages 3 to 12. Children under 18 may stay free in parent's room or purchase second room at 50 percent discount, depending on availability.
Meetings: Up to 600 people
Day Visitors: Yes
Handicapped Facilities: Fully accessible; dive program for disabled
Packages: Honeymoon, dive, wedding
Rates: Per person, daily, EP. *High Season* (mid-Dec–mid-Apr): from $595. *Low Season* (mid-Apr–mid-Dec): $335. $500 resort credit on a 5 night stay in high season; $300 on 4 night in low season.
Service Charge: 13.5 percent on room
Government Tax: 9.5 percent

THE BAHAMAS

An archipelago of more than 700 tropical islands stretches south from the eastern coast of Florida over 100,000 square miles of peacock-green and cobalt-blue seas. The Bahamas are so close to the US mainland that many people hop to them in their own boats or private planes for the weekend.

Proximity, together with the foreign but familiar cultural influence of Great Britain (which ruled the Bahamas for more than two centuries), helps make this island nation the tropical destination most visited by Americans—almost five million a year. Most people's introduction to the Bahamas includes Nassau, the capital and commercial center, and Paradise Island, across the harbor. Both bustle with activity day and night, but when you want to exchange the razzle-dazzle for tranquillity, you need only escape to the "other Bahamas," where life is so laid-back and serene that 10 people make a crowd. The Out Islands, as they are called, offer lazy, sunny days of sailing, snorkeling, scuba diving, fishing, windsurfing, or doing nothing at all. The Abacos: At the northern end of the archipelago, a group of islands is strung in boomerang fashion for 130 miles around the Sea of Abaco, whose sheltered waters offer some of the Bahamas' best sailing. Marsh Harbour is the hub, and New Plymouth is a Cape Cod–like village with palm trees.

Andros: Directly west of Nassau, Andros is the largest of the Bahamas but one of the least developed islands. The interior is covered with forests and mangroves. The Barrier Reef, third largest in the world, and, just beyond, the Tongue of the Ocean, 1,000 fathoms deep, lie off the eastern coast and attract divers and sport fishermen from afar. Eleuthera: First-timers in search of the other Bahamas will delight in the quiet and beauty of this island paradise with its 300 years of history, comfortable hotels, and good dining and sports facilities. Eleuthera, 60 miles east of Nassau, is a 110-mile-long slice of land never more than 2 miles wide (except for splays at both ends).

Governor's Harbour, near the center of the island, is the main town and commercial hub. Harbour Island, almost touching the northeastern tip, is one of the Bahamas' most beautiful spots and the site of Dunmore Town, its original capital.

Exumas: About 35 miles south of Nassau, the Exumas spread southeast across 130 square miles of the beautiful turquoise waters popular with yachtsmen, snorklers, and divers. Georgetown, the center, is a quiet village of fewer than one thousand people.

Information

Bahamas Tourist Office, 1200 South Pine Island Rd., Ste. 750, Plantation, FL 33324; (800) 4-BAHAMAS, (954) 236-9292; Fax: (954) 236-9282; www.bahamas.com (office also in Toronto)

GREEN TURTLE CLUB AND MARINA

Abaco, Bahamas

Set on a point overlooking White Sound on the south and Coco Bay on the north, and surrounded by white sand beaches and green forested hills, the Green Turtle Club has been a favorite of yachtsmen since it started as a boathouse bar in the 1960s.

The Charlesworth family, who formerly owned the resort, came to the Bahamas from Britain in search of a family vacation house and decided to stay. It has one of the most idyllic settings in the Abacos, if not the entire Bahamas. It was apparently enough to attract the new owners, Adam Showell and his sister, Ann Showell Mariner, who bought the hotel in September 2004. They also own "Castle in the Sand Hotel" in Ocean City, Maryland.

There is a variety of accommodations spread over the 14-acre property. The wooden cottages with deluxe rooms and suites are painted a fresh yellow with white trim; inside, the spacious rooms are furnished with attractive colonial-style mahogany furniture, Meissen prints, and Oriental rugs.

Some rooms and suites, as well as cottages with kitchens for up to four people, are located on a small rise by the swimming pool. Other villas directly on the water have private docks and kitchens and can accommodate up to 8 to 10 people.

A deluxe beach villa, Beau Soleil has three separate accommodations— all with kitchen—and can be rented together or as one unit. It has its own swimming pool for the use of the guests staying in the villa and their guests.

The Green Turtle Club Restaurant, long been know for good food, changes its menu daily; it is posted in the marina dock box and at the bar and the front desk. There are two seatings: 7 and 7:30 p.m., when dinner is served promptly. Guests can choose to eat inside in the air-conditioned, pine-paneled dining rooms, or outside on a screened patio at the water's edge. The restaurant accommodates the resort's many day visitors, mainly boaters, along with hotel guests. The restaurant also offers a la carte dining on the screened in patio from 6:30 until 8:30 p.m., where no reservations are necessary. The resort is constantly being refurbished and upgraded without changing its atmosphere. Among the recent additions are a 20,000-gallon-per-day watermaker and wireless Internet service, free for hotel and marina guests. Green Turtle has the ambience of a club, and indeed, it has a private membership club, Green Turtle Yacht Club, to which all hotel guests pay $1 per day temporary membership. It is associated with the Royal Yachting Association of England and the Palm Beach Yacht Club in Florida, with whom it has reciprocity.

The bar, with its dark wood and beamed ceiling, is in the original boathouse and decorated with flags from yacht clubs around the world. Its walls are papered with one-pound British sterling notes, US dollars, and other currency, maintaining a tradition begun in World War II when RAF pilots, about to depart on a mission, left money for a round of drinks in their memory in case they did not return. Just outside the bar is a patio restaurant.

The bar is the social center in winter, but in summer the crowd moves out to the pretty terrace by the marina. At sunset and after dinner, this is probably the liveliest place in the Abacos, particularly on the nights when there is live music for listening and dancing. Tucked in the corner to one side of the terrace is a quiet cove with a small beach where lounge chairs and thatched umbrellas draw sun worshipers during the day. Up a small hill where the rooms are located, there is a pretty, tiled lap swimming pool. For those who are more energetic, a path behind the cottages leads to secluded Coco Bay, a beautiful white-sand beach where there is good snorkeling. A narrow dirt road leads to New Plymouth, the main settlement on Green Turtle Cay, about an hour's walk from the resort. Water sports, boats for fishing, and dive excursions are available daily at Brendal's Dive Center.

Golf can be arranged at Treasure Cay, a 20-minute boat ride away.

The nearest airport is on Treasure Cay; from there you take a taxi to the ferry dock, a ferry to New Plymouth, and a water taxi to the club. But after a couple of the resort's famous Tipsy Turtle Rum Punches, you'll forget about the long trip and be happy that you discovered the club.

GREEN TURTLE CLUB AND MARINA ★ ★

Green Turtle Cay, Abaco, Bahamas Out Islands
Phone: (242) 365-4271; **Fax:** (242) 365-4272, (866) 528-0539 (message/toll free fax); (800) 254-2617; **e-mail:** info@greenturtleclub.com; www.green turtleclub.com

Owners: The Showell family

General Manager: Lynn Johnson

Open: Year-round

US Reservations: Direct to hotel (866) 528-0539 or its website

Deposit: 5 nights for Christmas/New Year's; 2 nights, balance of year; 30 days cancellation for holidays, 14 days balance of year

Minimum Stay: 5 nights during holidays, 2 nights balance of year

Arrival/Departure: Green Turtle Ferry Service can be arranged by hotel reception; $11 per person one way, payable locally. Taxi from Ferry Dock to airport, $4 per person with $8 minimum charge

Distance from Airport: (Treasure Cay Airport) 3½ miles; taxi and ferry, see information above

Distance from New Plymouth: 2 miles; water taxi daily

Accommodations: 34 rooms with deck or terrace in cottages and villas (all with queen or king); some with kitchens

Amenities: Air-conditioning, ceiling fans; 6 rooms have bath with tub, 22 have shower only; small refrigerator; no telephones, room service; 32-inch flat-screen television in 9 rooms, 9 deluxe and superior club rooms; television in lounge.

Sports: Freshwater swimming pool; boat rentals, snorkeling, diving, bonefishing, kayaking, deep-sea fishing available for a fee

Electricity: 110 volts

Dress Code: Casual

Children: All ages; cribs and babysitters can be arranged

Meetings: Up to 50 people

Day Visitors: Welcome; reservations required for meals

Handicapped Facilities: No

Packages: 3-night When Turtles Fly, from $499 per person. Also, see resort's website

Rates: Per night, one or two people, daily, EP: Deluxe Club and waterfront rooms from $99 to $240; 1-, 2-, and 3-bedroom villas from $199 to $489, depending on season. Guests who pay for 6 nights may get the 7th night free.

Service Charge: 25 percent

Government Tax: 25 percent

SMALL HOPE BAY LODGE

Andros, Nassau, Bahamas

The very antithesis of the glitz and glitter of Nassau and Paradise Island is Small Hope Bay Lodge, a rustic retreat in an idyllic setting on the eastern coast of Andros. Here, friendly conversation replaces casinos and floor shows, and natural means not only an almost undisturbed landscape but also genuine people and an ambience where guests blend into the "family" and love it—or quickly find they are in the wrong place.

When the late Dick Birch decided to give up cold Canadian winters and the fast track to create a resort on an undeveloped island, he found the ideal spot: a white-sand beach on Andros, facing the third longest barrier reef in the world, only an hour's flight from Florida.

Hidden under pine and palm trees on the shallow bay from which it takes its name, Small Hope Bay Lodge has 20 bungalows for 40 guests at the edge of a crescent beach. Birch, an engineer by profession, built the bungalows and lodge himself out of local pine and coral stone. The bungalows have large rooms with tiled floors and are decorated with colorful handmade batiks created at Androsia, the factory begun by Birch's former wife, Rosie, and now a mainstay of the island's economy. Hammocks wide enough for two are placed about the property. Romantic? You bet.

The lodge, the focal point of the resort, has a large living room rather than a hotel lobby. (Check-in means having your name hung up at the bar.) The homey lounge has a large stone fireplace and walls lined with well-read books: everything from scientific treatises to science fiction. An old fishing boat, the *Panacea,* serves as the bar (drinks are included in the all-inclusive price).

Meals are informal, in keeping with the resort's laid-back ambience. Breakfast always has a "Bahamian Special" consisting of down-home island tastes with a full continental buffet andl grill choices. Lunch and dinner are served buffet style. By early evening guests have gathered in the lodge for cocktails, along with conch fritters and a veggie platter served every evening before dinner.

Dinner is a communal affair at which guests dine family style with family members, dive masters, and staff. It is just slightly more formal than other meals, with Androsia table linens and the chef coming to the bar and announcing the details of the upcoming meal. The chef favors fresh seafood supplied by local fishermen, with fresh vegetables from the island's farms. At least once per week is Bahamian night with complete Bahamian fare.

Entertainment after dinner might be an impromptu party or slide show in the lounge. On cool winter evenings guests settle on huge cushions by a warm fire to continue their conversations. Others play chess, backgammon, or Ping-Pong. Someone strumming a guitar might bring on a song; a CD might inspire dancing. Nightly, there's viewing of the dive activities.

Children are easily included in the informal atmosphere. There is plenty for them to do, but they must be 10 years old to dive. Children 7 and under have a separate dinner hour. The star attraction is the 142-mile-long barrier reef,

less than 15 minutes from the lodge. A conservationist and record-setting diver, Birch (and his family) worked hard to have the Bahamian government declare the Andros reef a national reserve. The reef has a tremendous variety of coral and fish, and virgin dive sites are frequently found.

The dive center offers excursions several times daily, ranging from 10 feet on one side of the reef to "over the wall," a dive to 185 feet that looks down a sheer vertical 6,000-foot drop into the Tongue of the Ocean. You can have a personalized video of your dive made by the lodge's resident diver-photographer. Nondivers snorkel in shallow water either from shore or from the dive/snorkel boat out on the reef, or they can take a Discover Scuba course at no cost. Equipment is provided. A special program provides one-on-one or -two diving with a dive master to some of the Blue Holes, part of the intricate cave system beneath Andros. The center also offers shark diving under controlled, environmentally conscious conditions. It offers Nitrox and numerous advanced certifications.

Bonefishing is as popular as diving, and you can't find better waters for the sport than those of Andros. Small Hope can arrange everything you need, along with some of the best bonefishing guides in the Bahamas.

The resort has a variety of special week packages and guided tours: yoga groups, a birding and ecology week with experts, bonefishing clinics, safari into the interior of Fresh Creek, or overnight camping in the wilderness on western Andros.

Small Hope continues its environmental stewardship with zeal and pride reflected in its complete recycling program. For example, all beer bottles are sent back to the manufacturer, aluminum cans go to Nassau for "Cans for Kids" and steel cans are sent to a recycling company; vegetables are composted. The resort also has an Environmental Management System, to be sensitive and creative in making the 50-year-old property ever more sensitive to the environment. For example, it monitors all usage of electricity and water per person, and production of waste.

Small Hope operates as an all-inclusive resort; rates include accommodations, meals and hors d'oeuvres, open bar, hotel taxes, and use of windsurfers, bikes, sailboats, kayaks, nature trails, beachfront hot tub, self-guided bike and walking nature trails, and free introductory dive or snorkel lessons.

Following Dick's sudden death in 1996, his son, Jeff, and other members of the family have carried on the spirit of this unspoiled paradise, which is not just a business but a way of life. It's like spending the weekend at a beach cottage with friends from all over the world. While diving continues to be the main attraction, nondivers in search of tropical bliss and beauty, good food, and good company will be happy here, too. "Rest, relaxation, and rediscovery" is the resort's motto, and it delivers.

SMALL HOPE BAY LODGE
★ ★ 🐋

Fresh Creek, Andros Island; PO Box FC23301, Fresh Creek, Andros Island, Bahamas

Phone: (800) 223-6961, (242) 368-2014; **Fax:** (242) 368-2015; **e-mail:** SHBinfo@SmallHope.com; www.smallhope.com
Owners: The Birch family
General Manager: Jeff Birch
Open: Oct to US Labor Day in Sept
US Reservations: Direct to lodge, (800) 223-6961
Deposit: 1 night per person
Minimum Stay: 5 nights during Christmas/New Year's and Easter
Arrival/Departure: Taxi $20 for two plus $4 per person extra
Distance from Airport: 5 miles. Several reliable air services from Nassau to Fresh Creek (ASD). Service available from Fort Lauderdale via Continental and Watermakers. Be sure to bring passport. There is also ferry service from Nassau on Bahamas Ferries three times per week.
Accommodations: 20 cottages with twin beds or king (good mattresses), all with patios; 4 two-bedroom cottages for families with children
Amenities: Ceiling fans; bath with shower; oceanfront hot tub; tile floors; air-conditioning in most rooms (small energy surcharge); room service on request; no telephones, television, locks on doors
Fitness Facilities/Spa Services: Masseuse available; hot tub on beach
Sports: Diving and snorkeling (see text); windsurfing (equipment free), Laser sailboat, kayaks, Hobie catamaran; nature walks; birding; biking; no swimming pool; great bonefishing, $290 half day for two people, boat, guide, equipment; reef fishing, deep-sea fishing available; guided eco-trips available for extra fee

Electricity: 110 volts/60 cycles

Dress Code: Informal resort wear, day and evening. Small Hope has only one rule: no ties.

Children: All ages; cribs; playroom and supervised activities; babysitters available; children's rates; special rates for single parents; equipment and lessons for scuba/snorkeling for children under age ten

Packages: Scuba, wedding, fishing, family, honeymoon, snorkeling. Check website for specials.

Meetings: Small groups; up to 40 people when renting entire resort

Day Visitors: Welcome

Handicapped Facilities: Limited

Rates: All-Inclusive, per adult, per night, nondivers. *High Season* (mid-Dec–late Apr): $265. *Low Season:* $235. Divers rates, inquire. Rates for snorkelers and children are available.

Service Charge: Included; 6 percent discretionary gratuity added to bill

Government Tax: Included

SANDALS GRANDE EMERALD BAY

Great Exuma, Bahamas

Quietly settled on 470 acres, the resort blends in well with its Out Island surroundings of Great Exuma. This is, in fact, surprising, since the opening of Sandals (and its Four Seasons predecessor), completely transformed life on this small island. Happily, Great Exuma's people have embraced their new-found fame with genuine Bahamian grace.

Upon approaching the resort's main building in muted Bahamian British colonial style, the newly renovated 18-hole Greg Norman–designed golf course spreads out on both sides and behind. The resort manages to be elegant and seaside comfortable at the same time. The main building and centerpiece of the resort opens onto a lovely small lobby with the reception desk and tours service desk. Here, too, is Il Cielo, one of the resort's six restaurants. To one side of the main building is the Red Lane spa, the 29,000-square-foot oasis offering a full range of treatments in 17 indoor treatment rooms and 3 outdoor treatment cabanas. It also includes a fitness club and beauty salon.

Beyond the lobby, the true charm of the Sandals Emerald Bay becomes evident—the heavenly turquoise and blues of the waters of Emerald Bay spread in both directions in a crescent shape. At the center the large, free-form main pool meanders in different directions and is outlined by the yellow-and-white striped cloth cabanas that provide respite from the strong Bahamian sun. A quiet, freshwater pool is off to one side of the resort. To the left and right are lovely pale-yellow, 3-story buildings with white Bahamian sloped, tile roofs and shuttered soft pastel stucco that house the majority of the 183 guest rooms. These buildings are not directly on the water or beach but rather tucked a bit back, with large lawns separating them. In May 2011, they were joined by another 66 guest rooms, including 4 super elegant 1-bedroom suites, bringing the resort's total to 249 accommodations.

All of the guest rooms are tastefully done in understated elegance of classic, comfortable decor. The oversize rooms use light sky-blue or seagrass color schemes, accented by stone floors, custom area rugs, and dark-stained, handcrafted wood furnishings. The comfortable beds are available in king-size or two doubles. The rooms are equipped with television, DVD/CD player, iHome docking station, air-conditioning, ceiling fan, seating area, and louvered sliding doors out onto a balcony or terrace. Some higher-category rooms have a separate parlor area, as well. The large marble bathrooms have dual-sink vanities, deep-soaking tubs, separate glass-enclosed showers, and a separate toilet. The pristine beach is a wonderful stretch of sand that leaves one feeling as though there isn't any other place in the world. Activities include snorkeling, kayaking, windsurfing, and other nonmotorized water sports. The resort has 6 Har-Tru tennis courts.

To one side of the main pool is the casual Banana Bay Dino's Pizzeria, and to the other side, The Drunken Duck where you have choices ranging from a variety of grilled meat and seafood to pizza and sandwiches. The bar is popular for before- and after-dinner drinks and is a great place to mingle with other guests.

Sandals Grande Emerald Bay is meant to be the essence of Sandals new Luxury Included vacation concept that encompasses such elements as service with one of the resort industry's lowest guest-to-staff ratios and private butlers trained by the Professional Guild of English Butlers. Another element is that every resort has a minimum of

6 restaurants ranging from beachside casual to white-glove formal as well as a choice of cuisine such as Caribbean, Japanese, Italian, Mediterranean, English pub, and more, and featuring top brands of liquors and wines. Red Lane Spa is found at 15 Sandals Resorts, and Sandals Weddings by Martha Stewart are available at 18 resorts. Couples who book a minimum 6-night wedding stay in a premium category or higher get the wedding at no additional cost.

It almost goes without saying that the quality of the beach must be high with ample space for water activities and instruction. Sandals operates one of the largest PADI certification programs in the Caribbean, giving guests access up to as many as 30 dive sites and 8 dive excursions per day, per resort. Divers can be PADI certified at every level up to dive master.

For golfers, Sandals offers courses in Jamaica and Saint Lucia but the pride is the 18-hole Greg Norman–designed Sandals Emerald Reef Golf Club. The 7,000 yard, par-72 championship course has 6 stunning, signature ocean-side holes and a newly added golf lounge named the Shark Shack, in honor of Norman, who is currently the Lifestyle spokesman for Sandals Emerald Bay. The lounge is furnished with a poker table and seating on an outdoor deck. The course's renovations included a new state-of-the-art irrigation system, reshaping and edging of many bunkers, installation of new bunker drainage, and major landscaping. Check the website for promotional packages.

The 23-acre Marina at Emerald Bay, located a short distance from the resort, provides 160 wet slips and 190 dry slips and can accommodate mega-yachts of 260 feet in length. Serving as a point of entry for customs and immigration, the marina offers daily docking and full marina services, including water and electricity, telephone and cable television, fuel dock, dockmaster's office, the Harbormaster's Lounge restaurant, a ship's chandlery, a produce market, floating docks, and dry dock storage.

The true beauty of this resort is the beauty of the Bahamas and its people. Sandals has taken every opportunity to incorporate the local flavor and culture into its resort while still maintaining its well-established service and style.

SANDALS GRANDE EMERALD BAY ★ ★ ★ ★
PO Box EX29005, Great Exuma, Bahamas
Phone: (242) 336-6800; **Fax:** (242) 336-6801; www.sandals.com
Owner/Management: Sandals Resorts International
General Manager: Jeremy Mutton
Open: Year-round
US Reservations: (800) SANDALS
Deposit: $400, full payment 45 days prior to travel
Minimum Stay: None
Arrival/Departure: Transfers available. Great Exuma is served by American Eagle from Miami, Continental Connection from Fort Lauderdale, and Bahamas Air from Nassau.
Distance from Airport: (Exuma International) 15 minutes
Accommodations: 249 rooms and suites, all with either 1 king or 2 doubles

Amenities: Air-conditioning, ceiling fan; multiline phones; CD and DVD players, iHome docking station; safe; umbrellas; iron and ironing board; tea and coffeemaker, stocked minibar; cable television, high-speed Internet access; tiled bathrooms with separate tub and shower, 2 sinks, toilet, hair dryer

Fitness Facilities/Spa Services: See text

Sports: Greg Norman 18-hole golf course; diving, bone- and sports fishing, snorkeling, kayaking, windsurfing; tennis

Electricity: 110 volts

Dress Code: Smart casual

Children: None

Meetings: Yes (see text)

Day Visitors: Welcome, but guests have priority at all facilities. *Day Pass* (10 a.m.–2 p.m.): $180. *Evening* (6 p.m.–2 a.m.): $150. *Full Day* (10 a.m.–2 am): $310.

Handicapped Facilities: 2 guest rooms; property is wheelchair accessible

Packages: Romance, golf, others

2012 Rates: Per person, double, daily, All-Inclusive, from $295

Service Charge: Included

Government Tax: Included

THE DUNMORE

Harbour Island, Eleuthera, Bahamas

A new name, new owner, new pool, new fitness facility, new homes— it's easy to say that this historic boutique hotel, formerly Dunmore Beach Club, was almost a new hotel when it reopened in December 2010.

Set high above Harbour Island's famous pink-sand beach on 10 well-kept acres shaded by tropical trees and colorful flowers, The Dunmore is a small, quiet resort with 16 guest cottages, spaced far enough apart from one another to provide privacy. The structures are squares, more or less, of newly painted, crisp-white exteriors. But what they lack in architectural merit on the outside, they make up for in their comfortable interiors—all with pitched roofs, air-conditioning, modern bathrooms, and new furnishings and finishes along with some useful high-tech gadgets. The rooms are actually large suites and come in three categories: ocean front, ocean view, and garden view. Each unit has a breezy porch with fabulous views, where it is easy to spend hours reading, sipping a cool drink, snoozing, watching the changing colors of the beautiful sea, and feeling completely removed from the cares of the world.

All the cottages have a spacious bedroom with a large bath; some also have a living area or a separate sitting room with a daybed or a sleeper sofa. Garden view cottages are surrounded by a private flowering garden. The oceanfront cottages with views of the Atlantic Ocean have immediate access to the pink sand beach. The 2-bedroom oceanfront Ocean House, a large 2-story cottage, has a living area with kitchenette, small study, and a private sundeck with a spectacular view. It can be rented as a 2-bedroom house or as 2 private suites. All accommodations are air-conditioned and have a ceiling fan, cable television, telephone, flat-panel HD television, wireless Internet, iPod dock; private patio with umbrella and furniture; king-size bed with high-end

Sealy Posturepedic mattresses, luxury linens, down pillows, bathroom, robes, hair dryer, makeup mirror, and Molten Brown toiletries; safe, mini bar, coffeemaker, nightly turndown service. The entire resort has complimentary Wi-Fi and an Apple iPad is available to guests to check e-mail.

The newly renovated main house serves as clubhouse and restaurant/bar. It has a large, comfortable living room with a library. The bar, which is attended by full-time bartenders, quickly takes on a house-party ambience during pre-lunch and pre-dinner cocktail hours.

The resort's long established reputation for having the best cuisine on the island is being upheld by its new executive chef, Matthew Ono. Guests enjoy creative interpretations of Bahamian dishes and international classics based on seasonally available local produce and fresh seafood. Meals are served in the upgraded indoor dining room or, weather permitting, under the new dining tent on an outdoor terrace. Beachside food and beverage service is also available.

At dinner, the dining room gets dressier and more formal, as do the guests, with dining room tables dressed in white linen and candlelight, and meals served on fine china. The resort has a dress code. Children under age 12 must be seated to eat by 6:30 p.m. Reservations are required. The restaurant is closed on Tues for lunch and dinner.

From the dining room terrace, steps lead down to the beach—as nice a spot for walking or jogging as it is for sunning and swimming. Among the resort's newest amenities is an oceanfront pool, complete with a lounge area and open-air fitness facility. There are beach chairs with pretty aqua and white stripped hoods and umbrellas for lounging. The Dunmore has a tennis court and offers snorkel gear, kayaks, paddle boards, sand volleyball. Deep-sea fishing, bonefishing, sailing and scuba diving can be arranged for a fee.

In mid-2011, construction began on the first of six residential home sites with great ocean views and private beach access. "The Residences at The Dunmore" homeowners will enjoy the amenities and convenience of a full-service, luxury resort. Floor plans are available on The Dunmore's website.

The Dunmore's new owner, Gil Besing, a 25-year veteran of the commercial real estate industry, is the founder and chief executive officer of Cardinal Capital Partners, Inc.

DUNMORE BEACH CLUB ★ ★ ★

PO Box EL-27122, Harbour Island, Eleuthera, Bahamas
Phone: (242) 333-2200, toll free (877) 891-3100; **Fax:** (242) 333-2429; **e-mail:** info@dunmorebeach.com; www.dunmorebeach.com
Owner: RW Operations, LTD
General Manager: Omar and Quincie Stubbs
Open: Year-round except Aug 15 to Nov 15
US Reservations: Direct to hotel, toll free (877) 891-3100; toll free (242) 333-2200
Deposit: 3 nights; 30 days cancellation
Minimum Stay: 3 nights, 7 nights Christmas/New Year's Eve

Arrival/Departure: Concierge services from North Eleuthera Airport to hotel for fee.
Distance from Airport: (North Eleuthera International) 3 miles; from airport to ferry, 1 mile, $5; from dock to Harbour Island, 2 miles, $5; from Harbour Island to hotel via taxi, one-way, $4
Distance from Dunmore Town: ½ mile; taxi one-way, $4
Accommodations: 16 cottages, all with furnished patio; king-size beds with high-end Sealy Posturepedic mattresses
Amenities: Air-conditioning, ceiling fan, cable television, telephone, flat-panel HD television, Wi-Fi, iPod dock; umbrella; hair dryer, robes, Molten Brown toiletries; safe, mini bar, radio and clock; luxury linens, down pillows, bathroom, makeup mirror; coffeemaker, nightly turndown service; concierge, golf cart to explore Harbour Island.
Sports: Oceanfront swimming pool, free use of tennis court; kayaks, paddle boards, snorkel gear, sand volleyball. Deep sea fishing, bone fishing, sailing, and scuba diving arranged for fee.
Fitness Facilities/Spa Services: Open-air fitness facility; massage therapist available
Electricity: 110 volts
Dress Code: Long pants required in dining room. Jacket optional. Shorts allowed on dining terrace in summer.
Children: All ages; cribs, high chairs; babysitters. Children under 12 must be seated to eat by 6:30 pm.
Meetings: Up to 32 people
Day Visitors: For lunch and dinner with reservations
Handicapped Facilities: Yes, but beach access difficult

Packages: Special rates for weddings; inquire

Rates: Per room, two people, daily, *CP. High Season* (mid-Nov–Apr 30): $400–$740. *Low Season* (May 1–Aug 15): $340–$580. Additional 20 percent

applied to Mar and Dec 19–Jan 5 rates. For single, additional occupants, and children's rates, inquire.

Service Charge: 24 percent

Government Tax: 24 percent

BRITISH COLONIAL HILTON NASSAU

Nassau, Bahamas

In October 1999 Hilton International opened its first Bahamian property, the British Colonial Hilton Nassau, after completing an 18-month, $68 million restoration that converted the historic property into a deluxe business and leisure hotel with downtown Nassau's only private beach. A decade later, the hotel underwent another major renovation.

Located in the heart of downtown Nassau's business center, the British Colonial Hilton is the city's oldest continuously operating hotel, first opened

in 1922. It was part of a development project that housed the first stock exchange in the Bahamas, along with offices. Formerly known as the British Colonial Hotel and built on the historic site of old Fort Nassau, the 7-story Hilton preserves the Caribbean colonial charm of the old landmark while adding the amenities that today's travelers want and expect.

The latest renovations saw a makeover of all guest rooms, meeting rooms, restaurants, and a magnificent, redesigned lobby. Standard guestrooms have new bedding accessories and soft furnishings, 32-inch high-definition LCD televisions, marble floors, new lighting, mini refrigerator, desk, and ergonomically-designed chairs.

The sixth and seventh floors house 47 executive rooms and 10 suites, which were upgraded with soft furnishings and 37-inch high-definition LCD television added. The suites also have Nespresso coffee machines. The new Executive Lounge, where guests enjoy private check-in and check-out as well as complimentary continental breakfast, evening hors d'oeuvres, and drinks, has been relocated to the top floor, offering panoramic views over Nassau harbor. The space is 50 percent larger than the previous lounge and offers new facilities, including complimentary computer work stations, Wi-Fi Internet access, self-service kitchenette with all day refreshments, and large-screen televisions.

In addition to the private beach, the landmark property has a large freshwater swimming pool set in pretty tropical gardens, a fitness center, and a snorkeling facility. Aqua, the main dining room, serves a buffet and a la carte international selections for breakfast, lunch, and dinner. The outdoor Patio Bar and Grille offers Bahamian and American-style snacks. For evening cocktails there's Bullion and @1 Coffee Bar with evening entertainment on some evenings.

The British Colonial Hilton has a fully equipped business center. Its expanded meeting facilities include the spacious Governor's Ballroom, the Victoria Room with garden and ocean views, the Sir Harry Oakes Boardroom, Sir Milo Butler Boardroom, a larger, new Windsor Room, and 5 other meeting rooms.

Situated at Number One Bay Street, the hotel is within easy walking distance of Nassau's famous Straw Market, duty-free shops, historic sites, and the port. Golf and nightlife are only a few minutes away by car.

The British Colonial was the setting for two James Bond films with Sean Connery: *Thunderball* (1965) and *Never Say Never Again* (1983). (Connery currently has a home on the island.) The hotel can arrange for Stuart Cove (who trained the Bond movie doubles) to take divers down to see the 120-foot freighter that was sunk for the movie *Never Say Never Again* as well as the Valkin Bomber airplane from *Thunderball*.

BRITISH COLONIAL HILTON NASSAU ★ ★ ★

1 Bay St., Nassau, Bahamas
Phone: (242) 322-3301; **Fax:** (242) 322-9009; www.hilton.com
Owners: Adurion Capital Limited
Management: Hilton Hotels Corporation
General Manager: Pablo Torres
US Reservations: Hilton Reservations Worldwide, (800) HILTONS
Deposit: 1 night
Minimum Stay: None, except Christmas/New Year's 3 nights minimum stay
Arrival/Departure: Guests referred to local company for transfer service
Distance from Airport: (Sir Lynden Pindling International Airport) 10 miles; taxi one-way, $22

Accommodations: 288 rooms (including 47 executive level rooms, 23 suites, the Prime Ministers Suite, and the Executive Lounge)
Amenities: Air-conditioning; telephones; television; hair dryer, toiletries; room service, nightly turndown service; high-speed Internet; oversize desks; modems, fax machines on request
Sports: Beach, swimming pool; free non-motorized water sports and snorkeling facility on-site
Children: 18 and under stay free when staying with parents
Electricity: 120 volts
Dress Code: Business casual

Meetings: Facilities for up to 400 people; 5 meeting rooms; boardroom; business center
Day Visitors: Yes
Handicapped Facilities: Yes
Packages: Yes
Rates: Per room, double, daily: *High Season* (Jan–May 31): $239–$899. *Low Season* (June 1–Sept 30): $199–$899. *Shoulder Season* (Oct 1–Dec 21): $209–$899; *Christmas holidays* (Dec 22–31): $249–$899. Single rates available.
Service Charge: Maid gratuity, $5 per person per day
Government Tax: 18 percent
Energy Surcharge: $4 per person per day

GRAYCLIFF HOTEL

Nassau, Bahamas

If you are a romantic and care more about ambience, history, and in-town location than glitter, casinos, or the beach, Graycliff will be your kind of hotel.

Situated in one of the oldest structures in Nassau (and listed in the National Register of Historic Places), Graycliff is one of the most unusual hotels in the Bahamas, if not the Caribbean. Just up the hill from Bay Street, Nassau's main thoroughfare, and 1 block from Government House, the landmark mansion is thought to have been built around 1740 by Captain John Howard Graysmith, an infamous pirate who commanded the schooner, Graywolf, which plundered treasure ships along the Spanish Main. In 1776, when Nassau

was captured by the American navy, Graycliff became their headquarters and garrison—hence the bars on the windows of the hotel's wine cellar.

Graycliff was Nassau's first inn when it opened in 1844. During the roaring 1920s, Graycliff opened to the public again by then-owner Polly Leach, a close companion to Al Capone, and became a popular gathering spot for the rich and famous.

Later the mansion became the private residence of a wealthy Canadian couple who renovated it and added the swimming pool. In 1966, Graycliff was purchased by Lord and Lady Dudley, Third Earl of Staffordshire, who hosted such luminaries as the Duke and Duchess of Windsor and Sir Winston

Churchill. Lady Grace Dudley added priceless antiques, some of which still decorate guest rooms and public areas.

In 1973 Graycliff was purchased by its current owners, Enrico and Anna Maria Garzaroli, who turned the private home into the elegant hotel and restaurant that it is today. The hotel has 20 varied, newly renovated rooms and pool cottage suites, 2 restaurants, a gym, and 2 swimming pools.

Graycliff Hotel rooms are spread throughtout the original main building, the gardens, and a newer building, which now also houses the Graycliff Cigar Company (added in 1998). Rooms in the old section are named to evoke the romance of the tropics and Bahamian history; in the newer part, the names reflect the cigars made there. Each is different in arrangement and individually decorated, blending the old and the new; all are air-conditioned and have private baths. The old can be enjoyed in the Pool Cottage, where Winston Churchill stayed, and usually considered the bridal suite or the Baillou, the original master bedroom in the main house, with an enormous, elegant bedroom, parlor, and marble bathroom larger than most New York apartments. The new, huge Mandarino Cottage has an extra large bathroom with whirlpool and separate shower, and a dining terrace, especially popular with honeymooners. Luxury rooms and suites have sitting areas; the Graycliff Suite also includes a dining area, private balcony, and very large bathroom. The romantic setting makes Graycliff very popular for weddings which the wedding coordinator can customize.

Dining at Graycliff is a treat. The Graycliff Restaurant serves fine (and expensive) continental and Bahamian cuisine in very elegant surroundings (some might say a bit pretentious). The evening begins with cocktails in the Old World parlor while you peruse the menu and place your dinner order and enjoy piano music in the background. Be sure to try the house specialty. The restaurant has 4 air-conditioned dining rooms and an outdoor dining area. The decor reflects the era when Graycliff was a private home. Following dinner you are invited to relax and enjoy the evening with an after-dinner cognac or cigar. Dinner for two costs $150 and up. Graycliff Restaunt offers a Chef's Table in the kitchen and holds cooking classes for hotel guests from time to time.

Graycliff's award-winning Wine Cellar has an inventory of more than 200,000 bottles from more than 400 vintners in 15 countries, ranging from rare wines to popular vintages. Private tours of the wine cellar and Cigar Company are available and you can have a private cigar-rolling lesson for a fee. The wine cellar is also a venue for private wine tasting dinners for up to 18 people. The private room costs $1,000 plus the dinner and wine. You can also explore Graycliff's Wine Cellar online.

The second restaurant, Humidor Churrascaria, offers a complete change of pace and is a fun and festive dining experience. When the restaurant opened in 2005, it brought a brand-new concept to Nassau and was an immediate hit. The cuisine is Brazilian Churrascaria with a Bahamian flair. Churrascaria (Choo-RAH-scah-ree-ah) refers to a restaurant that specializes in *rodizio*—a Brazilian barbecue method of grilling, cutting, and serving several varieties of meats. The restaurant does not have a traditional menu; rather, a steady stream of energetic waiters bring you a large quantity and variety of meats such as chicken, pork, beef, and lamb hot from the grill. There's also a large salad bar, vegetables, and fresh fish. The all-you-can-eat prix fixe meal costs $39.95 per person. Dessert, drinks, and gratuities are not included. Dinner is served nightly Monday through Saturday. And coming soon, Graycliff will be transforming West Hill Street into what will be called Graycliff Heritage Village. Located across the street from the hotel, the new addition will have a chocolate factory, coffee roasting, and a craft village for local artisans. The hotel's other amenities include a gym with treadmills, bikes, free weights, weight machines with television or music, sauna, and Jacuzzi; and the Graycliff's Gift Shop & Gallery.

Although the surroundings are elegant, the ambience at Graycliff is friendly. And you don't really have to give up Nassau's glittering nightlife or gorgeous white-sand beaches. Both are less than 10 minutes away in almost any direction. Graycliff also has an agreement with Blue Lagoon Island for its guests to use the beach facilities on a complimentary basis.

GRAYCLIFF HOTEL ★ ★ ★

8–12 West Hill St., Nassau, NP, Bahamas; PO Box N-10246, Nassau, Bahamas

Phone: (800) 476-0446, (242) 302-9150; **Fax:** (242) 326-6110; **e-mail:** info@graycliff.com; www.graycliff.com
Owners: Enrico and Anna Maria Garzaroli
General Manager: Paolo Garzaroli
Open: Year-round, restaurants closed to public Christmas day.
US Reservations: (800) 476-0446
Deposit: 1 night
Minimum Stay: 1 night, except 3 nights from Dec 20–Jan 3
Arrival/Departure: Arranged on request for fee
Distance from Airport: 20 minutes from Nassau International; taxi one-way $22–$25
Distance from Nassau: Located in Nassau
Accommodations: 20 rooms and suites (9 with sitting areas; 6 with balconies or terrace; most have king bed; several with double beds)
Amenities: Air-conditioning, private bath (11 with Jacuzzis), minibar; safe; direct-dial phone, alarm clock, cable television; hair dryer, toiletries, iron and ironing board; daily housekeeping, evening turndown, room service, laundry/dry cleaning available; shop; free on-site parking; complimentary Wi-Fi throughout the property
Fitness Facilities/Spa Services: In-room massages available; weight room/gym (personal trainer on request)
Sports: 2 swimming pools; nearby tennis, golf, and water sports
Electricity: 110 volts
Dress Code: Dress code strictly enforced. For lunch, casually elegant. For dinner, resort elegant; jackets suggested but not required. No shorts

(dinner); shoes must be worn at all times.

Children: Allowed but no facilities

Meetings: Group dinners up to 300

Day Visitors: In restaurants

Handicapped Facilities: Limited

Packages: Wedding, honeymoon, romance

Rates: Per room, daily. *High Season* (mid-Dec–Apr 30): $375–$700. *Low Season* (May 1–mid-Dec): $325–$575.

Service Charge: $4.25 per person, per day on rooms; 18 percent on food and beverages

Government Tax: 18 percent on room

ONE&ONLY OCEAN CLUB

Paradise Island, Nassau, Bahamas

Paradise on Paradise. In the ups and downs of the Bahamas' development, the posh One&Only Ocean Club has been the one resort that's kept its panache. Located on 35 acres along a white-sand beach across the bridge from Nassau, this tony resort is one of the most beautiful in the Tropics. It has style.

Long a hideaway for the rich and famous, the club was originally the private winter home of a wealthy Swedish industrialist, who named it Shangri-La. In the 1960s A&P heir Huntington Hartford built the Ocean Club adjacent to Shangri-La, got government permission to rename the island Paradise Island (originally called Hog Island), and turned it into a premier resort for his wealthy friends. In 1968 Resorts International acquired the majority interest in Hartford's holdings and expanded Paradise Island into a major resort. In 1988, in a highly publicized deal with Donald Trump, the late showman/producer Merv Griffin bought Resorts International, which included the Ocean Club; and in 1994 Sun International bought out Merv Griffin and built the nearby mammoth resort complex, Atlantis. The Ocean Club was left in its secluded splendor. Now one of the One&Only group, the signature of Kerzner International luxury hotels, Kerzner reinvented the resort, preserving its timeless elegance while updating it with new facilities and amenities for the 21st century generation of travelers.

In addition to extensive renovations, beachfront rooms, a beachfront restaurant headed by a noted chef, an elaborate spa, a boardroom for 22 people, a logo shop, a family pool and a KidsOnly program were added and the golf course redesigned. The project was part of a $100 million development, which included the construction of Ocean Club Estates—luxurious homes, marina, and ultraluxury beachfront villas with an infinity-edge pool and dedicated butler.

Located on the eastern end of Paradise Island, a 40-minute drive from Nassau International Airport, hotel services begin upon your arrival at the airport with limo transfer (for a fee) to the resort. As soon as you turn into the long drive through gardens and manicured lawns to the main entrance, you know you have arrived at a special place. The club's style begins with check-in. If you have been a guest before, the staff will remember your name and probably your preferences.

The main building is a graceful 2-story mansion, with rooms set around a tropical garden courtyard with an ornamental pool and fountain at the center. The rooms overlook turquoise waters edged by 2 miles of beach along lawns where hammocks swing in the breeze under palms and giant eucalyptus trees. Rooms have verandas and are furnished in colonial-style mahogany.

The Crescent, made up of 5 two-story buildings by the beach, has 40 oceanfront rooms (each measuring a spacious 550 square feet) and 10 suites (each with a huge 1,100 square feet)—all with private balcony or terrace with unobstructed views of the club's long white-sand beach. In 2010, the Crescent Wing was renovated under the direction of famed interior designer Adam D. Tihany who created a fresh environment of vibrant colors. Burgundy, mustard, and sunny yellow in pillows and throws are set on white bedcovers against floors of Brazilian cherry wood and rugs in coordinated colors. Custom-made ebonized mahogany furniture with woven cane accents and campaign-style desks combine classic colonial influences and contemporary design. The accommodations have Frette linens, a pillow menu, large marble bathrooms, separate showers, double-sink vanities, and the latest technology—Internet access, portable telephone, DVD and CD players, and DMX music. Crescent suites also have steam shower, Jacuzzi bathtub, a bathroom television, a stocked minibar, and a Bose entertainment system.

All accommodations enjoy butler service, which includes packing and unpacking, dinner and activity reservations, personal wake-up calls, daily fruit bowl delivery, shoeshine service, afternoon tea, champagne, and strawberries delivered to guest rooms. There is thrice-daily maid service, including nightly turndown, and guests can borrow from the CD and DVD library. Laptops are available for guest in-room use. To the south is the freshwater swimming pool, which has a wonderful setting overlooking the terraced Versailles Gardens, which flow for ¼ mile in 7 tiers to an authentic 12th-century French cloister on the highest rise at the far southern end. The cloister, with its graceful arches and columns, was part of a monastery brought, piece by piece, from France to the United States by William Randolph Hearst. Hartford purchased the stone structure, shipped it from Florida, and had it reassembled here. The family pool is near the tennis courts and complimentary KidsOnly program, housed in its own facility. It offers imaginative half- and full-day interactive, educational, and recreational experiences for ages 4 to 12, daily throughout the year.

The beachfront restaurant, Dune, created by renowned chef and restaurateur Jean-Georges Vongerichten and designed by famed French interior designer Christian Liaigre, is stunning. Set in the dunes at the edge of the beach, the decor interprets the British-colonial heritage of the Bahamas in a modern context, rendering it casual and elegant at the same time. Liaigre, who is known as the most environmentally sensitive of designers, blends natural woods and fibers with a sophisticated patina of color that ranges from the ash of weathered wood around the bar to the slate of chairs and the charcoal of highly polished Ivory Coast hardwood table tops in the dining room. Running full length across the back of the restaurant is the display kitchen.

Daily at breakfast, lunch, and dinner, diners may sit inside under a high-pitched, beamed ceiling and look in one direction to the turquoise sea and in the other direction to the activity in the kitchen. Or they can dine under white umbrella tables on the outdoor patio overlooking the beach. At one end of the building is an outdoor white marble bar, which has become a popular rendezvous almost any time of day.

The menu offers Jean-Georges's signature dishes from his top-rated New York restaurants with Bahamian ingredients whenever possible. To underscore his commitment to using local products, Jean-Georges engaged Bahamian Teresa Kemp to create a garden of local herbs in front of the restaurant. Jean-Georges was also responsible for training the Bahamian staff.

The Ocean Club Golf Course is an 18-hole championship course revamped by pro golfer and course designer Tom Weiskopf. The course (7,123 yard/par 72), designed for every caliber of player, takes advantage of the Bahamian landscape and crosswinds, challenging golfers' accuracy. The course is available for play only to Ocean Club and Atlantis guests and villa owners.

The One&Only Ocean Club's spa, operated by Mandara, has an open air pavilion; 8 private spa suites, each with a garden Jacuzzi and outdoor water-fall shower. The spa suites use natural materials—Javanese teak massage tables, Thai-silk pillows, and coconut bowls filled with fresh flowers and floating candles. Mandara offers a full range of body and beauty treatments.

On the beach—one of the most beautiful in the world—you are served afternoon sorbet and cooled off with Evian misting; food and beverage services are available. Water sports include sailing, kayaking, and snorkeling; diving can be arranged. A fitness room has men's and women's lockers and changing facilities. Bicycles are available without charge. The Tennis Club has 9 Har-Tru courts (4 lighted for night play); a staff pro available for private lessons; and a pro shop with racquet rentals and full line of apparel.

One&Only Ocean Club guests have the best of both worlds: peace and tranquillity in a romantic setting and a glittering nightlife and restaurants at the nearby Atlantis. Free shuttles run every half hour to Atlantis, the golf course, and the casino. In addition to its romance, this fashionable resort appeals to people who like a quietly elegant and slightly European ambience.

ONE&ONLY OCEAN CLUB
★ ★ ★ ★

Box N-4777, Paradise Island, Nassau, Bahamas

Phone: (242) 363-2501, (800) 321-3000; **Fax:** (242) 363-2424; www.one andonlyoceanclub.com
Owner: Kerzner International Bahamas
General Manager: Alex Kim
Open: Year-round
US Reservations: Kerzner International, (888) 528-7157 or reservations@oneand onlyoceanclub.com
Deposit: 2 nights
Minimum Stay: None, except at Christmas/New Year's; inquire
Arrival/Departure: Transfer service via town car, $60 one-way
Distance from Airport: (Nassau International Airport) 40 minutes; taxi one-way, $22; 5 minutes from Paradise Island Airport
Distance from Nassau: 3 miles; taxi one-way, $6 plus $2.50 bridge toll; water taxi between Paradise Island and Nassau one-way, $2.50
Accommodations: 105 rooms and suites and 2 three-bedroom and 1 four-bedroom villa, all with terraces and king-size beds
Amenities: Air-conditioning, ceiling fans; television; marbled bath with tub and shower, hair dryer, toiletries; telephones; stocked minibar; terry robes, thrice-daily maid service; butler service; daily fruit bowl; laptop for use in suites and villas, shoeshine service. Crescent: Jacuzzi baths, steam shower, Bose entertainment system, in-room check-in; Internet access, DVD and CD player, iPods, DMX music
Fitness Facilities/Spa Services: Fitness room operated by New York-based La Palestra; men's and women's lockers

and changing facilities; full-service Mandara spa

Sports: Beach, 2 freshwater pools (1 for children); tennis, golf, walking paths, bikes, water sports

Electricity: 110 volts

Children: KidsOnly program; babysitters; Discovery Channel Camp operated by Atlantis

Dress Code: Casual but always chic; jackets requested in evening

Meetings: Small executive groups

Day Visitors: Not encouraged

Handicapped Facilities: Limited

Packages: Golf, tennis, honeymoon, wedding

Rates: Per room or suite, daily, EP. $500–$2,500; for villa rates, inquire

Service Charge: $7 per couple daily housekeeping gratuity

Government Tax: 12 percent resort tax based on room rate

BARBADOS

Barbados is an elegant place in a quiet sort of way. Whether it is the 300 years of British rule, the Bajans' pride and natural grace, or the blue-stocking vacationers who return annually like homing birds to their roost, this Caribbean island feels something like Masterpiece Theatre in the Tropics.

Independent since 1966, Barbados still seems as British as the queen. Bridgetown, the capital, has a Trafalgar Square, now renamed National Heroes Square. Bewigged judges preside over the country's law courts, hotels stop for afternoon tea, and a police band gives outdoor concerts.

The 166-square-mile island of green rolling hills even resembles the English countryside and is a pleasure to explore. On an island only 21 miles long, you can visit stately homes and gardens, more than 50 important historic sites, and the outstanding Barbados Museum.

A coral island 100 miles east of the Lesser Antilles, Barbados is the easternmost land in the Caribbean. Its western coast, fringed with attractive beaches, is bathed by calm Caribbean waters; the eastern shores are washed by the whitecapped rollers of the Atlantic. It is one of the main locations for windsurfing in the Caribbean and often a venue for international competitions. The island is surrounded by coral reefs good for snorkeling and learning to scuba dive. Sailing, fishing, golf, tennis, horseback riding, and polo are also available.

Barbados has one of the widest selections of accommodations of any island in the Caribbean, ranging from modest guest houses to ultraposh resorts. Their ambience is often more European than that found in hotels on Caribbean islands closer to the United States, because the majority of Barbados's visitors come from Britain and other European countries.

Information

Barbados Tourism Authority, 820 2nd Ave., New York, NY 10017; (800) 221-9831, (212) 551-4300; Fax: (212) 573-9850; www.visitbarbados.org

COBBLERS COVE

St. Peter, Barbados

This cozy complex of 2-story cottages in gardens overlooking the beach can induce love at first sight in those who want a casual, romantic resort with just enough history to lend it charm—but with attractive, modern, spacious accommodations to boot.

The centerpiece of this quiet resort is a pale pink villa built in the early part of the 20th century by a Bajan sugar baron as a summer home. The former living room, similar to an English country drawing room, now serves as a reading lounge with daily US and European newspapers.

The villa's open-air, seaside terrace doubles as the dining pavilion and bar, a favorite meeting place for hotel guests and local friends. During the winter season you'll hear a strong British upstairs accent, but in summer the voices are likely to have a more familiar American ring.

In the evening the pavilion and another terrace next to the lounge become romantic settings for candlelight dining. Blending traditional European dishes with fresh local products, the chef has developed an innovative, sophisticated cuisine. Because all dishes are cooked to order, guests give their selections to the head waiter while they enjoy a drink at the bar adjacent to the dining terrace. Friday night is particularly special with a seafood (fresh catch from Barbados waters) and caviar (from around the world) dinner. Cobblers Cove has a dinner exchange with some other deluxe island hotels.

The cottages, each with 4 suites, sit snugly in a V in 3 acres of tropical gardens alongside the main house and around a small pool overlooking the Caribbean. The pool area can be crowded when the hotel is full, but a large wooden deck provides space for lounging near the beach, only 10 yards away.

All accommodations are suites with large bedrooms, ample closets, upgraded bathrooms, and special drying racks for wet bathing suits and towels. Each suite overlooks the garden or sea and has a wet bar and separate sitting room with louvered doors that, when folded back, open onto a furnished patio or balcony to create one large, airy space.

The most sensational accommodations are the bilevel Camelot and Colleton Suites on the top floor of the main villa by architect Ian Morrison, known for his handsome design of nearby Royal Pavilion hotel. These posh love nests offer the ultimate in privacy, along with marble floors; a king-size, canopied four-poster bed; and a lounge area with a settee, writing desk, and chaise lounge—all in fresh blue and white decor. The huge bathrooms have whirlpool tubs, twin sinks, bidets, and his and hers showers with twin showerheads. Each suite has a small plunge pool and wet bar that overlooks a wonderful view of the sea.

The resort's sports facilities include complimentary water sports and day and night tennis. You can go snorkeling directly off the beach. Cobblers has a gift shop, exercise room, and spa facilities housed in a pair of colorful chattel houses. Also in a chattel house is an Internet room on the top floor and on the first floor, a kids corner, which operates in the summer and during holidays.

Life at Cobblers Cove is pleasantly low-key. There's the manager's weekly cocktail party and occasional live musical entertainment, but essentially the resort is a friendly, easy-living sort of place where guests meet and mingle or go their own way. The resort's informality is suited to families, while its cozy, romantic ambience attracts couples of all ages. Cobblers Cove is a member of the prestigious Relais et Châteaux.

COBBLERS COVE ★ ★ ★
Road View, St. Peter, Barbados
Phone: (246) 422-2291; **Fax:** (246) 422-1460; **e-mail:**reservations@cobblers cove.com; www.cobblerscove.com
Owner: Hayton, Ltd.
General Manager: Randall Wilkie
Open: Year-round except Sept–mid-Oct
US Reservations: Karen Bull Associates, (800) 890-6060; **Fax:** (404) 237-1841
Deposit: 7 nights in winter; 1 night in summer; 30 days cancellation in winter, 14 days in summer
Minimum Stay: 14 nights during Christmas/New Year's
Arrival/Departure: Transfer service arranged for fee
Distance from Airport: 18 miles (45 minutes); taxi one-way, $40
Distance from Bridgetown: 12 miles (25 minutes); taxi one-way, $20
Accommodations: 40 suites in 2-story cottages (22 garden view, 16 deluxe and oceanfront) with twin beds in 10, all with terraces and patios; 2 superdeluxe suites with plunge pool
Amenities: Air-conditioning, ceiling fans; direct-dial telephones; individual safes; television arranged on request; radio at front desk; bath with tub and shower, hair dryer, terry robes, basket of

toiletries; stocked minibar, ice service, room service 8 a.m.–9 p.m.

Fitness Facilities/Spa Services: Fitness facility with exercise equipment and spa services with new treatment rooms and expanded treatments

Sports: Freshwater swimming pool; free waterskiing, windsurfing, Sunfish, snorkeling, tennis; special fees for golf at Sandy Lane and Royal Westmoreland courses; diving/water sports can be arranged

Electricity: 110 volts/50 cycles

Dress Code: Informal by day; elegantly casual in evening; men wear slacks and open-neck shirts. Jeans, shorts, and swimwear are not allowed in bar area after 7 p.m.

Children: All ages except mid-Jan–mid-Mar, when none under 12 years old; cribs; babysitters with advance notice

Meetings: No

Day Visitors: With reservations

Handicapped Facilities: Yes

Packages: Honeymooners, gourmet, golf, summer

Rates: Per room, two people, daily. *High Season* (early Jan–mid-Apr): $870–$1,250; Camelot and Colleton Suites, $2,490 and $2,910. *Low Season* (mid-Apr–Sept 30): $530–$695; suites, $1,165 and $1,290. EP *Shoulder Season* (Oct 1–mid-Dec): $580–$775; suites, $1,290–$1,505. Single, 2-bedroom, Christmas, MAP, low, and shoulder rates available; inquire.

Service Charge: 10 percent included in all rates; additional at guests' discretion

Government Tax: Included

CORAL REEF CLUB

St. James, Barbados

This is a family affair. The O'Hara family—mother, two sons, a daughter, two daughters-in-law, and a son-in-law—own and operate this resort and give it a special cachet.

The Coral Reef Club, together with the Sandpiper, its sister hotel next door, enjoys a coveted location on Barbados's Caribbean coast, amid a string of fashionable resorts and trendy restaurants. Spread over 12 acres of flowering trees and gardens and fronting a mile of casuarina- and mahogany-shaded powdery sands, the resort blends an upscale British style with a comfortable, relaxing, friendly atmosphere.

Coral Reef Club was born almost by accident in the 1950s when an Englishman and owner of Coral Reef's original coral-stone house, began taking in guests to help defray expenses. Over the next three decades, the beachfront property grew from a 4-bedroom beach house to a 69-room resort. The late Budge O'Hara, the patriarch of the family who arrived as manager with his bride, Cynthia, in 1956, eventually acquired both hotels.

After their father passed away in 1995, the younger O'Haras and their spouses assumed day-to-day management of Coral Reef and Sandpiper, refurbishing, updating, and expanding the properties.

Patrick and Mark jointly manage Coral Reef, along with sister Karen, Patrick's wife, Sharon, and Mark's wife, Maria, an artist, who all help with refurbishing, housekeeping, and gardening. Sharon's sister, Sue Jardine, is sales and marketing manager, and Karen's husband, Wayne Capaldi, manages the Sandpiper. As we said, Coral Reef is a family affair.

A tree-lined drive leads to the original coral-stone villa overlooking the beach, passing the cottages and the newer, 2-story buildings nesting in the gardens. The main building houses the island- and antique-dressed lobby, lounge, restaurant, and bar, which open onto a balustrade terrace overlooking the beach and gardens.

Accommodations are in garden rooms and cottages providing the most privacy; rooms in the main house; and some, built around a large swimming pool, house luxury junior suites and luxury plantation suites. Another group of 13 luxury cottages/suites have their own plunge pools and wraparound terraces. Located in the front half of the gardens toward the sea, they are well suited for families as they have a separate living room where two children can sleep. Also, there are 2 four-bedroom villas with kitchens. A few single rooms with double bed are also available.

All accommodations have tile floors, patios or balconies, king-size or twin beds, air-conditioning, ceiling fans; small refrigerators, direct-dial telephones, safes, hair dryers, CD players, clock radios, and homey touches, such as toasters, a shelf of paperback books, and fresh flowers.

The resort's most posh accommodations are 5 enormous, superdeluxe Plantation Suites with private pools. Situated on the second floor of two separate buildings with sea views, plus a fifth by the sea, the beautifully furnished, luxury suites have four-poster canopied beds, spacious living rooms, a dressing area, huge bathrooms with separate tub and large shower, and a complimentary starter bar. Two similar posh suites have been added to Sandpiper.

The breeze-cooled restaurant serves all three meals plus afternoon tea and a Sunday brunch buffet; during the winter season it also serves a buffet lunch daily. Dinner offers an a la carte menu nightly except Monday, when a buffet of Bajan dishes, plus English standards of roast beef and Yorkshire pudding, are featured. For a change of scenery, Coral Reef has a dining exchange with neighboring Sandpiper, as well as with Cobblers Cove up the road. Room service for meals is available during restaurant hours.

The main bar is open 24 hours, and musical entertainment and dancing are offered nightly in the winter, less frequently in other months. A folklore show and beach barbecue are staged weekly. The resort has a television room, billiards room, and Wi-Fi and a computer/Internet-access room for guests to use. A boutique in the style of a Barbados chattel house is found in the gardens. A complimentary shuttle to Bridgetown goes daily for shopping.

Those in search of an active vacation will find 2 freshwater swimming pools and 2 lighted tennis courts, as well as a 10-station, air-conditioned exercise room. They can enjoy free use of small sailboats, kayaks, and equipment for water skiing and for snorkeling on the resort's reef, only a few yards from the beach. They have access to a 32-foot catamaran, and scuba diving can be arranged for a fee, as can golf at nearby courses.

In 2008, the resort added a full-service spa and a new tennis court. The lovely spa building in a garden setting is a departure from the colonial style of the accommodations and has an understated, slightly modern look and reflects a Zen-like atmosphere. Coral Reef has many loyal fans who, like the owners, are into the second and third generations. Most are Brits but many are affluent Americans who appreciate the resort's certain Old World character blended into a New World setting and its friendly family ambience. Many of the staff have been with the hotel for years. The O'Haras usually greet guests on arrival, invite them to their home for the manager's cocktail parties, and give gifts to those staying at Christmas.

CORAL REEF CLUB ★ ★ ★ ★
St. James, Barbados
Phone: (246) 422-2372; **Fax:** (246) 422-1776; **e-mail:** reservations@coral reefbarbados.com; www.coralreefbarba dos.com
Owners: O'Hara family
Managing Directors: Patrick and Mark O'Hara
Open: Year-round except mid-May– mid-July and Sept
US Reservations: Ralph Locke Islands, (800) 223-1108; **Fax:** (310) 440-4220
Deposit: 3 nights, 7 at Christmas; 28 days cancellation winter, 14 in summer
Minimum Stay: 14 days at Christmas, 7 nights February 1–29, Easter, Thanksgiving

Arrival/Departure: Airport transfers arranged. Regular car, $75, luxury car, $115 one way

Distance from Airport: 18 miles (45 minutes); taxi one-way $40

Distance from Bridgetown: 8 miles (20 minutes)

Accommodations: 88 units, all with terraces, patios, or balconies (25 king or twin double; 4 singles; 6 superior junior suites; 33 luxury junior suites; 13 cottage suites with living room and plunge pool; 5 Plantation Suites with sundeck and plunge pool; 2 four-bedroom villas)

Amenities: Air-conditioning, ceiling fans; direct-dial phones; safe; refrigerator, toaster; hair dryer, bath with tub and shower, bathrobes, basket of toiletries; daily newspaper; nightly turndown service; television on request; hair salon; boutique; 24-hour room service; e-mail and Internet access

Fitness Facilities/Spa Services: New spa and fitness (see text)

Sports: 2 freshwater swimming pools; 2 tennis courts with free pro program, lighted; snorkeling, Sunfish, kayaking, and waterskiing included; golf, diving, deep-sea fishing arranged for fee

Electricity: 110 volts/50 cycles

Dress Code: Smart casual by day; elegantly casual in evening; jacket and tie or black tie Christmas and New Year's

Children: Children welcome year-round except Jan 15–Mar 15 when those under 12 years old cannot be accommodated; children under 5 not allowed in restaurant or lounge after 7 p.m.

Meetings: Up to 24 people

Handicapped Facilities: Certain accommodations suitable

Packages: Honeymoon, wedding

Rates: Per room, for two, including breakfast, service charge and taxes. *High Season* (Dec 15–Apr 21): $805–$2,725. *Low Season* (Apr 22–Oct 9) $440–$1,365; (Oct 10–Dec 14): $465–$1,365. For 2-bedroom, single, third person, and children rates, inquire.

Service Charge: Included

Government Tax: Included

FAIRMONT ROYAL PAVILION

St. James, Barbados

Set amid 11 acres of immaculate tropical gardens directly on a white-sand beach in a quiet cove, the pastel pink Royal Pavilion, designed by famed architect Ian Morrison, combines Spanish mission and Mediterranean elements in its design. An imposing avenue of royal palms leads to the flower-encircled portico of the main entrance. There you step into a marbled reception hall with a concierge desk and a colonnaded Andalusian courtyard cooled by a fountain. If you wish to have your arrival match the hotel's grand entrance, you can be met at the airport by a luxury car and have access to the airport's VIP lounge.

In 2010, The Fairmont Royal Pavilion completed a two-month renovation that introduced a new room category: 900 square-foot Beachfront junior suites with private terraces and dedicated butler services. The interior decor of the 24 new suites takes its inspiration from Barbados' heritage in typical plantation house style with soft hues and rich walnut tones of the traditional furnishings and commissioned artwork. All suites have free Wi-Fi, 42-inch flatscreen satellite television and media panel with a DVD/CD player. Junior suite guests also benefit from escorted airport fast track service, personalized check-in/checkout, and daily evening canapés. All the resort's accommodations are large, deluxe rooms with balconies or terraces facing the sea. Completing the roster is a villa with 3 additional accommodations. The lobby is wireless-equipped, and 2 laptop computers are available for guests' use.

Royal Pavilion's triumph is The Palm restaurant, an elegant, pink marble dining room by the sea. Here the romantic palm-court effect is enhanced by living palm trees that are part of the decor. Adjacent to the restaurant is a spacious lounge with graceful arched doorways and windows opening onto views of the gardens and sea. Here guests enjoy afternoon tea, cocktails, and after-dinner drinks. The Palm Terrace restaurant and bar have a casual but sophisticated atmosphere. The restaurant serves local fresh fish with a contemporary flair.

On the northern side of the resort, Taboras is a casual, open-air bistro where breakfast, lunch, dinners, and themed evening are presented, as well as offering a beach and poolside snack menu. It is named for Fernando Tabora, a well-known Latin American landscape architect who designed the exquisite gardens for Royal Pavilion. Taboras is terraced by the sea on one side, with the swimming pool, a Jacuzzi, and a large sunning deck on the other. One of the resort's courtyards has a cluster of fashionable boutiques and a hair salon. Guests are offered spa treatments in their rooms.

During high season, children under 13 are not permitted, but from April to October, when the hotel offers complimentary daily children's activities, all ages are welcome. The hotel has 2 hard-surface tennis courts (lighted) and provides complimentary non-motorized water sports including snorkeling, wakeboarding, sea floats, Sunfish sailing, and kayaking. Through a partnership with the nearby Royal Westmoreland Club, Royal Pavilion guests have access to that club's championship golf course,

designed by Robert Trent Jones II.

The Fairmont Royal Pavilion is tony but not snobbish and enjoys a high number of repeat guests, mostly from Britain and the US. It is well suited for those who want a relaxing vacation in a stylish yet relaxed ambience, where the emphasis is on pretty surroundings, comfort, and sophisticated cuisine.

FAIRMONT ROYAL PAVILION ★ ★ ★ ★

Porters, St. James, Barbados, BB24051
Phone: (246) 422-5555; **Fax:** (246) 422-0118; www.fairmont.com
Owner: Fairmont Hotels & Resorts
General Manager: Wayne Kafcsak
Open: Year-round
US Reservations: Fairmont Hotels, (800) 441-1414; (866) 540-4485
Deposit: 3 nights, 30 days cancellation in winter; 1 night, 14 days cancellation in summer
Minimum Stay: 10 nights during Christmas
Arrival/Departure: Luxury car and limousine transfer services arranged for fee
Distance from Airport: 12 miles; taxi one-way, $40
Distance from Bridgetown: 8 miles; taxi one-way, $25
Accommodations: 72 oceanfront deluxe rooms and suites with king-size beds and private balconies in 2 three-story buildings; 1 garden-view 3-bedroom villa
Amenities: Air-conditioning; bath with tub and shower, hair dryer, basket of toiletries, bathrobe; direct-dial telephone, radio, cable television; Internet access; DVD player; safe; stocked minibar; twice-daily maid service, 24-hour room service; concierge

Fitness Facilities/Spa Services: Air-conditioned fitness center; in-room treatments and massage
Sports: Freshwater swimming pool; complimentary tennis and equipment (lessons extra), Hobie Cats, Sunfish, snorkeling, waterskiing, windsurfing. Diving and motorized water sports additional charge; golf, fishing arranged
Electricity: 110 volts/50 cycles
Dress Code: Informal by day, casually elegant in evening; for dining, jeans, T-shirts, rubber shoes, sneakers not accepted; no shorts in Palm restaurant
Children: No children under 13 years old except from Apr 1 to Oct 31; cribs; babysitters

Meetings: Up to 50 people; equipment available
Day Visitors: With reservations
Handicapped Facilities: Limited; 1 ground-floor room
Packages: Honeymoon, wedding, family, bed-and-breakfast
Rates: Per room, daily, EP. *High Season* (mid-Dec–mid-Apr): $864–$1,669. *Low Season* (May 1–early Nov): $519–$669. *Shoulder Season* (Apr 7–30): $1,209–$1,479. Inquire for 2- and 3-bedrooms rates.
Service Charge: 10 percent, included
Government Tax: 8.5 percent on room, included

BONAIRE

The second largest island in the Netherlands Antilles, Bonaire is located 50 miles north of Venezuela and 86 miles east of Aruba. For decades it has been a haven for divers, who come to enjoy the island's remarkable marine life. The entire coastline, from the high-tide mark to a depth of 200 feet, is a marine park with more than 80 dive sites.

Most island hotels cater to divers and have excellent operations on their premises. In some places the reefs are so near you can wade to them; others are only a swim or short boat ride away. Thus, divers can enjoy unlimited diving from the beach at any time of day or night—the kind of ease and convenience few places in the world can duplicate. Indeed, there's no better place in the Caribbean to learn scuba.

Even for travelers with no higher aspiration than snorkeling, this 24-mile crescent-shaped island offers plenty. Two of its attractions are certainly unusual, if not unique, and easily accessible. The hilly northern end is covered by the Washington/Slagbaai National Park, a 13,500-acre wildlife sanctuary that includes the island's highest point, 784-foot-high Brandaris Hill. The park is a showcase of island flora and fauna with a variety of unusual formations and 130 species of birds.

The flat, dry southern part of the island has an equally interesting attraction. Salt pans, more than 150 years old and covered with white sparkling mountains of salt, are worked commercially, but amid the pans is a 135-acre flamingo sanctuary and breeding ground for about 10,000 birds. You can tour the perimeter of the pans to watch and photograph the birds.

A quiet island of 10,400 inhabitants, Bonaire's peaceful ambience belies its turbulent past. Discovered in 1499 by Amerigo Vespucci—for whom the Americas were named—it was colonized by the Spaniards, who carted off the entire Arawak population to Hispaniola. Later the island was captured by the Dutch, fought over by the French and British, and leased to a New York merchant. Finally, in 1816, the Dutch took it over and kept it.

Kralendijk, the capital, is a colorful miniature city with distinctive Dutch colonial architecture. Among the oldest structures is historic Fort Oranje and the original administration building, which dates to 1837, and restored as the Government Office. The island has a surprising variety of good restaurants.

Information

Tourism Corporation of Bonaire, 80 Broad St., Ste. 3202, New York, NY 10004; (212) 956-5911, (800) BONAIRE; www.tourismbonaire.com; usa@tourismbonaire.com

CAPTAIN DON'S HABITAT

Kralendijk, Bonaire, N.A.

A resort for divers, Captain Don's Habitat was founded by a diver who has become a legend in his own time.

I met Don Stewart, a salty California expatriate, on my first trip to Bonaire in the early 1970s, long before Habitat was born. He had wandered into Bonaire in 1962 from a 70-foot schooner called the Valerie Queen because, as he said in his wry way, "I was thirsty and heard they had water." The good ship *Valerie* sank; Stewart stayed. He started Bonaire's first hotel and later opened his own very rustic inn for divers, one of the first of its kind.

Stewart, known to all as Captain Don, bent my ear most of the day and evening on the wonders of scuba diving, the unique qualities of Bonaire, the need to protect the marine environment, and anything else that came to his mind. He was not a man at a loss for words.

Since then not much has changed, except that this interesting character has managed to get enough of the right people to listen. Today, after almost four decades of adhering to careful management of its reefs and sea life, Bonaire has one of the most magnificent marine parks in the world; diving is its number one industry. On the 30th anniversary of his arrival on the island and in appreciation for his contributions, the Bonaire government honored Stewart by proclaiming "Capt. Don Week" with all the associated fanfare; a memorial plaque sponsored by the Council of Underwater Resort Operators was placed on a reef bearing his name.

Along the way Stewart's once dinky little inn grew into quite a nice resort. Perched on a coral bluff north of town, overlooking a ½-mile shoreline of great diving, Captain Don's Habitat is a very casual, relaxed resort. It is designed as clusters of white stucco town houses, some in attractive Dutch colonial architecture with high-pitched red roofs, others more modern with Spanish features such as courtyards and dark wood doors and windows.

In the past several years, the hotel has been substantially updated, upgraded, and expanded, offering enough variety and flexibility to meet almost any need. In 2011, marking the resort's 35th anniversary, it opened a wing of 12 new deluxe oceanfront junior suites, named for the late Albert E. J. Romijn, an environmentalist and one of Habitat's visionaries. Every detail of the new buildings were designed to have the least impact on the local environment from the low-impact construction methods, to the use of solar water heaters and energy saving devices, to a state-of-the-art wastewater treatment system. The rooms and facilities are set in carefully designed, lush landscaping and maintained to eliminate harmful runoff into the fragile marine eco-system just off shore.

The suites use energy saving lights and appliances while maintaining the look and comfort of a deluxe suite. All rooms are air-conditioned and furnished with one king-size bed with pillow-top mattress, queen-size sleeper sofa also with pillow-top mattress, coffee table, work desk with chair, flat-panel television, clock-radio with iPod dock,

refrigerator, microwave, granite-top wet bar with refrigerator, microwave, coffeemaker, full bath with tub, hair dryer, covered patio or balcony with breakfast table with chairs and sun lounges.

The resort also has 2-bedroom garden-view cottages with kitchenettes set back from the water; deluxe ocean-view rooms with 2 queen-size beds, a refrigerator, and a furnished balcony or patio overlooking a large freshwater swimming pool; and 2-bedroom/2-bathroom garden-view apartments with kitchens each with a balcony or patio; and 3- and 4-bedroom villas. All rooms have air-conditioning and cable television.

The interiors are spacious, particularly those with wood-beamed ceilings and French doors leading to a patio overlooking the sea. Separated from their neighbors by greenery and walkways, these units convey a feeling of privacy and offer an unexpected level of luxury for their moderate rates. The guest rooms are tastefully furnished, mostly with rattan. Another group of island-style of cottages, renovated and upgraded in 2007, has 2 bedrooms and 2 baths.

Wireless Internet service is available throughout the resort, and guests can enjoy massage and spa services at the Spa at Habitat, located on the property.

Happy hour at the Decompression Stop Bar, the oceanfront watering hole, attracts divers from far and wide. Rum Runners, the open-air seaside restaurant, offers an eclectic menu of Italian, Cajun, and local dishes, along with freshly made thin crust pizza from a stone-fired oven. The Monday barbecue after the

"Meet the Captain" cocktail party is a well attended merry evening.

The dive operation is one of the main PADI five-star training facilities in the Caribbean. An environmental-awareness philosophy was also the basis for the design of the resort's new Dive and Conference Center, opened in 2009, and part of a recently completed two-and-a-half-year expansion and modernization project. Conveniently located next to the restaurant and bar and only a few steps from the dock and shore diving areas, the larger state-of-the-art dive operation, rental, and retail center boasts a more spacious and modern conference area, classrooms with upgraded audio and visual equipment, and wireless Internet.

In addition to PADI, the dive operation is a NAUI and SSI training facility and a SDI/TDI Professional Development Center. Also located in the new dive center is RecTek Scuba owned and operated by Walt Stark, well-known technical diving instructor on Bonaire. All of Habitat's technical diving operations are coordinated here by Walt. Everything for the most technical of tech divers can be found here.

You can dive at Captain Don's 24 hours a day, any day of the year. The resort has 3 state-of-the-art boats and a photo shop and offers every level of instruction, including underwater photography courses. Most guests come on packages that include tank, weights, belt, unlimited free air, and at least one boat dive daily. One such weekly package, "7th Night Free" available from late April through June is priced from about $778 per person, based on double occupancy and includes ocean-view accommodations, buffet breakfast daily, welcome drink, manager's rum punch party, 6 single-tank boat dives, 6 days of 24-hour unlimited shore diving, tanks, weights and belt, government taxes, service charges, and energy surcharge.

Although Habitat caters mainly to divers and would-be divers, it offers other diversions such as ocean kayaking and windsurfing. You can swim in the main pool, set into a wooden deck by the sea, or soak up the sun on the resort's tiny strand of sand, appropriately named Seven Body Beach. Couples between the ages of 30 and 50 and families with kids old enough to dive make up the majority of guests. Most come on packages, which represent good value. You should, too. Captain Don, as loquacious as ever, is still a man with a mission, although retired from the daily operation of Habitat. He often appears for special nights with Stetson, fringe, and his custom-made peg leg. You can't miss him.

CAPTAIN DON'S HABITAT
★ ★ 🐋

PO Box 88, Kralendijk, Bonaire, N.A.
Phone: (599) 717-8290; **Fax:** (599) 717-8240; **e-mail:** captaindon@maduro.com; www.habitatbonaire.com
Owner: Maduro Holdings, Ltd.
General Manager: Jack Chalk
Hotel Manager: Claire Sealy
Open: Year-round
US Reservations: Captain Don's Habitat, Maduro Dive FantaSeas, (800) 327-6709, (305) 981-9113; **Fax:** (305) 981-9397

Deposit: $100 per person; full payment 31 days prior to arrival
Minimum Stay: None, except Christmas/New Year's, 7 nights
Arrival/Departure: Transfer normally included in packages
Distance from Airport: 6 miles; taxi one-way, $20
Distance from Kralendijk: 1 mile; taxi one-way, $10
Accommodations: 62 rooms and suites in cottages and villas (variety of sizes and layouts from studios to 2 bedrooms/2 bathrooms); 12 new deluxe junior suites (see text)
Amenities: Air-conditioning, ceiling fans; some baths with tub, most with shower, toiletries; television; coffee-maker; hair dryer; safe big enough for laptop; telephones in deluxe ocean-view rooms and cottages; photo shop; no room service; wireless Internet
Sports: Freshwater swimming pool; full scuba program (see text); boating, kayaking, snorkeling, windsurfing, deep-sea fishing, hiking arranged
Electricity: 127 volts; 50 Hz
Dress Code: Bathing suits and shorts appropriate at all times
Children: All ages, but must be 10 or older to scuba dive
Meetings: Up to 100 people; seminar and conference facilities
Day Visitors: Yes
Handicapped Facilities: Yes
Packages: Divers, nondivers, family
Rates: Per room, per night double (excluding meals, transfers, or diving). *High Season* (mid-Dec–Mar 31): $191–$499. *Low Season:* $150–$452. For a minimal cost, car rental can be added and Harley-Davidson motorcycles are available for rent. Inquire for weekly dive packages.
Service Charge: Included
Government Tax: Included

BRITISH VIRGIN ISLANDS

This archipelago of about 50 green, mountainous islands and cays scalloped with idyllic coves of white-sand beaches is spread over 59 square miles along Drake's Channel and the Anegada Passage between the Caribbean Sea and the Atlantic Ocean. Mostly volcanic in origin and uninhabited, the British Virgin Islands are almost as virgin as the day Christopher Columbus first saw them. Popular hiding places of pirates in olden days, these gems are today favorite hideaways of yachtsmen for their good anchorage and of vacationers fleeing the crowd.

The largest and most populated islands of this British Crown Colony are Tortola, the capital, and Virgin Gorda, to the east of Tortola. Several islands, such as Guana Island off Tortola's northeastern coast and Peter Island to the southeast, have been developed as private resorts.

Tortola is best known as a yacht-chartering center. Its main town and port, Road Town, is the British Virgin Islands' commercial and residential hub. Other entry points are West End, where ferries from St. Thomas stop, and the airport on Beef Island, connected to Tortola's eastern end by a small bridge.

Virgin Gorda's largest settlement, Spanish Town, is located about midisland. Little more than a hamlet a decade ago, the town has grown by leaps and bounds as the island has prospered from sheltering several of the Caribbean's most celebrated hideaways.

The B.V.I., as aficionados call them, do not appeal to everyone. They have no golf courses or casinos, and nighttime activity is very low-key. But they more than make up for the lack of razzle-dazzle with fabulous scenery and facilities, particularly for water sports.

Information

British Virgin Islands Tourist Board, 1 West 34th St. at Fifth Ave., Ste. 302, New York, NY 10001; (212)563-3117, (800) 835-8530; Fax: (212) 563-2263; e-mail: info@bvitourism.com; www.bvitouristboard.com; www.bviwelcome.com

SANDCASTLE

Jost Van Dyke, B.V.I.

Feel like dropping out? Want to hide out for a few days? Try Sandcastle. It's on tiny Jost Van Dyke, a remote island northeast of Tortola that's home to only 275 people.

That number is just fine for those who find their way to this heavenly haven. There are no casinos, no native floor shows, no discos here. And electricity came only in the 21st century. All rooms have electricity for lights and fans; the newest two rooms, in a storm-resistant building, even have air-conditioning.

Sandcastle sits on White Bay, a gorgeous ½-mile stretch of powdery white sand with a lot of palm trees and tropical flowers, which seem to grow where they will. You stay in one of the four cottages, two of which have two rooms, or in one of two new spacious rooms. They are modestly but adequately furnished with almost everything you'd need on a castaway island: king-size beds, daybed, comfy chairs, a coffee table, books, and an efficient toilet.

The water comes from heaven and the resort or island's desalinization plant. Outdoor shower stalls are attached to each cottage. The newest rooms have full baths with indoor hot-water showers. All accommodations have hot-water showers.

The Soggy Dollar, the beachfront restaurant and bar, is the hotel's focal point and the food one of its highlights. Dinner finds many other guests from yachts anchored offshore sitting down to savor dishes such as grilled fish and key lime pie.

Sandcastle's reputation for super food is well known in yachting circles; sailors simply pull their boats into the bay and transfer to shore via their dinghies. There is no dock; you must usually take a step or two in the water before hitting dry land. It's all very romantic. Conversation can be lively or quiet, depending on the mix of guests.

You won't be at Sandcastle long before you'll be tempted to try the hotel's specialty drink, the Painkiller. This yummy concoction (rum, coconut cream, fruit juices, and nutmeg) originated here. Have two at midday and it's hammock time.

There's wonderful snorkeling on a reef within swimming distance of the beach. The first reef is in only 12 feet of water; the sea bottom then slopes to about 40 feet for a second reef, and about 400 yards farther is a wall with an 80-foot drop. It's great diving, if you come with dive gear.

For excitement it's a 45-minute walk or a quick taxi ride to Foxy's Tamarind Bar, the most famous watering hole in this part of the Caribbean. Foxy, the consummate Caribbean character, has a well-deserved reputation for his quick wit and talent on the guitar.

You could take an excursion or two to neighboring islands, but for most people the combination of sand, sea, and sun, along with the great cooking, is enough.

Getting to Sandcastle requires a bit of scheduling and a lot of determination. You can fly to Tortola or St. Thomas. From Beef Island Airport on Tortola, it's a 45-minute taxi ride to the West End Ferry dock. From St. Thomas a ferry to West End several times daily takes one hour. At West End the Jost Van Dyke ferry boat meets you, and a half hour or so later, you'll kick off your shoes and hit the sand. Alternatively, from Red Hook on St. Thomas, the Mona Queen runs via St. John twice on Friday, Saturday, and Sunday directly to Jost Van Dyke in 45 minutes.

Pack light. You won't need much—bathing suits and shorts. This is barefoot living at its best. Obviously, Sandcastle is not for everyone, but for some it's as near paradise as they need to be.

SANDCASTLE ★

6501 Red Hook Plaza, Ste. 201, St. Thomas, U.S.V.I. 00802
Phone: (284) 495-9888; **Fax:** (284) 495-9999; **e-mail:** relax@soggydollar .com; www.soggydollar.com
Owners/Managers: Jerry and Tish O'Connell
General Manager: Tina Chinnery
Open: Year-round
US Reservations: Direct to hotel

Deposit: $500 to confirm reservations; 60 days cancellation
Minimum Stay: 3 nights during winter
Arrival/Departure: See text
Distance from West End: (Tortola) 30 minutes by boat; from Red Hook, St. Thomas: 45 minutes
Accommodations: 4 cottages (2 directly on beach with sitting rooms, king-size beds); 2 garden rooms with kings and air-conditioning
Amenities: Electricity for lights and fans; outside shower stalls connected to each cottage; gift and sportswear shop
Sports: Kayaking and snorkeling equipment included; hammocks on beach
Electricity: 110 volts/60 Hz (as in US)
Dress Code: Casual: bathing suits and bare feet
Children: None under 16 years of age
Meetings: No
Day Visitors: Welcome at restaurant and bar
Handicapped Facilities: No
Packages: 7-night MAP, including transportation from Tortola
2012 Rates: Two people, daily, EP. *High Season* (mid-Dec–mid-May): $285–$310. *Low Season:* $210–$250. MAP and singles rate available; inquire.
Service Charge: 7 percent on room
Government Tax: 7 percent on room

GUANA ISLAND

Guana Island, B.V.I.

A secluded resort tucked into a far-from-it-all setting, Guana Island is one of the Caribbean's true hideaways. Located off the northeastern coast of Tortola, 850-acre Guana Island began as a private club in the 1930s. After purchasing it in 1975, its present owners modernized the facilities while retaining its homey style and made it into a private nature sanctuary, leaving all but the 70-acre resort area crowning the topmost ridge and some lowland orchard and sports areas undeveloped.

White-washed stone cottages, surrounded by gardens of hibiscus, oleander, and flowering trees, accommodate a total of 32 guests. The cottages vary in size and layout, but each has its own special appeal. Most have fabulous views across the island and sea and in the evening take in 200 degrees of magnificent scenery bathed in sunset orange and red.

The guest rooms are actually junior suites with large verandas and all were recently refurbished and upgraded. Guana has never looked better. The rooms are earthy, airy, and cozy, furnished with local art against whitewashed stucco walls, set off by wood-beamed ceilings. All accommodations are very comfortable and the bathrooms modernized and most now have white sculptured walls, providing a contemporary effect. Two generators supply the island's power, and a reverse osmosis system along with rainwater provides drinking water. A biological sewage treatment plant enables the resort to treat and recycle all waste, using the final clear water, high in nitrates, for the "orchard" and vegetable garden where papaya grows to the size of footballs. The garden produces most of the fruits and vegetables used by the resort and is a big attraction for guests who go there to learn from Dr. Liao, the caretaker who shows them around and offers them tea, coconut milk, and freshly picked fruit.

North Beach Cottage, a very private, 1-bedroom house with a living room, kitchen, and bath is on its own ⅓ mile of beach with a private freshwater pool and a sea pool. North Beach Cottage is surrounded by open and covered decks for lounging or sunbathing and dining. Meals can be arranged there, or you can eat at the resort's main dining terrace. The trail to the cottage from the main resort winds along an old Quaker stone wall. North Beach Cottage guests are provided with a golf cart to drive across the Flat to White Bay Beach.

Among the most recent additions are Harbour House and Jost House, 2- and 3-bedroom villas, each with their own pools and hot tubs plus use of a golf cart and villa services. The 3-bedroom Jost House, the most modern in design, is also the most posh with a large heated infinity pool, stone and marble bathrooms, large separate living room and dining room, and its own staff. Harbour House rents as a 2-bedroom unit with the pool or as 2 separate guest rooms without it. The 3-bedroom Anegada House Villa has an ideal hillside location with a lovely terrace and pool overlooking White Beach and expansive views. It can be rented as a villa or 3 separate, 1-bedroom units.

Guest cottages have no phones, but guests may use their cell phones or rent one from the resort to use, so long as they do not use it within "sight or earshot of other guests." Guana has Wi-Fi Internet service for guests who bring their own computers, or they can use the guest computer in the Guest Office. There's no television, except in the villas, but the resort offers outdoor "Old Movie Nights" upon guests' request.

The main house, Dominica, is the social center. It includes a homey lounge with an honor bar, a library where a rare winter evening chill could be warmed by a fireplace, and dining terraces where all meals and afternoon tea are served.

The lively atmosphere during cocktails in the lounge before dinner is more like a weekend house party than a hotel. Dinner seating, normally on the open-air terrace, is arranged by the manager nightly. You may choose to dine with other guests or on your own. You dine by candlelight on a menu that includes fresh seafood, home-baked breads, locally grown fruits and vegetables, and good wine. There is a weekly beach barbecue with music and crab races.

Guana Island boasts 6 untrampled porcelain beaches. Reef-protected White Bay, the "arrival" beach below the main house, is a powdery ½-mile crescent bathed by gin-clear waters ideal for swimming and snorkeling. A golf cart or club jitney will shuttle you to and fro, or you can walk on one of the island's two paved roads. The more isolated beaches can be reached on hiking trails or by boat; 2 are accessible only by boat. A stone stairway of about 150 steps wanders down a cliff on the northern end of Guana and leads to Chicken Rock—so named because it looks like a sitting hen—where at the end of a long hike you can cool off in pristine sea pools.

The owners' interest in conservation led them to make Guana a nature and wildlife preserve and garnered them awards from major magazines for their stewardship. They underwrite programs that, due to the island's unusual nature—an ecosystem almost undisturbed for a century—brings a small army of scientists from prominent universities, The Conservation Agency, and other institutions from afar to study and document its rich flora, fauna, and marine life. They are also helping to restore the natural environment and reintroduce native species, including a half-dozen or so flamingo, the red-legged tortoise, and the rock iguana.

About 50 bird species and 31 butterfly species can be seen regularly, and another 50 bird species come at different times of year. The pristine reefs near shore have about 125 species of fish and dozens of species of coral. Maps of the island's two dozen trails are available. Be sure to bring comfortable walking shoes or sneakers with tread and binoculars.

While the personable managers are attentive and the friendly staff—most of whom have been at Guana for years—are helpful, no one pampers you. You set your own pace, doing as little or as much as you want. There's lots of walking—hiking would be more accurate—to get to meals and the beach. (Transportation is available, too.) But then, nature is what Guana is all about. If you need entertainment or waiters at your beck and call, this is not the place for you.

Guana is designed for travelers who seek tranquillity and can operate on their own juices. Your company will be mostly Americans, with a few British and other Europeans mostly in the 30 to 60 age group. Younger guests and honeymooners tend to come in spring and summer. If it's privacy you want, you can rent the entire island—as CEOs, wedding parties, and families on reunion often do.

GUANA ISLAND ★ ★ ★ 🐚
Guana Island, B.V.I.
Phone: (284) 494-2354; **Fax:** (284) 495-2900; **e-mail:** guana@guana.com; www.guana.com
Owners: Henry and Gloria Jarecki
Resident Managers: Frits and Jenny Hannenberg
Open: Year-round except Sept–Oct
US Reservations: Guana Island, (800) 54-GUANA, 212-GUANAIS; **Fax:** (917) 591-8861
Deposit: 3 nights room and 17 percent tax per booking; 30 days cancellation unless resort is able to rebook accommodation. Policy differs for Christmas/New Year's; inquire
Minimum Stay: 4 nights with round-trip transfers; otherwise none
Arrival/Departure: Guests met at Beef Island Airport by Guana Island representative and taken to nearby dock to board resort's launch for 10-minute ride

to island; $60 per person, round-trip transfer fee added to final bill for stay of 3 nights or less.

Distance from Airport: 10 to 12 minutes by boat

Distance from Road Town: 45 minutes by boat and road; from launch dock to town one-way, $60

Accommodations: 15 rooms in 7 hillside cottages, all with twin or king-size beds and verandas; 1 bedroom in North Beach Cottage; 2 bedrooms Harbour House; 3 bedrooms Jost House (a total of 42 guests can be accommodated)

Amenities: Bathrobes, hair dryers, shower amenities; welcome gifts; cell phone, Wi-Fi service, ceiling fan; shower-only baths, some with air-conditioning; no radio, television; villas have phone and television

Sports: 2 tennis courts (clay and all-weather Omni-turf); self-service beach bar with water-sports equipment, dressing and restrooms, lounging chairs, hammocks; use of courts, racquets, fishing rods, snorkeling gear, sailboats, kayaks, water skis, windsurfers; deep-sea fishing charters and diving arranged

Fitness Facilities/Spa Services: Beach spa for massage and other treatments; also available in room

Electricity: 110 volts

Dress Code: Casual; cover-up and shoes at breakfast and lunch; dinner smart casual

Children: Inquire in advance; children are free in July and Aug

Meetings: Up to 42 people can rent whole island

Day Visitors: No

Handicapped Facilities: Very limited; inquire

Packages: Romance, honeymoon

Rates: 2 people, daily, **AP.** *High Season* (Dec 20–Jan 3): $1,550; (Jan 4–Mar) $1,250. *Shoulder Season* (Apr 1–May 31): $950. *Low Season* (June 16–Aug 31): $695. North Beach Cottage and Villas, inquire. *Entire Island* (daily up to 42 people): $21,050–$31,750, depending on the season

Service Charge: 10 percent; no additional tipping

Government Tax: 7 percent room tax

PETER ISLAND RESORT

Road Town, Tortola, B.V.I.

Set on some of the most beautiful beaches in the Caribbean and surrounded by forested hills with pretty vistas at every turn, posh Peter Island has evolved from a small, exclusive yacht haven created in 1971 into a full-scale resort and spa.

Covering 1,050 of the private island's 1,800 green, hilly acres, Peter Island is perennially named as one of the Caribbean's top resorts. It was all but blown away by Hurricane Hugo in 1989. But it was rebuilt by its then-owners, Amway Hotel Corporation, and has had several major renovations over the years, each upgrading the resort and making it better. The last added a large, elaborate spa on its own separate beach. Ownership of Peter Island Resort passed to family members of the

Amway owners in 2000 and is privately owned.

The resort is laid out in two areas: the original A-frame cottages overlooking the yacht basin, and the more deluxe suites hidden beneath a forest of palm trees on Deadman's Bay, the main beach. The latter have the spacious beachfront junior suites that were improved with an open floor plan with large windows and doors that look out at the lush surroundings and ocean views. The rooms have lavish bathrooms with imported Spanish tile and original hand-laid stonework, walk-in double showers, Jacuzzi tubs, and walls of glass that open on to ocean or garden views.

In 2009, all 32 ocean-view rooms and 20 beachfront junior suites were refurbished with a new look inspired by the Caribbean setting and featuring bright colors for accents against white bedding and combined with whimsical design elements. The design uses one of two color schemes: turquoise, lime and light green, shades of brown and taupe; or a palette of sunset orange, peach, and magenta with contrasting lime. BVI-inspired paintings by Caribbean-based artist Debi Carson adorn the walls. New carved and woven wood headboards add a contemporary edge. In the lounge area of the Beachfront Junior suites, daybeds add comfort and practicality.

Although the resort has not abandoned its long-standing policy of no-television-in-guest-rooms, Peter Island is looking to the future—fiber-optic cable lines and dataports in room and telephones were part of the upgrading. Some signature items such as Peter Island beach sandals and a compact disc of Caribbean music await you upon check-in.

The A-frames are less expensive than the beachfront rooms. Each cottage has 4 large bedrooms: 2 on the ground floor with patios and 2 above with high, beamed ceilings and decks overlooking the harbor on the south and Drake's Channel on the north. Peter Island also has villas, each more spectacular than the other. The Crow's Nest is a fabulous villa with 4 bedrooms, each with a private balcony and bath with Jacuzzi tubs, game room, entertainment system, and pool surrounded by flagstone terraces, as well as an enormous living room and dining room. It is staffed with a housekeeper, butler, and private chef, and a personal villa manager. Situated on the crest overlooking the Sir Francsis Drake

Channel with spectacular views, its price is spectacular, too.

Another hillside villa, Hawk's Nest, is suitable for families. It has 3 bedrooms, living room, television, kitchen, sundeck, plunge pool, air-conditioning and a separate nanny's apartment. This villa is the most centrally located to the resort and enjoys views over the marina and harbor.

Falcon's Nest a 6-bedroom residence, has its own chef, housekeeper, valet and butler, and villa manager. Perched 350 feet above the Caribbean maximizing spectacular views, the villa combines a sophisticated, tropical island feel with a contemporary structure by interior designer Cooper Carry. Among its features are a custom-made 12-person, hand-crafted Tiger maple dining room set, flat-screen television that rises out of a built-in cabinet, 2-story living room with elevated terrace, large outdoor living space with covered dining area, BBQ and swim-up bar; zero-entry pool with a waterfall, grotto, and large Jacuzzi. Each of the 6 bedroom suites has a terrace and luxurious bathroom with indoor/outdoor space, panoramic views, and rain shower. There's a couples spa treatment room; state-of-the-art exercise room; nanny quarters, chef's kitchen and quarters. Private charters, special menus and rare vintage wines are some of the special services Peter Island's villa program can offer guests.

At the resort, the open-air lobby, next to the infinity pool, is convenient to the dock and A-frame cottages. The adjacent library has a flat-screen television that carries CNN and other cable programs. The air-conditioned

Tradewinds restaurant has large waterfront windows with views of Drake's Channel and Tortola. Tradewinds, which also has outdoor dining, offers weekly vintner's wine-pairing dinners, focusing on a particular region to showcase wines from that area. Each course is prepared to complement the wines being served. The cost is $75 per person for hotel guests and $115 including wine for nonguests.

The Beach Bar and Grill on Deadman's Bay Beach, a casual setting for lunch, has an open kitchen and wood-fired oven. It offers an interesting menu as varied as pizza, roti, and fresh fish, along with a salad bar and dessert table. Tea is served daily in the bar area near the pool. Dinner by candlelight is set in both the main dining room and alfresco by the pool, weather permitting. Menus are changed daily, with light fare and a classic as well as a contemporary repertoire.

Peter Island's lovely spa with 12 treatment rooms, is set in gardens on its own beach. Two are in separate, small thatched-roof cottages directly by the sea. Two extraordinarily large treatment rooms with their own whirlpool are designed for couples. Based as it is away from the main resort, it has a superb, tranquil setting in a natural environment. There is a large infinite-edge swimming pool (with very cold water), outside showers encased in natural stone, and an outdoor terrace where lunch is served.

In 2009, the Spa introduced Ayurvedic "Science of Life" wellness programs based on the traditional medicine native to India and overseen by Indian doctors, Dr. Sabari Sabereesan and Dr. Raja Mannar, who are experts in the field of yogic science and naturopathic medicine. A treatment menu as well as multi-day packages, is available. The spa also has a newly developed facial department with Ingrid Millet Paris, the caviar-based, luxury skincare that offers 13 specialty facials. Products sold at the new Spa boutique are also available on the resort's website.

Peter Island operates as an all-inclusive resort. In addition to meals and tea, water sports, tennis, mountain biking, and use of the fitness center are included. Hotel guests must reserve for dinner, because the dining terrace is a popular stop for yachts sailing around the Virgin Islands.

Each of Peter Island's 5 beaches is memorable. On Deadman's Bay Beach you will find thatched umbrellas and lounge chairs near the bar and water-sports center; hammocks are hidden among the trees. The fitness center, with an array of exercise equipment, is at the eastern end of Deadman's Bay Beach. Farther east, Little Deadman's Bay is a mini-mirror image of the main beach, and farther on, secluded Honeymoon Beach has a thatched umbrella and 2 chairs. It's for all romantics, not just honeymooners, but only one couple at a time, please.

PETER ISLAND RESORT ★ ★ ★ ★
PO Box 211, Road Town, Tortola, B.V.I.; or PO Box 9409, St. Thomas, U.S.V.I. 00801
Phone: (284) 495-2000, (800) 346-4451; **Fax:** (284) 495-2500; **e-mail:**

reservations@peterisland.com; www
.peterisland.com
Owner: Van Andel family
General Manager: Wilbert Mason
Open: Year-round
US Reservations: Peter Island Resort
Worldwide; **Phone:** (800) 346-4451,
(616) 458-6767); **Fax:** (616) 458-6641
Deposit: 3 nights at time of reservation
Minimum Stay: 10 nights during
Christmas/New Year's
Arrival/Departure: Guests arriving at
Beef Island Airport transfer directly to
resort's motor launch for 6-mile trip
across Drake's Channel to Peter Island.
Resort also operates up to 8 round-
trips of free ferry service to its dock at
Baughers Bay in Tortola. Transfer by
helicopter directly to resort's lighted
helipad can be arranged from St.
Thomas, San Juan, or other islands.
Distance from Airport: (Beef Island)
Approximately 6 miles
Accommodations: 52 rooms (22 in
A-frames with kings; 20 junior suites
in beachfront buildings with kings); 1
three-bedroom villa with two-bedroom
guest apartment; 1 four-bedroom and 1
six-bedroom villa, all with verandas and
pools
Amenities: Air-conditioning, ceiling
fans; minibar, coffeemaker; telephone;
bath with double sinks, tub, shower,
hair dryers, bathrobes, toiletries; room
service for continental breakfast; no television; beachfront juniors have showers
and Jacuzzis for two
Fitness Facilities/Spa Services: Fitness
center with exercise machines; The Spa
(see text)
Sports: 4 tennis courts (2 lighted),
tennis pro, equipment; small boats,
windsurfers, and free introductory lessons; fishing charters and motor launch
sightseeing; snorkeling gear free; on-site
dive operator
Electricity: 110 volts
Dress Code: Resort wear for men and
women
Children: Inquire
Meetings: Entire island can be rented
for up to 130 people
Day Visitors: Welcome
Handicapped Facilities: Limited
Packages: Honeymoon, wedding, dive,
sailing, 4 and 7 nights off-season
Rates: FAP, double occupancy, per day.
High Season (Jan 4–Mar 31): $980–
$1,415. *Low Season* (June 1–Oct 31):
$610–$930. For Apr–May and Nov 1–
Mar and Villa rates, inquire.
Service Charge: 11 percent
Government Tax: 8 percent

SUGAR MILL HOTEL

Apple Bay, Tortola, B.V.I.

Set on a hillside overlooking Apple Bay on Tortola's quiet northern coast, Sugar Mill is a cozy country inn as well known for its restaurant as for its hotel. It is owned and operated by veteran travel and food writers Jinx and Jeff Morgan.

Sugar Mill is divided into two sections by the small road that skirts the northern coast of Tortola. Instead of a lobby, at the hotel entrance you will find an outdoor gazebo-lounge all but concealed in a riot of flowers and tropical greenery. It is adjacent to the bar, which doubles as the reception area, library, and boutique, and leads to an open-air terrace where breakfast is served. Behind it is the restored remnant of a 370-year-old sugar mill for which the inn is named and that houses the Sugar Mill Restaurant.

Hugging the steep hillside above the mill are clusters of 2-story buildings containing the hotel's rooms and suites—all with balconies overlooking the lovely gardens and a small terraced, freshwater swimming pool. The rooms, furnished mainly in wicker, are comfortable but not fancy. They have air-conditioning, ceiling fan, private bathroom, hair dryer, iron, ironing board, clock radio, and a choice of king or twin beds. The rooms contain small kitchen units that families with children particularly appreciate.

Plantation House, near the hotel entrance gazebo, designed with fine stonework has two deluxe air-conditioned bedrooms, each with a patio, that can be rented individually or as a two-bedroom unit. Each has an open-plan layout, and is furnished with a king-size bed, a living room area with sofa and chairs, cable television, large bathroom with double sinks, and kitchenette and coffee maker.

The Cottage, a one-bedroom suite in classic Caribbean decor with mahogany furniture, has a queen-size, four-poster bed and sitting area as well as television, kitchenette, a bathroom with outside stone shower, and a garden veranda with table, chairs, and lounger.

The newest accommodations are four air-conditioned, pool suites decorated in warm tones, with bedroom (king or twin), living room with queen-size sofa-bed, television, breakfast-bar kitchenette, bathroom with twin sinks and a stone-faced outside showers with its own garden. The large balconies have ceiling fans with table and chairs overlooking the fresh water pool.

The resort also has a deluxe villa with 2 air-conditioned bedrooms with bathroom, living area with a queen-size sofa bed, a full kitchen, cable television, and large balcony with a wide-angle views of the ocean and neighboring islands. Pictures and helpful descriptions of the accommodations are available on Sugar Mill's website.

The lower section of the hotel sits at the edge of the sea alongside a small reef-protected beach with lounging chairs; here, too, is Islands, an informal, open-to-the-breezes restaurant where, as the name suggests, the specialties are Caribbean fare. It is open for lunch daily.

The old stone sugar mill, under a high roof with ceiling fans, the warm glow of candlelight, fresh flowers, colorful Haitian paintings, and classical music playing in the background—all this makes up the inviting setting in which you will enjoy the inn's celebrated cuisine. The Sugar Mill is usually filled with patrons from other hotels and residents of Tortola.

Menus are a la carte and change daily. There are 4 appetizers and 5 entrees from which to chose, featuring such specialties as grilled shrimp on coconut risotto with sesame sauce; cashew crusted halibut with mango and jalapeno sauce, and pumpkin risotto, to name a few. Many of the recipes are included in the Sugar Mill Caribbean Cookbook.

Given Jeff's expertise in California wines (he has written three books on the subject), the extensive wine list highlights California vintages. Jeff has provided brief descriptions of each wine to help guests make their selections.

Sugar Mill gets a great variety of guests—celebrity friends, movie stars, artists, writers, and just plain folks. Many are repeaters—Americans, Canadians, and British—who appreciate the food and enjoy the inn's homey, informal atmosphere. Some come for the workshops conducted by established artists and sponsored by the Morgans from time to time.

Sugar Mill is a bit remote—for many that's part of its charm. Car rental can be arranged.

SUGAR MILL HOTEL ★ ★
Box 425, Road Town, Apple Bay, Tortola, B.V.I.
Phone: (284) 495-4355, (800) 462-8834; **Fax:** (284) 495-4696; **e-mail:**

sugmill@surfbvi.com; www.sugarmill
hotel.com

Owners: Jinx and Jeff Morgan

Managing Director: Patrick Conway

Open: Year-round except Aug–Sept

US Reservations: (800) 462-8834,
(284) 495-4355

Deposit: 3 nights; 30 days cancellation
in order to issue full refund

Minimum Stay: 7 nights during
Christmas/New Year's; 3 nights rest of
high season

Arrival/Departure: Transfer arranged
on request for fee

Distance from Airport: (Beef Island
Airport) 18 miles (45 minutes); taxi
one-way, $50

Distance from Road Town: 10 miles,
taxi one-way, $27; from West End ferry
dock, 3 miles, taxi one-way, $15

Accommodations: 23 rooms (including
studios; deluxe villa, The Cottage; 19
double rooms with terrace and kitchen;
4 family suites); 1 two-bedroom villa; 2
Plantation House suites); twin and king-
size beds

Amenities: Ceiling fans, air-
conditioning; bath with shower only,
hair dryers; telephone with dataport;
clock-radio; iron and ironing boards;
refrigerator and coffeemaker; microwave
in all rooms; wireless Internet

Sports: Freshwater swimming pool,
small beach, beautiful long strands
nearby; free snorkeling gear; scuba,
deep-sea fishing, hiking, other sports
arranged

Electricity: 110 volts/60 cycles

Dress Code: Casual

Children: Over 11 years old in winter;
babysitters

Meetings: No

Day Visitors: Welcome in small
numbers

Handicapped Facilities: Inquire

Packages: Honeymoon, adventure

Rates: 2 people per unit, daily, EP. *High
Season* (mid-Dec–mid-Apr): $340–
$385. *Shoulder Season* (mid-Apr–May
31 and Nov 1–mid-Dec): $275–$335.
Low Season (June 1–July 31 and Oct
1–31): $255. Two bedroom, $690 and
$695 winter; $535 summer. Single,
triple, and quad rates are also available.

Service Charge: 10 percent

Government Tax: 7 percent

BIRAS CREEK RESORT

Virgin Gorda, B.V.I.

A masterpiece of understatement far off the beaten path, Biras Creek is a hideaway in every sense. Small and secluded, the quietly posh resort is designed for relaxing and luxuriating in privacy in a casual, unpretentious, yet sophisticated ambience.

Much of the resort's privacy is all but guaranteed by its location: It's accessible only by boat or helicopter and reached by the resort's private launch—or by your own yacht. Set in 140 acres of nature preserve on an isthmus of green hills that brackets the northern end of Virgin Gorda, the resort overlooks North Sound, a huge deep-water bay that has long been a yachtsman's mecca. On the north and east is the Atlantic, and to the west—the side where you arrive—the Caribbean.

When you approach from the water, all you see is a fortresslike stone structure with a steep carousel roof atop a small rise at the center of the property. Built in terraces and approached by several sets of interconnected stone steps, the "castle" serves as reception, dining, and social center with an indoor-outdoor terraced restaurant and bar commanding a lovely panoramic view.

The resort's size and layout also help ensure privacy. Hidden under enormous almond and sea grape trees that provide shade and maximize privacy are 17 cottages, each with 2 suites. They skirt the crest of Bercher's Bay, where the Atlantic roars in—too rough for swimming but great for cooling breezes to lull you to sleep. Cottage 11A is so close to the sea, it's like being on a ship—in a storm.

Each suite has a large bedroom and sitting room with comfortable chairs, ottoman, and mountains of pillows. Sliding glass doors open onto an ocean-view terrace with lounging chairs—the perfect nook for afternoon reading or dozing. The bathroom features a delightful open-air shower with a tropical garden, enclosed by an 8-foot patio wall but open overhead to blue skies.

Terra-cotta tile floors and the ocean breezes sailing through the screen doors and louvered windows keep the tree-shaded rooms cool. Near your cottage door are two bicycles for your exclusive use.

In 2006, after being bought by Pam and David V. Johnson, owners of Michigan-based Victor International Corp, a real estate, resort development, and management company, Biras Creek was given a million-dollar update without changing its character. All the guest rooms were converted into nonsmoking rooms. They have 300-thread-count cotton linens, Sealy Plush pillowtop mattresses, feathered down pillows, oversized cotton towels, tropical robes, free Wi-Fi, and iPod sound systems. Among other nice touches, the oceanfront room patios have low railings and terra-cotta tiles line the patios and entrances.

The grand suites—17A and 17B—are superdeluxe with a private plunge pool, luxuriously spacious sitting room, bedroom, and bath and handsome, decor. A premier suite, ideal for a family, has 2 bedrooms, 2 baths, and a spacious living area bordered by 3 terraces.

The Arawak Room, a lounge, has Donghia furniture and Janus et Cie outdoor furniture on the Arawak deck—an ideal spot to relax and enjoy afternoon tea. The Arawak has wireless Internet connection for guests. Across from the Arawak room is an air-conditioned fitness center with Nautilus elliptical and treadmill machines. Nearby is the spa, in its own separate building, with 3 treatment rooms and a full roster of services.

Running from the castle to the hillsides are 25 landscaped acres watched over by Biras Creek's gardener, Alvin Harrigan, who has tended the gardens since the resort opened in 1974. Harrigan guides guests on a weekly garden tour. Most of the remaining 115 acres of the estate have been left to nature and include hiking trails and walking paths. However, on the properties' north side overlooking the Atlantic is Oil Nut Bay, a 400-acre peninsula being developed by Biras's owners, as a residential community.

Biras Creek's freshwater pool, at the foot of the castle, has lounge chairs and thatched-roof sun shelters. A secluded beach at tranquil Deep Bay is a 10-minute walk or a 5-minute bike ride from your cottage. En route you pass the tennis courts and a small estuary, a favorite spot for bird-watchers. Next to the beach a large thatched-roof pavilion has a bar (open daily) and picnic tables where lunch barbecues are served. Further on is probably the most improbable addition at Biras Creek—a stable with five Paso Fino horses from Puerto Rico. It apparently came naturally to the Johnsons, who have a passion for horses and keep Tennessee Walking Horses at their farm in Michigan.

Biras Creek's open-air dining room in the hilltop castle is cheerful by day, with sunlight flooding the open terraces, and romantic by night, with candlelit tables and soft background music. The restaurant serves 3 meals daily, as well as afternoon tea. There also is a private dining room for exclusive dining for 12 people. The room can accommodate private meetings and small conferences.

From its inception Biras Creek established a reputation for fine cuisine and an impressive wine list. The bar adjoining the main dining room is a delightful open-air lounge and a popular gathering spot before dinner. There's a weekly manager's party, and music for dancing under the stars several nights.

As your boat approaches Biras Creek from Gun Creek, you will see the Yacht Club Costa Smeralda Marina, another development by the Biras owners on the south side of the resort. Slips for several dozen yachts up to 100 meters (328 feet) and up to 9.1 meters (30 feet) draft are available and a large clubhouse and marine supply facility are nearing completion. Biras offers several packages in the off-season that are good values. Among the most popular is the Sailaway package for the best of both worlds—a stay at the resort plus overnight sailing through the British Virgin Islands on the resort's own crewed yacht. The resort has its own helicopter landing pad.

BIRAS CREEK RESORT
★ ★ ★ ★ ⚲

Box 54, Virgin Gorda, B.V.I. 1150
Phone: (284) 494-3555; **Fax:** (284) 494-3557; **e-mail:** biras@biras.com; www.biras.com
Owners: Pam and David V. Johnson
General Manager: Rik Blyth

Open: Year-round, except late Aug to mid-Oct
US Reservations: (877) 883-0756; **Fax:** (248) 364-2471; or Relais et Châteaux, (800) 735-2478
Deposit: 3 nights
Minimum Stay: 10 nights during Christmas
Arrival/Departure: Transfer from Virgin Gorda Airport can be arranged, $90 round-trip, and includes a 25-minute jitney bus ride to dock at Gun Creek on northern end (almost length of Virgin Gorda). There, resort's water taxi picks you up for 10-minute ride to Biras Creek. From Tortola the resort's water taxi zips you from dock near Beef Island Airport directly to Biras Creek, $95
Distance from Airport: (Spanish Town) 8 miles; taxi one-way, $30; ferry from Beef Island one-way, $40. A ferry schedule is available on Biras's website.
Accommodations: 31 suites in 17 cottages with twin or king-size beds; 1 two-bedroom ocean-view suite; 3 suites interconnect—one with plunge pool
Amenities: Ceiling fans, air-conditioning in bedrooms; coffeemakers, small refrigerator; phones; iron and ironing board; free Wi-Fi; in-room dataport; safes; hair dryers, showers; robes; no locks on doors or room service; all nonsmoking rooms
Fitness Facilities/Spa Services: Small spa
Sports: Freshwater pool; 2 lighted tennis courts with free use, equipment; sailing, snorkeling, windsurfing equipment and instruction; hiking trails; motorized Boston Whalers; snorkeling trips three times a week and frequent trips to nearby secluded sands; fishing charters, day and sunset cruises; dive courses with certification arranged for fee; Dive BVI

dive masters conduct free introductory scuba lessons

Electricity: 110 volts/60 cycles

Dress Code: Casual by day; cover-up and footwear required in dining room and bar; informally elegant for evening; tie and jacket not required

Children: Over 6 years old

Meetings: Up to 16 people

Day Visitors: With prior arrangements

Handicapped Facilities: None

Packages: Off-season, honeymoon, Sailaway, family, wedding, weekend

Rates: Per suite, double, daily, FAP. *High Season* (mid-Dec–early Apr): $980–$2,450. *Low Season:* $700–$1,950. Rates include use of tennis courts and water-sports equipment. For 2-bedroom, weekly and single rates, inquire.

Service Charge: 10 percent

Government Tax: 8 percent

THE BITTER END YACHT CLUB

Virgin Gorda, B.V.I.

Although the Bitter End Yacht Club shares the waters of North Sound with Biras Creek, the two resorts are as different as you could imagine. Bitter End, stretching almost a mile along the northern shore of the sound, is as big and busy as Biras Creek is small and serene.

The 89-acre Bitter End began in the 1960s as a watering hole for yachtsmen. In 1972, Chicago businessman, Myron Hokin, sailed by on a fishing trip. He recognized the value of Bitter End's superb anchorage—the last outpost before the Atlantic—and bought the property, originally as a family retreat.

In 1988, Bitter End merged with neighboring Tradewinds, a more upscale resort, and overnight doubled in size. In addition to more facilities and rooms, Bitter End gained a wider range of style, broadening its appeal and transforming it from a boating haven to a full-scale resort.

Only steps from the beach, the original thatched cottages and Beachfront Villas, which continue to be the most popular accommodations, were renovated, modernized, and greatly upgraded as part of the resort-wide multimillion-dollar renovation, introducing a bit of island sophistication to the resort's once traditional decor, without compromising the hideaway's historical charm and unpretentious, barefoot elegance.

The decor, created by well-known Miami-based interior designer Barbara Hulanicki, integrates Italian-tiled bathrooms, teak vanities, custom-designed bedroom and common area furniture with all materials designed by Hulanicki exclusively for the Bitter End. Using bright blue, orange, and gold colors, the Asian and Caribbean–inspired fabrics in the bedspreads and pillow are coordinated with the art on the walls. All enjoy air-conditioning inside and sea views from a wraparound porch and hammock outside.

Climbing the wooded hillsides above the Clubhouse restaurant to the southeast are the deluxe North Sound Suites in jungle gardens; they're connected to one another by wooden walkways and catwalks, much like tree houses. Similar to the Beachfront Villas, each of the

North Sound Suites villas has 2 accommodations with balconies and fabulous views of the sound. The 2 units—one with 2 queen-size beds and one with a king—can be combined into a 2-bedroom villa. The rooms have peaked, wooden ceilings and are tastefully decorated in wicker with rich fabrics and grass-cloth wall coverings. They are air-conditioned and have telephones, refrigerators, coffeemakers, and king- or queen-size beds. The Estate House is a posh, secluded 2-bedroom villa above the Clubhouse with a large living room, separate dining area, screened porch, and wraparound veranda.

On the beach below the North Sound Suites is a freshwater pool, with bar and lunch service poolside. On "Main Street," Bitter End's Pub is a full-service restaurant, featuring a brick pizza oven. In addition to its great pizza, the pub wins for its flying fish sandwiches and rotis, the West Indian version of a curry wrap. The pub also serves as a sports venue with five flat-screen television sets, broadcasting sporting events from around the world. It also has a pool table, foosball, and several dart boards, making the pub a hangout of the yachting crowd which regularly ties up at the marina.

The Clubhouse Grill, an open-air restaurant, has been a favorite rendezvous for yachties for years. The menu features generous buffets as well as table service for breakfast, lunch, and dinner, and cocktail service on the terrace all day and evening. The meal plan for resort guests includes dining at the Clubhouse or on the Almond Walk, an idyllic setting for numerous events each week, such as Seafood Night and West Indian Night, with dining and dancing under the stars to the resort's own steel band, The Reflections. It is also one of several locations for weddings. The Emporium, a provisioning center catering to yachtsmen for over 20 years, is housed in a charming Caribbean-style building. It offers homemade baked goods from Bitter End's bakery, fresh fish and meats, and wines, rums and other essentials.

The Spa at Bitter End is a full-service facility with 4 treatment rooms and a team of spa professionals providing manicures and facials to herbal wraps and aromatherapies at the spa or in the privacy of one's room. The spa also offers private and group yoga sessions on the beach. The spa is open 12 hours a day, 7 days a week; packages for bridal parties and wedding day preparations are available.

Even with its expansion, Bitter End remains above all a family owned and operated yachting club. Nautical themes are everywhere, and the flags of yacht clubs from around the world hang in the Clubhouse. The resort's fleet of more than 100 crafts is available to guests for their unlimited use. It includes Boston Whalers, Rhodes 19s, Lasers, Mistral Sailboards, and Sunfish, among others. The resort offers 15 weekly excursions aboard its private fleet as well as custom-tailored deep-sea fishing boats, day, snorkeling, and sightseeing charters.

The resort completed a brand-new and improved Quarterdeck Club Marina facility, replacing the old one, and designed particularly to accommodate larger charter catamarans and private megayachts that frequent its anchorage and docks. The new facility has wider slips, improved hybrid/composite decking surfaces, and a better layout to accommodate a wider variety of boat sizes and shapes, along with other improvements.

And if you don't know the difference between a jib and a spinnaker, Bitter End provides free introductory sailing lessons, along with windsurfing and snorkeling instruction. The Bitter End Sailing School holds classes for boaters of all skill levels. The Fall Sailing Festival each November is a month-long, action-packed promotion of Bitter End's sailing facilities and includes Women on the Water Week, Family Thanksgiving Week, and other themed weeks. During the Annual Pro-Am Regatta, guests get to sail with America's Cup–winning skippers and Olympic medalists. It's said to be the only event of its kind in the world.

A Junior Sailing Program is offered year-round for kids 6 years old and over. The resort also has a children's program with supervised water sports, crafts, and hikes. Daily dive classes for beginners and trips for certified divers are also available.

Bitter End's easygoing atmosphere attracts sports enthusiasts of all ages— singles, couples, honeymooners, and families. Most are affluent, active, and somewhat preppie Americans, but there is a sprinkling of Europeans. Life here is so water oriented that those who have no interest in sailing or water sports should look elsewhere. But if you love the sea, this little corner of the Caribbean is paradise.

THE BITTER END YACHT CLUB ★ ★ ★

North Sound, Virgin Gorda, B.V.I.
Phone: (284) 494-2746; **Fax:** (284) 494-4756; **e-mail:** binfo@beyc.com; www.beyc.com
Owner: Dana Hokin
General Manager: Sandra Grisham-Clothier
Resort Manager: Mary Jo Ryan
Open: Year-round, except late July–mid-Oct
US Reservations: Bitter End Yacht Club, (800) 872-2392, (312) 506-6205; **Fax:** (312) 506-6206
Deposit: 3 nights; 30 days cancellation
Minimum Stay: None, except Christmas holiday, 7 days minimum
Arrival/Departure: Transfers cost $70 round-trip
Distance from Airport: (Virgin Gorda Airport) 30-minute taxi ride (one-way, $35), plus 10-minute boat ride; or from Beef Island Airport via Bitter End's own North Sound Express high-speed ferry, a 30-minute scenic trip from the airport directly to the resort, $35 per person ($70 round-trip)
Accommodations: 85 rooms and suites with verandas (45 in beachfront cottages; 38 in North Sound Suites with twin, queen-size, or king-size beds; 2-bedroom villa); 4 live-aboard boats
Amenities: Air-conditioning in North Sound Suites and 10 Beachfront villas, ceiling fans; bath with shower only, hair dryers on request; coffeemaker, refrigerator; television/VCR in North Sound suites; towels changed daily, nightly turndown service; phones; shops and mini-market; no room service
Fitness Facilities/Spa Services: Full service spa
Sports: Sailing, windsurfing, kayaking, water sports (see text); one swimming pool, 3 beaches; jogging and exercise trail; yoga, aerobics; daily snorkeling excursion; kiteboarding; marina with 70 moorings and 25 slips; large complimentary fleet of watercraft; sailing and windsurfing school
Electricity: 110 volts/60 cycles
Dress Code: Informal
Children: 6 years and older; supervised activities; sailing lessons; babysitters
Meetings: Up to 100 people; conference center; audiovisual equipment
Day Visitors: Welcome
Handicapped Facilities: Limited
Packages: Honeymoon, family, weddings, dive, sailing school, wind-surfing, theme weeks
Rates: 2 people, daily, FAP. *High Season* (early Jan–Apr 30): $720–$1120. *Low Season* (May–late July): $570–$890. *Sailing Season* (early Oct–mid-Dec): $520–$890. For Christmas/New Year's holiday, rates are almost double those above. For Estate House, inquire
Service Charge: 11 percent
Government Tax: 7 percent

ROSEWOOD LITTLE DIX BAY
Virgin Gorda, B.V.I.

Opened in 1964, RockResorts—exclusive enclaves renowned for their spectacular natural settings, begun by conservationist pioneer Laurance Rockefeller (hence the name)—became the standard against which all other Caribbean resorts were measured.

Understated and environmentally sensitive long before conservation became fashionable, they were a new kind of resort, where less is more. The accommodations were almost spartan in their simplicity: no phones, air-conditioning, radios, television, or room keys. Peace, privacy, and natural beauty—not man-made trappings—were their special appeal.

But times have changed, even at Little Dix, and since 1992 (when the Rosewood group of Dallas took over),

Rosewood Little Dix Bay, as it is known today, has undergone a renewal that has made it better than ever. Each phase added more amenities and facilities, including large, luxurious villas and junior suites, an oceanside swimming pool, a fabulous spa, and Wi-Fi throughout the property.

Little Dix is set in a 500-acre garden paradise along a half-mile white-sand beach on the southwestern side of Virgin Gorda, with the green slopes of Gorda Peak as a backdrop. Still exclusive but not quite as snooty as in its formative years, Little Dix's service and country club atmosphere begin as soon as you step off the plane at the tiny Virgin Gorda Airport where the runway was recently paved and lengthened. There you are met, registered, and driven to the resort's ferry for a 20-minute ride to the Little Dix dock and taken directly to your beachside room, where you will find fresh flowers, a bottle of rum, and soft drinks.

Camouflaged under dense tropical foliage, Little Dix's spacious guest rooms, each with its own terrace overlooking the sea, are in clusters of cottages—some hexagonal and cone topped, some conventionally shaped—with two to four rooms. Those rooms behind the beachfront cottages are perched on stilts like tree houses to catch the trade winds; they have ground-level patios and hammocks.

The rooms make use of native stone and island hardwoods in their decor, and the results are fabulous. Without changing the tranquil spirit or character of Little Dix, the designers put together an eclectic mix of traditional and contemporary decor in the wonderful manner of understatement that is Little Dix. The rooms are light and elegant yet comfortable and inviting. There are good reading lamps—all the more useful with Little Dix's service, "Hot Type," which enables guests to obtain advance copies of select novels without charge. The junior suites have a large outdoor covered living area, and oversize bathrooms with indoor and outdoor showers.

Perhaps even more telling about changing times are Little Dix's luxurious villa suites, each with 3 bedrooms and a private pool. They are located at the west side of the resort on a small beach. Each has an oversize living area, spacious bathrooms with outdoor showers, a private pool, and dining pavilion.

The exotic spa treatment rooms are in simple, thatched huts. It has my vote for the most beautiful spa in the Caribbean. The spa treatments that use local ingredients are right up there, too. Both the villas and spa were designed by Roger Downing, whose firm is based in the British Virgin Islands and who has a keen sense of harmonizing the structures with their natural environment and maximizing their setting. The spa sits at the edge of a bluff that commands spectacular, wide-angle views. It is centered by an open-air pavilion beside a vanishing-edge pool. From here rock-lined paths wind through tropical gardens to a series of individual, thatched roof cottages housing treatment rooms.

Daytime activities—most included in the room rate—can be as strenuous as lazing on a bright blue float on smooth azure water (a protective reef keeps it that way) or more demanding: Sunfish sailing, waterskiing (extra charge), and scuba lessons. A water taxi will take you to one of seven pristine beaches to snorkel, sunbathe, and picnic. The most fun of all may be a tennis challenge, with 6 or more people kept in constant motion by the Peter Burwash–trained pro.

As with many other exclusive resorts, the need to attract younger guests and cater to the ever-increasing family market led Little Dix to add a children's facility, the Children's Grove, which operates year-round.

The center of life at Rosewood Little Dix Bay is the Pavilion, a terrace with 4 interconnected dining and lounge areas topped with a soaring, 4-point shingled roof where lavish breakfasts and lunch buffets, afternoon tea, and candlelight dinners are served. For Thursday lunch, guests are taken by Boston Whalers to

Spring Bay for a beach party. The resort can also arrange private dinners on the beach with full service, tiki lights, and steel pan music, at an extra cost. The Sugar Mill Restaurant and Bar, adjacent to the main terrace, is a dinner alternative, and the service is first-class all the way. Indeed, service is one of Little Dix Bay's strengths. Most employees are Virgin Gorda natives who have been at Little Dix for more than two decades, giving the resort a sense of family.

ROSEWOOD LITTLE DIX BAY

★ ★ ★ ★ ★

PO Box 70, Virgin Gorda, B.V.I.
Phone: (284) 495-5555, (888) 767-3966; **Fax:** (284) 495-5661; **e-mail:** littledixbay@rosewoodhotels.com; www.littledixbay.com
Owner/Management: Rosewood Hotels and Resorts
Managing Director: Duncan Hogarth
Open: Year-round
US Reservations: Rosewood Hotels and Resorts, (888) ROSEWOOD; **Fax:** (214) 871-5444
Deposit: 3 nights; 28 days cancellation
Minimum Stay: Applies in high season; inquire in advance.
Arrival/Departure: Upon arrival at Tortola airport (EIS), Little Dix rep takes guests to private boat for 20-minute ride to the resort. Welcome drinks are served while guests register. Cost: $95 per person, round-trip (50 percent off for children 5 to 12; 4 and under free). Fly BVI air taxi to Virgin Gorda available from St. Thomas, $250 per person, one-way for minimum of 2 persons. Via St. Maarten, connect to Winair or Liat to Beef Island

Distance from Airport: (Virgin Gorda Airport) About 2 mile
Distance from Spanish Town: 2 miles
Accommodations: 78 double rooms, 16 junior suites, 1 two-bedroom, and 2 three-bedroom villas
Amenities: Ceiling fans, air-conditioning; bath with double sinks, tub and shower, bathrobes, slippers, toiletries, hair dryers; telephones; CD player; minibars; safes; nightly turndown service, towels changed and ice service two times daily; room service, Wi-Fi.
Fitness Facilities/Spa Services: Fitness center with cardiovascular equipment; spa (see text)
Sports: Swimming pool; 7 tennis courts (2 lighted), clinics, resident pro; hiking trails; sunfish, Hobies, kayaks; dive trips for fee
Electricity: 110 volts/60 cycles
Dress Code: Gracious informality; trousers, collared shirts, and closed-toe shoes (no beach attire) required after 6:30 p.m.; jackets and ties not required
Children: All ages; year-round program (see text); nanny service
Meetings: Up to 20 people
Day Visitors: Individuals welcome with reservations
Handicapped Facilities: No
Packages: Honeymoon, wedding, spa
Rates: 2 people, daily, **EP.** *High Season* (early Dec–Apr 1): $650–$1,900. *Shoulder Season* (Apr 1–31 and mid-Nov–mid-Dec): $525–$1,300. *Low Season:* $375–$1,000. Villa rates: inquire
Service Charge: 18 percent on food and beverages
Government Tax: 7 percent
Resort Fee: 10 percent

CAYMAN ISLANDS

Known as the Mount Everest of diving, the Cayman Islands are a British Crown Colony tucked under the western end of Cuba. The group is comprised of three low-lying islands almost completely surrounded by reefs: Grand Cayman, the resort and commercial center; Cayman Brac, a string bean of untamed wilderness, 89 miles to the northeast; and Little Cayman, the smallest, 5 miles west of Cayman Brac.

One of the most prosperous places in the Caribbean, the islands have excellent communications and their own airline and currency—and a population of only 50,000. Early in their history they were a favorite hiding place for pirates, and Pirates' Week, held in October, is a frolicking annual commemoration of the islands' history.

Grand Cayman, with the capital at George Town, is the largest of the trio. Seven Mile Beach, where the majority of the hotels are located, is a magnificent crest of powdery white sand just north of George Town. The 22-mile-long island rises only 60 feet above sea level and is made up largely of lagoons and mangroves rich in bird life.

Across one of these areas, North Sound, lies a barrier reef, and just inside the mouth is one of the Caribbean's most unusual sites. Dubbed Stingray City, it offers divers and snorkelers a thrilling opportunity to touch, feed, and photograph a dozen or more friendly stingrays in only 12 feet of water.

Grand Cayman also has the world's only sea turtle farm, where you can see turtles at various stages of development in their breeding pans. For a nominal fee you can sponsor a turtle for release to the ocean.

Under the sea the Caymans are surrounded by extensive cliffs, slopes, and valleys of submerged mountains, collectively known as the Cayman Wall, and densely encrusted with forests of corals, giant sponges, and other marine life. Nondivers can see the Caymans' underwater splendors thanks to recreational submarines.

Cayman Brac is 12 square miles of untamed tropics yet to be discovered by nature buffs for its hiking, fishing, birding, and caving. Little Cayman is even less developed. The 10-mile-long island has large expanses of mangroves and lagoons and is surrounded by long stretches of white-sand beaches, extensive reefs, and spectacular walls that some experts consider make up the finest diving in the Western Hemisphere.

Information

Cayman Islands Department of Tourism, Empire State Building, 350 Fifth Ave., Ste. 1801, New York, NY 10118; (212) 889-9009; www.caymanislands.ky

THE RITZ-CARLTON, GRAND CAYMAN

Seven Mile Beach, Grand Cayman

When The Ritz-Carlton, Grand Cayman, opened in December 2005, it raised the bar for all resorts in the Cayman Islands. Ideally situated on Grand Cayman's famous Seven Mile Beach, the resort's 144 acres stretch from sea to sea, from the Caribbean-washed beaches across the island to the world-renowned dive waters of the North Sound. Designed in classic British-colonial architecture and surrounded by tropical gardens, the $500 million Ritz-Carlton is 20 minutes from the airport and only 66 minutes by air from Miami.

The resort offers a wide choice of deluxe accommodations; a restaurant by highly regarded chef Eric Ripert of New York's Le Bernardin; 2 retail stores; a full-service La Prairie Spa—the first in the Caribbean; Ambassadors of the Environment program by Jean-Michel Cousteau; a Nick Bollettieri tennis center with clay courts lighted for evening play, grass court, and a small tennis stadium court with professional instruction; and an unusual 9-hole golf course, designed and built by the PGA legend Greg Norman that is open only to hotel guest and residence owners.

In 2007, the Ritz-Carlton Grand Cayman owner purchased the Safe Haven golf course, which lies adjacent to the hotel, and renamed it The North Sound Club. It operates as an independent 18-hole course. The resort's 365 guest rooms include 36 suites and the premier Ritz-Carlton Suite. The beautifully appointed rooms offer a choice of king-size or double beds, a large desk, stocked honor bar, marble baths, deluxe toiletries, sewing kit, lighted makeup mirror, hair dryer, and bathroom scales. Oceanfront rooms have views of the Caribbean, beach, and pool; Resort rooms, located on the North Sound side of the property, overlook the golf course and the waterway pool. Guest rooms are charged a $45 per day per room resort fee that covers the use of certain facilities and amenities, such as complimentary dining for children 5 years and younger in 4 restaurants. Other amenities include Wi-Fi access; use of laptops; valet parking; use of floating Aqua Lounge dining tables and Aqua bed lounges; access to spa steam rooms, saunas and whirlpools; fitness center and daily fitness classes; certain water sports equipment; introductory sailing lesson; snorkel gear and lessons; golf course putting green and tennis center hitting area; outdoor nightly movies and access to DVD library.

Accommodations in The Ritz-Carlton Club level have the option of ocean, beach, or resort views. Club guests have a private Club Concierge, 24-hour room service, twice-daily housekeeping, overnight laundry service, and morning newspaper. They also have elevator key access, an exclusive lounge, and five food presentations daily. The elegant Ritz-Carlton Suite, with panoramic ocean-view rooms, has a master bedroom, one-and-a-half baths, living room, dining areas and butler's pantry, and seafront balcony.

Six super deluxe 5-bedroom, 5-bath homes known as The DeckHouses have been built as part of a planned 19 gated single-family residences community situated within a latticework of canals

between The Ritz-Carlton and North Sound. Each has full access to the services and amenities of the hotel.

Jean Michel Cousteau's Ambassadors of the Environment provides a supervised program of children's activities, centered on multifaceted learning and recreational experiences designed to immerse children in the natural aspects of the Cayman Islands. Eco adventure programs are offered for kids as young as 4 years of age. Several water-based activities including mangrove kayaking, night snorkeling, and underwater photography are designed for older children and adults.

The resort has 6 dining and entertainment choices. Blue by Eric Ripert is the resort's gourmet restaurant in a formal setting with a poolside alfresco bar and grill overlooking the lagoon. Other dining options include 7, an oceanfront cafe, offering open-air all-day dining overlooking the Caribbean Sea and Periwinkle, a more casual alfresco bistro with a Mediterranean focus. In the evening, 7 Prime Cuts & Sunsets specializes in high quality steaks. Cocktails, a wine bar, and light fare, including traditional tea on weekends, are served at Silver Palm. Sushi and the island's largest sake collection are offered at Taikun. The lively beachfront pool bar, Bar Jack, is a popular sunset gathering place. There's also 24-hour in-room dining service.

Silver Rain, the 20,000-square-foot La Prairie Spa, has 17 treatment rooms and a full range of pampering and relaxation treatments and spa services. There also is a fitness center.

The resort's large meeting facilities brought another new dimension to Grand Cayman with the ability to cater to corporate executive meetings at the luxury level. The flexible facilities include the largest ballroom in the Cayman Islands, an elegant boardroom, and 5 meeting rooms. The resort's grounds and terraces provide options for outdoor functions.

THE RITZ-CARLTON, GRAND CAYMAN ★ ★ ★ ★

PO Box 32348, Seven Mile Beach, Grand Cayman, Cayman Islands
Phone: (345) 943-9000; **Fax:** (345) 943-9001; www.ritzcarlton.com
Owner: Michael Ryan
Management: The Ritz-Carlton Hotel Company, Atlanta, Georgia
General Manager: Marc Langevin
Open: Year-round
US Reservations: Ritz-Carlton, (800) 241-3333
Deposit: Varies by season; inquire
Minimum Stay: Varies by season; inquire
Arrival/Departure: Transfer service; inquire
Distance from Airport: (Owen Roberts International) 4.3 miles
Accommodations: 365 guest rooms, including 36 suites with king-size or 2 doubles; 1 Ritz-Carlton oceanfront suite; 36 Ritz-Carlton Club level rooms; 24 two- and three-bedroom oceanside residential suites
Amenities: Air-conditioning; safe; stocked bar; marble bathrooms; cable television, digital clock/alarm radio, CD player; dual-line phones and dataports, wireless Internet; bathrobes and slippers; twice-daily housekeeping, 24-hour room service; Ritz-Carlton Suite: living room/dining area, pantry, master bathroom, one-and-one-half bathrooms
Fitness Facilities/Spa Services: Fitness center; La Prairie Spa (see text)
Sport: Swimming pool, snorkeling, diving, fishing, boating; tennis; golf (see text)
Electricity: 110 volts
Dress Code: Casually elegant
Children: All ages; Cousteau Ambassadors program; babysitting
Meetings: Up to 1,000 people
Day Visitors: Yes
Handicapped Facilities: Special rooms
Packages: Golf, wedding, spa
Rates: Per room, double, per day, EP. *High Season* (mid-Dec–Apr 30): $599–$1,149. *Low Season:* $249–$499, plus $45 resort fee (see text). For suite rates, inquire.
Service Charge: 10 percent
Government Tax: 10 percent

PIRATES POINT RESORT

Little Cayman, Cayman Islands, B.W.I.

Unusual if not unique, Pirates Point is a diver's resort owned and operated by Gladys Howard from Tyler, Texas.

What's unusual about that?

Gladys happens to be an award-winning cookbook author and a Cordon Bleu chef who studied with Julia Child, James Beard, and Lucy Lo. And she operated an international cooking school and gourmet catering service in East Texas for 20 years.

When you arrive at the Edward Bodden Airstrip, Gladys' staff will meet you in a white van for the half-mile ride to the resort. The airport strip has been tarmaced, but the terminal is still a wooden shack; Little Cayman has a total population of about 100 people.

Pirates Point consists of a central pavilion that includes the front desk, lounge and bar, dining room and outdoor barbecue, and 5 cottages constructed of cut stone and wood. They're only 20 steps from the beach. Three of the cottages have 2 units each, one has 4 units, and one is reserved for single guests. Two cottages have large verandas. The family cottage has a king and 1 or 2 twins in a trundle.

The little resort is immaculate. Rooms are spacious and surprisingly pleasant and comfortable, given their rustic setting. They have pastel stucco and wood-paneled walls and high wood-beamed ceilings. Furnished in wicker, they have either 2 twin beds or 1 king. In the bathroom you'll find fluffy towels, terry robes, and a shower with hot and cold water. Pirates Point has its own reverse-osmosis plant, which helps ensure a freshwater supply. The resort has a guest telephone and VCR and DVD players in the lounge. DVD movies and videos are available.

Each year Gladys repaints all guest rooms and buildings as well as overhauls and refits the *Yellow Rose III,* the resort's 42-foot custom dive boat. The resort has a large freshwater pool and a 10-person Jacuzzi surrounded by an 8-foot deck. The bar is air-conditioned and complimentary wireless Internet service is available. There is a dedicated computer for guest use in the clubhouse, or guests can use their own laptops within about a 50-yard radius of the clubhouse.

The complex is shaded by large almond, sea grape, and coconut palm trees. Along the path by the cactus garden leading to the reception area, you will notice some sculptures made from coconuts, driftwood, and other natural material. What started as a pastime has developed into a wacky tradition, and now these "works of art" by guests decorate the bar and add character to the inn. Since 1988, Gladys has run an annual contest for the most original creation; the prize is a week's vacation at the resort.

You can count on the food to be good. Gladys uses whatever she can get and works miracles in her kitchen. It is difficult to get products locally, except fish. Her supplies come by boat from Grand Cayman, and she flies in fresh fruits and vegetables.

For this caterer and gourmet chef, dining is serious business. There's no roughing it here: You'll dine with crystal stemware and linen napkins even at picnics. Lunch, an outdoor buffet under the sea grape trees, is in your swimsuit, and dinner offers a buffet and table service in the dining room. There is a barbecue on Thursday and a Happy Hour special Champagne and Sushi reception at Gladys's house every Friday night—and this lady is the ultimate hostess. If you are a hotel guest during Pirate Week (in late Oct or early Nov), the Cayman Islands's annual carnival bash, you will surely get involved in helping to construct the resort's float and join the party and the parade. It's great fun.

A coral atoll 10 miles long and 1 mile wide, Little Cayman is one of diving's last frontiers. Its Bloody Bay Wall is one of life's great diving experiences. Rising to within 20 feet of the surface and plunging in sheer cliffs more than a mile deep, these pristine formations offer marine life found nowhere else. There are giant sponges, trees of black coral, elaborate sea fans, and eagle rays, to name a few. The late Philippe Cousteau called it one of the three finest dive areas in the world.

Pirates Point is located only 2 miles or a short boat ride from the wall and with its fast boat can easily reach the most dramatic dive sites. The resort has a full scuba operation with 6 instructors on staff who handle everything from a short resort course to full certification and advanced training. The resort offers 2 dives daily and night dives by request. The dives do not have time limits and are done safely, opting for longer quality dives, rather than quantity. Good shore snorkeling (gear costs extra) can be enjoyed directly in front of the resort. The resort has a sandy beach, but the entrance into the water from shore is rocky and better made from its small pier, which puts you into about 3 feet of water. Pirates Point can arrange fishing and group-dive programs on request.

Gladys, as avid an environmentalist as she is a gourmet chef, founded the Little Cayman National Trust, which has created trails for hiking and bird-watching. The Caymans are a flyover for North American birds, and Little Cayman is a sanctuary for the red-footed booby and frigate bird. It also has its own island lake for tarpon fishing, with an endemic subspecies.

Pirates Point operates as an all-inclusive resort. The certified dive package includes accommodations with private bath, 3 meals daily with wine, an open bar with unlimited drinks, 2 boat dives daily, tanks, weights, belt, guide, transfer to/from the airport, and use of bicycles, beach towels, and terry robes. Add the experience of diving at Little Cayman and Gladys's food, and Pirates Point tallies up as one of the best buys in the Caribbean.

PIRATES POINT RESORT ★ ★ 🐾
Box 43LC, Little Cayman, Cayman Islands, B.W.I.
Phone: (345) 948-1010; Fax: (345) 948-1011; e-mail: piratept@candw.ky; www.piratespointresort.com
Owner/Manager: Gladys B. Howard
Open: Year-round except for early Sept–late Oct
US Reservations: Direct to hotel
Deposit: Half total package rate within 10 days of booking; 30 days

cancellation, refund half of deposit; fewer than 30 days, deposit forfeited
Minimum Stay: 3 nights
Arrival/Departure: Complimentary transfer service
Distance from Airport: (Edward Boden Airport) ½ mile; no taxi service (Little Cayman is 90 miles northeast of Grand Cayman; Cayman Airways, 800-422-9626, provides daily flights from George Town)
Distance from South Town: ¾ mile
Accommodations: 11 rooms in bunga-lows (7 air-conditioned; 6 oceanfront); doubles have twins or king; maximum of 20 divers
Amenities: Ceiling fans, floor fans; 7 rooms with air-conditioning; baths with shower only; custom 42-foot Newton dive boat; daily maid service, no room service
Sports: See text
Electricity: 110 volts
Dress Code: Very casual
Children: Over 5 years of age, but must be over 12 to dive
Meetings: Up to 20 people
Day Visitors: Welcome, with reservations
Handicapped Facilities: Limited
Packages: All-inclusive, dive, honeymoon
Rates: Per person, double, weekly pack-age, FAP. High Season (mid-Dec–mid-Apr): $2,095 diver; $1,695 nondiver. Low Season: $1,895 diver; $1,595 non-diver. Single supplement, $100 per day or request single room.
Service Charge: 15 percent
Government Tax: $8 per room daily

CURAÇAO

Only 39 miles off the coast of Venezuela, the cosmopolitan capital of the Netherlands Antilles is noted for its commerce, diversity of restaurants, and fashionable shops with goods from around the world. These features are found side by side with the colorful colonial harbor of Willemstad, making it easy and fun to explore on foot.

At the heart of the compact historic old city are Fort Amsterdam, the Governor's Palace, the 18th-century Dutch Reform Church, and, nearby, Mikve Israel-Emanuel Synagogue, the oldest synagogue in the Americas (founded in 1654).

Juxtaposed against the sophisticated city center is the little-known landscape of windswept shores, chalky mountains, and rugged terrain, as well as two of the best nature parks in the Caribbean. In the 3,500-acre Christoffel National Park, cactus grows as tall as trees. Dominated by the rocky peak of 1,238-foot Mount Christoffel, the park has 20 miles of roads with color-coded routes for self-guided tours and hiking trails.

Curaçao is completely surrounded by reefs with an extraordinary variety of coral and fish that are only now being discovered by divers. The 1,500-acre Curaçao Underwater Park, stretching for 12½ miles from the SuperClubs' Breezes Resort to the eastern tip of the island, protects some of Curaçao's finest reefs. Many areas can be enjoyed by snorkelers as well as divers. East of the marine park is the Curaçao Aquarium, a private facility where 400 species of marine life native to Curaçao waters are displayed.

Quiet seas wash Curaçao's western shores, but wild surf crashes against the windward north. The coast has many small coves with beaches and large bays or lagoons with very narrow entrances and wide basins. These waterways are among Curaçao's most distinctive features. Some lagoons are used for commerce, others for sport.

On the east, Spanish Water, the location of the Hyatt Regency Curaçao is one of the island's largest, prettiest lagoons with a long, narrow opening to the sea. It has hilly green fingers and coves, islands, and beaches, and is the boating and fishing center with marinas and water-sports facilities. The constant northeastern trade winds that cool the island have made windsurfing one of Curaçao's most popular sports, with international recognition and an Olympic champion. Annually in June the Curaçao Open International Pro-Am Windsurf Championship attracts world masters.

Information

Curaçao Tourism Corporation, 1 Gateway Center, Ste. 2600, Newark, NJ 07102; (973) 353-6200; Fax: (973) 353-6201; e-mail: northamerica@cura cao.com; www.curacao.com

CURAÇAO MARRIOTT BEACH RESORT & EMERALD CASINO

Curaçao, N.A.

When it opened in 1992, the Curaçao Marriott Beach Resort & Emerald Casino was something of an homage to the island's architecture and rich history. The hotel's stately facade of deep ochre stucco and white gabled trim to the traditional red tile roof and colonnaded promenades are echoes of the island's past.

More so than other former colonies, Curaçao's Dutch heritage is evident throughout the island in its architecture. The colorful stucco buildings that line the harbor and streets of Willemstad, the capital; the historic *landhuis,* or manor houses, that dot the countryside; the homes in the Scharloo area, during the 19th century a lively neighborhood of

wealthy merchants—all are relics of the colonial era. In addition to the Dutch touch, the architecture was shaped by the spirited colors and exuberant flair of Spanish, Latin American, and African influences. All served as the inspiration for original designers Mary Jane Rosa and John Olson, who spent days combing neighborhoods, noting details, and even collecting paint chips to re-create authentic colors. The results are subtle and sophisticated—a modern interpretation of historical tradition.

Set on Piscadera Bay, the tropically elegant 3-story resort stretches along a white-sand beach on the southern coast of the island, 10 minutes from the airport and from downtown Willemstad and next door to the World Trade Center Curaçao.

A circular driveway fronted by a massive gabled roof, fountain, and garden driveway makes for a grand entrance. As you walk up a set of steps into the hotel, you can see through the open-air lobby to a fabulous view of the white sandy beach and the turquoise Caribbean waters.

On the periphery of the hotel, a shaded promenade of bellied columns, symmetrically bowed in Curaçao style, frames ocean views and blurs the line between indoor and outdoor living. The lobby, with its rich wooden ceiling and weathered brass fixtures, is meant to recall the Curaçao of the 18th and 19th centuries, when it was a major hub for trade ships cruising between Europe and South America. The result was the Curaçao style, an eclectic blend of decorative themes and products from all over the world.

The lobby's front desk is made entirely of wood panels crisscrossed with carved, rope-style moldings. Sturdy unfinished wooden furniture with carved detailing and textured upholstery in deep colors lends a Dutch flavor to the sitting areas.

Recalling the elegant Scharloo courtyards, tiled pathways—lined with more white columns and flaming bougainvillea—lead to the plush guest rooms. The large, air-conditioned rooms, with furnished balconies or terraces and full or partial ocean views, are dressed in contemporary colors.

The immense pool and beach area, graced with fountains and lush tropical greenery, is the center of the hotel—and the action. Comfy chaise lounges ring the free-form pool, which has a swim-up bar, a wading pool, and 2 large whirlpools. A shack dispenses beach towels, and an outdoor grill serves up burgers and barbecued chicken.

The man-made beach is wide, long, and studded with thatched shelters under which you can escape the hot sun. Caribbean Sea Sports, which operates directly on the beach, offers snorkeling, waterskiing, windsurfing, sailing, kayaking, and scuba diving lessons and equipment rentals. It also has a lobby shop.

For breakfast and dinner, Portofino, a glass-enclosed restaurant with high ceilings and palm-frond fans, also offers alfresco dining on its patio. The dinner specialty is northern Italian cuisine and a selection of fresh pasta. The Emerald Lounge, an upscale mojito bar, serves seafood and pizza and features light jazz music in the evening.

Across from it the Emerald Casino—fashioned after the patios or courtyards at the center of Scharloo homes—glitters with elegance and sophistication. An opulent French crystal chandelier 8 feet in diameter sparkles overhead against a white-clouds-on-blue-sky mural. In front of the casino, the casual Voila Delicatessen, a relaxing sitting area, is open for 3 meals daily. Another recent addition is the Boardroom Beach Bar, a casual pub for lunch and dinner that's particularly popular for cocktails at sunset. At Seabreeze, you can take drinks at its swim-up bar or dine for lunch and dinner on international selections at its restaurant. The resort has a kosher kitchen.

In addition to water sports, the resort's sports and fitness facilities include 2 lighted tennis courts, a health club with a gym, 2 saunas, 2 steam rooms, and a massage room. There are aerobics classes, Universal machines, exercise bikes, stair climbers, and free weights. The fitness center provides exercise and strength-training equipment and is enhanced by its natural surroundings. The resort has a beauty salon, shopping arcade, and a state-of-the-art, 24-hour business center offering full business services. The hotel offers shuttle service to town.

Meeting facilities are centered on the Queen's Ballroom, which has a distinctly Spanish flavor and Old World, formal atmosphere. It takes its cue from the Scharloo salas, rooms saved for special celebrations filled with music and dancing.

On a clear night—and every night in Curaçao is clear—there's a touch of Caribbean magic when you sink your body into the bubbling waters of an outdoor Jacuzzi and watch moon shadows dance upon the yellow gables, white columns, and crimson tiles of this most modern yet delightfully traditional resort.

CURAÇAO MARRIOTT BEACH RESORT & EMERALD CASINO ★ ★ ★ ★

Piscadera Bay, PO Box 6003, Curaçao, N.A.
Phone: (599) 9-736-8800; Fax: (599) 9-462-7502; www.paradisebymarriott .com
Owner: Reef Resorts
General Manager: John Toti
Open: Year-round
US Reservations: (800) 223-6388

Deposit: 1 night with credit card; 3 days cancellation in high season
Minimum Stay: Christmas/New Year's/Easter/Carnival
Arrival/Departure: Airport transfers not available but free transportation, subject to availability, twice a day to downtown
Distance from Airport: 10 miles; taxi one-way, $25
Distance from Town: 5 miles; taxi one-way, $25
Accommodations: 247 rooms and 10 suites, with balconies or patios (8 terrace suites and 2 Presidential Suites with ocean view; 124 rooms with king, 123 with queens)
Amenities: Air-conditioning; bath with tub, shower, toiletries, hair dryer; remote control television with cable; radio; fridge (upon request); telephone; safe; iron and ironing board; casino; turndown service on request, room service 6 a.m.–midnight
Fitness Facilities/Spa Services: Fitness center with aerobics classes, Universal equipment, steam rooms, massages, saunas; beauty salon
Sports: Freshwater swimming pool, 2 outdoor whirlpools; 2 free, lighted tennis courts; water-sports center for snorkeling, waterskiing, windsurfing, sailing, kayaking, and diving lessons and equipment rentals
Electricity: 110 volts and 220 volts
Dress Code: Casual by day; casually elegant in evening; jackets and ties not required
Children: Up to 2 children under 12 years old free in parents' room, including meals; cribs, high chairs; babysitters

Meetings: Up to 400 people; hotel adjacent to the World Trade Center Curaçao
Day Visitors: May use pool, beach, fitness center, tennis courts, and other facilities for $75 per person; limited if hotel is busy
Handicapped Facilities: Available on request

Packages: Family, romance
Rates: Per room, EP. *High Season* (early Jan–Mar): from $319. *Low Season* (Apr–mid-Dec): from $239. Meal plans available
Service Charge: 12.98 percent
Government Tax: 9 percent

HOTEL KURA HULANDA SPA AND CASINO AND LODGE KURA HULANDA AND BEACH CLUB

Willemstad, Curaçao

Kura Hulanda means "Dutch courtyard" in Papiamentu, the native language of Curaçao. Given that the island is the architectural crown jewel of the Dutch Caribbean, this simple term perfectly denotes the distinctive, charming environment of the Hotel Kura Hulanda Spa and Casino, an extraordinary fusion of "urban renewal," Caribbean style, and one man's vision.

Opened in late 2001, the hotel is the centerpiece of Project Kura Hulanda, which includes 65 historic buildings, mostly former private homes, in an

8-block complex. Project Kura Hulanda showcases meticulously restored 18th- and 19th-century Dutch colonial Caribbean architecture and includes an internationally recognized cultural museum, as well as a conference center, casino, spa, and retail shops.

Dutch millionaire Jacob Gelt Dekker, along with his longtime partner John R. Padget, made his fortune in rental-car and one-hour-photo businesses in Europe. On a trip to Curaçao after he and Padget had sold off their major business interests at huge profits, Dekker fell in love with the island's extraordinary architecture. Almost overnight, he drew up plans for Project Kura Hulanda. In a run-down neighborhood of dilapidated houses and broken streets, Dekker and his team carved out, quite literally, an architectural and cultural oasis.

Hotel Kura Hulanda is conveniently located in the center of the Otrabanda section of Willemstad, Curaçao's capital, only 15 minutes from the airport. The brightly colored compound, located above St. Anna Bay near the Queen Emma Bridge, is within easy walking distance of Punda, Willemstad's major downtown district across the retractable pontoon bridge.

The hotel gives the impression of a peaceful village, with tree-lined lanes carefully crafted of imported stone and a tour-book façade with some interesting architectural flourishes, such as perfect replicas of historic houses Dekker saw on his travels to Suriname and a charming central courtyard between the lobby and the restaurants and shops. Elsewhere around the property there is a series of intimate courtyards that include an African sculpture garden and an herb and fruit garden.

Kura Hulanda's spacious, nicely appointed accommodations include double rooms and suites. Because the units are adapted from renovated private homes, no two are the same. As a decorative motif, each room displays a wall with a handpainted design by a local artisan. Custom-made furniture, including a four-poster bed, is handcarved from the finest mahogany and old teak; the handwoven linens are from India; bathrooms are of Indian marble.

Two signature suites are a 996-square-foot, 2-story, 1-bedroom presidential suite that includes an entertainment center with big-screen television and a fully equipped kitchen; and a sexy yet sophisticated bridal suite with handcrafted furniture made of hammered sterling silver, including a canopied, handcarved bed worthy of Cleopatra. A pair of duplex luxury spa loft suites have huge bathrooms.

Amenities include air-conditioning, ceiling fans, waffle-weave bathrobes, hair dryers, cooler, cable television, portable CD system, high-speed Internet, and teak butler stands for clothing and comforter. The hotel's international appeal is reflected in its telephone system with modem and voice mail available in English, Dutch, French, and Spanish.

Kura Hulanda has 2 swimming pools, including the "eco-pool," a grotto surrounded by natural rock formations and fed by a waterfall, and a more traditional pool near a sculpture garden. Hotel guests enjoy access to a private beach club and preferential golf privileges at a golf club nearby. Kura Hulanda offers complimentary transportation to these clubs. An air-conditioned and fully equipped fitness center has free weights and the latest machines and a sauna and steam room.

Next to the fitness center is the hotel's spa, where guests can enjoy facials, massages, manicures, and pedicures for an additional charge. In-room services are also available. The hotel has a business center, and among its most important facilities in today's post–September 11 world is an unobtrusive state-of-the-art security system that monitors the grounds around the clock.

For dining, Kura Hulanda offers a number of options, from casual to elegant. The hotel's Indian influence is carried through at Jaipur, its signature restaurant serving tandoori oven specialties from traditional chicken and naan breads to shrimp and lamb. The restaurant, set by the rock grotto eco-pool, also has a cozy, alfresco bar. The AstroLab Observatory restaurant, with a courtyard filled with museum-quality navigational instruments, serves breakfast and dinner. Jacob's Bar offers tapas and cocktails in a Spanish setting with an outdoor dining terrace overlooking the central courtyard. Both the hotel and its Sculpture Garden restaurant were awarded the prestigious AAA Four Diamond rating for 2011.

The Mansion Executive Lounge serves as the Executive floor found in upscale city hotels. Situated in a house overlooking the Kura Hulanda Village Square and enjoying a private entrance, the Lounge is furnished with items from a private collection including artwork.

It offers wireless Internet, 2 computers and a printer, and wide-screen HD television. Complimentary coffee, tea, and fresh fruits are provided in the morning; wine, coffee, and snacks in the late afternoon. For rates, inquire from the hotel.

The Museum Kura Hulanda houses the largest African collection in the Caribbean and a stunning, eye-opening exhibit that chronicles the history of slavery.

For travelers interested in history and culture and like being within easy walking distance of Curaçao's main attractions, Hotel Kura Hulanda is an ideal option. To say that Kura Hulanda is charming—which it is—would be an understatement. It's truly a rare jewel and like no other hotel in the Caribbean.

Kura Hulanda also offers another option—the **Lodge Kura Hulanda and Beach Club,** a resort on the island's west end, located about 45 minutes from the airport. The beachfront haven offers pleasantly appointed villas, suites and guest rooms—all with balconies or patios overlooking the ocean or gardens. The lodge, facing a natural reef off of its beach, has an on-site dive shop offering snorkeling, diving courses, and daily excursions. Scuba gear, snorkeling equipment, Sunfish, and kayaks are available for rental. "Best of Both Worlds," a town and country package, combines the hotel and the lodge. Daily complimentary scheduled transportation between the two is available.

The lodge proved to be so popular it expanded with 18 more villas after its first year. Set atop a stone bluff, each of the 2,300-square-foot, 3-bedroom,

3-bath villas, offers sea views, a 2-story great room, marble floors, top-of-the-line appliances, and a plunge pool. The master suite has a waterfront patio, walk-in closets, and a Jacuzzi tub.

HOTEL KURA HULANDA SPA AND CASINO AND LODGE KURA HULANDA AND BEACH CLUB ★ ★ ★ ⌁

Langestraat 8, Willemstad, Curaçao
Phone: 011-5999-434-7700; **Fax:** 011-599-9-434-7701; **e-mail:** hotel@kura hulanda.com; www.kurahulanda.com
Owners: Dr. Jacob Gelt Dekker and John R. Padget
President/Managing Director: Peter Heinen
Group General Manager: Stefan Dubbeling
Open: Year-round
US Reservations: (877) 264-3106; **e-mail:** reservations@kurahulanda.com
Deposit: Only credit-card guarantee required; cancellation up to 72 hours in advance
Minimum Stay: None
Arrival/Departure: Transportation available by taxi; Kura Hulanda can arrange transfers to/from the airport for a fee
Distance from Airport: (Hato International Airport) 8 miles; taxi one-way from airport to hotel, $25; taxi to Lodge, $65
Accommodations: Hotel, 80 rooms and suites (17 deluxe, 12 superior, 14 standard rooms; 14 junior, 3 one-bedroom, 5 deluxe one-bedroom suites; 1 presidential, 1 bridal, 1 executive, and 2 spa loft suites). Lodge, 74 villas, suites and rooms

Amenities: Air-conditioning, ceiling fans (in some rooms); marble bathroom, hair dryer, bathrobes; stocked cooler; cable television; teak clothing and comforter butler stand; portable in-room CD player/stereo; 110-outlet by desk, multilingual telephone system with modem and voice mail; high-speed Internet; safe; room service (7 a.m.–11 p.m.); nightly turndown service
Fitness Facilities/Spa Service: Fitness center, spa (see text)
Sports: 2 swimming pools; transportation to and from private beach club and golf club. Lodge: Tennis, diving, snorkeling, bicycles, water sports
Electricity: 110/220 volts
Dress Code: Casual; shorts and T-shirts not allowed at dinner
Children: All ages
Day Visitors: Yes
Handicapped Facilities: Inquire
Meetings: 2 conference rooms for up to 50 people; auditorium for 160; executive boardroom for 20 with adjacent dining room; closed-circuit television; audiovisual equipment; interpreter/translator system for Dutch, English, French, and Spanish. Lodge: room for up to 45 people and with state-of-the-art audiovisual equipment
Packages: Spa, golf, dive, museum, honeymoon, hotel/lodge combinations
Rates: Per person, double, per day, **EP.** *High Season* (Jan 3–Apr 7): $155–$1,200. *Low Season* (Apr 8–Dec 23): $150–$1,000. Third adult, children, and MAP rates available. **Lodge:** *High Season* $175–$490; *Low Season* $155–$455. For 2 and 3 bedroom rates, inquire
Service Charge: 12 percent
Government Tax: 7 percent

RENAISSANCE CURAÇAO
RESORT & CASINO
Willemstad, Curaçao

Opened in historic Willemstad in 2008, the Renaissance Curaçao Resort & Casino is as colorful as Curaçao's famous waterfront with an architectural design that takes its cue from the historic setting, blending it with contemporary features. But what makes this resort truly unusual is a different piece of history—it's built into the Rif Fort, a 19th-century landmark designated as a UNESCO World Heritage site. Equally unusual is its manmade elevated beach.

The Renaissance Curaçao is part of a retail and entertainment complex adjacent to the cruise port. It has a waterfront promenade and The Renaissance Mall with 15 restaurants, including a full-service one, lounges and bars, shops, a casino, and movie theater complex where the latest releases are shown.

To arrive at this hotel at night could be disorienting. Yes, the water, waves and palm trees are familiar tropical Caribbean. But walk through the front door and into the brightly lit lobby and you might be caught off-guard. The scene is sophisticated, contemporary, and chic with large, modern wall art, sleek chandeliers, and colorful fabrics on chairs and couches. Add the lights and clatter of slot machines from the Carnaval Casino, directly across the lobby from the check-in desk, and you will find it's not a typical Caribbean lobby. But then, the Renaissance is no ordinary hotel.

In morning's light, the details coalesce. Your ocean-view balcony overlooks the resort's signature "eternity beach," a marvel of modern maritime engineering. The beach, complete with mature palm trees and sand barged in from Aruba, is on the roof of a 1-story building that is part of the Renaissance Mall complex.

Open to hotel guests only, the beach is attached to an infinity pool with a waterfall and overlooks the Caribbean Sea beyond and below. The sandy bottom of the infinity pool is home to large starfish and a few schools of small fish, which act as vacuum cleaners to keep the water clean. Food and drinks are served at the beach bar, and from a chaise lounge, you have an up-close view of the activity at the cruise ship dock. The hotel's 237 accommodations come in 3 categories of guest rooms and 4 types of suites, and they either overlook the hotel atrium or have balconies with island or ocean views. The spacious rooms are air-conditioned and come with a queen bed awash in comforters, pillows, and a duvet; safe; separate shower and tub; coffee/tea maker, flat-screen television, Internet access, and a computer workspace with an outlet console at desk level; evening turndown service, and newspaper delivery on request. The Renaissance Curaçao is a nonsmoking hotel.

Business and corporate travelers figure into the guest mix, along with leisure travelers. The meetings rooms and function space are geared to them and include a 3,600-square-foot atrium, a 2,700-square-foot ballroom, two boardrooms, coffee lounge, business center, and indoor and outdoor function space. The pool and beach area provide additional space for outdoor events.

The 4-story Renaissance Curaçao, stretching along a cobblestone street, blends with the 18th-century, brightly painted, colonial-style architecture that dominates Willemstad's harborfront without appearing to be phony. Across from the main entrance is a green, 2-story building that will fool you completely. It is Curaçao's first pay-to-park garage, hidden behind a facade of old Willemstad.

Within the hotel is the Express-O Coffee Shop; the 15,000-square-foot casino with its Carnaval decor; the Blue Lobby Bar, a lively meeting place with a selection of signature drinks and novel snacks; the casual Nautilus Restaurant, an all-day eatery serving buffet and a la carte international cuisine; and the beachside Infinity Beach Bar serving cool drinks, lunch, and dinner.

A 2-minute walk from the lobby along a winding, cobblestone pathway brings you to the arched stone entrance of Rif Fort. Built in 1828, it was one of the three forts that guarded the entrance to Curaçao's natural harbor; the original cannons are at the fort's entrance. The fort had been abandoned for years until a group of developers created its new concept.

Inside the fort is a village-within-a-village—a large, tree-shaded courtyard bordered by Douwe Egberts Cafe, Indi's Spice Bar, Anchor Bar and Seafood Restaurant, the Chihuahua Cantina, the Bistro Le Clochard, one of Curaçao's leading and long established restaurants; an ice cream shop, an herb store, Le

Creperie and the Sopranos Piano Bar, which offers a fun photo op for a picture of Tony and a tourist. There are also retail shops, art galleries, a 6-theater cinema complex, the hotel's tour excursion desk, a dive center, car rental outlet, the Aqua Spa offering a wide range of treatments, and the fitness center fitted with treadmills, step machines, workout stations, exercise cycles, and weights.

The Renaissance Curaçao's location is its greatest asset. It's a destination-within-a-destination with nightlife, entertainment, gaming, dining, and shopping in one place and giving its guests the best of both worlds: A beach resort for sun, sand, sea, and starfish with historic Willemstad, the capital, at its front door.

RENAISSANCE CURAÇAO RESORT & CASINO ★ ★ ★

Baden Powellveg #1, Otrobanda
Curaçao, Netherlands Antilles
Phone: (011) 599-9-435-5000; **Fax:** 599-9-435-5025; www.renaissancecuracao.com; **e-mail:** info@curacaorenaissance.com
Owner: Metacorp N.V.
General Manager: Maylin Trenidad
Open: Year-round
US Reservations: (888) 778-4722
Deposit: 1 night with credit card; 3 days cancellation in high season
Minimum Stay: Christmas/New Year's
Arrival/Departure: Transfers not available
Distance from Airport: 10 miles; taxi one-way, $20
Distance from Town: 5 miles; taxi one-way, $20
Accommodations: 237 rooms and suites, most with balconies

Amenities: Air-conditioning; bath with tub, shower, bathrobes, toiletries, hair dryer; flat-screen cable television with CNN, ESPN, HBO, movies/videos; radio; minifridge; coffee/tea maker; telephone with voice mail; safe; iron and ironing board; down comforters, custom duvets, premium linens; turndown service on request, concierge, room service 6 a.m.–midnight; business center, Internet, newspapers on request; nonsmoking
Fitness Facilities/Spa Services: Fitness center; on-site spa
Sports: Freshwater swimming pool; Infinity Beach Club, spa cabanas. Watersports center for snorkeling, waterskiing, windsurfing, sailing, kayaking, and diving for fee.
Electricity: 110 volts and 220 volts
Dress Code: Casual by day; casually elegant in evening; jackets and ties not required
Children: Up to 2 children under 12 years old free in parents' room, including meals; cribs, high chairs; babysitters
Meetings: 4 meeting rooms, 8,600 square feet of total meeting space; full-service business center
Day Visitors: Use of pool, beach, fitness center, tennis courts, and other facilities for $95 per person but limited when hotel is busy
Handicapped Facilities: Available on request
Packages: Family, 4-nights Sand Dollar, others
Rates: Per room, double, daily: *High Season* (Jan 2–Apr 12): $348–$421. *Low Season* (Apr 13–Dec 21): $220–$267
Service Charge: 12.84 percent
Government Tax: 7 percent

DOMINICAN REPUBLIC

The Dominican Republic is a land of superlatives: the oldest country of the Caribbean, with the tallest mountains and the lowest lake. Historic Santo Domingo was the first Spanish settlement in the New World. Here the Spaniards built their first cathedral, first hospital, first university, and first fortress.

The Old City has been beautifully restored and is alive with restaurants, shops, art galleries, and museums. Columbus Square boasts the oldest cathedral in the Americas.

Modern Santo Domingo, the fun-loving, sophisticated capital with Old-World charm, has more than one million people and about the lowest prices in the Caribbean. The modern Plaza de la Cultura is the heart of the capital's cultural life. It includes the National Theatre, where plays, concerts by the National Symphony Orchestra, jazz ensembles, and visiting artists are held.

But Santo Domingo is far more than history and culture. Dominicans are warm and friendly and love to have a good time, and their city bounces with every sort of entertainment, from piano bars and smart supper clubs to brassy cabarets. One of the city's most unusual attractions, Los Tres Ojos ("the three eyes") Park, is a subterranean cave with three lagoons, each with different water: sweet, salt, and sulfur.

From the rolling terrain of the east and south, the land rises toward the island's center in two tree-covered spines where two national parks contain the country's highest peaks—more than 10,000 feet high with trails.

In the northeastern corner Samana Peninsula and Bay is one of the most beautiful and least developed areas. From December to March whales play at the mouth of the bay. On the Rio Limon, in the center of the peninsula, a footpath leads to a magnificent waterfall, all but hidden amid the savage beauty of the thickly forested mountains. On the southern side of the bay, Los Haitises National Park is a 100-mile karst region with dense mangroves, estuaries, and tiny cays that are rookeries for seabirds.

Over the last three decades, the Dominican Republic has been developing its coastal areas, along the north and east coast where resort development at Punta Cana continues nonstop. Most resorts are large all-inclusives catering to the mass market. Recently, both areas have welcomed small, boutique resorts.

Information

Dominican Republic Tourist Office, 136 E. 57th St., Ste. 805, New York, NY 10022; (888) 374-6361 or (212) 588-1012; Fax: (212) 588-1015; or 848 Brickell Ave, Ste. 405, Miami, FL 33131; (888) 358-9594, (305) 358-2899; Fax: (305) 358-4185; www.godominicanrepublic.com

CASA DE CAMPO
La Romana, Dominican Republic

Think big. Four golf courses, 13 tennis courts, over a dozen restaurants, 3 polo fields and 150 polo ponies, a 300-station sport shooting center, fitness and water-sports centers, a fleet of sport-fishing boats, a 350-slip marina and yacht club, a 5,000-seat amphitheater, 2 museums, an art and design school, a replica of a 16th-century Mediterranean village, an international airport, a cruise port, 45 retail shops, a spa, 267 guest rooms, and 1,500 private villas on 7,000 acres.

Yes, it's big. But Casa de Campo is never overwhelming or noisy or crowded, as megaresorts often are. On the contrary, it's tranquil and very private. *Casa de Campo* means "a house in the country" in Spanish, and despite its size, Casa actually has that feeling to it.

Set in pretty rolling countryside in the southeastern corner of the Dominican Republic near the sugar-producing town of La Romana, Casa de Campo began in the early 1970s as a private retreat for local sugar barons, who played polo and golf on a preserve owned by Gulf & Western, whose founder, the late Charles Bluhdorn, developed the property into a sprawling resort. Later Gulf & Western sold it to the present owners, brothers Alfonso and Jose "Pepe" Fanjul, who developed it further. Today it is something of a sophisticated amusement park and a posh country club with Caribbean attractions and Spanish charm, appealing to families, honeymooners, sportsmen, incentive winners, and just about anyone who wants a vacation with lots of choices at affordable prices.

As part of the resort's 2-year $40 million redesign completed in late 2010, the lobby and the entire main area of the hotel area were modernized with floor-to-ceiling windowed walls and mahogany paneling, accented with locally crafted metalwork by El Artistico, modern art and neutral-colored furnishings surrounded by tropical flora. The lobby holds the guest services area, Excel Concierge-VIP lounge, transportation center, and library. The new La Caña Restaurant & Lounge by Il Circo for fine dining is in the former space of the La Caña Bar. Also new is a Carmen Sol New York boutique for designer fashions and a bridal salon for booking weddings. Adjacent to the central building is the spacious new pool terrace, furnished with contemporary private cabanas and lounge chairs; canopy-covered seating areas and platforms for yoga classes. Of the resort's accommodations, 155 guest rooms and 10 suites were transformed into a new luxurious Elite category with new furnishings and locally-inspired decor by Dominican designer Patricia Reid and Mayra Gonzalez, with fine details using marble, native corolina stone, and precious woods. The rooms have 42-inch LCD flat-screen cable television with Blu-Ray disc player, alarm clock with iPod and iPhone docks, Wi-Fi, mini-bar with coffee/espresso machine, safe, and walk-in closet. The spacious bathrooms have tubs and glass-enclosed showers.

All guest rooms are furnished with 2 double beds or a king and have a private balcony or terrace with views of the golf courses or gardens. All are air-conditioned and equipped with a Bose Wave radio, direct-dial telephones with voice mail and dataport, a separate vanity and dressing area, a hair dryer, and an iron and ironing board. Luxury rooms have extra amenities such as Serta pillowtop mattresses, a cozy seating area, bathrobes, a dressing area with a marble-topped vanity, a lighted makeup mirror, 3 phones, and a writing desk.

The resort's private villas, located throughout the resort—near the tennis club and the Equestrian center, around the golf courses, and in the country-side—have 2 to 7 bedrooms, each with air-conditioning and private bath. Each villa has cable television, a pool or whirlpool, a comfortable living room, a dining room, a fully equipped kitchen, and a screened terrace, in addition to maid and butler services. A private chef can be added. Villa guests booked through the hotel have full access to all Casa de Campo facilities and preferential golf rates. The villas are particularly popular with families and friends and golfing buddies traveling together. Of the group, some 20 sumptuous, commodious Exclusive Villas have 4 to 6 bedrooms and an array of high-end features and amenities.

The resort's Cygalle Healing Spa is an eco-friendly sanctuary that offers indoor and outdoor spa services, using natural body-treatment products made in small batches at the on-site spa pharmacy from indigenous ingredients. Guests can receive treatments in a lush Zen garden, an outdoor private gazebo on the beach, in a private cabana by the pool, or in their hotel room or villa. Designed by Dominican Myra Gonzalez, the spa is located in the main area of the resort.

Casa de Campo is a member of the prestigious Leading Hotels in the World group.

Perched on a cliff overlooking the Chavon River, several miles from the main hotel, Altos de Chavon is a replica of a 16th-century Mediterranean village conceived by Bluhdorn and created by Italian cinematographer Roberto Copa to foster the culture of the Dominican Republic—a vision that thrives today. Begun in 1976, with local artisans building the village of stone, wood, and iron by hand, it was completed and officially inaugurated with a concert by Frank Sinatra in its 5,000-plus-seat amphitheater in 1982. The amphitheater is home to the school's performing arts department and has hosted Andrea Bocelli, Julio Iglesias, among others. At the heart of the village in a cobblestone square stands the Church of St. Stanislaus, a frequent venue for weddings.

Nearby, the Regional Museum of Archaeology houses a comprehensive collection of artifacts of the Taino Indians (the island's inhabitants at the time of Christopher Columbus's arrival); the World of Amber Museum, and the Altos de Chavón Art Studios by Emilio Robba, offering beautiful ceramic, weaving, and serigraphy collections hand-made by local artists. Three art galleries showcase the works of Dominican, European, and American artists. Altos de Chavon School of Design, in affiliation with New York's prestigious Parsons School of Design, offers degrees in various design fields and the arts. Casa de Campo guests can take classes in summer when students are on break. Along the narrow streets, local shops sell

handmade jewelry, pottery, and Dominican crafts. There's a new trendy dance club and Casa Montecristo, a chic cigar lounge by Tabacalera de Garcia, the largest hand-made cigar factory in the world. Free tours of the factory are available for hotel guests.

The variety and quality of sports are among Casa de Campo's prime attractions. Its four 18-hole championship Pete Dye–designed courses (one for private membership only) attract players from around the world and regularly host international tournaments. The Teeth of the Dog course, with 7 holes skirting the Caribbean, is one of the most beautiful in the world and has been named the top course in the Caribbean by *Golf* magazine. The open-air Lago Grill, which sits under a tall thatched roof and overlooks the famous golf course, is the most popular restaurant for breakfast and lunch with all-you-can-eat buffets. The Links is an inland, rolling course with water coming into play on 5 holes. Casa de Campo's fourth golf course (third resort course), known as Dye Fore, is laid out around Altos de Chavon with wide-angle views of the Chavon River, the surrounding countryside, and the Caribbean. It has the distinction of being planted with 2 new strains of grass, or paspalum, that thrive on saltwater and can be watered directly from the ocean. The 19th Hole Bar serves light fare and is an ideal watering hole after a round of golf. A new 9-hole course is being created adjacent to the Dye Fore. La Terraza Tennis Center offers 13 Har-Tru tennis courts, 10 lighted for night play. Ballboys are available, and games are guaranteed at all times for all levels of expertise. Clinics and private lessons are offered.

Casa de Campo's equestrian and polo facilities are without rival. The Equestrian Center offers guided rides along trails and the Dominican countryside, along with jumping, riding, and dressage lessons for beginners and experienced riders; it is the venue for authentic rodeos. The facility has more than 150 trained polo ponies and equipment for players of any level.

For skeet, trap, and shooting clays, the 245-acre Sporting Clays Center is outstanding. Shaun Snell, a famed British marksman, is a sought-after instructor.

Casa de Campo has plenty of water toys with 3 swimming pools, including a children's pool and a pool with a swim up bar. Water sports are featured at the resort's private Minitas Beach, and there are trips to the offshore islands of Saona and Catalina.

Casa de Campo's children's program, Kidz 'n Casa, is a day camp offered daily year-round from 9 a.m. to 4 p.m. for children ages 3 to 8. There is a separate program for children ages 9 to 12, teens 13 to 18, and a new one for toddlers, 1 to 3 years with nannies, day and night.

Casa de Campo offers many dining choices. The new Beach Club by Le Cirque at Minitas Beach is an upscale, breezy outdoor restaurant specializing in the cuisine of the famous New York eatery with local variations and featuring a chef from Le Cirque. In the main hotel area above the pool is the new La Caña Restaurant & Lounge by Il Circo. The Safari Club at the shooting center is dressed in African decor with carved wood furnishings and hand-painted ceilings under a 30-foot thatched roof. The club is open for lunch and dinner during high season.

Some of the resort's best restaurants are located at Altos de Chavon, where nighttime offers floodlit views over the ravine several hundred feet below. La Piazetta is an Italian restaurant with strolling musicians; Gino's Pizzera is a new open-air gourmet pizza parlor, and OneBurger features designer hamburgers.

Another major feature of the resort is the Marina and Yacht Club, a boating and residential community at the mouth of the Chavon River where it empties into the Caribbean Sea. Designed by Italian architect Gianfranco Fini to resemble an Italian seaside village, the development consists of a private yacht club and marina with 350 slips for yachts up to 280 feet in length. The marina has a fleet of 31-foot Bertram sport-fishing boats for deep-sea fishing, and others for river fishing and sailing. Marlin is the main catch on the ocean, while you can fish for snook in the Chavon River with a local guide. It has a residential community, shops, galleries, a movie theatre with first-run movies in English, and 2 popular resort restaurants: Chinois for Pan-Asian flavors and fresh sushi and La Casita for fresh seafood and Spanish cuisine.

The heart of the complex is the Italian Plaza, an oceanfront 2-story structure with restaurants, a bakery, delicatessen, pizzeria, ice-cream shop, and piano bar on the first floor and 2- and 3-bedroom apartments on the upper floor. Behind the plaza on a single level are a drugstore, bank, travel agency, art gallery, beauty parlor, gift shops, and boutiques—all open to Casa de Campo resort guests. The other residential areas in the Marina area are Ensenada with 2- and 3-bedroom apartments with boat slips in front; and the even more luxurious Darsena with 14 villas in 3-, 4-, and 5-bedroom configurations and 41 boat slips (30 feet to 50 feet). Each villa has its own pool.

Casa de Campo is the Good Life—a fun-filled destination, especially for families, providing options, privacy, security, and the kind of friendly service usually associated with smaller resorts.

CASA DE CAMPO ★ ★ ★ ★

PO Box 140, La Romana, Dominican Republic

Phone: (809) 523-3333; **Fax:** (809) 523-0000; **e-mail:** res1@ccampo.com .do; www.casadecampo.com.do

Management: Premier Resorts and Hotels, Claudio A. Silvestri, President and CEO

General Manager: Daniel Hernandez

Open: Year-round

US Reservations: Premier World Marketing, 2600 SW 3rd Ave., Miami, FL 33129; (800) 877-3643, (305) 856-7083, (305) 856-5405; **Fax:** (305) 858-4677; **e-mail:** res1@ccampo.com.do

Deposit: 2 nights within 7 days of booking; balance 14 days prior to arrival

Minimum Stay: 7 nights Christmas/ New Year's

Arrival/Departure: Direct flights daily from Miami to Casa de Campo's international airport of La Romana (LRM) via American Airlines; American Eagle daily from San Juan

Distance from Airport: From La Romana: 10 minutes; from Santo Domingo: 1 hour and 15 minutes

Distance from Santo Domingo: 1½ hours

Accommodations: 267 superior and Elite hotel rooms in 2-story buildings with balcony or terrace; 150 two- to four-bedroom classic and exclusive villas—all with pool or whirlpool and some with both

Amenities: Hotel rooms: Air-conditioning, ceiling fan; minibar, coffeemaker; cable television, Bose Wave clock-radio, direct-dial telephones with voice mail and dataport; hair dryer, separate vanity and dressing area; baths; walk-in closet, safe, iron and ironing board; golf cart. Supplemental option: maid and butler, concierge from 8 a.m.–10 p.m.

Fitness Facilities/Spa Services: Fitness center, free weights, exercise equipment. New spa (see text)

Sports: Four championship 18-hole golf courses (1 private membership); 13 Har-Tru tennis courts (10 lighted); shooting center; equestrian center, polo; marina, water sports, river fishing, boating

Electricity: 110 volts

Dress Code: Smartly casual

Children: All ages

Meetings: Up to 500 people

Day Visitors: Yes with reservations

Handicapped Facilities: Limited

Packages: Golf, villa, inclusive meals

Rates: Per person, double, per night, EP. *High Season* (Jan 4–Apr 24): from $495. *Low Season:* from $345. For 2-bedroom Elite suites and villa rates, inquire.

Service Charge: 16 percent

Government Tax: 10 percent

CASA COLONIAL BEACH & SPA

Puerto Plata, Dominican Republic

Old world grace and contemporary elegance were combined to create Casa Colonial Beach & Spa, the first luxury boutique hotel on the Dominican Republic's north coast, previously known for large, all-inclusive resorts.

Located a few miles east of Puerto Plata on the beach at Playa Dorada, the elegant all-suite hotel, opened in late 2004, and was designed in colonial architectural style by Sarah García, a noted Dominican architect and interior designer and daughter of Isidro García, who owns VH Hotels & Resorts, which operates Casa Colonial as well as two adjacent resorts.

Casa Colonial's white colonnaded buildings, set in magnificent tropical gardens that add to its gracious ambience, reflect the area's Spanish-colonial past.

The design, enriched with Dominican historical and cultural elements, gives the hotel its special character and enhances the guests' experience.

The front of the *casa,* or home, resembles a classic Dominican plantation estate. But upon entering, you are greeted by a cool, modern lobby made all the more elegant by very high ceilings, Italian marble floors, and rich wood accents against white walls. Local materials such as Dominican coral stone and mahogany are incorporated into the decor. Quality and attention to detail are evident throughout.

Upon arrival, you are welcomed by a friendly staff and given a refreshing, cold, scented towel. Instead of the traditional reception, there is a sophisticated, contemporary lobby-lounge and a concierge desk, whose attendant handles check-in and just about any other need a guest may have. A few steps farther on in the center of the next lounge area is a large glass bar, which is illuminated in the evening (another bar is located at the beach). To one side is Lucia, the gourmet restaurant, named for another daughter.

Beyond the bar is a second building, all but hidden in the hotel's lush gardens, that houses the resort's oceanfront guest rooms and suites. Along the hallways leading to the guest rooms are displays of handsome old clay jars once used on the Garcia family's farm to keep water cold. Room numbers on guest room doors are embroidered on linen and framed, in the manner of an old Dominican tradition.

The 50 spacious accommodations range from junior and 1-bedroom suites to a presidential suite. They have generous balconies with views of the ocean or gardens and are furnished with table and chairs and lounger. The bedroom is fitted with a 4-poster king or 2 queen-size beds with custom-made Serta mattresses, which the resort calls the "best sleep in the Caribbean." They are very comfortable, indeed.

Junior suites extend to a comfortable sitting area and balcony (some with an additional sofa bed and/or dining area). Deluxe suites have a separate living room and dining alcove. With the addition of an adjoining suite, 3 deluxe oceanfront suites and 2 garden ones can be made into 2-bedroom master suites with a private entrance. The rooms have custom-designed, Caribbean-inspired furnishings and fine linens.

All accommodations have air-conditioning and marble floors, ceiling fans, high-speed Internet (a laptop is available for rent), flat-screen cable television (most channels in Spanish), Bose radio/alarm clock/CD-player, original art, 3 phones with international direct dialing and voice mail, and 24-hour room service. Rooms are equipped with a minibar, coffeemaker, hair dryer, bathrobe and slippers, iron and ironing board, umbrella, and in-room safe (large enough for a laptop). The large marble bathrooms have double sinks, walk-in shower, separate toilet, and a big bathtub alongside a louvered window that looks into the bedroom and, in some cases, the gardens and ocean. The Penthouse and Presidential Suites each have a crow-foot bathtub on a tree-shaded, open-air terrace off the bathroom.

Casa Colonial's gourmet (read: expensive) restaurant, Lucia, is open for dinner only. Adjoining it is the wine cellar and small dining room that is used for private parties and wine tastings. The Veranda, an inside/outside restaurant overlooking the beach, offers 3 meals daily, and also services the rooftop snack bar, where light fare is available at lunch. The bar is beside the hotel's pretty rooftop infinity pool and 4 hot tubs that overlook the beach.

The Bagua Spa is a beautiful space of gleaming white marble and offers indoor treatment rooms including 2 private couples therapy rooms with a Jacuzzi, and outdoor treatment pavilions set over a tropical pond with a waterfall. Treatments include massages, wraps, aromatherapy, and facials. The spa also has a sauna, steam room, and an ocean-view fitness center with Cybex equipment. Special classes and a personal trainer are available.

The hotel has a meeting room, a wedding pavilion on the beach, and provides private transfer to the 18-hole Robert Trent Jones championship golf course nearby. It also provides valet parking, golf-club storage, newspapers via Internet, and laundry service. Casa Colonial is a member of the Small Luxury Hotels of the World. Frequently named as a favorite hideaway by travel and fashion magazines, Casa Colonial was apparently to the liking of fashion jetsetter Donatella Versace, enough for her to spend two weeks with her two children there.

CASA COLONIAL BEACH & SPA
★ ★ ★ ★

PO Box 22, Puerto Plata, Dominican Republic
Phone: (809) 320-3232; **Fax:** (809) 320-3131; **e-mail:** reservascc@vhhr .com; www.casacolonialhotel.com
Owner: VH Hotels & Resorts
General Manager: Basilia Diaz
Open: Year-round
US Reservations: (866) 376-7831 or contact@epoquehotels.com
Deposit: Secured with credit card
Minimum Stay: 7 nights from Christmas/New Year's
Arrival/Departure: Airport transfer provided for fee
Distance from Airport: 15 minutes from Puerto Plata Airport; 45 miles from Santiago
Distance from Santo Domingo: 110 miles

Accommodations: 50 suites (42 junior, 2 one-bedroom, 4 deluxe, 1 penthouse, and 1 presidential)
Amenities: Balconies, Frette linens, bathrooms with double sinks, Kohler tubs, walk-in showers; robe and slippers, minibar, high-speed Internet, safe; flat-screen television; wireless Internet access in lobby and rooftop; three phones, coffeemaker, hairdryer, CD player, iron/ironing board, umbrella, 24-hour room service.
Fitness Facilities/Spa Services: Spa with 10 treatment rooms and 3 ocean-front pavilions, sauna, steam room; rooftop pool and 4 ocean-view hot tubs; fully equipped gym, classes, personal trainer
Sports: Pool; nearby Playa Dorada Golf Course and Playa Grande Golf Course; Ocean World Aquatic Park; windsurfing
Electricity: 110/220 volts
Dress Code: Casually elegant
Children: All ages, but no facilities
Meetings: Up to 50 people, audio/visual equipment; wireless Internet; private dining room
Day Visitors: Yes
Handicapped Facilities: Yes
Packages: Weddings, honeymoon, golf, spa, romantic, extreme sports
Rates: Per suite, per night, double, *High Season* (Jan 4–Apr 3): $350–$1,300; *Low Season:* Apr 4–Dec 23) $286–$968. Christmas/New Year's (Dec 24–Jan 3, 2013) $450–$1,600.
Service Charge: 10 percent
Government Tax: 16 percent

TORTUGA BAY AT PUNTACANA
RESORT & CLUB
Punta Cana, Dominican Republic

Simple elegance is simply the best way to describe Tortuga Bay, the boutique hotel with a large hotel complex, that opened in December 2005 on the eastern shores of the Dominican Republic.

Located at the heart of the PUNTA-CANA Resort & Club, a 15,000-acre Caribbean resort where Julio Iglesias and other international celebrities keep vacation homes, Tortuga Bay is a private enclave of 14 luxurious 2-story villas with 1- and 2- bedroom suites. All the interiors—which are fabulous—were designed by renowned fashion designer Oscar de la Renta, who, too, is one of the resort's owners.

The gracious and spacious villas—custard yellow with white trim—are set on a 1,200-foot-long beach (a segment of the PUNTACANA Resort & Club's 5-mile stretch) and are very practically, as well as prettily, designed. You can book the entire villa with 3 or 4 bedrooms or only the ground level, which has a 2-bedroom apartment; or one of the very large junior suites on the second floor. The junior suites have large verandas facing the beach and on the side, bathing it in sunlight; some have Jacuzzi.

De la Renta's decor takes full advantage of the space with four-poster canopied beds (king or 2 doubles), a large comfortable easy chair and ottoman, desk, and chest of drawers. Most of the furniture is in dark wood set against white walls and bed covers with just the right touch of color in decorative throws and throw pillows. The result: simple but elegant, or as one might say in Spanish, *muy simpatico*.

Suites have ceiling fan, minibar, flat-screen plasma television, CD/DVD player, Internet connection, laptop rental, direct-dial phone/voice mail, microwave, coffee/tea maker, fully stocked bar, walk-in closet, umbrella, safe, pillow menu, and laundry service. The large bathrooms are fitted with twin sink vanities, whirlpool bathtubs, separate showers, bathrobe and slippers, hair dryer, deluxe toiletries, makeup mirror, iron/ironing board, daily newspaper, and room service.

Upon check-in guests get their own golf cart to use during their stay. They also meet their villa manager (butler by another name)—a personable young Dominican (one for every two villas) who attends to all your requests from check-in to departure. The villa manager accompanies you to your villa, familiarizes you with its gadgets, and gives you a cell phone and number to call when you need him. He will book your dinner or spa reservations, tee-times, horseback riding excursions or lessons, and take care of your shoe shine or ironing.

Tortuga Bay has its own private reception area, which also houses the bar and restaurant, Bamboo, also decorated by De la Renta, a cozy place with an elegant touch. Bamboo serves 3 meals—either in the pretty air-conditioned interior or outside on a terrace by the swimming pool. The menu is international; a Dominican menu is also available from room service from 7 a.m.

to 11 p.m. Afternoon tea (or excellent Dominican coffee) is served on the restaurant/bar patio. The Bar is also the place to try one of the famous Dominican rums and a Dominican cigar.

On one side of the patio in the garden is a whirlpool and just beyond, the well-equipped Fitness Center. The resort has a 1,200-square-foot boardroom with state-of-the-art audio visual equipment including wireless Internet. Other amenities include wireless Internet access in the lobby and the restaurant, bar, and pool areas and laptops for rent. The resort also has full-time nanny service for a fee.

In addition to Bamboo, Tortuga Bay guests may dine at any of PUNTACANA Resort's 8 restaurants and bars using an electronic key card programmed for their exclusive use, avoiding the need for cash or signatures. They also have access to PUNTACANA Resort's sports and recreational facilities that include La Cana golf course designed by Peter Dye, a full-service marina and water-sports center, a horse ranch, a private nature reserve, and International Biodiversity Center. The nature reserve has 11 hiking trails, several leading to spring-fed natural pools that are great for a refreshing swim.

Another of the shared facilities is the Six Senses Spa, located in the handsome Clubhouse about a mile north of Tortuga Bay's reception center. The full-service spa offers a wide range of treatments, administered by therapists, mostly from Thailand, as well as yoga, Reiki, and tai chi classes.

Personalized service begins for Tortuga Bay guests upon arrival at the

Punta Cana International Airport, which the resort also owns. (Indeed, it was the opening of the international airport two decades ago that launched Punta Cana's incredible resort development where now more than 3 million visitors vacation annually.) Tortuga Bay's guests are met, whisked through immigration by the resort's staff, and driven in an air-conditioned minivan to the resort, 5 miles away. On departure, guests get preferred use of the airport's VIP lounge. A VIP terminal is available for those who arrive by private aircraft.

The resort also has a selection of private residential villas with 3 to 6 bedrooms located on the La Cana Golf Course. All villas have complete kitchen, private pool, golf cart, and daily housekeeping service. Villa descriptions are available on the Tortuga Bay website.

In 2011, Tortuga Bay was given AAA's prestigious Five Diamond Award—the first in the Dominican Republic and only four in the Caribbean—and very well deserved.

TORTUGA BAY AT PUNTACANA RESORT & CLUB ★ ★ ★ ★
Phone: (888) 442-2262, (809) 959-2262, ext. 7237; **Fax:** (809) 959-3951; e-mail: reservationstb@puntacana.com; www.puntacana.com
Owner: Green Diamond Inc.
General Manager: Vincenzo Calcerano
Open: Nov to Sept
US Reservations: (888) 442-2262
Deposit: Christmas and Easter, 1 night secured with credit card
Minimum Stay: 4 nights, President's Week and Easter; 10 nights Christmas/New Year's

Arrival/Departure: Airport meet/assist services and resort transfers; use of VIP airport lounge on departure included in rate.
Distance from Airport: (Punta Cana International Airport) 5 miles
Distance from Santo Domingo: 3½-hour drive
Accommodations: 14 Villas/32 suites (can be configured as 10 three-, 4 four-bedroom, or 14 two- or 18 one-bedroom suites)
Amenities: See text
Fitness Facilities/Spa Services: Fitness center, outdoor whirlpool; spa, yoga, Reiki, and tai chi classes
Sports: Swimming pool, bicycles, kayaks, tennis; use of Punta Cana water sports, Ecological Reserve; La Cana golf and access to Clubhouse
Electricity: 110 volts
Dress Code: Smart casual
Children: Complimentary program, children's pool, cots and cribs; full-time nanny service (for fee)
Meetings: Yes
Day Visitors: No
Handicapped Facilities: No
Packages: Golf, honeymoon, spa
Rates: Per room, per night, FAP. *High Season* (Jan 7–early Apr): $670–$870. *Low Season* (mid-Apr–Dec 23): $580–$755. *Easter:* $790–$975. For 2- to 4-bedroom villa, inquire. Rates include airport transfers, meet/assist and use of airport VIP lounge, and golf cart for complete villa.
Service Charge: 26 percent mandatory
Government Tax: 26 percent mandatory

RENAISSANCE SANTO DOMINGO
JARAGUA HOTEL & CASINO

Santo Domingo, Dominican Republic

Robert Redford once spent weeks here while filming *Havana*. So what else do you need to know? Yes, it's big and brassy, but it's also wonderfully Dominican.

Located on the Malecon, Santo Domingo's popular seashore boulevard overlooking the Caribbean, the Jaragua (pronounced Ha-RAG-wa) offers the best of two worlds: a resort set in 14 acres of tropical gardens in the heart of the capital and a city full of history, culture, and fun.

The Jaragua doesn't have a beach (there are no beaches in Santo Domingo), but it has lagoons spilling into a huge swimming pool, a health club and spa, a tennis complex, several restaurants and bars, a casino, shops, and spacious guest rooms. And it's all within easy reach of any of Santo Domingo's many attractions.

Opened in 1987 on the site of the first Jaragua, a popular Havana-in-the-old-days hotel with outdoor gardens and a splashy nightclub, this Jaragua is today. A modern high-rise of 10 floors combined with garden low-rise buildings, its design is sleek and the decor sophisticated, with stylish art deco details throughout. You will be impressed by the quality and high standards. Marble floors and satiny, hard-finished fixtures are kept polished to such a shine, you'll think they're mirrors. The Jaragua puts the city's other hotels to shame and demonstrates what Dominicans can do with a hotel when they set their mind to it.

You arrive at the hotel by way of a grand driveway graced with fountains and gardens and step from a large portico directly into the lobby. Prepare yourself for the experience. On your left is the huge, open casino, brimming with action and bouncing with merengue music most of the time. To your right is the quiet, elegant reception area with soft indirect lighting that highlights the lobby's art deco features. The contrast of the two sides is amazing. But it's so Dominican and it works.

The guest rooms are in two areas: the majority in the main 10-story tower, with the others in 2-story garden buildings on the western side of the main building. All are large and attractive, and the penthouse suites with their own Jacuzzis are small palazzos. The stylish appointments of contemporary design include plush upholstery, draperies, and new deluxe bedding of down comforters, designer duvets, and fine cotton linens.

The rooms, designed as much with business travelers in mind as tourists, each have a desk and 3 phones, including one in the marbled bathroom. The tower rooms, most with views of the sea, are for those who want to be at the center of the action. The top floors of the tower are dedicated to the executive rooms and suites and the Club Lounge.

Being more removed, the garden rooms provide greater privacy and quiet and are particularly popular with guests enrolled in the fitness center program. Directly in front of the guest-room tower is the Jaragua Club, housing the fitness center and a full service spa, which was recently renovated and offers saunas, steam room, Jacuzzi, 7 massage rooms, and offering a full range of treatements. The hotel has packages for a full beauty program. The public areas, guest rooms, and meeting rooms have Wi-Fi. The hotel, which is popular for conferences, has 13 meeting rooms. Beyond the lagoon and gardens is the swimming pool, which is now part of the Jaragua Club. To the rear is the tennis complex with 4 lighted clay courts, a viewing stand, and a pro shop.

The Jaragua has several dining outlets: Coffee Corner is located off the lobby and offers several types of coffee and a variety of pastries from the hotel's bakery. Quisqueya Restaurant is located in a corner on the main floor. It is the main venue for breakfast and lunch and offers American entrees along with their Spanish counterparts. Las Cascadas, overlooking the waterfalls and lagoon, now hosts the casual Blue Bar & Lounge, offering dinner with international and local cuisine and tapas. Champions Sports Bar offers good food, good sports, and good times, and is open for dinner. The grill and bar by the pool serves lunch and snacks.

The Jaragua jumps in the evening, and there's plenty of opportunity to be part of the action. In addition to the casino and the casino bar, the 1,200-seat La Fiesta Room often has headline entertainers. Merengue Bar is the place for cocktails, live music, and dancing. The Jaragua indeed has glamour and style—not so much Caribbean as Latin—and is as popular with Latin Americans as it is with gringos. This hotel is not for the traveler who wants a laid-back Caribbean retreat on a beach. If you prefer having the facilities and services of a large luxury hotel, thrive on a glittering, lively nightlife, and like to be in the center of the action, though, you'll love the Jaragua.

RENAISSANCE SANTO DOMINGO JARAGUA HOTEL & CASINO ★ ★ ★

367 George Washington Ave., Apartado Postal 769-2, Santo Domingo, Dominican Republic
Phone: (809) 221-2222; **Fax:** (809) 686-0528; www.marriott.com/sdqgw
Owner/Management Company: Marriott International
General Manager: Eduardo Reple
Open: Year-round
US Reservations: Renaissance Worldwide, (800) 468-3571; or direct to hotel, (800) 331-3542; **Fax:** (809) 221-8271
Deposit: 1 night
Minimum Stay: None
Arrival/Departure: Transfer service arranged for charge
Distance from Airport: (Santo Domingo Las Americas International Airport) 20 miles (40 minutes); taxi one-way, $40
Distance from Old City: 1 mile; taxi one-way, $10

Accommodations: 300 rooms and suites with double or king-size beds (200 deluxe rooms, including 9 suites in 10-story tower; 100 in 2-story garden buildings)

Amenities: Air-conditioning, bath with tub and shower, hair dryer, makeup mirror, basket of toiletries, bathrobe; cable television, radio, direct-dial telephone, high-speed Internet access; minibar and refrigerator, ice service; nightly turn-down service; concierge; 24-hour room service; Jacuzzis in penthouse suites; business center with Internet access

Fitness Facilities/Spa Services: See text

Sports: Freshwater swimming pool; free use of tennis courts; tennis rental equipment and lessons for fee; golf, horseback riding, water sports, fishing arranged through concierge

Electricity: 110 volts

Dress Code: Casual

Children: All ages; cribs, high chairs; babysitters; up to two children under 18 stay free in garden room with parents

Meetings: Up to 1,000 people

Day Visitors: Yes, for casino and restaurants

Handicapped Facilities: Yes

Packages: Spa, honeymoon, golf, adventure, other Renaissance standards

Rates: Per room, single or double, daily, EP. Year-round: $89–$429

Service Charge: 10 percent

Government Tax: 16 percent

GRENADA

Known as the Spice Island, Grenada is a tapestry of tropical splendor where banana trees by the side of the road grow as tall as the palm trees fringing the powdery beaches and trade winds nourish the lush mountainous interior.

St. George's, the capital and one of the Caribbean's prettiest ports, is set on a deep horseshoe-shaped bay. Clinging to green hillsides behind it are yellow, blue, and pink houses topped with red roofs and historic buildings climbing to a series of colonial forts built to protect the strategic harbor.

Grand Anse Beach, south of St. George's, is a lovely 2-mile crescent of white sand bathed by calm Caribbean waters. It is the island's main resort and water-sports center, with snorkeling, sailing, diving, and windsurfing. Bay Gardens, a hillside botanic oasis, has trails covered with nutmeg shells that wind through woods of an estimated 3,000 species of tropical flora.

The main cross-island highway from the capital winds up the mountains to the Grand Etang Forest Reserve, crossing it at 1,910 feet within a few hundred yards of Grand Etang, an extinct volcano whose crater is filled with a lake.

The Grand Etang National Park, part of Grenada's national park system protecting most of the interior mountains, has hiking trails around the lake, through surrounding rain forests, and up to mountain peaks that showcase the island's exotic vegetation, birds, and wildlife.

North of St. George's, the road hugs the leeward coast, passing fishing villages and winding along the edge of magnificent tropical scenery on mountains that drop almost straight into the sea and hide little coves with black-sand beaches.

Grenada is one of the world's largest producers of nutmeg and just about every fruit known in the Tropics. In Gouyave you can visit the country's major nutmeg processing station. In the same vicinity Concord Falls, a triple-stage cascade set deep in the central mountains, is about an hour's hike; it requires some rock hopping, but your reward is a lovely waterfall that drops through jungle-thick vegetation to a pool where you can enjoy a refreshing swim.

Information

Grenada Tourist Board, Grenada Board of Tourism, PO Box 1668, 1801 N.O. St., Lake Worth, FL 33460; (800) 927-9554, (561) 588-8176; Fax: (561) 588-7267; www.grenadagrenadines.com

THE CALABASH HOTEL

St. George's, Grenada, W.I.

Having a private maid prepare your breakfast isn't a bad way to start a vacation—and she'll serve it to you in bed, if you like.

Since it opened in 1961, the Calabash has been the last word in British gentility, attracting lords and ladies and an occasional prince or princess, who fly in on their private planes. Once they've checked in, though, no one (except the staff, of course) will know who they are or see them being treated differently from you or me. This is true though times and owners have changed.

In 1989, when the new, young British owner, Leo Garbutt, took over, he updated, upgraded, and expanded the rather staid resort, making it much better (would you believe exciting?), but without diluting any of its grace. Among

the improvements were more units with private pools and the addition of a keyhole-shaped swimming pool in a quiet area near the main building, which has men's and women's restrooms and showers. The tennis court was lighted, and the beach bar moved to a more convenient location at the center of the beach. More recently, the resort added the Heaven and Earth Spa at The Calabash Hotel in its own bungalow by the beach.

The resort has regular live entertainment and a full range of water sports, included in the room rates. Telephones are installed in all rooms but—as the management is quick to tell you—you may have yours removed if you consider it a nuisance. Now that's gentility. Television was added, too, but you can close the cabinet door and never look at it, if you prefer. A computer with Internet is available for guests' use at no charge; guest rooms have Wi-Fi access.

The Calabash is spread over 8 landscaped acres overlooking a quiet bay. Accommodations, each named for a tropical flower that grows in the gardens, are in 1- and 2-story cottages arranged in a half moon around a broad, open green with the main building at the center. Each of the spacious, airy units has a bedroom and a bathroom, sitting area, and patio or balcony. In the older, cozier units, where the decor has been updated in soft green and aqua decor, retaining a Caribbean feeling, the bedrooms and sitting rooms are separate. In the newer units they are combined in one spacious room and sport a contemporary look. Adjacent to or, in some cases, within each unit is a small pantry where the maid appointed to your room prepares your breakfast each morning.

In the newer 2-story units, 6 on the ground floor have small, private pools; those on the second floor have whirlpools. They also have pitched roofs, which make them seem all the larger and airier. Two units with pools were specially designed to accommodate handicapped guests. Each unit has a garden view leading down to the sandy beach, where fruit juice is served each morning and where you will find lounge chairs and lots of shade trees as well as a beach bar and a casual restaurant where lunch is available.

The most spacious accommodation is the Thorneycroft Suite, named for Lord Peter and Lady Carla Thorneycroft, who have spent many holidays at the Calabash. The suite, which has more than 2,000 square feet, has a large master bedroom leading out to a balcony, a huge marble-tiled bathroom with double shower and large double whirlpool bath, a walk-in closet, and a dressing area. A large and well-appointed lounge leads to a sundeck beside the private pool. The suite's luxurious interiors were created by Penny Barnard, a well-known designer from St. Lucia. The Thorneycroft Suite has a spiral staircase that can connect with the Calabash Suite below; the 2 suites can be booked as one family unit.

Amber Belair is The Calabash's luxurious villa community on 19 acres next to the resort on a peninsula that marks Grenada's most southerly point. Several of the initial homes, which set the style for the new development, were designed by the late Arne Hasselqvist, who created most of the famous posh homes on the island of Mustique. Owners have access to all of the facilities of the Calabash. Some of the villas are available for rent.

Rhodes Restaurant, named for the award-winning British chef who designed its kitchen to his specification, created menus that favor the use of local products, and trained the staff for a year under the direction of a top Rhodes chef based at the resort.

The hotel manager invites all the guests to cocktails at the beach bar on Wednesday, and there is live entertainment on different nights. Afternoon tea is served in the main bar and cocktail canapés are delivered to all suites every evening. Each guest may get a complimentary head, neck, and shoulders massage at the Heaven and Earth Spa.

Despite the assorted royalty that drops in, do not get the idea that the Calabash is a posh pleasure palace. Heaven forbid. It's anything but. Rather, the Calabash is unpretentious and understated. It appeals to a wide range of visitors: couples, honeymooners, families with children, and nature lovers. Most come from the United States and Britain, with a sprinkling of Europeans. All appreciate the quality that has long made the Calabash one of the best in the Caribbean.

THE CALABASH HOTEL ★ ★ ★

PO Box 382, L'Anse Aux Epines Beach, St. George's, Grenada, W.I.

Phone: (473) 444-4334, 020 8977 6099; **Fax:** (473) 444-5050; **e-mail:** reservations@calabashhotel.com; www.calabashhotel.com

Owner: The Garbutt family

General Manager: Clive Barnes

Open: Year-round, except Aug 12 to Oct 5

US Reservations: Direct to hotel or reservations@calabashhotel.com; (201) 244-7723

Deposit: 3 nights; 21 days cancellation

Minimum Stay: 7 nights during Christmas and February

Arrival/Departure: Upon request, hotel can send transportation to airport to pick up guests

Distance from Airport: (Maurice Bishop International Airport) 3 miles; taxi one-way, $16

Distance from St. George's: 5 miles; taxi one-way, $17

Accommodations: 30 suites, all suites have balcony or patio and whirlpool baths (1 Thorneycroft suite with private pool; 7 private pool suites; 10 superior suites; 6 West side suites; 6 Whirlpool suites)

Amenities: Air-conditioning, ceiling fans; most baths with tub and shower, robe, hair dryer, toiletries; telephone; safe; minibar, CD player; tea/coffeemaker; iron/ironing board; nightly turndown, room service 11 a.m.–8:30 p.m.; concierge; boutique; repeat guests greeted with fruit basket and bottle of wine; television, iPod dock, DVD player; small library; free Wi-Fi

Fitness Facilities/Spa Services: Fitness center with exercise equipment. Full service spa, treatments available for fee

Sports: Freshwater swimming pool; free use of 2 lighted tennis court, racquets, balls; snooker and billiards room; shuffleboard and beach boules; snorkeling equipment, Sunfish, kayaks, windsurfing, and other nonmotorized water sports from beach concessionaire free of charge; fishing, diving, yacht charters, and hiking with guide in national park arranged; free green fees at Grenada Golf Club

Electricity: 220 volts

Dress Code: Casual

Children: Over 12 years old in Feb, all ages other times; cribs, high chairs; babysitters

Meetings: No

Day Visitors: With reservations

Handicapped Facilities: Yes

Packages: Honeymoon, wedding, romantic escapes, gourmet getaways

Rates: Per person, daily. *High Season* (mid-Dec–early Apr): $710–$1,255. *Low Season:* $385–$855. Single rates available.

Service Charge: Included

Government Tax: Included

LA SOURCE

Pink Gin Beach, St. George's, Grenada, W.I.

Located on the southeast corner of the island on 40 hillside acres overlooking Pink Gin Beach, La Source combines the facilities for an active beach vacation with pampering of body and mind of a spa. The resort was all but blown away during a hurricane in 2004. After extensive rebuilding, refurbishing, and upgrading, this all-inclusive resort reopened in February 2008. Designed by Miami-based architect and interior designer Lane Pettigrew, the resort reflects Grenada's British and French heritage with West Indian and Victorian–inspired architecture and colonial-style interior decor upgraded and modernized by the resort owners. The French connection in the name was inspired by La Source, a painting by the 19th-century neoclassic French artist Jean Ingres, known for his portraits and nudes. The resort's signature image— a female figure similar to that of a woman bathing in Ingres's painting, is incorporated into the design of the outdoor tiles and elsewhere throughout the resort.

The layout, set around a central courtyard with fountains and sculpture, is meant to suggest a West Indian colonial village; the main building would have been the governor's residence, complete with a clock tower permanently set at 5:10 p.m., the traditional time of the governor's cocktail hour in colonial days. The resort's 100 guest rooms were renovated extensively and all now have large, contemporary marble bathrooms and air-conditioning units, among other upgrades.

Four restaurants provide guests with a variety of dining options. Oscar's Beach Bar and Restaurant is an open-air beachside restaurant and tropical lounge serving lunch and dinner with a la carte choices. Guests can also enjoy breakfast, lunch, and dinner at the Garden Restaurant and dinner and a la carte options at the Great House. The Cafe Deli offers soups, salads, sandwiches, and other lunch choices. Room service for continental breakfast is available. The Beach Bar, Piano Bar, and Terrace Bar feature entertainment.

La Source rates include 3 meals plus afternoon tea, red and white wines at lunch and dinner, and all beverages (except for champagne and wines ordered from the wine list), as well as taxes and gratuities. Tipping is not allowed. Transfers to/from the airport and use of the resort's safety deposit box and book exchange are also included.

The Oasis Spa, a focal point of the La Source experience, was completely transformed and now boasts 17 treatment rooms, including 3 wet rooms, 2 Vichy shower rooms, and 1 hydro-tub, in addition to a new salon with cushy manicure and pedicure chairs. Prior to the spa's reopening, 30 new spa technicians completed an intensive training program. The resort's rates include one prearranged spa treatment per day, following the day of arrival. These body and beauty treatments from the "Mind, Body, and Spirit" program range from facials and massages to body wraps and exfoliating polishes. You can also take more unconventional treatments such as reflexology at an additional cost.

An expanded deck and boardwalk surround the swimming pool and whirlpool, providing additional room for sunbathers. The pool and beach area look out at a spectacular view of Grenada's coast—all the way to St. George's, the capital. A larger, redesigned fitness center and a boutique round out the updates.

La Source's all-inclusive program includes three dives in a week's stay for certified divers, an introductory dive course for first timers, and a variety of sports, such as tennis, par-3 golf, volleyball, fencing, archery, windsurfing, sailing, and more. A regular schedule of yoga, tai chi, and Pilates classes, as well as special ones taught by masters in these fields, are available during designated weeks throughout the year.

The latest addition is a scuba-yoga program, said to be the first in the Caribbean, and based on the idea that yoga and scuba diving complement each other. It's especially helpful to those who have initial fears of diving, according to the resort's resident holistic program director. Participants can select 3 morning dives over a 7-night stay. The dives are then balanced with Pranyama yoga techniques, meditation exercises, and underwater buoyancy lessons to enhance the overall dive experience. Participants learn breathing exercises to strengthen the lungs and enhance their ability to breathe with continuity, among other techniques.

LA SOURCE ★ ★ ★
Pink Gin Beach, PO Box 852, St. George's, Grenada, W.I.

Phone: (473) 444-2556, (800) 544-2883; **Fax:** (473) 444-2561; **e-mail:** lasource@theamazingholiday.com; www .theamazingholiday.com
Owner/Management: Liberty Club Limited
General Manager: Mark Grabby
Open: Year-round
US Reservations: (888) 527-0044, (954) 949-2163; **e-mail:** reservations@ eliteislandresorts.com
Deposit: 30 percent, 42 to 31 days cancellation; 60 percent, 30 to 16 days; 75 percent, 15 to 6 days; 100 percent, 5 to 0 days
Minimum Stay: None
Arrival/Departure: Transfer included
Distance from Airport: 5 minutes from Point Salines International Airport, taxi one-way, $8
Distance from St. George's: 7 miles; taxi one-way, $20
Accommodations: 90 rooms and 10 suites, including some single rooms, all with terrace, most with ocean views, in 3 buildings of 3 and 4 stories; furnished with 2 double or king-size beds
Amenities: Air-conditioning, ceiling fan, telephone, CD/clock/radio, safe, minifridge, walk-in closets, marble bath with tub and shower, hair dryer, makeup mirror, bathrobe, basket of toiletries; iron/ironing board, room service for continental breakfast; nightly turndown service; boutique, hair salon; no television
Fitness Facilities/Spa Services: Weight training, jogging, hikes, aerobics, stretch and dance classes, yoga, tai chi, stress management—all with instruction; personal trainer. Oasis Spa: Loofah rubs, body and foot massage, seaweed wraps,

facials, reflexology, and aromatherapy; beauty salon extra charge

Sports: Free-form pool, large whirlpool; 2 lighted tennis courts; fencing; ping-pong; archery; volleyball; golf (9-hole, non-regulation, par 3); snorkeling, wind-surfing, sailing—all with instruction; complimentary introductory dive course; PADI certification additional cost

Electricity: 220 volts; rooms have one 110 volt outlet

Dress Code: Sports/beachwear by daytime; casually elegant in evenings

Children: Minimum age 16 except May 1–Sept 15, when minimum age is 10 years. Rate for children age 10 to 12 is 50 percent, if sharing room with parents.

Meetings: None

Day Visitors: *Day pass:* for 10:30 a.m.–6:30 p.m., $100, includes lunch, drinks, and scheduled activities. Spa treatments subject to availability and priced separately. *Dinner Pass:* $100 includes dinner, drinks, and scheduled nightly entertainment

Packages: Weddings complimentary for guests staying 7 nights minimum. Honeymooners receive a couple's massage, complimentary bottle of sparkling wine, and fresh flowers.

Handicapped Facilities: No

Rates: Per person, daily, All-Inclusive. *High Season* (Dec 21–mid Apr), starting from $420. *Low Season* (mid-Apr–Dec 20): from $250. Single rates starting from $520 and $470, respectively.

Service Charge: Included

Government/Hotel Tax: Included

MOUNT CINNAMON

Grand Anse, Grenada, W.I.

At Mount Cinnamon, the fun boutique resort by Peter de Savary, there are 21 one-bedroom ocean view suites and two- and three-bedroom white villas with red tiled roofs and arched balconies, terraced down a hillside overlooking the sea as bougainvillea, hibiscus, and other tropical flowers spill over walls.

Everything about the rebirth of this 20-year-old villa property, a 10-minute drive from the airport and from St. George's, conspires to amuse with happy hues of lemon, fuchsia, lime, and whimsical touches that make you smile, like gaily painted tin fish wall hooks holding wicker beach bags and wood oars standing in tall wicker baskets.

A canvas of white walls, crisp white linens, and red tile floors show off joyful colors that cover the beds, furniture, puffy pillows, carpets, and locally produced art work; adobe walk-in showers are hand-rubbed with fuchsia or gold or blue; and Roman-striped pillows.

All accommodations are air-conditioned and have airy sitting rooms with kitchen, breakfast bars, and outdoor living-space. Most bedrooms also have large balconies and all have separate dressing areas with adobe-walled showers.

The retro-looking fridge in the kitchen is tangerine orange or electric blue; French doors open onto a large patio with arches framing wide-angle views of the sea and Grand Anse Beach is just a 5-minute walk away.

Savvy, the resort's stylish restaurant with a delightful poolside setting, is surrounded by tropical flowering gardens and panoramic views. Its menu offers pub favorites and Creole dishes served with contemporary flair and has received rave reviews since it opened.

The pool, off the open-air lounge area of the main building and reception, is only a few steps from the villas. White canvas umbrellas and orange, turquoise, and green wicker-style lounge chairs add splashes of color to the patio. The Savvy Beach Club & Cabana with a poolside cocktail bar and a spa are open daily from 10 a.m. until the sun goes down. Set up with a covered patio, tables, lounge chairs, it has a dining area where you can enjoy lunch and drinks. Fresh fish and other favorites are on the grill from noon until 3 p.m.

Moi Spa at Mount Cinnamon is small, but like everything else here, designed to evoke the senses with lots of candles, abstract art work, and subdued lighting.

A wide range of water sports including kayaks, sailing, diving, and fishing, as well as tennis, boat excursion, guided island hiking tours, river-tubing, plantation tours, and children's programs can be arranged.

Peter de Savary's $555 million Port Louis Grenada—an investment twice the annual budget of Grenada—is a mixed-use seaside development. It will have a 300-slip marina for mega-yachts; individual homes and villas; and several hotels (www.portlouisgrenada.com).

In summer of 2011, Mount Cinnamon joined the Elite Resorts group, which also includes Galley Bay in Antigua and Palm Island in the Grenadines, resorts which are also in this book.

MOUNT CINNAMON ★ ★ ★

PO Box 3858, St. George's, Grenada, W.I.
Phone: (473) 439-9900; **Fax:** (473) 439-7000; www.mountcinnamongre nada.com; **e-mail:** info@mountcinna mongrenada.com
Founder/Chairman: Peter De Savary
General Manager: Cynthia O'Connell
Open: Year-round
US Reservations: Direct to hotel or **e-mail:** reservations@mountcinnamon grenada.com
Deposit: 7 nights; 21 days cancellation
Minimum Stay: 7 nights during Christmas and February
Arrival/Departure: Upon request, hotel can arrange transfer for a fee
Distance from Airport: (Point Salines Airport) 4 miles; taxi one-way, $25
Distance from St. George's: 6 miles; taxi one-way, $25
Accommodations: 21 total 1-bedroom and 2- and 3-bedroom (in villas), all with terrace, most with ocean views, furnished with king-size beds; 2-bedroom villas, 1 king and 2 twin beds

Amenities: Air-conditioning, bath with shower, hair dryer, toiletries; telephone; safe; BOSE sound system; tea/coffeemaker; iron/ironing board; mini-refrigerator, cable television; Internet
Fitness Facilities/Spa Services: Gym, spa
Sports: Freshwater swimming pool; free use of lighted tennis court; snorkeling, windsurfing; fishing, golf, diving, hiking with guide in national park arranged for fee
Electricity: 220 volts; 120 volts
Dress Code: Casual by day; elegantly casual in the evening
Children: Up to age 12 free
Meetings: Small groups up to 12 people
Day Visitors: No, except restaurant
Handicapped Facilities: None
Packages: Honeymoon, wedding, romantic escapes
Rates: Per suite, daily, EP: *High Season* (Jan–Apr): $750–$1,375. *Low Season:* $520–$895. Children up to age 12 free
Service Charge: 10 percent
Government Tax: 15 percent

SPICE ISLAND BEACH RESORT

St. George's, Grenada, W.I.

Spice Island Beach Resort opened in 1961 as a rustic, laid-back inn that defined the very notion of a Caribbean escape. In 1988, it was bought by some local businessmen headed by managing director Sir Royston Hopkin, K.C.M.G., who was the 1991 Caribbean Hotelier of the Year and honored by Queen Elizabeth II in 1995 and 2005. Spice, now a Hopkin family enterprise, is more than triple its original size.

After a hurricane devastated the island of Grenada in 2004, Spice closed for 15 months to rebuild. It reopened in December 2005, after a $12 million reconstruction, as practically a new resort and better than ever. In the process, all the accommodations and facilities were upgraded and updated, starting with the elegant new entrance,

which sets the upscale tone for the resort. A landscaped swimming pool near the beach was enhanced, and there's a full-service spa housed in its own separate building, a Cybex fitness center, a children's center, a business center with Internet access, and two upscale boutiques—one for women's fashion and one for men. The central building housing the dining room, bar, open-air terrace, reception area, lounge, and kitchen was completely redesigned and rebuilt, opening it from the entrance to the sea.

The Spice welcome begins at the front entrance where you are greeted upon arrival with a Spice Island Classic, a cooling drink of sparkling wine and sorrel juice.

The resort offers 7 types of guest rooms, ranging from 620 to 1,500 square feet. Stretching along the beach on both sides of the main building and the pool are 1-story cottages, which were rebuilt from the ground up and are fabulous. Each houses 4 Sea Grape junior suites; 2 also have a master suite—the posh Cinnamon and Saffron Suites, which recently were enhanced with a Bose Lifestyle Home Entertainment System and iPod docking station. The master and junior can be combined into a 2-bedroom suite. The junior suites, with handsome contemporary Caribbean decor, have a large bedroom with a king bed (and the most comfortable pillows I've ever had in a hotel). The room extends to a sizeable seating area furnished with a daybed-style sofa that turns into a double bed. The room opens onto a patio, only a few steps from the beach. The huge marble bathroom has a double sink, large whirlpool tub, and a louvered window that looks out to the bedroom and the beach.

Behind the beachfront suites are the honeymooners' favorites: suites with private pools a step away from a bedroom with a king-size bed. To the left of the main building and also set back from the beach are 2-story bungalows whose ground-level suites have plunge pools. All accommodations are air-conditioned and have ceiling fans, flat-screen cable television, DVD players, iPod dock, CD-clock radio, minibar, hair dryer, iron and ironing board, direct-dial phone with Internet access, safe, and coffee/tea maker. Further enhancing the luxury, guests in all suites sleep on fine Frette linens and enjoy Molton Brown toiletries.

The pool suites, spacious and airy with marble floors and glass doors, are furnished in more regal decor than the beachfront ones. All rooms have whirlpools big enough for two, found either in a tiny garden atrium open to the sky or in a corner of a large bathroom with a skylight. Four are ultra-posh Royal Collection Pool suites with pools that are surrounded by high walls and are large enough for laps—albeit short laps—and secluded enough for skinny-dipping. The Royal Collection suites, thought to be the only ones with a large, redwood cedar in-room sauna for two at a Caribbean resort, have another unusual feature—a canopied fitness area, set in the gardens, with an exercise bike. Each has a sundeck with chaise lounges and patio table, along with a flower garden. Each suite, measuring 1,500 square feet, has a separate living room, a bedroom with a king-size bed, and a marble tile bathroom with double sinks and double whirlpools. They also have a stocked minibar, flat-screen television, music center, phone, iPod dock, coffeemaker, hair dryer, safe, ceiling fan, and iron and ironing board.

Breakfast and lunch are served in the open-air beachside restaurant or from room service, which is available from 7:45 a.m. to 10 p.m. Dinner in Oliver's Restaurant is a 5-course menu with two or three choices of continental and local dishes. On Friday night a steel band livens up the evening and a Caribbean buffet highlights the most popular native dishes. On Sunday, guests enjoy a barbecue lunch buffet. During the winter season there is music for dancing several nights.

Guests at Spice spend lazy days on the 1,600 feet of beach, occasionally cooling off in the languid waters or reading and dozing under leafy sea grape trees. Or they can luxuriate in Janissa's Spa, where they will find a full range of face, hair, and body treatments. If they are a bit more ambitious, they can try the Cybex equipment in the fitness center, or enjoy tennis, water sports, a game of golf, or a bicycle ride.

To maintain the setting's serenity, motorized water sports are not available in this section of Grand Anse Beach.

The Nutmeg Pod is the children's center, open daily from 9 a.m. to 5 p.m. for kids age 3 and up. It has a weekly schedule of organized activities.

In keeping with the resort's impressive environmentally conscious stewardship, Spice Island became a completely nonsmoking resort in December 2008. The move includes the restaurant, bar, and all indoor/outdoor facilities, as well as the guest rooms.

Spice Island operates as an all-inclusive resort with rates covering accommodations, 3 meals and afternoon tea, bar service, house wine at dinner; nonmotorized water sports such as snorkeling, kayaking, and Hobie Cat sailing; tennis; golf greens fees at the Grenada Golf Club; and concierge and room service. There is also a half-board option that includes only breakfast and dinner.

SPICE ISLAND BEACH RESORT

★ ★ ★ ★ 🐚

Grand Anse, PO Box 6, St. George's, Grenada, W.I.

Phone: (473) 444-4258; **Fax:** (473) 444-4807; **e-mail:** spiceisl@spiceisle .com; www.spiceislandbeachresort.com
Owner/Managing Director: Sir Royston O. Hopkin, K.C.M.G.
General Manager: Brian Hardy
Open: Year-round
US Reservations: Direct by phone or e-mail
Deposit: 3 nights in winter; 1 night in summer; 30 days cancellation prior to arrival, mid-Dec–mid-Apr, except during Christmas holidays and Feb when it is 45 days; 14 days in summer
Minimum Stay: 7 nights Christmas holidays and Feb; none in summer (mid-Apr–mid-Dec)
Arrival/Departure: Transfer service not available due to Taxi Association regulations
Distance from Airport: (Pointe Salines Airport) 4 miles; taxi one-way, $19
Distance from St. George's: 6 miles; taxi one-way, $20
Accommodations: 64 rooms and suites, most beachfront and ocean view, all with whirlpools; 17 suites with private swimming pools (6 luxury pool suites, 7 private-pool suites, 4 royal private-pool suites), each with king-size beds
Amenities: Air-conditioning, ceiling fans; whirlpool tub, shower, hair dryer, basket of toiletries; television, telephone with Internet access; clock-radio; stocked minibar, coffeemaker; iron and ironing board; safe; nightly turndown service; room service for meals and beverages/delivery charge applies; boutique; Internet access
Sports: Tennis court, balls, racquets; snorkeling gear, Hobie Cats, kayaks,

windsurfers provided; boating, diving, fishing, hiking arranged

Fitness Facilities/Spa Services: See text

Electricity: 220 volts

Dress Code: Casual by day; elegantly casual in evening

Children: All ages; none in pool suites year-round. Children's center for age 3 and older; cribs; babysitters

Meetings: Up to 65 people; business center with Internet access and business equipment

Day Visitors: Yes

Handicapped Facilities: Limited

Packages: Honeymoon, wedding, renewal of vows

Rates: Two people, daily, **All-Inclusive.** *High Season* (mid-Dec–mid-Apr): $750–$1,990. *Low Season:* $600–$1,265. Children and single rates are available.

Service Charge: 10 percent

Government Tax: 15 percent

TWELVE DEGREES NORTH

St. George's, Grenada, W.I.

Joe Gaylord, who has lived in Grenada since 1967, gave up the real estate business in New York for his patch of paradise. He created Twelve Degrees North—which takes its name from Grenada's latitude—out of the frustration of not finding the resort he wanted for his vacation. His nest is the most unhotel hotel you are ever likely to find. Joe believes it is unique in the Caribbean, and perhaps it is. It's also one of the Caribbean's best bargains.

The small complex has only 8 units of 1 and 2 bedrooms. They are situated in 4 two-story buildings that are interconnected by steps. The rooms have terra-cotta floors and are decorated with rattan furniture.

The bedrooms have a king or 2 twin beds joined by a king-size headboard. The 2-bedroom suites have 2 baths and large living rooms. The suites on the second floor have pitched ceilings, which make them seem more spacious. All the units have kitchens and terraces with picture-postcard views of the Caribbean; all face west, making your terrace the ideal perch at sunset for enjoying the rum punch you will find in your refrigerator upon arrival. And that's not all you'll find in it.

Your refrigerator and pantry will be fully stocked with beverages and food—chicken, fish, fruit, vegetables, bread, and other staples—for your stay. The reason for this horn of plenty is one of the features that make Twelve Degrees so unusual: Namely, for your entire stay you will have a personal attendant (a combination maid, cook, and housekeeper) assigned exclusively to your suite.

Joe has devised a system that seems to work like magic for them, the women attendants, and their guests. Each attendant's sole job is to care for the occupants of her unit and her unit only, year in and year out. She is available from 8 a.m. to 3 p.m. daily and will keep your room immaculate, change the linens, do your personal laundry, and cook and serve your breakfast and lunch.

If you don't want her to come as early as 8 a.m., it's no problem; just say so. If you don't need her to hang around to serve you lunch, just tell her. She can make your lunch and leave. For the evening you are on your own, but if you would like her to prepare your dinner in advance, she will do that too. If you don't care to bother with making dinner, there are restaurants nearby.

You pay for the provisions that are stocked for you in advance of your arrival. If you do not intend to use certain items, you can tell Joe or your attendant, and they will be deducted from your bill.

You will find that these women are good cooks and are pleased to introduce you to Grenadian cuisine, but if you prefer your own style of cooking, they will prepare meals as you request.

Joe's care in selecting his location and staff extends to getting the right kind of guests—namely, ones who are suited to the quiet, intimate ambience of this resort. He does not welcome children, for example, simply because his guests do not want them around. Most people come for the tranquillity; anyone who needs activity or entertainment would definitely be in the wrong place.

Twelve Degrees North—the 12th degree north line actually runs through the property—is about as low-key and laid-back as the Caribbean gets. It is set in a little cove on a hillside of tropical woods and gardens that slope to a small beach. A stone path leads from the cottages downhill to the beach. There you find an ample-size L-shaped freshwater pool, 3 hammocks, lounging chairs, a built-in gas barbecue, and a thatched hut with a self-service bar and library of well-read books. Pick a spot and spend the day. You might converse with some of the other guests around the pool or by the beach. Most will be from the States—professionals, a university professor, a stockbroker, a television producer—and most are good company.

They usually are experienced travelers who have tried many of the better-known, ritzier places in the Caribbean. They probably heard about Joe's place from a friend or their own research. To the right of the beach is a 100-foot pier with a gazebo and benches. It juts out into the sea where the water is deep enough to swim (by the beach the water is very shallow), and there's a reef for snorkeling. The use of snorkeling gear, Sunfish, and kayaks, as well as the tennis court, is included in the rate. Scuba diving and waterskiing can be arranged for a fee.

There's a 720-square-foot over-the-water sundeck. When you look up from the beach or pier, you will see Joe's home. If you think you have a wonderful view, wait until you see his. And you are likely to do so: Joe often invites guests to join him for cocktails. Most consider it the highlight of their visit. The house sits out on a point; the entire front is open to the view.

Oh, I forgot to mention: Twelve Degrees North has no office; it's in Joe's house. But if he knows you are coming, he will be standing by the driveway to greet you when you arrive. You can count on it.

TWELVE DEGREES NORTH ★

PO Box 241, St. George's, Grenada, W.I.
Phone: (473) 444-4580; **Fax:** same as phone; **e-mail:** 12degrsn@spiceisle.com; www.twelvedegreesnorth.com

Owner/Manager: Joe Gaylord
Open: Year-round
US Reservations: Direct to hotel
Deposit: 3 nights
Minimum Stay: 7 to 10 nights during Christmas and Feb
Arrival/Departure: No transfer service
Distance from Airport: (Pointe Salines International Airport) 3 miles; taxi one-way, $16
Distance from St. George's: 5 miles, taxi one-way, $18; from Grand Anse, 2 miles, taxi one-way, $8
Accommodations: 6 one-bedroom suites; 2 two-bedroom suites, all with terrace, kitchen, and twin beds or king
Amenities: Ceiling fan; kitchen; bath with shower, basket of toiletries, hair dryer, shampoo and conditioner dispenser; complimentary rum punch; personal maid-cook
Electricity: 220 volts
Sports: Freshwater swimming pool; use of tennis court, snorkeling gear, kayaks, Sunfish included; scuba, fishing, waterskiing for fee; trail hiking, birding arranged
Dress Code: Casual
Children: None under 15 years old, year-round
Meetings: No
Day Visitors: Not suitable
Handicapped Facilities: No
Packages: No
Rates: Two people, 1-bedroom, daily, FAP. *High Season* (mid-Dec–mid-Apr): $225. *Low Season:* $165. Four people in 2-bedroom unit, $350 plus $70 per person per day and $285 plus $60, respectively
Service Charge: 10 percent
Government Tax: 8 percent

JAMAICA

From the 7,400-foot peaks of the Blue Mountains, where the famous coffee is grown, Jamaica's terrain drops to foothills of banana groves and sugarcane fields and orchards of mangos and limes. Brilliant flowers, vivid birds, exotic fruit, gentle people whose voices lilt as though they are singing—these are the charms with which this Caribbean beauty seduces her admirers.

Jamaica, the land of reggae, is the quintessence of the Caribbean and offers diversity—in landscape and lifestyle, culture and cuisine, sports and attractions—that few islands can match. There are waterfalls to climb, mountains to hike, trails to ride, golf, tennis, polo, diving, fishing, plus attractions that are unique to Jamaica, such as rafting on the Rio Grande and trips into the mountainous Cockpit country that once sheltered the Maroons, runaway slaves who defied British rule.

Jamaica, 144 miles long and 49 miles wide, is located 90 miles south of Cuba. The third largest Caribbean island, Jamaica was called Xaymaca, meaning "land of wood and water," by the Arawaks who populated the island when Columbus arrived in 1494.

The British took Jamaica in 1655 and stayed for the next 300 years. Although the colonial trappings disappeared on the road to nationhood since independence in 1962, vestiges of the British, such as cricket and croquet, tea parties and polo, are still very much a part of the Jamaican fabric, incongruous as they may seem.

If its British past was the stock for the Jamaican bouillabaisse, the traders, slaves, and settlers who came to the island were the ingredients that created a culture as diverse as its scenery. Jamaica's influence in art, dance, and music extends far beyond the Caribbean.

Jamaica's diversity enables every visitor to find a niche. From the laid-back beaches of Negril on the west to the quiet coves and busy resorts along the 100-mile northern coast to Port Antonio on the east, there are resorts to suit most travelers, regardless of interest and budget.

Information

Jamaica Tourist Board, 5201 Blue Lagoon Dr., Ste. 670, FL 33126; (800) 233-4582, (305) 665-0557; www.visitjamaica.com

STRAWBERRY HILL

Kingston, Jamaica, W.I.

One of the most enchanting Caribbean havens is not on a beach but rather, it is perched high in the Blue Mountains of eastern Jamaica, where eco-green must have been invented.

Strawberry Hill is the dream-come-true of Island Records mogul Chris Blackwell, who launched Bob Marley, U2, and others to superstardom and helped create the hip image of Miami's South Beach with his art deco hotels. Set amid gardens and wooded hills at an elevation of 3,000 feet near Irish Town, Strawberry Hill is a former coffee plantation whose manor house commands one of the island's most enviable views, with the mountains over 7,000 feet as the background and the sea at your feet.

The great house, renovated to serve as the centerpiece of the hotel, has a lounge and restaurant. Its decor is designed around Island Records memorabilia dating from the company's beginning in 1962 and including its many gold records and awards as well as items from its stable of recording stars. There's a library and a small conference room for up to 30 people. Wi-Fi service is available for no charge in the common areas.

Most accommodations are found in 12 veranda-encircled 1- and 2-story cottages. Designed by Jamaican architect Ann Hodges in a modified gingerbread-trimmed West Indian style and painted in neutral colors, they have 1- and 2-bedroom cottages with beautifully finished, local wood interiors.

Rooms are furnished in country-casual fashion by Tanya Melich, a

British-by-way-of-the-Bahamas designer. They feature four-poster beds and antiqued, handmade island furniture. The cottages are positioned to take maximum advantage of their heart-stopping views. Each has a terra-cotta bathroom and a small kitchen nook—intended as a convenience for an early-morning or late-evening repast rather than serious cooking. If you have a hammock on your veranda, it will be hard to resist for an afternoon nap or a cocktail-hour perch to watch the sun drop into the sea and Kingston light up for the evening show.

Each guest can enjoy videos and recordings from a stocked library. Electronic gear enables you to stay plugged into the outside world, should you need to disrupt the serenity of this very private escape. In your room, you will find a television, a CD/DVD player, coffeemaker, minibar, large writing desk (that's to lay a guilt number on writers who goof off), and heated mattress pads (can you believe it actually gets cold at night in Jamaica!) on the huge four-poster beds. These pads are set on low to prevent mildew as well as to warm guests. Huge white pillows, down-filled comforters, and sheer mosquito netting—not necessary but aesthetically pleasing—make the beds very inviting.

Wooden walkways connecting the cottages wind their way up to the manor house and its crowning glory—a 60-foot swimming pool set in gardens on the highest point of the 45-acre property with vistas to infinity.

The Strawberry Hill Living Spa provides a wide range of treatments and services that encourage wellness. A perfect complement to the resort's idyllic setting, it utilizes natural ingredients in a variety of services, including hydrotherapy, facials, and body care, as well as Aveda massage treatments based on Ayruyedic philosophies. The first step is to determine your unique "aroma identity" and formulate a personal aroma blend, which is used in all of your treatments. In addition to massage and stress-relieving treatments, the spa offers manicure, pedicure, and facials. It also organizes hiking, mountain biking, and other outdoor activities in the Blue Mountains.

Chef Kingsley McGregor creates unique and outstanding dishes that combine *nouvelle cuisine* techniques with traditional Jamaican cooking and uses herbs and spices grown in the resort's vegetable garden, such as spearmint, lemongrass, dill, and cilantro, as well as mangoes, Otaheite apples, naseberry, jack fruit, sweet sop, and other fruits from the resort's tropical orchard. Meals can be enjoyed in the sun-dappled, high-ceilinged main dining room, which manages to be formal yet casual and relaxing all at the same time. Continental breakfasts (huge plates of fresh fruit, toast, and Blue Mountain coffee) are served, weather permitting, on the covered veranda that's just a few steps away. The restaurant, open from 7 a.m. until 10 p.m., serves all 3 meals, as well as afternoon tea and Jamaican Sunday brunch. Room service is available from 7 a.m. to 10 p.m.

The grounds at Strawberry Hill are interesting and historic as the property was a coffee farm since around 1890. To date, the resort has catalogued 350 endemic and exotic plant species. The main canopy is of juniper *(Juniperus barbadea)* lining the old driveway with specimens of cedar *(Cedrela odoratissma),* eucalyptus *(Eucalyptus nicolae),* and mango *(Mangifera indica).* The gardens are an ongoing process as only 4 acres out of a possible 10 acres of terraced land have been defined, along with a further 35 acres of slopes.

Strawberry Hill has an all-inclusive option that includes all meals, beverages, and a customized minibar stocked daily with juices, bottled water, and herbal waters; taxes and service charges are additional.

Although Strawberry Hill is 5 miles from Kingston, the drive can take 30 minutes or more because of the narrow mountain roads. From the Kingston Airport on the far side of the city, you need to allow for at least a 50-minute drive, depending on the traffic. Those who do not care to make the drive can arrive by helicopter (a 7-minute ride)—if cost is no object.

If you fall in love with Strawberry Hill and can't bear to leave, ask about monthly rates—particularly if you're a writer.

STRAWBERRY HILL ★ ★ ★ 🐟
Irish Town, Jamaica, W.I.
Phone: (876) 944-8400; **Fax:** (876) 944-8408; **e-mail:** reservations@island outpost.com; www.islandoutpost.com
Owner: Island Outpost
Chairman: Jonathan Surtees
Managing Director: Paula Surtees
Hotel Manager: Tanisha Henry
Open: Year-round
US Reservations: (800) OUTPOST

Deposit: Determined by length of stay
Minimum Stay: None
Arrival/Departure: Upon request, hotel can arrange transfers by car for a fee; helicopter service available (7-minute flight) for fee (very costly)
Distance from Airport: (Kingston Airport) 15 miles (50-minute drive on mountain roads)
Distance from Kingston: 5 miles (30 or more minutes on mountain roads)
Accommodations: 11 villas with 13 rooms (4 studio suites; 4 one- and 2 two-bedroom villas, and 1 deluxe one-bedroom villa); 4 kings, 8 queens, 2 twins; all with balcony or veranda; some with kitchenette
Amenities: Bath with tub and shower; coffeemaker, minibar; nightly turndown service, room service; telephone, hair dryer, television, CD player/DVD
Fitness Facilities/Spa Services: See text
Sports: Hiking; mountain biking in Blue Mountains; sightseeing excursions, coffee plantation tours; swimming pool
Electricity: 110 volts
Dress Code: Casual
Children: Allowed but no programs; can use swimming pool and explore nature trails
Meetings: Small conference room for up to 30 people; state-of-the-art audiovisual equipment
Day Visitors: Welcome for breakfast, lunch, and dinner with reservations. Visitors may tour property; see manager at front desk upon arrival.
Handicapped Facilities: Not recommended for handicapped persons
Packages: Honeymoon, wedding, spa
Rates: Per room, for two people, per night, seasonal, starting at $195 for 1

bedroom; $295 for studio and $395 for 2-bedrooms and deluxe villa. All-Inclusive rates begin at $495 per night. Monthly rates available; inquire.

Service Charge: 10 percent
Government Tax: 10 percent

HALF MOON
Montego Bay, Jamaica, W.I.

Set in carefully tended lawns and gardens at the edge of a 2-mile stretch of white-sand beach, Half Moon is one of the most complete resorts in the Caribbean. Since it opened in 1954, it has grown from a cluster of cottages around Half Moon Bay—truly a perfect crescent—to a vast resort spread over 400 acres. It boasts a wide range of accommodations and extensive sports facilities, including a championship golf course, tennis and squash complex, and fitness center, along with an array of activities and services.

The entrance leading to the porte cochere is a long, flower-festooned driveway, a wedding cake of arches and filigree wrapped in bouquets of exuberant tropical flowers. It's so pretty that you barely notice you've passed security gates. Walls are camouflaged with flowered hedges to protect this fairyland of snow-white villas and gazebos.

From the porte cochere you are greeted by a large marble-paved lobby open all the way to the sea. This elegant lobby, furnished with Queen Anne–style mahogany chairs and other pieces, has a front desk with computerized check-in facilities and a private check-in lounge for VIP guests. Beyond is a lobby bar and open-air lounge next to the Seagrape Terrace,

the main indoor-outdoor restaurant by the sea.

Half Moon's plantation-style buildings house spacious guest rooms, most with sitting areas, large suites, and baronial 1- and 2-story villas with patios and balconies. The accommodations are furnished with a contemporary Caribbean theme and have large, modern bathrooms, large verandahs, dataport/Internet access, minibar, television/VCR, and electronic safe, among other signature amenities. The villas have kitchens, large tiled bathrooms, and separate dressing areas; some have private or semiprivate pools. Each of the 32 Royal Villas, the most luxurious of the accommodations, has a private pool. They offer privacy, but they are quite a distance from the main restaurant and bar. Two golf carts come with each villa, making it easy to cover the distance. The villas also come with a cook, butler, and housekeeper. There is a grocery shop in the hotel's shopping arcade.

Throughout the resort, British colonial architecture harmonizes with English country house interiors, using furniture made in Jamaica. Most rooms have four-poster beds.

The large, tree-shaded Seagrape Terrace restaurant and its breezy bar directly by the beach are the center of activity throughout the day. In the evening the setting, especially pretty for candlelit dining under the stars, offers a wide selection of continental and Caribbean-Jamaican cuisine. Next to the Terrace is Il Giardino, serving Italian cuisine. The Sugar Mill, on the hillside above Half Moon, has an enchanting garden setting next to a 200-year-old waterwheel, and offering its own original Caribbean haute cuisine.

Half Moon's beach is not deep, but it is long. Swimmers also have a choice of 4 large freshwater pools. Guests in some villas enjoy one of the 17 private or semiprivate pools. Snorkeling, scuba diving, sailing, windsurfing, and deep-sea fishing (all at additional charge) are available from the water-sports center. The resort, a popular venue for weddings, has an open-air interdenominational wedding chapel on Sunrise Beach.

Half Moon's beautiful 18-hole championship golf course, designed by Robert Trent Jones, is one of Jamaica's best. Built on undulating terrain in the foothills and by the sea, the 7,115-yard, par-72 course is made difficult by the tricky breezes that blow in off the ocean. There's a pro shop and a custom-built teaching academy.

The Fern Tree Spa at Half Moon is housed in the luxury villa for which it was named. There are 6 beachfront spa suites, each with a large bedroom, sitting area, and oversize bathroom, along with a sea-view patio with an outdoor soaking tub and shower and a studio for ensuite treatments or yoga. The spa boasts a spa elder versed in the art of holistic healing, who created a treatment menu that reflects traditional remedies and current spa techniques. Treatment rooms are set in tropical gardens open to a private garden terrace. A couples massage room has a private patio with dipping pool. The spa has a relaxing lounge, hydrotherapy pool and yoga pavilion.

Half Moon's fitness center, upgraded with the latest exercise equipment; offers Yoga and aerobics classes daily; a personal trainer is also available. A championship tennis pavilion adjoins the tennis complex, which has squash and tennis courts. There are jogging and biking paths and horseback-riding trails.

The Anancy Children's Village at Half Moon, the children's center, is centered around the Jamaican folk hero, Anancy, and attended by a staff of trained counselors. Open daily, each of four age groups has its own playhouse, and a center facility has a kitchen where kids learn to make cookies and other items. It offers arts and crafts, nature walks, and other activities. It has a swimming pool, swings, tennis courts, playhouses, sandboxes, and a duck pond.

Half Moon is the very definition of barefoot elegance, combining a certain glamour and style with a laid-back Caribbean ambience. Guests are the most international you'll find at any of Jamaica's resorts: British and European princes and princesses—not to mention Hollywood ones—captains of industry, and sportsmen as well as business-meeting participants and Japanese honeymooners. Somehow it all seems to fit together.

HALF MOON ★ ★ ★ ★
PO Box 80, Rose Hall, Jamaica, W.I.

Phone: (876) 953-2211; Fax: (876) 953-2731; e-mail: reservations@half moon.com; www.halfmoon.com
Owner: Half Moon Bay Ltd.
Managing Director: Richard Whitfield
Open: Year-round
US Reservations: Direct to hotel (24-hour service), (800) 626-0592; (888) 830-5974
Deposit: 3 nights
Minimum Stay: 14 nights during Christmas/New Year's
Arrival/Departure: Transfer service arranged for fee
Distance from Airport: (Montego Bay Airport) 5 miles; taxi one-way, $20
Distance from Montego Bay: 7 miles; taxi one-way, $30
Accommodations: 398 units (34 superior rooms; 119 deluxe, junior, and imperial suites; 60 royal suites with private pools; 32 villas of 5- to 7-bedrooms, all with private pool and terrace); all doubles with 2 double beds or kings
Amenities: Air-conditioning, ceiling fans; direct-dial telephone, television; safe; bath with tub and shower (some with bidet, too), hair dryer, basket of toiletries; bathrobe in royal suites; minibar or refrigerator, kitchen in villas; nightly turndown service, room service 7 a.m.–midnight

Fitness Facilities/Spa Services: Fitness center and spa (see text)
Sports: 4 large freshwater swimming pools, 49 private or semiprivate pools, children's pool; 4 squash courts (lighted), 13 Laykold tennis courts (all lighted), free use, lessons, equipment for fee; windsurfing, Sunfish, diving, snorkeling, guided horseback riding for fee; 50 percent discount on golf for hotel guests; pro, pro shop, equipment, caddies, carts for fee; bikes for rent
Electricity: 110/220 volts
Dress Code: Casual by day, but long-sleeved shirts after 6 p.m. in winter; informal in summer, but shorts, T-shirts, jeans not allowed at dinner
Children: All ages; cribs, high chairs; Children's Center with playground and supervised activities; babysitters; children's menus and discounts
Meetings: Up to 1,000 people
Day Visitors: Welcome
Handicapped Facilities: Yes
Packages: Golf, honeymoon, wedding; Platinum (All-Inclusive)
Rates: Per person, daily, EP. *High Season* (mid-Dec–mid-Apr): $400–$1,650. *Low Season:* $250–$1,100. For Royal Villa rates, inquire.
Service Charge: Included
Government Tax: Included

THE RITZ-CARLTON GOLF & SPA RESORT, ROSE HALL, JAMAICA

Montego Bay, Jamaica, W.I.

Located east of Montego Bay in the Rose Hall plantation area on Jamaica's north coast, is the Ritz-Carlton Golf & Spa Resort, Rose Hall. The resort is on 1,500 feet of waterfront and is 15 minutes from Sangster International Airport in Montego Bay and within easy reach of several shopping villages and the new Jamaican Convention Center.

Owned by an affiliate of the Rollins Group of Wilmington, Delaware, Jamaica, and opened in 2000, the layout is centered by a main building with a spacious lobby, looking out to the gardens and sea, and two separate wings with guest rooms that stretch along the gardens to sea. The off-white stucco buildings with rust-colored roofs frame the swimming pool and the resort's tropical gardens and fountains. Arched doorways, vaulted ceilings, tall columns, and open-air spaces are architectural features throughout the hotel, which together with the British-colonial interior decor reflect the style of Jamaica's historic plantation homes. Over two years in two phases, the AAA Five Diamond resort got a multimillion-dollar renovation throughout.

All guest rooms and suites have private, covered balconies with balustrade fronts. Tropical floral prints, mahogany bedposts, and rattan furniture are elements in the casually elegant decor. All rooms are equipped with complimentary Internet access and have flat-screen plasma television, gourmet coffeemaker, and minibar. Bathrooms with white marble floors and walls have double sinks in a long white marble counter with the usual array of Ritz-Carlton toiletries, hair dryer, and separate shower stall, tub, and toilet.

The Ritz-Carlton Club, accessed by elevator key only, has a dedicated concierge and elegant, private lounge where complimentary food and beverages are offered five times daily. It has 33 rooms, including 2 wheelchair-accessible, 3 suites, and the Presidential Suite.

The resort's 18-hole, 6,800-yard championship golf course, White Witch, is named after the famed storybook, *The White Witch of Rose Hall*, by Herbert G. de Lesser. Designed by Robert Von Hagge and Associates, the course is situated across more than 200 acres of lush green mountainsides and rolling country with 16 holes embracing dramatic views of the Caribbean Sea and several holes with water hazards. The clubhouse has an open-air restaurant with a 1,700-square-foot veranda and takes in views of the golf course, the ocean, and the mountains. There's a resident pro, pro shop, and men's and ladies' locker rooms.

The Ritz-Carlton's outdoor swimming pool area, located between the central gardens and the beach, is crowded with lounge chairs. A small Jacuzzi is hidden in the foliage near the pool. A walkway from the pool area leads to the beach where a variety of water sports is available. In another area of the grounds, you find 2 tennis courts and a tennis pavilion; and a tennis pro.

The spa and fitness center, one of the resort's most popular amenities, has 11 treatment rooms, adorned with beautifully painted murals of the blue sky on the ceiling. The spa offers a menu of island-inspired treatments featuring local ingredients, plant extracts, and essential oils, such as Jamaican Coffee Scrub and Sugarcane Body Polish. It also offers the full array of body treatments including deep-tissue massage, reflexology, shiatsu, and Ritz-Carlton's signature facials.

The spa's wet rooms feature a rainforest bath as well as scrub, seaweed, and mud therapies and wraps. Massages, facials, and wet treatments are also given in rooms designed specifically for two—couples, mothers and daughters, and siblings. Therapists are on hand to train spa guests to perform massage techniques on each other at home. The salon offers hair and nail services for men and women.

A fitness center, which overlooks the lush tropical gardens of the West Wing, has cardiovascular and weight-training equipment and treadmills with personal television and cross trainers with made-for-iPod and USB port connectors. Ladies' and men's relaxation lounges are outfitted with soft plush recliners. A steam and sauna and cold plunge area has shower facilities and lockers.

The Ritz-Carlton's dining options include Horizon for breakfast and dinner indoors in air-conditioning or on an outdoor patio, located on the lower level of the lobby overlooking the gardens; and Mangos, a casual poolside bar and restaurant with a wide selection of local and international choices for lunch and dinner. For a taste of Jamaica,

The Reggae Jerk Centre offers barefoot casual dining for lunch with island specialties on the hotel's west beach, while the White Witch Restaurant takes you into the hills of the golf course to enjoy sunset cocktails, lunch, or dinner on the terrace.

Cohoba, the lobby lounge and outdoor terrace, has a rustic coffee station, where morning guests can enjoy Jamaica's famous Blue Mountain coffee. In the evening, it is transformed into a tapas bar with live local entertainment. Off the lobby is a boutique.

The hotel's extensive meeting and banquet facilitiesinclude a 10,800-square-foot ballroom, 12 total meeting rooms and 42,000 square feet of outdoor and pre-function space with a covered terrace. The hotel also sells the famous Rose Hall Great House, one of Jamaica's prime attractions, which won the Phoenix Award, the highly coveted recognition for historic preservation and conservation given annually by the Society of American Travel Writers. The lower level of the house has a bar and the manor house is available for weddings and special events.

THE RITZ-CARLTON GOLF & SPA RESORT, ROSE HALL, JAMAICA ★ ★ ★ ★

1 Ritz-Carlton Dr., Rose Hall, St. James, Jamaica, W.I.
Phone: (876) 953-2800; www.ritzcarlton.com
Owner: Rose Hall LLC
Management: The Ritz-Carlton Hotel Company, L.L.C., Washington, D.C.
General Manager: Tony Mira

US Reservations: Ritz-Carlton, (800) 241-3333
Deposit: 1 night, except during holiday season
Minimum Stay: 5 nights Christmas/New Year's with 60 days full, nonrefundable prepayment
Arrival/Departure: Transfer service by Jamaica Tours Ltd., for $45 shuttle and $175 for exclusive town car round-trip
Distance from Airport: (Montego Bay) 7 miles
Accommodations: 427 guest rooms and suites with private balconies (260 king; 118 double-doubles; 51 executive suites; 1 Ritz-Carlton suite) with garden, pool, mountains, and partial or full ocean views; 33 Ritz-Carlton Club rooms and 3 suites and private lounge
Amenities: Air-conditioning; safe; stocked bar; marble bathrooms with separate shower and tub and dual sinks; cable television, digital clock/alarm radio, 3 telephones with dual lines and data ports, computer and fax hookups; free high-speed Internet access, Wi-Fi in public areas, pool and beach; terry bathrobes and slippers, goose-down pillows; 24-hour room service; Ritz-Carlton Suite: living room/dining area, pantry, foyer with powder room, master bathroom, dressing area, walk-in closet, twice-daily maid service
Fitness Facilities/Spa Services: See text
Sports: Swimming pool, water sports, tennis; golf, see text
Electricity: 120 volts
Dress Code: Casually elegant
Day Visitors: Yes
Handicapped Facilities: Special rooms
Children: All ages; Ritz Kids program
Meetings: Up to 800 people

Packages: Golf, wedding, spa, honeymoon, weekend, all-inclusive, special occasion, and meal plan
Rates: Per person, double, per day, EP. *High Season* (Jan 4–Apr 7): $359–$729.

Low Season (Apr 8–Dec 22): $209–$569. Call for rates for Christmas/New Year's.
Service Charge: 14 percent
Government Tax: 10 percent

ROUND HILL HOTEL AND VILLAS

Montego Bay, Jamaica, W.I.

If you like the idea of sunset cocktails around the same piano Cole Porter once played, or dining on the terrace next to Ralph Lauren or the queen of Norway, Round Hill may be just the place for you.

Nothing is guaranteed, of course, but for almost six decades this hillside enclave has been one of the Caribbean's most cherished retreats for the rich and famous. It's still not a bad place to hang out, if you think Paul McCartney—a recent guest—makes good company.

You can't mistake the roadside entrance to Round Hill: white pillars with round (what else?) tops. The road along the 110-acre peninsula rounds the hill at the crest before descending quickly to the main building by the sea. Housed in a replica of the Good Hope carriage house, the reception with its white-and-black checkerboard tile floor and mahogany furnishings looks through to the gardens and sea, setting a gracious tone for arriving guests.

Round Hill was opened in 1953 by John Pringle, a prominent Jamaican who purchased the property. After selling land to some titled Europeans and affluent Americans, he created a deluxe resort by getting his celebrity friends to become shareholders and build houses there. Noël Coward, Adele Astaire, the William Paleys, and the Oscar Hammersteins were among those who flocked here in the 1950s and came to regard Round Hill as their club.

Set amid acres of marvelous gardens, the villas cascade from the hilltop to the beach. Practical as well as pretty, villas are made up of two to five separate suites. Each has a private entrance, but they share the kitchen. You can rent the entire villa or a suite and still have your privacy, along with the services of the villa staff: a cook, maid, and gardener. Of the 27 villas, 23 have private swimming pools.

The exteriors are similar in design: All are 1-story stone and white clapboard structures with shingled roofs and louvered shutters and doors opening onto terraces and seaward views. Inside, no two villas are alike, but most merit a spread in House Beautiful. Your housekeeper prepares and serves breakfast on your private terrace, from which you can feast on Jamaica's beauty framed by the flowering gardens that surround you.

Pringle's original hotel is now the beachfront Pineapple House, a white 2-story building at the water's edge. All rooms have been completely reconstructed and redesigned into large junior suites. Those on the ground floor have screened louvered doors that open onto wooden balconies furnished with a table

and 2 chairs. Rooms on the second floor do not have balconies, but they have high-pitched roofs, making the rooms seem larger and airier and they enjoy unobstructed views of the sea and coastline. With handsome decor by Round Hill homeowner Ralph Lauren, the rooms are all white from ceiling to their white Brazilian mat-tile floors. They are comfortably furnished with a desk and four-poster beds (king or 2 doubles) made in Jamaica from big bamboo painted black and dressed in white woven spreads. A touch of color is added in bright blue or fuchsia pillows and throws. The sitting area has a coffee table and overstuffed chair and a Lauren-designed chaise longue. Pineapple House takes its name from Round Hill's logo, a Caribbean sign of welcome and a reminder that this was once a pineapple plantation. The emblem is everywhere: embossed on menu covers, shaped into lamps, and printed on all stationery. Pineapple House guests can breakfast in their rooms or at the seaside dining terrace.

Lunch for all is served alfresco on the hotel's tree-shaded dining terrace overlooking the bay. Award-winning Chef Martin Maginley, one of the Caribbean's most creative chefs, turns out some of the best cuisine of any hotel in Jamaica.

The Restaurant at Round Hill is an elegant dining venue housed on a spacious terrace above the main dining area and features contemporary Caribbean cuisine for which Chef Martin is known. The restaurant is open 5 nights a week and for brunch on Sunday during the winter season. Advanced reservations are recommended.

The Grill at Round Hill, redesigned by Ralph Lauren, reopened in 2010 as an entirely new restaurant with fresh interiors and updated menus created by Chef Martin, noted for his modern Caribbean cuisine based on local products and the resort's organic garden when possible. The decor of the new dining space features classic black granite floors, white columns, and brass lanterns, combining the property's history with modern design for a clean, unpretentious effect.

Evenings at the resort begin with cocktails in the piano bar, which was decorated by Ralph Lauren. Dinner settings change from Monday night's barefoot picnic on the beach to Saturday night's dinner dance in the Georgian Pavilion. Four nights a week, dinner in the dining terrace is followed by entertainment from the resident band and local artists, with dancing under the stars. Friday is Jamaica Night, featuring a folklore group and reggae band, while a steel band livens up the Monday scene.

In the past, the beautiful, large infinity pool by Pineapple House compensated somewhat for Round Hill's small beach, but in 2010, using reclaimed sand from the water directly in front of the property, the beachfront has been expanded three-fold. A coral reef lies within swimming distance of shore, and use of snorkel gear is included in the rates (as are use of the tennis courts and transfers to nearby golf at Tryall). The air-conditioned business center has computers with high-speed Internet access and laptop dataports.

The Spa at Round Hill, the resort's full-service facility, is housed in a restored 18th-century plantation house on 10 waterfront acres. It has 10 air-conditioned treatment rooms, an indoor/outdoor fitness center, and a beauty salon. The spa offers a comprehensive program of face and body treatments, using Elemis aromatherapy products. Among the services are stress-reduction aromatherapy massage; Reiki; reflexology; and body wraps. The Spa's newest addition is an 80-minute hot stone treatment that concludes with a traditional massage.

Round Hill also has a children's program called Pineapple's Kids' Club, open daily from 9 a.m. to 5 p.m., with a full daily schedule of activities for all ages. Childen under 3 years old must be accompanied by a nanny anywhere else. New amenities include Xbox, a foosball table, and entertainment for young adults as well as children. Also available are half and full-day kids camps with traditional Jamaican folklore storytelling, craft-making, and sport and sea activities. Some new family programs offer a stargazing beach picnic with s'mores and hot chocolate for the children and wine for the parents, as well as excursions and other activities to be arranged through the concierge.

Times have changed, and so have the owners of the villas, but Round Hill is still glamorous in a way that's hard to find.

ROUND HILL HOTEL AND VILLAS ★ ★ ★ ★
PO Box 64, Montego Bay, Jamaica, W.I.
Phone: (800) 972-2159, (876) 956-7050; **Fax:** (876) 956-7505; **e-mail:**

reservations@roundhilljamaica.com;
www.roundhilljamaica.com
Owner: Round Hill Developments Ltd.
General Manager: Josef F. Forstmayr
Open: Year-round
US Reservations: Direct to hotel, (800) 972-2159; Elegant Resorts of Jamaica, (800) 237-3237
Deposit: 3 nights
Minimum Stay: Christmas/New Year's, President's Weekend, Easter, and Thanksgiving holidays, inquire
Arrival/Departure: Transfer service arranged for fee
Distance from Airport: (Montego Bay Airport) 10 miles; taxi one-way, $35; free daily shuttle to town once daily
Accommodations: 110 rooms (36 in Pineapple House, 13 with 2 double beds, 23 king; 74 rooms and suites in 27 private villas with twins and kings; all villas staffed, 23 with private pools)
Amenities: Air-conditioning, ceiling fans; bath with tub and shower, bathrobes, basket of Elemis toiletries; telephone; kitchen in villas; ice service; nightly turndown service, room service 7:30 a.m.–9:30 p.m. (additional charge); beauty salon; Pineapple House rental with VCR or DVD, $30 per day; radio; boutiques; afternoon tea in cocktail bar; Internet access service for a fee
Fitness Facilities/Spa Services: Fitness room with exercise equipment; aerobic, exercise, yoga classes; jogging trail, weekly nature walk; beauty salon, spa (see text)

Sports: Infinity-edge swimming pool, 23 private pools for villas; 5 Laykold tennis courts (2 lighted), equipment free, proper tennis attire required; snorkeling gear; kayaks, golf arranged at four Montego Bay courses; free transfers to Tryall for golf daily at 9 a.m.; a shopping bus weekdays at 10 a.m.; water sports for fee; deep-sea fishing, horseback riding arranged
Electricity: 110 volts
Dress Code: Casual during day; dining areas, long trousers and collared shirt for gentlemen, no shorts after 7 p.m., except Mon
Children: All ages; cribs, high chairs; babysitters; children's dinner served from 6 p.m. May 1–Oct 31; half price meal plans for children under 12; Kids Club (see text) and more
Meetings: Up to 120 people for weddings
Day Visitors: Welcome; reservations for lunch or dinner required
Handicapped Facilities: No
Packages: Honeymoon, wedding, family packages, Platinum (All-Inclusive)
Rates: Two people, daily, EP. *Christmas* (Dec 18–Jan 3): $729–$1,399. *High Season* (Jan 4–mid-Apr): $599-$1,149. *Low Season* $379–$789. Villas with 2- to 6-bedrooms, including FAB daily, $1,100–$6,000 and $800–$3,600, respectively. Weekly rates available, inquire.
Service Charge: Included
Government Tax: Included

TRYALL CLUB

Montego Bay, Jamaica, W.I.

To take afternoon tea on the terrace of the 19th-century Great House at tradition-rich Tryall is to glimpse the grand style of colonial life in bygone days. (No wonder the British didn't want to give up the empire!)

To spend a week in a villa at Tryall is to peek at the lifestyle of the rich, more than the famous—and today more American than British.

To play golf on Tryall's famous 18-hole championship course, one of the best in Jamaica, is to experience the island's beauty while being humbled by the difficulty of these benign-looking greens. And to travel the 2,200 acres of this former sugar and coconut plantation is to understand why its aficionados say, "There will never be another Tryall."

Located on the northern shores of Jamaica, Tryall, awarded AAA Four Diamonds, is an exclusive luxury suite and villa resort of great distinction. Its vast acres flow from forested mountainsides through manicured gardens to the sea. At the center the restored 19th-century manor house sits high on the hillside with gardens sloping down to the beach. The site catches a constant breeze and commands breathtaking, wide-angle views.

The gracious Great House, with parlors, dining room, and broad terraces, is the hub of the resort's social life. Two long 1- and 2-story wings perpendicular to the Great House houses the hotel's spacious, elegant 13 Great House villa suites of 1- and 2-bedrooms, which are among the finest in the Caribbean. All overlook the gardens and the fairways, with magnificent, expansive views stretching to Montego Bay. Some are duplex suites, others are on one level; all have living and dining areas and fully equipped kitchens. The upper floors of the duplexes have small balconies; those below have terraces.

The guest rooms are individually furnished in British-colonial style, accented with a museum collection of antiques and art belonging to individual owners. Recently all the rooms and suites were refurbished with handsome new fabrics and posh marble bathrooms, several with Jacuzzi baths.

You can take breakfast in your room (your housekeeper will cook breakfast and lunch for you at no additional charge; an excellent food shop is on the property) or in the Great House. A casual lunch can be taken in the delightful setting of the Beach Cafe.

The 73 estate villas, ranging from 2 to 8 bedrooms, are Tryall's crown jewels. All in harmonious, traditional design, the privately owned mansions, with names like Linger Longer, Tranquillity, and No Problem, are exquisitely furnished and fully staffed. They are set in spacious lawns and gardens, providing greater privacy than the Great House suites. Each villa has its own pool and staff: cook, chambermaid, laundress, and gardener. The 4- to 7-bedroom villas have a larger staff. You may choose to dine in your villa or at the Great House.

On Wednesday down by the beach, an early-evening barbecue features Jamaican dishes, entertainment by a Jamaican folklore group, and a crafts fair. The setting for dinner—weather permitting, on the lamp-lit terrace—may be more spectacular than the food, although menus are changed daily, relying more on fresh, seasonal ingredients. The service is exemplary. Dinner might be followed by light entertainment. Guests usually adjourn to the popular bar. Monday night guests are invited to the general manager's cocktail reception, where they can meet and mingle with guests and club staff. A spacious and well-equipped center houses Tryall's Hummingbird Kids Club, where the kids enjoy fun activities such as treasure hunts, face painting, crab races, and sessions on Jamaican folklore that score high with young families.

Tryall's tennis center, rated among top resort facilities worldwide, has a resident pro, Richard Ferdinand, who organizes weekly tournaments and helps put together foursomes. He also oversees the resort's popular Junior Tennis Camps.

The golf course, familiar to television audiences as the host of the Johnnie Walker Championships, tops the list of Tryall's sports facilities. The attractive course runs along Tryall's 1½ miles of seafront and through palm groves and rolling terrain, with fairways bordered by fruit and flowering trees, and rises to forested hills before returning to the sea. There is a jogging track near the Great House and a range of water sports by the beach.

The beauty salon near the Great House offers a variety of spa services, while massage treatments are available in villas. For fitness enthusiasts, Tryall has a fitness center, an activities coordinator, and yoga, aerobic classes, and dance lessons in reggae and soca. Marine biologist T. J. Jett heads up the Tryall Nature & Wildlife program, which takes guests on rain forest hikes and coastal reef exploration. And for those who had something less strenuous in mind, Tryall is an official bird sanctuary.

Tryall is tony, gracious living at its best with the facilities of a modern resort. Honeymooners and romantics of all ages will not find a more beautiful place, and families are among the most dedicated fans. But Tryall is a resort with a clubby ambience. If you are a part of the club, you will love it. If not, come with friends.

TRYALL CLUB ★ ★ ★

PO Box 1206, Montego Bay, Jamaica, W.I.

Phone: (876) 956-5660; **Fax:** (876) 956-5673; www.tryallclub.com
Owner: Privately owned units
Managing Director: Gerald Giarla
Open: Year-round
US Reservations: Karen Bull Associates, (800) 238-5290; **Fax:** (404) 237-1841; **e-mail:** karenbull@mindspring.com
Deposit: 25 percent; 60 days cancellation in winter, 30 days in summer
Minimum Stay: 14 nights at Christmas; 7 nights in villas; applicable at other times, inquire
Arrival/Departure: Transfer service on request
Distance from Airport: (Montego Bay Airport) 14 miles; taxi one-way, $35 for 1 to 4 passengers
Distance from Montego Bay: 12 miles; taxi one-way, $30 for 1 to 4 passengers

Accommodations: 13 Great House villa suites of 1 and 2 bedrooms; 59 estate villas with 2 to 7 bedrooms
Amenities: Great House: air-conditioning, ceiling fans; telephones; bath with tub and shower, hair dryer, basket of toiletries, bathrobe; beauty and massage salon, gift shop, cigar shop, art/craft gallery, convenience store; room with computer/Internet connection and fax for guest's use; for villas, inquire
Fitness Facilities/Spa Services: See text
Sports: Freshwater swimming pool; 9 Nova cushion tennis courts (4 clay and 5 Nova cushioned hard courts, 5 lighted), equipment rentals, resident pro; golf, caddies required, pro, pro shop; jogging trail; Sunfish, windsurfing, paddle boats, snorkeling; scuba diving, fishing, waterskiing, sailing, horseback riding arranged
Electricity: 110 volts
Dress Code: Casual by day; elegantly casual for evening with long trousers and collared shirts for men year-round
Children: All ages; cribs, babysitters; Kids Club daily program
Meetings: Up to 100 people; breakout rooms and team building activities
Day Visitors: Welcome
Handicapped Facilities: Limited
Packages: All-inclusive, golf, tennis, and others available
Rates: Great House, two people, daily, EP. *High Season* (early Jan–Apr 16): $440–$550. *Low Season:* $275–$395. Inquire for villa prices. Temporary Membership, per adult: $100 per week or $20 per day
Service Charge: Included
Government Tax: Included

BREEZES GRAND NEGRIL RESORT & SPA

Negril, Jamaica, W.I.

Do you want it all on a vacation? To leave your worries on the doorstep? Then Breezes Grand Negril might be the answer. It guarantees everything under the sun. In fact, it even guarantees the sun.

Breezes Grand Negril is the Super-Club flagship of its nine resorts. In late 2009, SuperClubs underwent a rebranding of its properties, renaming some and changing the amenities offered in others. For example, the Negril property has shortened the hours for room service and made it only available to upper-category suites; neither complimentary laundry nor the sample spa treatment are offered, but at the same time, prices were lowered. With Breezes label, the best known and most popular of the group, SuperClubs is aiming for consistency, the benefits of name recognition, and a broader audience.

Set in 22 acres of tropical gardens just north of Negril on Jamaica's southwest shore, the resort curves around a 2-mile crescent of white-sand beach on Bloody Bay and is made up of several components, each with different architectural details.

You enter under a modern, glass-topped porte cochere to a pink stone and marble passageway with ponds and fountains and a colonnaded courtyard with a gigantic floral display at the center. Its pink stone walls are enlivened with paintings by local artists from Kingston-based Chelsea Galleries. From here, you step into a large lobby with the desk where you check-in in one corner, a concierge desk in another, and, as incongruous as it may seem, a huge water-wheel turning slowly and spilling water into nearby pools. Farther along, a sidewalk opens onto the large open-air, main restaurant, bar, and the main swimming pool to one side and a series of specialty restaurants on the other. Parts of these areas are faced with glass brick walls, an art deco feature from the 1930s. Tucked under the lobby on the ground floor are slot machines, a game room, and a business center with Internet access.

Cupping the crescent-shaped beach, almost from one end to the other, are the Mediterranean-style 2-story semi-detached cottages housing the all-suite accommodations. They include spacious junior suites, 1-bedroom suites, a Royal suite, a Presidential suites, and 8 luxury beachfront Jacuzzi suites. All offer comfortable living areas furnished in mahogany and private terraces with a view of the beach, ocean, or manicured gardens. Some 52 rooms are reserved for the clothes-optional beach tucked discreetly at the southwestern end of the resort.

The majority are beachfront split-level junior suites with king-size or twin beds and a step-down living room area with sofa, coffee table, desk, and patio or balcony. All are air-conditioned and have cable television, CD player, small refrigerator (stocked with water and soft drinks daily), safe, direct-dial telephone, hair dryer, iron and ironing board, tile and dark green marble bathroom with Jacuzzi bathtub or multihead Euro-flux shower.

In addition to accommodations, all meals, airport transfers, taxes, and gratuities (no tipping allowed), Breezes Grand Negril's all-inclusive rates include special amenities such as premium brand cocktails, instruction and equipment for most water and land sports, daily recreational activities and nightly entertainment, and complimentary weddings (see below for details). A registered nurse is also on the premises.

The resort's 6 restaurants provide a broad selection that includes the open-air Gran Terrazza serving breakfast and lunch buffets and afternoon tea, plus 2 dinner events—the Beach Party on Monday and Grand Gala Buffet on Friday. La Pasta, an inside/outside "sidewalk" cafe, offers Italian fare; and next door, The Grand Cafe serves continental dishes at dinner in a casually elegant atmosphere (no shorts). Open for dinner only are Reggae Cafe, a Jamaican eatery, specializing in jerk chicken and pork, roast fish, and other local delicacies; Piacere, the gourmet restaurant that offers French and Italian nouvelle cuisine; and best of all, Munasan, a Japanese restaurant with teppanyaki stations and sushi bar. Reservations are required for the latter two. After dark the beat goes on at Amici, the piano bar, and Atlantis, the disco, as well as themed parties in the Gran Terrazza.

Tucked away in the gardens under the shade of a gigantic, beautiful old cotton tree is a tree-house snack bar at the center of the property and one of the resort's 7 bars. It is open 24/7 and serves light fare. Up in the trees with it is one of the resort's 3 large, outdoor Jacuzzis.

Nearby, too, is the Blue Mahoe Spa and fitness center. The spa has 3 air-conditioned treatment rooms and steam and sauna rooms, encircling a plunge pool for cool, post-sauna dips. There are also 4 cliff-side gazebos for open-air massages by the sea. Treatments are a la carte. The gym, open 24/7, has 2 air-conditioned exercise rooms with Cybex equipment including free weights and Olympic barbells, treadmills, Stairmasters, and stationary bikes. There is also a padded aerobic platform overlooking Bloody Bay. The gym offers daily classes for power walking, aerobics, aquacise, body sculpting, weights, and stretch. Aerobics sessions include soca and reggae dancing. The facility has licensed resident and visiting instructors and certified personal trainers.

At the beach, the water-sports shop offers diving, Hobie Cat sailing, snorkeling, water-skiing, windsurfing, kayaking, beach volleyball, indoor games room, and glass-bottom boat rides. Tennis lessons and tournaments are arranged by the resident pro; scuba resort course costs $70 and a PADI certification, $350; additional scuba diving is free.

Breezes Grand Negril is big on weddings and even has a wedding coordinator to attend to the details. Its complimentary wedding package for a minimum 3-nights' stay includes marriage license, minister, witnesses, bouquet of tropical flowers and boutonniere, champagne and traditional Jamaican wedding cake, and arrangements for the ceremony. All a bride and groom need to do is pick a location in the gardens, on the beach, or at a cliff-top gazebo. A photographer can be arranged at an additional cost, and couples are responsible for the necessary legal fees. The resort has specials for honeymooners or couples celebrating an anniversary or renewing their vows—for a minimum of 6 nights, they get free legal fees. Breezes Grand Negril is designed for couples, singles, and families with children 16 years and older.

Oh, and about those guarantees—it's something like having year-round weather insurance. The Sunshine Guarantee: For every day the sun doesn't show its face during your stay, SuperClubs will give you a credit voucher equal to that day's Super–Inclusive room value, good for one year toward another SuperClubs vacation. No Hurricane Guarantee: Should a hurricane strike the resort, guests will receive reimbursement for the value of disrupted nights and a voucher for a future stay for the same number of disrupted nights.

There's also a Satisfaction Guarantee. If you are not 100 percent satisfied with your holiday at the resort, and if, after notifying the general manager of the problem, he is unable to rectify the situation by the second night of your stay, SuperClubs will issue you a credit voucher for the value of the unused portion of your stay, good for up to one year at a SuperClubs resort.

BREEZES GRAND NEGRIL RESORT & SPA ★ ★ ★

Norman Manley Boulevard, PO Box 88, Negril, Jamaica, W.I.
Phone: (876) 957-5010; **Fax:** (876) 518-5147, (876) 957-5517, (800) 467-8737; **e-mail:** info@superclubs .com; www.breezes.com/resorts/ breezes-grand-negril
Management: SuperClubs
General Manager: Roberto Pellicia
Open: Year-round

US Reservations: (800) GO-SUPER, (800) 467-8737
Deposit: Secure with credit card
Minimum Stay: 3 nights; 5 nights Christmas/New Year's
Arrival/Departure: Airport transfers included in rate
Distance from Montego Bay: 55 miles; 90-minute drive from Sangster International Airport in Montego Bay
Distance from Kingston: 3½-hour drive
Accommodations: 210 suites private patio or balcony (presidential suite, 8 luxury beachfront Jacuzzi suites; 200 beachfront, ocean view, or garden split-level junior suites and 1 bedroom, with king or twin beds)
Amenities: Business center with Internet access; private terraces, air-conditioning, cable television, CD players, room refrigerators, safes, hair dryers; complimentary laundry; spa services; valet and dry cleaning services; fitness center; sauna, Jacuzzis; Sunshine, No Hurricane, and Satisfaction guarantees
Fitness Facilities/Spa Services: Spa with treatments for fee; Cybex gym; power walks, aquacise, and aerobics classes; reggae and soca dance classes; 5 Jacuzzis
Sports: 2 pools (1 in main beach area, 1 at au naturel beach); 4 tennis courts (2 lighted) with lessons and tournaments; golf with transfers and green fees included, scuba resort certification ($70 charge; PADI $350), snorkeling, water-skiing, windsurfing, Hobie Cat sailing, kayaking, beach volleyball, indoor games room, 5 Jacuzzis, glass-bottom boat rides
Electricity: 110 volts/50 cycles
Dress Code: Resort casual; cover-up for Gran Terrazza; shoes and slacks for men required for Piacere
Children: None under 16 years of age
Meetings: Meeting facilities for up to 800 people
Day Visitors: Yes, must be booked in advance; day pass $79, 10 a.m.–6 p.m.; night pass $99, 6 p.m.–2 a.m.
Handicapped Facilities: Yes
Packages: Wedding, honeymoon, golf, Epicurean weekend
Rates: Per person, per night double, *High Season* (Jan 1–mid–Apr): $260–$355. *Low Season:* $225–$350.
Service Charge: Included
Government Tax: Included

COUPLES SWEPT AWAY

Negril, Jamaica, W.I.

If 10 tennis courts, a fully equipped gym, 2 racquet courts, a squash court, an aerobics center, an Olympic-size swimming pool, unlimited golf, and yoga sessions hit the right buttons, you'll think you're in heaven when you arrive at this spiffy resort, which sweeps around the white sands of Negril Beach. And these marvels are part of an all-inclusive package: You pay nothing extra for meals, beverages, use of sports facilities, or even transfers and gratuities.

Couples Swept Away has found a niche within the niche of Jamaica's all-inclusive resorts. Not as frenetic or glitzy as most, but more romantic than some of its neighbors down the beach, Couples Swept Away enjoys a laid-back, serene ambience geared to people interested in keeping fit even when on vacation.

You don't really have to be a health and fitness nut to enjoy Couples Swept Away—mildly interested will do. No one will push you to rise at 7 a.m. and hit the courts before the sun gets too hot (besides, the courts are lit for night play) or note if you don't show up for aerobics. The marvelous sports facilities are right here, on the premises, when—or if—you want to work out and use them.

Here you vacation in sync with nature. Wind chimes fill the air; flowers and tropical foliage dress the grounds. The Veggie Bar serves up incredible fresh fruit and vegetable drinks that look more like works of art than beverages.

The architecture and decor throughout show a sense of style. Low-key and in stellar good taste, the guest rooms as well as public areas make use of the best examples of Jamaica's superior-quality furniture, crafts, and art. Earth-toned fabrics, natural woods and ceramics, and rattan pieces contrast well with the terra-cotta floors, which are practical as well as attractive.

The guest rooms, clustered tightly between the road and the beach, are in villa-style buildings of cream stucco trimmed with rich, dark hardwood and linked by a labyrinth of garden walkways. Floor-to-ceiling louvered doors and windows, helped by ceiling fans, encourage sea breezes to cool your suite. Spacious verandas with built-in divans and comfy rattan lounges lure you to laze away the hours gazing out to sea.

There are three categories of accommodations in the original section of the resort, comprising 140 suites. Garden Suites are the farthest from the beach. Atrium Suites, on or close to the beach, are in groups of 4 rooms that share a central garden. These can be a bit noisy if your neighbors have loud voices. Both the garden and atrium suites have huge verandas. The third type is villas directly on the beach. Each has 2 beachfront suites upstairs with a separate veranda, and 1 suite on the ground floor, also with a private veranda.

A major expansion in 2006 added 172 new suites, all with king beds, television, and minibar, plus the addition of a large conference room, a full-service spa, a disco/piano bar, Internet cafe, wine bar, logo shop, pool with swim-up bar, 2 Jacuzzis, a beach grill, and a large open-air restaurant with a show kitchen.

Directly across the road from the resort's front entrance is the 10-acre Sports and Fitness Complex, the most comprehensive facility of its kind in Jamaica—if not the Caribbean. In addition to the air-conditioned racquetball and squash courts and the lighted tennis courts (hard and clay), the fully staffed facilities include a 25-meter lap pool, a complete gym with Cybex, an aerobics center with an ExerFlex floor (it gives when you bounce), a basketball court, aquacise, saunas, steam rooms, whirlpools, bicycles, a jogging track, and a pro shop. The complex hosts trendy fitness workout classes including "butts, guts, and thighs"; boxing and instruction; superabdominals, basketball clinics and games, Step 101; stretch classes; and a circuit cardio routine. All these are in addition to a mind-boggling daily schedule of exercise sessions and clinics, from aerobics and power walks to tennis and yoga. The center offers fitness assessments and evaluations and has personal trainers available by appointment.

Water sports include Sunfish sailing, windsurfing, waterskiing, snorkeling, and scuba diving—all with instruction. A dive resort course is included; PADI certification is extra. A free-form pool and a whirlpool are alongside a great beach. Unlimited golf at nearby Negril Hills Golf Club is included; transportation is provided.

The expanded Oasis spa has 9 treatment rooms, including 3 couples massage rooms, a hydrotherapy room, and a Vichy room with a 9-head shower and offering a wide range of treatments including the new Bamboo Fusion massage and its signature "Reggaesage" treatment. Beauty and body services are an additional charge. Wedding spa packages are also available.

Buffets feature international fare with a Jamaican flair, and table service is available. Pizza lovers might easily get swept away with the fresh renderings in the Patois Patio, an open-air restaurant with a large show kitchen. Feathers, the resort's top restaurant, is open in the evening, offering sophisticated international and Caribbean selections with French influences. The Seagrape Cafe in a romantic, open-air setting by the beach features grilled fare with Jamaican flavors. There's also Lemongrass, a Thai specialty restaurant, and a 24-hour grill. The piano bar is lively in the early evening, and a resident band plays nightly for dancing. Varied entertainment—a native floor show or a Jamaican band with a cabaret singer—is scheduled throughout the week. You'll find a game room with billiards and cable television.

Most guests come from the United States and Canada, but the number coming from Europe, other Caribbean islands, and Latin America is growing. In addition to its obvious appeal to fitness-oriented couples, Couples Swept Away has great charm for honeymooners and romantics of all ages.

COUPLES SWEPT AWAY ★ ★ ★
Norman Manley Boulevard, Box 3077, Negril, Jamaica, W.I.
Phone: (876) 957-4061, (876) 957-4040; Fax: (876) 957-4061; e-mail: inquiry@couples.com; www.couples.com
Owner: Issa Hotels and Resorts
General Manager: Ricardo Bowleg
Open: Year-round

US Reservations: (800) COUPLES (268-7537); online booking available at www.couples.com
Deposit: $400, 45 days cancellation
Minimum Stay: 3 nights
Arrival/Departure: Transfer included in all-inclusive package
Distance from Airport: (Montego Bay Airport) 60 miles, 1½ hours by car
Distance from Negril: 3 miles; taxi one-way, about $10
Accommodations: 312 rooms in 2 sections. Original 26 two-story villas, all suites with king beds and verandas; 64 garden; 56 atrium; 20 beachfront. New section are all suites with king bed, television, and minibar (48 Garden Verandah; 48 Ocean Verandah; 48 Beachfront Verandah; 24 Great House Verandah; 4 Great House Jacuzzi)
Amenities: Air-conditioning, ceiling fans; bath with shower only, hair dryer, basket of toiletries; telephone, iPod/MP3 docking station, CD player, coffeemaker; iron and ironing board; room service for continental breakfast, ice service, nightly turndown service; spa (extra charge for treatments)
Fitness Facilities/Spa Services: See text
Sports: See text
Electricity: 120 volts
Dress Code: Casual by day; casually elegant in evening
Children: No
Day Visitors: $100 per day provides access to Sports Complex and Resort
Meetings: Up to 200 people; also for weddings
Handicapped Facilities: No
Packages: All-inclusive, honeymoon, wedding ceremony complimentary

($250 government license and processing fee extra)
Rates: Per couple, per night, **All-Inclusive.** *High Season* (mid-Dec–mid-Apr): from $530. *Low Season:* from $385.
Service Charge: Included
Government Tax: Included

ROCKHOUSE HOTEL AND RESTAURANT

Negril, Jamaica, W.I.

Rockhouse was one of Negril's first hotels. Flower children put this then-undiscovered hideaway on the map in the early 1970s. But in 1995 Inhouse Hotels, owned by three enterprising young Aussies, purchased the old Rockhouse and renovated and upgraded it to such a degree that it became a new hotel.

Situated in the rocky area of the west coast on 4 acres at the top of a cliff that drops precipitously to the sea, Rockhouse is comprised of 20 thatched-roof, octagonal cottages of rock and wood in a jungle of exotic gardens. It reminds some people of a South Seas island and others of an African village.

Two particularly welcome amenities that the new owners added were a restaurant (the old hotel never had one) and a cliffside, freshwater swimming pool (which replaced a small, saltwater tidal pool). The pool, carved from rock at the edge of the cliff, pleases former guests who might not have cherished diving into the sea from the rocks, although the water here—aptly named Pristine Cove—is perhaps the cleanest

177

and clearest in Negril. Ladders and stairs carved into the rock provide easy access to the water for swimming and snorkeling on the nearby reef. There is no beach but many sunning places. These cozy corners, built out over the rocks, have two lounge chairs and an umbrella and provide greater privacy and direct access to the sea. They also make a fine perch for watching dolphins or sunsets. An outside pavilion is used for yoga and special events. The restaurant, built of stone with a thatched roof, has a cantilevered balcony suspended over the cove. It serves 3 meals daily and features local specialties, as well as a broad wine list. There is also a full room-service menu; with the installation of a phone system, guests can order from the restaurant to have food served in their room or anywhere on the property.

Recently, Rockhouse opened Pushcart for casual dining, located on the old Pirates Cave property that adjoins the hotel. Taking its inspiration from Jamaican street food, the restaurant's menu includes such treats as peppered shrimp, a specialty of the Black River area; fish with bammy, like that sold by vendors in Port Royal; and other homecooking favorites. Pushcart, which is open to the public, has an open kitchen design, as well as a rum bar, and great sunset views. It complements the Rockhouse Restaurant, which provides a more refined Caribbean epicurean experience. The resort's executive chef, Kevin Broderick, was award the 2010 Jamaican Chef of the Year.

Even with all the changes, the resort maintains its seclusion and Jamaican flavor as a rustic escape with a primitive

charm, light-years away from the action of Negril.

Regardless of how rustic the accommodations may look from outside, they are quite comfortable inside. The stone and wood, peaked-roof cottages have sliding glass doors that provide great vistas and lead outside to a terrace. They have an indoor toilet and sink and an enclosed outdoor shower open to the skies. The cottages are set far enough apart to offer privacy, too. Most are situated near the water's edge so you can fall asleep to the sound of the surf.

The original cottages are furnished with comfortable beds, and electricity runs the air-conditioning, ceiling fans, and minibars. All cottages have queen-size beds. Four cottages have a sleeping loft with 1 double and a twin bed. Some of the cottages have stone facing on the outside and inside. The modern bathrooms are separated from the sleeping area by an attractive stone partition. Other cottages have brightly painted exteriors and terraces.

Perhaps the biggest change came to Rockhouse when air-conditioning was added to all the accommodations along with safes, CD players, and free wireless Internet access available 24/7.

Rockhouse has another 14 rooms in 2 two-story cement-block buildings (well disguised with colorful exteriors and wooden slat doors under thatched roofs). Less expensive rooms in the block farthest from the sea have small indoor bathrooms; more deluxe rooms are found in the building near the pool. The latter has 8 rooms with tiled baths and large patios at the front and back, each separated from the others by an outdoor shower and tropical garden. The rooms are outfitted with furniture designed for Rockhouse and made from local woods.

Eight premium villas, larger than the existing ones, were built over the water on the cliff's edge, facing west with sunset views. Each thatch-roofed villa has an enclosed outdoor shower open to the skies and a spacious, wraparound private terrace and sliding glass doors providing great vistas of Pristine Cove. All rooms have ceiling fans, safes, and minibars. Another new category, the garden villa, consists of 2 villa rooms and has water views, but not on the cliff edge; these are slightly less expensive than other villas.

Rockhouse has a pressurized water system with master tank storage, while power from backup generators ensures continuous service. The entire property runs on solar-heated water with electrical backup. There's a Rockhouse boutique and a sunset bar.

The Rockhouse Spa works with spa consultant Linda Hall and Jamaican-based Caribbean Essentials to develop new local spa wraps, scrubs, and oils. Spa treatments are undertaken "on-the-rocks" in the cliff-edge massage cabana, at the Caribbean drench hut (which feels like a warm Jamaica rainfall), inside the 8-room garden spa, or in one's room. Yoga classes are offered daily in a specially built yoga room. Rockhouse has its own wedding specialist, Inise Lawrence, who is also resident general manager.

Rockhouse's commitment to the environment earned it Green Globe Certification in 2010. The hotel's commitment to sound environmental practices covers its entire operation to reduce its use of natural resources, minimize air emissions and use of hazardous materials, and give preference to locally sourced products. A commendable effort of the resort is Rockhouse Foundation, a US–chartered nonprofit organization established in 2003, primarily focused on support for education in childhood. Thus far, the foundation has invested in excess of $1 million on Negril area community projects including the renovation and expansion of the Negril All Age and Basic Schools, building a new library for Negril, and the current capital project, the renovation and expansion of the Little Bay School. In each of these learning environments, students were sitting in overcrowded classrooms under leaky roofs, with poor wiring and other problems, adding up to an inadequate learning environment.

Rockhouse has built a reservoir of loyal fans, particularly behind-the-scenes people from the movie and music world, such as producers and directors. But now, with the greater amenities, almost anyone who wants a close-to-nature experience, without giving up comfort and still able to be at the heart of the action in Negril, could be happy here.

ROCKHOUSE HOTEL AND RESTAURANT ★ ★ ⌣
PO Box 3024, West End Road, Negril, Jamaica, W.I.
Phone: (876) 957-4373; **Fax:** (876) 957-0557; **e-mail:** info@rockhousehotel .com; www.rockhousehotel.com
Owner: Inhouse Hotel, Ltd.
General Manager: Charlotte Wallace
Open: Year-round
US Reservations: Direct to hotel at bookings@rockhousehotel.com

Deposit: 3 nights
Minimum Stay: 3 nights during US public holidays
Arrival/Departure: Transfer by car from Montego Bay $80 for up to 4 people, by bus $20, one-way
Distance from Airport: (Montego Bay Airport) 56 miles (2-hour drive); bus one-way, $80 up to 4 people
Distance from Negril: 2½ miles; taxi one-way, $5–$8
Accommodations: 34 rooms (8 premium villas; 12 cottages, 5 studios of which 2 have bunk beds, 9 standard rooms), all with terrace or balcony and queen-size four-poster bed; 4 cottages with additional sleeping loft with double bed and twin
Amenities: Ceiling fan, stand fan, air-conditioning; safe, CD player in villas; minibar; telephone; bath with shower,

hair dryer and iron available; room service; video monitor
Sports: Swimming pool, daily yoga classes; horseback riding, tennis, golf, sailing, snorkeling, diving, and other water sports arranged
Electricity: 110 volts
Dress Code: Informal
Children: 12 years and older; no charge for third-person
Meetings: None
Day Visitors: Welcome to restaurant and spa
Handicapped Facilities: No
Packages: No
Rates: Per room, double, EP. *High Season* (mid-Dec–mid-Apr): $160 to $425 (villa). *Low Season* (mid-Apr–mid-Dec): $125 and $350
Service Charge: 10 percent
Government Tax: 10 percent

TENSING PEN

Negril, Jamaica, W.I.

It's my idea of paradise," the *New Yorker* poet and librettist told me when I asked her why she kept coming back to Tensing Pen. "And I really enjoy the people who come here. My husband and I always meet such interesting people here," she explained.

For a long time Tensing Pen has attracted writers, artists, musicians, and executives with high-stress jobs looking for a place to cool out. They have come to the right place.

It is set atop the cliff on Negril's West End, only 100 yards from Rick's, the town's most famous bar/restaurant,

if not Jamaica's, and a mecca for visitors at sunset. But those at Tensing Pen don't need to move: They have their own front-row perch for sunset watching.

Hidden in a jungle of lush foliage are 22 rooms, far enough apart to provide the ultimate privacy and connected by pebble and stone paths that meander through the dense tropical setting edged by the blue Caribbean Sea.

Four cottages called "Pillars" rest on a high stone base, giving the effect of treehouses. The upper level has a bedroom, bath, and terrace that captures the view and the breezes; below on the ground level is an enclosed outdoor shower.

All the cottages are topped with high, pointed, thatched roofs that from a distance resemble an African village hidden in the jungle. But their rustic exteriors belie their comfortable interiors. Inside, the handsome, airy rooms of white stucco walls are surrounded on three sides by wooden louvers of Jamaican cedar. The dark wood furniture includes a four-poster bed, either queen- or king-size, with mosquito netting (you'll be happy to have it after a rainy spell) draped from the top. The rooms have a basic clean and easy-to-live-with look. All cottages have roomy baths with either a marble or tiled deep shower.

One of the cottages, called the Longhouse, has 3 bedrooms, a large living room and dining room, and is particularly suited for a family or group of friends traveling together. South House is a 2-story cottage, somewhat different from the others. It has 2 separate bedrooms and large furnished balconies with fabulous views. Both levels have a refrigerator. Red Birch Cottage, a villa, is located on the north side of the property and has 2 bedrooms and 2 baths.

Tensing Pen has dining options. Continental breakfast (included in the rate) is always a casual affair. Lunch and dinner are available daily in The Lodge, an open-sided dining room/lounge.

The resort offers moderately priced spa treatments in its "massage hut" on the far north side of the property. Yoga sessions are held there on Tuesday and Thursday; private yoga lessons are also available. Tensing Pen has a freshwater pool.

Tensing Pen is the essence of laid-back Negril. Relaxed, comfortable, friendly, being here is like visiting a friend. It's no wonder that its devotees think it is paradise.

TENSING PEN ★ ★
PO Box 3013, West End Road, Negril, Jamaica, W.I.
Phone: (876) 957-0387; **Fax:** (876) 957-0161; **e-mail:** reservations@tensingpen.com; www.tensingpen.com
Owners: Karin and Richard Murray; Sam and Anne-Marie Petros
General Manager: Joseph and Evelyn Smith
Open: Year-round
US Reservations: Direct to hotel, toll free (800) 957-0387
Deposit: 50 percent of total stay
Minimum stay: 3 nights during US public holidays only
Arrival/Departure: Transfer by van for 1 to 2 people, $70 one-way; add $25 per person based on minimum of 3 persons
Distance from Airport: (Montego Bay Airport), 58 miles (1½ hour drive); Negril Airport, 9 miles, 15-minute drive (taxi one-way, $15)
Distance from Negril: 3 miles; taxi one-way, $10
Accommodations: 17 cottage rooms, a 2-bedroom/2-bath villa, and a 3-bedroom cottage; most rooms double occupancy with queen- or king-size beds; 1 room with 1 queen and 2 singles; 1 room with 1 queen, 1 single; Longhouse: 2 queen suites, 1 single, 2-and-a-half baths, full kitchen with housekeeper
Amenities: Ceiling fan, stand fan; private baths with shower; refrigerator in

all rooms; hair dryer available; safe, CD player in Longhouse, Red Birch Cottage, and main dining area; hammock huts overlooking the sea; sea floats; boutique with beverages; no telephones or televisions in rooms; free Wi-Fi Internet service property-wide

Fitness Facilities/Spa Services: Spa services and yoga on property

Sports: Snorkeling on property, other water sports; horseback riding, tennis, gym, golf; fishing, diving, and tours arranged

Electricity: 110 volts

Dress code: Casual

Children: Longhouse and Red Birch suitable for families with supervised young children; children over 12 accommodated in other rooms

Meetings: Open-air facility at SeaSong Hut for 10 to 12 people

Day visitors: Guests from other Negril hotels welcome for dinner, yoga, and spa services with 24-hour advance reservations

Handicapped Facilities: No

Packages: Customized wedding packages available for 2 or entire property takeover.

Rates: Per room, daily, AP; *High Season* (mid-Dec–mid-Apr): $140 (Garden Cabin)–$629 (Longhouse). *Low Season:* $110–$460 (Great House).

Service Charge: 10 percent

Government Tax: 10 percent

COUPLES SANS SOUCI

Ocho Rios, Jamaica, W.I.

Romance toujours. It's always in the air at Couples Sans Souci. Is it the gorgeous setting or the mellow air of tradition? Or is it the ambience of *sans souci?*

In French sans souci means "without a care," and you will not have many in this pink palazzo by the sea. One of Jamaica's oldest resorts, Couples Sans Souci is nestled tightly in terraced gardens between the mountains and sea on a bluff. Enormous African tulip trees form umbrellas beside a mineral spring that spills down the rockbound cove to the sea. The springs, the centerpiece of the resort's spa, were known for their curative powers as far back as the 1700s. Recent tests found them to be on a par with the most famous spa waters in Europe.

The current resort was born in the 1960s when a Jamaican company created a luxurious beachside residential complex to replace an earlier spa on the site. Stanhope Joel, one of Britain's wealthiest men, teamed up with well-known Caribbean architect Robertson "Happy" Ward to design Sans Souci with a charming blend of Georgian colonial and Italian Renaissance styles. At Ward's request Berger Paints created an exclusive color—Sans Souci Pink—for the hotel, which is still used today. In all, 43 apartments were built and sold to wealthy and titled British travelers.

Ward's plans, advanced for the times, put electrical and phone wires underground; an outdoor elevator from the lobby level to the mineral pool below for easy access; and an oversize outdoor chessboard on the terrace with 2-foot-high pieces (carved by a local Rastafarian who had never seen a chess set!).

The complex changed ownership several times over the years, but the major transformation came in 1984, when a Jamaican businessman formed the Sans Souci Hotel and Club. His wife, an interior designer, renovated the entire complex, dividing the apartments into deluxe rooms and 1-bedroom suites. Her signature, the charming Balloon Bar with its tiny papier-mâché figures of famous balloonists, remains. Jamaica-based Issa Hotels and Resorts, which owns the all-inclusive Couples group, purchased Sans Souci in 2005 and in 2008, completed a multimillion-dollar refurbishing of the resort.

Between 1991 and 1998, Sans Souci was expanded by adding a complex of 72 beachfront Jacuzzi suites, divorced from the older hotel, on a 400-foot private white-sand beach at the western end of the property. They have folding French doors that separate the bedroom from the sitting room; other doors open onto the terra-cotta tile terrace. The bathroom, marbled from top to bottom, has twin sinks, a Jacuzzi tub, and a separate shower. The suites were recently renovated with new furnishings and flat-screen televisions and iPod/MP3 docking stations added.

The units are convenient to the tennis courts, the pool, and Ristorante Palazzina, a casual air-conditioned indoor restaurant with covered terrace where buffet breakfast and lunch are served. The informal setting is convenient for sunbathers (often topless Europeans, who need only add a top for lunch). In the evening Palazzina serves French and Italian cuisine, with reserved seating from 6:30 to 9:30 p.m. Other options include the Beach

Grill for snacks and traditional Jamaican specialties; the Terrace for afternoon tea; Bella Vista, where Jamaican cuisine is served in a casual setting under the stars less than 10 feet from the water's edge (no reservations required); and Casanova, serving gourmet cuisine in a sophisticated atmosphere (reservations required). The resort has a separate, private au naturel beach where there's a pool with swim-up bar and a grill.

Accommodations in the older wings include veranda suites and 1- and 2-bedroom suites with large bedrooms and living rooms. Food service is available 24 hours, and in-suite dining is available from 6 a.m. to 11 p.m.

The main lobby has elegant carved-wood furniture. A game room by the lobby has a pool table, backgammon, chess, and various board games. From the lobby several terraces (one for dining, another with a freshwater pool) shaded by pink-and-white-striped umbrellas and huge tulip trees step down to quiet lanes through the gardens. They lead to the mineral pool, spa, and beachside pavilion with a gym and exercise room.

Charlie's Spa, named for a giant green sea turtle that lived in the mineral springs, is professionally staffed and offers massage, body scrubs, facials, reflexology, saunas, as well as manicures and pedicures in the beauty salon at additional charge.

Live nightly entertainment showcases some of Jamaica's finest cabaret artists, musicians, and cultural shows. Weekly themed galas are also on the entertainment roster and include casino night on Monday, an herbal remedy course for common ailments with local Jamaica herbs, and mixology and cooking classes.

And with a restaurant named Casanova offering candlelight-and-wine dinner and music for dancing under the stars, what else is there but romance in the air "without a care"?

COUPLES SANS SOUCI ★ ★ ★
PO Box 103, Ocho Rios, Jamaica, W.I.
Phone: (876) 994-1206; **Fax:** (876) 994-1408; www.couples.com
Owner: Issa Hotels and Resorts
General Manager: Pierre Battaglia
Open: Year-round
US Reservations: (800) COUPLES (268-7537) or online at www.couples.com
Deposit: $400 to confirm the reservation. Full payment required 45 days prior to arrival.
Minimum Stay: 3 nights
Arrival/Departure: Transfers by air-conditioned bus from Montego Bay included. Intra-island flight transfer arrangement from Montego Bay Airport to Ocho Rios (Boscobel Airport) for one-way, $85 per person, which can be booked with your hotel reservations.
Distance from Airport: (Montego Bay Airport) 60 miles; taxi one-way, $120; $30 round-trip in an air-conditioned minibus. Boscobel Airport: 10 miles; taxi one-way, $20
Distance from Ocho Rios: 2 miles; taxi one-way, $10
Accommodations: 150 suites, most with balconies, in 7 two- and three-story buildings (23 veranda suites, 8 ocean suites, 35 one-bedroom ocean balcony suites, 72 one-bedroom beachfront Jacuzzi suites; 10 penthouses, and 1 stand-alone Hibiscus Cottage—all kings)
Amenities: Air-conditioning, ceiling fans; bath with tub and shower, hair

dryer, basket of toiletries, bathrobe, slippers; radio, CD player, telephone, television; minibar, tea and coffeemakers; iron and ironing board, ice service, nightly turndown service, 24-hour food service

Fitness Facilities/Spa Services: Charlie's Spa and gym with Universal equipment (see text); hair salon

Sports: 4 swimming pools (3 freshwater, 1 mineral water); 3 whirlpools; 2 lighted tennis courts; Sunfloats, snorkel gear, kayaks, windsurfing; diving, fishing arranged; complimentary green fees at Upton Golf and Country Club; Jacuzzi; au naturel beach

Electricity: 110 volts/50 cycles

Dress Code: Casual by day, but cover-up and shoes required in Ristorante

Palazzina for breakfast and lunch, and more elegantly casual in evening

Children: None under 18 years of age (adult couples only)

Meetings: Up to 140 people style; multimedia capability; wedding, too

Day Visitors: Day pass includes food, water sports, tennis, beach, and more (but not the spa), $100 from 10 a.m. to 6 p.m. and $200 to 11 p.m.

Handicapped Facilities: No

Packages: Honeymoon, wedding, all-inclusive

Rates: Per couple, per night, All-inclusive. *High Season* (late Dec–late Mar): from $520. *Low Season:* from $415, double occupancy.

Service Charge/Gratuities: Included

Government Tax: Included

GOLDENEYE HOTEL & RESORT

Oracabessa, Jamaica

After a two-year renovation and expansion, the GoldenEye Hotel & Resort on Jamaica's north coast by the quiet village of Oracabessa, reopened in late 2010.

Owned by Chris Blackwell, founder of Island Records who made Bob Marley famous, GoldenEye was the Jamaica home of author Ian Fleming and the place where he penned all 14 James Bond novels. Fleming's original desk still stands in his former villa today. Through careful preservation, the ambience of Fleming's home endures.

Fleming first came to Jamaica during World War II, sent by British Naval Intelligence to investigate U-boat activities in the Caribbean. He bought the property on Oracabessa Bay and built his dream house, naming it after one of his war missions, Operation GoldenEye.

For decades, this hideaway played host to famous writers, musicians, celebrities, and heads of state. Among those who have planted trees here are Michael Caine, Kate Moss, Quincy Jones, Johnny Depp, and Bill and Hilary Clinton. They were following a tradition started by Anthony Eden, England's prime minister in the 1950s. Today, guests can continue the tree-planting tradition with a $1,000 donation to the Oracabessa Foundation, the GoldenEye-supported charity that educates and encourages sustainable development in the local community.

Set along secluded beaches washed by the Caribbean and surrounded by tropical gardens and the calm waters of the resort's lagoon, the 52-acre estate now had 23 units—11 new Beach Cottages, 6 new Lagoon Suites, Fleming's original villa, and 5 villas built by Blackwell.

GoldenEye, an Island Outpost property, provides contemporary Jamaican-style luxury while preserving the iconic romance of the property's past. The 5 original villas built by Blackwell, with 1- to 3-bedrooms, have been artfully renovated and updated. The innovative design team behind Blackwell's original villas, Ann Hodges, one of Jamaica's leading architects, and Barbara Hulanicki, a well-known interior designer, designed the new accommodations, blending them into the existing resort.

The Lagoon Suites extend 4 feet out over the lagoon—almost as though they were floating atop the water. Each suite provides guests with direct access to the water from a private dock; it also has a secluded garden with an outdoor lounge. From the bathroom, a guest can access the private outdoor shower.

The barefoot-chic, 1- and 2-bedroom Beach Cottages, situated on Low Cay Beach, open directly onto the sand. These cottages have a total living area of 1,110 square feet, Lagoon Cottages, 1,711 square feet, and open directly onto the beach or lagoon. The cottages have a large porch, louvered windows, and double doors, which invite indoor and outdoor living. The bathrooms have a deep, claw-foot tub and double washbasins. The kitchens feature polished concrete countertops and the latest appliances from Smeg's 50s style retro line; the oven and stovetop are designed by Italian architect, Renzo Piano.

The Fleming Villa accommodates groups of up to 10 guests, and includes the original 3-bedroom home (all refreshed and with an outdoor shower) plus 2 new cottages (1 poolside and the other overlooking the sea); a private swimming pool, media room and bar, sunken garden, and direct access to private Fleming Beach.

All villas, cottages and suites are outfitted with custom-designed furniture, bath and beauty products made using local wild-grown botanicals, Royal Hut's fine handmade linens, and flat-screen television with over 200 international channels. With a nod to Blackwell's illustrious history in the music industry, all accommodations feature a Logitech Squeezebox sound system stocked with music produced by Island Records. Complimentary Wi-Fi is available throughout the resort. All units have the latest Panasonic Inverter air-conditioning technology, which utilizes 40 percent less energy. The library has backgammon, chess, and games for kids as well as books.

The menus at GoldenEye's 2 new restaurants, headed up by Chef Conroy Arnold, are created in classic Jamaican style and deliver a bounty of local specialties. Perched on the western arm of Low Cay Beach is Le Bar Bizot, a casual restaurant only steps from the beach and fresh- and seawater swimming pools. The bar is named after Jean-Francois Bizot (1944–2007), the journalist, musical taste-maker, founder of the Paris-based world music station, Radio Nova—and friend of Chris Blackwell—who often visited GoldenEye. The bar serves breakfast, lunch, and dinner and light bites, cocktails, and wines all to the cool sounds of Radio Nova played here regularly.

The Gazebo, the newly designed second restaurant, has an all-day lounge and a dinner-only eatery, serving local fare with an international twist. Built in an aerie, tree house–style on the eastern bank of the lagoon entrance, it overlooks lagoon waters and Low Cay beach beyond. Facing west, the Gazebo is the ideal setting to take in Caribbean sunsets.

FieldSpa at GoldenEye, under the direction of Iona Wynter, a Jamaican Olympic tri-athlete, handles island-inspired activities. Wynter's fun, fitness-focused options range from bay rafting and Jet Ski leg and ab workouts, to triathlon training. A range of beauty and body therapies using locally farm- and wild-grown herbs and flowers are available. The spa is set by the lagoon; guests can kayak or swim through the lagoon to arrive at the spa.

GOLDENEYE HOTEL & RESORT
★ ★ ★

Oracabessa Bay, St. Mary, Jamaica
Phone: (876) 975-3354; **e-mail:** gold eneye@cwjamaica.com www.goldeneye .com
Owner: Chris Blackwell/Island Outposts
General Manager: Jenny Wood
Managing Director: Nick Simmonds
Open: Year-round
US Reservations: (800) OUTPOST (US, Canada) or (876) 622-9007; reser vations@islandoutpost.com
Deposit: 3 nights with reservation; 45 days cancellation prior to arrival, deposit

refunded in full; if less than 45 days, deposit nonrefundable

Minimum Stay: 3 nights

Arrival/Departure: Ground transfer from Kingston (Norman Manley) Airport or vice versa, $200; from Montego Bay (Sangster's) Airport or vice versa, $165; Ian Fleming International Airport or vice versa, $40

Distance from Airport: 90-minute drive from Montego Bay Airport; 10-minute drive from Ian Fleming International Airport (good for private planes); ground transportation, private plane, helicopter available on request

Distance from Capital: 2-hour drive Kingston; 20-minute drive east of Ocho Rios

Accommodations: 21 units (9 beach cottages, 2 lagoon cottages, 6 lagoon suites, Fleming's villa and 3 original villas)

Amenities: Custom-designed furniture; bath/beauty products from local-grown botanicals; fine linens. Bathroom with claw-foot tub, double washbasins, polished concrete countertops and floors; free Wi-Fi throughout property

Fitness Facilities/Spa Services: See text

Sports: Fresh and saltwater swimming pools, 500 feet beach, flood-lit tennis court; snorkeling, kayaking, Jet Skiing, paddle boarding, glass bottom boating, bird-watching, coconut carving, nature walks; deep-sea fishing, scuba diving, boating trips arranged for fee

Electricity: 110 volts; standard US plugs

Dress Code: Casual

Children: All ages; babysitting available upon request

Meetings: No facilities. Fleming Villa could be configured for a small meeting.

Day Visitors: Yes, to restaurants (with reservations)

Handicapped Facilities: Limited

Packages: None

Rates: Per room, per night, double, **FAB:** *High Season* (Jan 8–Apr 30): $840–$1,500. *Shoulder Season* (Nov 11–Dec 14): $670–$1,170. *Low Season* (May 1–Oct 31): $560–$975. For Fleming and other villas, inquire.

Service Charge: 10 percent

Government Tax: 10 percent

JAMAICA INN

Ocho Rios, Jamaica, W.I.

Located by a pretty beach on Jamaica's northern coast, this unpretentious inn has an elegance and timeless grace that can only be acquired through years of not trying to be anything more than it is—simply the best.

Set on a 6-acre rise, it overlooks a cove with a crest of golden sand anchored by rocky fingers at each end. A reef, within swimming distance of shore, protects the waters and the beach, and a gentle breeze cools the air.

Built originally in 1950 as a 4-room inn, Jamaica Inn is owned and operated by the second generation of Morrows from New England, Peter and Eric, who grew up here and consider it their home. They have inherited a fine tradition along with a fine inn, and their pride shows in every minute detail.

The staff, as polished as the silver with which you dine, is part of the attraction. Most have been here at least 10 years and underscore the inn's continuity. When you have breakfast on your terrace—and don't even think of doing anything else—a courtly waiter will lay out a starched white damask cloth, set the table, and provide fresh fruit and home-baked bread.

The inn's exterior is painted a distinctive blue—deeper than Wedgwood—mixed specially for the hotel. It's trimmed with snow-white balustrades and louvered windows. Guest rooms are located in wings that extend from each side of the house to embrace the lawn, pool, and beach.

The hotel's crowning glory is its accommodations. Your bedroom opens onto a large balustraded veranda with a beautiful view. No hotel in the Caribbean has verandas quite like these. Fully furnished as a living room, each balcony has a sofa, wingback chair, breakfast table, antique writing desk, drying rack, and large beach towels. It's like living in a villa. The bedrooms are tastefully furnished with Jamaican antiques and period pieces. You can request king or twin beds.

Room categories—premier, deluxe, superior—are determined by location: on the beach, on the water, or viewing the beach and sea. Each location has something going for it, but the rooms in the 1-story West Wing (Rooms 16 to 20) are very special. They are right at the edge of the sea, with the water lapping the rocks at the foot of your veranda. The water is so clear that you can see to the bottom.

Every year, Jamaica Inn closes for 6 weeks to refresh, renovate, and update guest rooms and facilities around the property as needed. Most recently, the bathrooms of the balcony suites were updated with new tubs, shower glass panels, porcelain sinks on wooden countertops, and accented by oversized mirrors in iridescent glass mosaic frames.

The inn's special suites include the Blue Cottage, directly on the beach, and the stylish Cowdray Suite on the second floor. Then there's the legendary White Suite, on a promontory with its own pool; over the years it has served as the haunt of European royalty, an occasional prime minister, a famous poet, and a galaxy of media stars.

And, there are more choices. Six airy and stylish cottages, which the inn acquired in 2002, were completely rebuilt and refurbished, with decor that combines Jamaican tradition with Indonesian touches. Situated near the spa, the cottages are set in gardens of Jamaican fruit trees and flowering shrubs. Two have 2 bedrooms and terraces overlooking the sea or beach, while Cottage Three and Cottage Four were made into large, luxurious 1-bedroom suites. Sitting at the edge of the bluff, the free-standing suites have wide French doors opening onto spectacular views of the Caribbean Sea. They are furnished with a king-size mahogany bed and a bamboo chaise. White covers contrast with the dark furnishings and flooring; gold and beige pillows add earth tones; and flowers and plants bring a fresh note. Most of the furniture was made in Jamaica. The oversize bath with marble floor has a separate shower and tub. Each suite has an outdoor shower, and Cottages One to Five have small infinity pools just off the bedroom.

If you can pull yourself away from your comfortable room, you will find the beach to be one of Jamaica's finest. You can take up residence under a thatched umbrella; the pretty oval pool and sea are only steps away.

If you are more energetic, there's a croquet lawn, tennis next door, and terrific snorkeling off the beach. Sunfish, sea kayaks, and snorkeling equipment are available without charge, as is the expanded gym with new equipment. Anthony, the beachman, will take you sailing, or if you had something less strenuous in mind, the resort's KiYara Ocean Spa offers an eclectic menu of treatments from around the globe. The spa is housed in thatched-roofed huts with hand-carved wooden pillars overlooking the sea. And for the e-mail addicted, there's a computer in the library, as well as wireless there and on the terrace.

Dining at Jamaica Inn is a special experience, whether in the romantic ambience of evening or breakfast on your veranda. The resort's young chef has added lighter contemporary fare and Jamaican specialties to the traditional repertoire.

Guests gather for cocktails at 7 p.m. on the front terrace and dine at 7:30 p.m. on the lamplit lower terrace, where the soft music of the resident band sets the mood. The palms sway gently overhead, and the band serenades with quiet tunes for dancing under the stars. It's straight out of a Dick Powell or Myrna Loy late-night movie: the romance of the Tropics. It's pure schmaltz. And it's wonderful.

While some might find Jamaica Inn a bit old-fashioned, most guests want it no other way. The Morrows frequently ask their guests—most from the United States—if they want less formality. The answer is always, "Don't change a thing." I agree.

JAMAICA INN ★ ★ ★ ★ ★

PO Box 1, Main Street, Ocho Rios, St. Ann, Jamaica, W.I.
Phone: (876) 974-2514, -2516; (800) 837-4608; **Fax:** (876) 974-2449; **e-mail:** jaminn@cwjamaica.com; www .jamaicainn.com
Owners: Eric and Peter Morrow
General Manager: Mary Phillips

Open: Year-round
US Reservations: (800) 837-4608; **Fax:** (876) 974-2449
Deposit: 3 nights; 50 percent on booking and balance 45 days in advance for Christmas/New Year's; full stay deposit for Feb, 30 days in advance
Minimum Stay: 10 nights Christmas/ New Year's; 5 nights, midweek in Feb; 4 nights, Thanksgiving Week. Cancellation, 30 days winter, 14 days summer; 45 days Christmas/New Year's and Feb
Arrival/Departure: Transfer service arranged for charge
Distance from Airport: (Montego Bay Airport) 1½-hour drive by private car, with refreshments, one-way, $115; by shuttle bus, $25 per person
Distance from Ocho Rios: 2 miles; taxi one-way, $10
Accommodations: 47 rooms and suites in 1- and 2-story wings with terrace; king beds convertible to twins; 4 two-bedroom cottages
Amenities: Air-conditioning, ceiling fans; bath with tub and shower, hair dryer; direct-dial phone with Internet access; nightly turndown service, ice service; room service with $5 charge 7:30 a.m.–11 p.m.
Fitness Facilities/Spa Services: Fitness room with exercise equipment; full service spa
Sports: Freshwater swimming pool; free tennis nearby; water sports; special rates for golf at Sandals Golf and Country Club; horseback riding arranged
Electricity: 110 volts
Dress Code: Informal during day. After 7 p.m., shirt with collar required (jacket optional). In Feb men wear black tie for

dinner; women, long dresses; neither required

Children: No children under 12 years old in winter; none under 10 in summer.

Meetings: Off-season, may book entire hotel

Day Visitors: Yes, with charge, based on availability

Handicapped Facilities: No

Packages: Honeymoon, weddings; Jamaica Inn/Round Hill combination

Rates: Two people, daily, **EP.** *High Season* (mid-Dec–mid-Apr): $503–$818. *Low Season:* $307–$456. White Suite and Cottage Three: $1,805 winter, $934 summer. Inquire for other suites and cottages.

Service Charge: 25 percent

Government Tax: 25 percent

SANDALS ROYAL PLANTATION

Ocho Rios, Jamaica, W.I.

What's old is new and what's new is old—that could be the tagline for Sandals Royal Plantation.

Quietly elegant and stylish, the Sandals Royal Plantation is a beach hideaway set on 17 acres of manicured tropical gardens on 2 private white-sand beaches overlooking the Caribbean Sea.

Built almost five decades ago in classic British colonial style, the historic resort, formerly Plantation Inn, was acquired in 2001 by Butch Stewart, who is best known for his all-inclusive Sandals group. Stewart renovated and reopened the resort as Sandals Royal Plantation, to be the flagship of a new group of luxury resorts aimed at recapturing the grace of days gone by, with less formality, modern amenities, and activities not imagined 50 years ago.

Situated on the north coast a few miles east of Ocho Rios, the resort is 90 minutes by car from Sangster International Airport in Montego Bay. Guest transfers by private taxi are included in the rate.

From the entrance, you step into a checkerboard, marble foyer and bar and a large game room decorated with fine Jamaican antique mahogany furniture and a large-screen television. The game room opens onto a big balcony with a large dining terrace and lounge area with views of the sea. The resort has a spa, dining options from casual to white-glove service, and a variety of sports and recreation.

Sandals Royal Plantation's accommodations include spacious, very comfortable suites with ocean views and most with balconies, and a 3-bedroom villa. There are seven categories of suites. The well-appointed rooms have custom-crafted mahogany furniture, king-size beds, air-conditioning, ceiling fans, dataports, safes large enough for laptops, satellite television, CD players, and large bathrooms faced with colorful tiles. The posh 3-bedroom Villa Plantana has a private pool and comes with a personal butler and chef.

Sandals Royal Plantation's top accommodations are the 2-bedroom Prime Minister Suite (2,100 square feet), atop the west wing overlooking the property's west beach; and the one-bedroom Governor General Suite (1,500 square feet), which is almost identical

but without a second bedroom. The spacious master bedroom has its own patio and is furnished with a four-poster mahogany bed and large-screen television. The marble bathroom has a deep Jacuzzi tub and separate mosaic shower. The second bedroom with its own private entrance may be booked separately.

Other top category suites are the 1-bedroom Honeymoon Plantation and Honeymoon Grand-Luxe (600 square feet) located on the first to third floors of the east wing, others in the west wing. All have king beds and large balconies, separate living area with large television and VCR, marbled bathroom, and walk-in closet. A special feature is a romantic Roman Spa room outfitted with a marble bar, Cleopatra chaise longue, a whirlpool tub, and wall-to-wall French windows looking out to the sea.

Other suites—luxury, premium, and deluxe—vary by location, but all have a king or 2 double beds (pillow menu is available), sitting area, walk-in closet, spacious bathroom with marble double vanities, whirlpool bath, and separate marble shower. Some have balconies; others have French balconies and all have ocean views.

The Red Lane Spa offers an array of body treatments including an outdoor moonlight couples massage, aromatherapy, and reflexology. Facials, hairstyling, and manicures are also available. Treatments have an additional cost. The facility has steam rooms and a relaxation room. The Fitness Center schedules a variety of classes such as evening yoga classes on the Gazebo Pier.

The resort has a freshwater swimming pool, 2 whirlpools, and 2 private beaches where beach butlers provide food and beverage service right to your beach chair. The resort also offers equipment and instruction for tennis on floodlit courts and for canoeing, kayaking, sailing, windsurfing, snorkeling, and diving.

A daily program of inviting events includes such activities as learning to cook the Jamaican way, watching hand-rolled cigars being made, enjoying Jamaican hot chocolate on the beach, and classical concerts in the elegant drawing room with its Steinway grand piano. Nightly entertainment might be as varied as a jazz trio, pianist, calypso band, or cultural show.

Sandals Royal Plantation's three restaurants with well-developed wine lists, overlook the sea and provide 24-hour-room service. Le Papillon specializes in seafood and boasts a Five-Star Diamond Award. It offers white-gloved service in a formal setting. Reservations are required, as are jackets for gentlemen. The C-Bar, a champagne and caviar bar, is situated within Le Papillon.

La Terrace features a la carte outdoor dining. The Royal Cafe serves grilled items, fresh salads, open-faced sandwiches, and ice cream.

For meetings, the Plantation Room accommodates up to 212 people theater-style and can be divided into 2 rooms.

The resort offers personalized butlers who become the "manager" of your suite during your stay, coordinating and supervising any service that you want for $200 per day.

Sandals Royal Plantation is a smoke-free resort. Smoking is permitted outdoors and in designated rooms. The popular Jamaican cigar-rolling classes led by an in-house expert continue to be offered on Friday afternoon.

Sandals Royal Plantation appeals most to romantics and those who appreciate its "grand tradition" in ambience and service, complemented by modern amenities and creative activities.

SANDALS ROYAL PLANTATION ★ ★ ★ ★
PO Box 2, Main Street, Ocho Rios, Jamaica, W.I.
Phone: (876) 974-5601; **Fax:** (876) 974-5912; **e-mail:** rpmail@jm.royal plantation.com; www.royalplantation.com
Owner: Sandals Resorts International
General Manager: Peter Fraser
Open: Year-round
US Reservations: (888) 487-6925
Deposit: Secure with credit card
Minimum Stay: 7 nights, Christmas/New Year's
Arrival/Departure: Private transfer
Distance from Airport: (Montego Bay) 1½-hour drive
Distance from Kingston: 2-hour drive
Accommodations: 74 suites in 6 categories
Amenities: See text
Fitness Facilities/Spa Services: The Royal Spa; gym
Sports: Swimming pool, water sports with instruction; golf with greens fees and transfers
Electricity: 110 volts
Dress Code: Casual elegance; no jeans, hats, tank tops, shorts, sneakers, or bare feet permitted
Children: Age 18 and older
Meetings: Up to 180 people

Day Visitors: Yes; day pass rates available on request
Handicapped Facilities: No
Packages: Honeymoon, wedding, Fourth Night, others
Rates: Per person, per night, All-Inclusive from $636. Rates include airport transfers from Montego Bay. Free night sales and the "up to 65 percent off" promotions likely to apply
Service Charge: Included
Government Tax: Included

BREEZES RESORT, SPA & GOLF CLUB, RUNAWAY BAY

Runaway Bay, St. Ann, Jamaica, W.I.

This Breezes resort got such a thorough renovation, redesign, and expansion in 2007, it's practically a new resort. Among the major additions were 2 freshwater swimming pools for a total of three; 2 new restaurants for a total of 5; an expanded spa, a new water-sports center, and new rooms and suites with plunge pools.

But the resort's Number One asset has not changed—its golf program. It sets Breezes Runaway Bay apart from its Breezes cousins and all-inclusive competitors.

Located next to the resort, the 18-hole golf course, which SuperClubs owns, is available to guests staying at this Breezes to enjoy free, unlimited greens fees. Better yet, Breezes offers the Golf Academy, supervised by a PGA pro. When it was inaugurated in 1990, it was the first year-round golf school in the Caribbean. It is available to Breezes guests for free; non-Breezes guests pay $45 for half-hour instruction, $90 for 1 hour.

You can have up to 42 hours of golf instruction weekly; the facility has a practice sand bunker, and a chipping green. Golf clubs and carts are available for rent at the pro shop. On the western side of the resort's entrance is a 9-hole putting green; to the east is the golf clubhouse. Travelers who don't know a wood from a five-iron need not fear: Breezes has a lot more going for it.

The resort, set on 27 acres, fronts a wide 2-mile stretch of golden sand on Jamaica's northern shore in Runaway Bay. In addition to the Olympic-size main pool, a freshwater swimming pool serves the group of rooms on the western beach, while another pool with a swim-up bar and misting pool is set along the eastern shore.

Other sports facilities include 4 lighted tennis courts—and instruction; a full water-sports program including snorkeling, windsurfing, sailing, kayaking, and scuba for certified divers, plus a resort course for beginners with certification for a $70 fee. Divers can experience the Jamaica's Canyon wall, located just beyond the beach.

The gym has Nautilus and Cybex equipment and an aerobics and exercise program 5 days per week. There is a jogging track, cricket, volleyball, bicycles and bicycle tours, and a nature

walk. The resort has a games room, a croquet lawn, billiards, and table tennis, and there are enough scheduled activities daily to keep you busy into the night, even if you never get near a fairway. You might try your hand at arts and crafts or the Circus Workshop featuring flying and swinging trapeze and trampoline clinics. There are horse-and-carriage rides, glass-bottom boat rides, themed nights, and beach parties. And when you want to take a break from all the activity, you'll find plenty of hammocks strung throughout the property.

The week starts on Sunday with an orientation and the introduction of the young, cheerful staff, and the the Repeat Guest's cocktail party on Tuesday. The new dining options include the casually elegant Munasan with a sushi bar and Teppanyaki stations, where chefs cook dinner to order; reservations are required; and the casual Reggae Cafe, serving Jamaican specialties 11 a.m. to 6:30 p.m. near the beach. Buffet meals are served in the Beach Terrace, a large open-air pavilion conveniently located at the center of the resort by the beach. Martino's is an air-conditioned, casually elegant Italian restaurant for dinner; reservations are required; and the Starlight Grill serves Asian fusion cuisine for dinner. Midnight snacks are also available at the Reggae Cafe.

The piano bar opens for cocktails, and different entertainment is presented every evening: beach on one night; nightclub or folklore show on another; staff and guest talent night on another; and a cabaret featuring Jamaican performers on intervening nights. The

Club Hurricane disco opens at 10:30 p.m. and goes until the last person leaves.

Guest rooms are located in several 2-story buildings on both sides of the main building and the expansive gardens, connected by "Breezeways." On the western beach is the new block of rooms introducing 30 oceanfront rooms and suites, including 6 one-bedroom suites and 8 veranda suites with private plunge pools. On the eastern courtyard, garden-view rooms were expanded and transformed into 32 veranda rooms, each with plunge pools.

The original guest rooms—all comfortable and with private balconies overlooking gardens and beach—were spruced up with new mahogany furnishings, LCD flat-screen televisions, and high-speed wireless Internet access for a fee. Bathrooms sport a fresh new look, too. The resort's attractive gardens have their own "rain forest."

The Blue Mahoe Spa was revamped into a full-service facility as part of a new Blue Mahoe Spa signature line at other Breezes resorts and offers a wide range of treatments at additional cost.

Breezes is one of the few all-inclusive resorts that welcomes singles. The resort is popular with honeymooners (weddings are offered without additional charge, but there's a mandatory government tax of $250), and it's a bargain for any sports enthusiast. Rates include accommodations, all meals, snacks, premium brand drinks, wine with lunch and dinner; sports with instruction and equipment; golf greens fees; entertainment; full-service weddings; and airport transfers. No tipping is allowed. Airfare is not included.

There are other Breezes resorts in Jamaica, Curaçao, Brazil, and Nassau, Bahamas. As in the other resorts, Super-Clubs backs up its claims with guarantees for credit or money back in case of a hurricane, days without sunshine, and other considerations.

BREEZES RESORTS, SPA & GOLF CLUB, RUNAWAY BAY ★ ★ ★
PO Box 58, Runaway Bay, St. Ann, Jamaica, W.I.
Phone: (876) 633-4000; **Fax:** (876) 633-4123; www.breezes.com
Owner: Innovative Resorts, Ltd.
General Manager: Franklyn Eaton
Open: Year-round
US Reservations: SuperClubs, (800) 467-8737 (877) BREEZES; **Fax:** (954) 342-4462
Deposit: $250 per person within 7 days of reservation; balance due 30 days prior to arrival or on arrival
Minimum Stay: 3 nights; 5 nights during Presidents' Week, Easter, and Christmas
Arrival/Departure: Complimentary transfer service from Montego Bay Airport
Distance from Airport: (Montego Bay Airport) 42 miles (75 minutes by car)
Distance from Ocho Rios: 15 miles (20 minutes by car)
Accommodations: 266 guest rooms and suites (4 ocean-view suites; 30 oceanfront of which 6 are 1-bedroom suites and 8 veranda suites with plunge pools; 32 revamped garden rooms with plunge pools), all with terraces; twin or king-size beds

Amenities: Air-conditioning; bath with tub or shower, hair dryer, toiletries; telephone, television, radio, CD player; wireless Internet connection and Internet cafe for fee; coffeemaker; iron and ironing board; room service for continental breakfast

Fitness Facilities/Spa Services: Blue Mahoe Spa and gym (see text)

Sports: See text

Electricity: 110 volts/50 cycles

Dress Code: Casual; beachwear on Beach Terrace; no shorts or T-shirts in Martino's

Children: 14 years and older

Meetings: Up to 320 people

Day Visitors: Day pass, $65; evening pass, $75

Handicapped Facilities: Yes, wheelchair accessible

Packages: All-inclusive, including greens fees

Rates: Per person, per night, All-Inclusive. *High Season* (Jan 1–mid-Apr): $200–$325. *Low Season:* $175–$300. (See text for amenities included.)

Service Charge: Included

Government Tax: Included

MARTINIQUE

As French as France and equally stylish, Martinique, the island of flowers, is a seductive beauty of savage mountain scenery and sophisticated resorts. From the north the land drops from razorback peaks covered with rain forests and an active volcano to flowing meadows and pastureland, to bone-dry desert. Whitecapped Atlantic waves crash against eastern shores; quiet, dreamy beaches hide in coves on the west. And it's all within a day's drive.

Fort-de-France, the pretty capital, is a shopper's favorite for French perfumes and designer fashions. La Savanne, the central square overlooking Fort-de-France Bay, is bordered by historic buildings and 18th-century town houses. South of Fort-de-France the Caribbean coast is scalloped with white-sand beaches. Pointe-du-Bout, a finger in Fort-de-France Bay, is the island's main tourist center, with hotels, marinas, a Robert Trent Jones golf course, restaurants, bistros, and a casino. The two sides of the bay are connected by frequent ferries.

On the southern shore overlooking Diamond Rock, a 2-mile stretch of palm-shaded beach is popular for windsurfing. Sainte-Anne, an idyllic colonial village around a tree-shaded square, is known for its seafood restaurants. Grande Anse des Salines at the southern tip has the island's most idyllic beaches.

Dominating the northern profile of Martinique is 4,584-foot Mont Pelée, usually crowned with swirling clouds. Its eruption in 1902 was one of the most devastating ever recorded. A north-country tour often returns via the extraordinary memorial of St. Pierre, the town buried in seconds under Mont Pelée's ashes.

Route de la Trace, a central highland road between Fort-de-France and Mont Pelée, winds northward through rain forests; each hairpin turn looks across sweeping views of the capital and coast. On a hillside at 1,475 feet is Le Jardin de Balata, a private botanic garden with more than 1,000 varieties of tropical plants.

On the northern skirt of Mont Pelée, Grand' Rivière, an old fishing village of spectacular scenery, is reminiscent of a Gauguin painting. Big volcanic rocks from Mont Pelée rest at the edge of black-sand beaches where vertical cliffs carpeted with wind-sheared foliage drop to the sea and huge whitecaps roll in from the Atlantic.

Information

Martinique Promotion Bureau/CMT USA; 825 3rd Ave., 29th Floor, New York, NY 10022; (212) 838-6887; Fax: (212) 838-7855; www.martinique.org; e-mail: info@martinique.org

BAKOUA HOTEL

Member of the M'Gallery Collection

Martinique, F.W.I.

The first time I visited Martinique, more than three decades ago, the Bakoua was the only hotel of any size or merit in the area of Pointe-du-Bout—all 30 rooms of it. Today the Bakoua has more than quadrupled in size, and Pointe-du-Bout has mushroomed into the center of Martinique's tourism industry, with many hotels, restaurants, shops, and water-sports centers.

Of course, the ambience of the hotel and its environs has changed completely. If you like to be at the heart of the action rather than sequestered in a quiet retreat, and if you prefer the conveniences of a large resort to the intimacy of a small inn, then you will be happy at the Bakoua.

The lobby captures a panoramic view of the Bay of Fort-de-France. The dining room, with its open-air Creole architecture, embraces the tropical setting that faces the cove of Anse Mitan. You can watch the yachts at breakfast and have a romantic view of the distant lights of Fort-de-France in the evening.

The accommodations are distributed across 4 large buildings. Three are located in a 3-story, large, long white stucco buildings topped by red roofs, all with balconies, overlooking either the gardens or the sea. The buildings are in the gardens on a rise above the bay; the fourth is a 2-story block directly on the hotel's small beach.

The deluxe rooms are fitted with "MyBed"—a soft, feather over-mattress, duvet, and 4 pillows treatment (MyBed bedding is hypoallergenic). If you fall in love with MyBed, you can buy one online at www.soboutique.com.

The guest rooms and suites have modern, minimalist decor while retaining their rich mahogany colonial-style furniture—including some carved headboards on four-poster beds and cane-backed chairs.

In addition to its pretty, oval-shaped swimming pool perched on a terrace overlooking the beach and the bay, the Bakoua offers tennis, windsurfing, an introductory dive lesson, and exercise equipment and aerobics classes in the fitness center. Water sports are available from a nearby dive shop for a fee.

The Bakoua provides thrice-daily shuttle service to the nearby 18-hole golf course designed by Robert Trent Jones (the island's only golf course). Sailing excursions on the hotel's own boat, jeep excursions, hiking, deep-sea fishing, and horseback riding can be arranged. The Bakoua has its own dock where visiting yachts tie up and from which you can take an odyssey of a day or longer.

From the lobby and dining level at the top of the rise, steps lead down to the beach and water sports. Le Coco is the beach bar at the water's edge; La Sirène, a casual but not inexpensive beachside restaurant, serves snacks and a light lunch of salads, fish, and grilled meats. Le Châteaubriand, the main restaurant, offers a buffet breakfast and gourmet dining in the evening, featuring French Creole and international cuisine, as well as nightly musical entertainment. Guests can enjoy steel bands on one night, the Ballet de la Martinique on another, a salsa parade or a fashion parade on others.

Le Gommier, the open-air cocktail lounge off the lobby, offers a ringside seat for sunset along with music for listening. The cozy lounge, with its circular sunken bar, is something of the hotel's social center. The balmy tropical air, the convivial ambience, and the wonderful views of the sailboats in the bay impart the warmth and friendliness of the old Bakoua.

The Bakoua's biggest attraction is its location at the center of Pointe-du-Bout resort life, yet quietly secluded in its own gardens. It's connected by frequent ferries to the heart of the capital directly across the bay and offers the services of a modern resort hotel in the French milieu of Martinique. You might want to brush up on your French.

BAKOUA HOTEL ★ ★ ★
La Pointe-du-Bout, 97229 Les Trois Ilets, Martinique, F.W.I.
Phone: (596) 66-02-02; Fax: (596) 66-00-41; e-mail: H0968-RE@accor.com; www.accorhotels.com/gb/hotel/0968-hotel-bakoua
Owner: Accor/Resort Hotels
General Manager: Frederic Massoubre
Open: Year-round
US Reservations: (800) 221-4542; Fax: (914) 472-0451

Deposit: 10 nights at Christmas; 3 nights in winter, 1 night in summer, 30 days in advance; 21 days cancellation in winter, 7 days in summer
Minimum Stay: None
Arrival/Departure: Meeting service at the airport
Distance from Airport: (Lamentin Airport) 10 miles; taxi one-way, approximately €40 ($54) day, €60 ($81) night
Distance from Fort-de-France: 20 miles (45 minutes by road; 20 minutes by ferry); ferry one-way, €7 ($9.50) round-trip
Accommodations: 132 rooms and suites (including 39 beachside, 53 ocean view, 39 garden view; 38 connecting; 38 family) in 3 three-story buildings and 1 two-story block, all with balconies or patios; king-size or twin beds
Amenities: Air-conditioning; direct-dial telephone, cable television, Wi-Fi, radio; safe; bath with tub and shower, radio, hair dryer, makeup mirror, basket of toiletries; minibar; room service when restaurants operating; concierge; shop
Fitness Facilities/Spa Services: Fitness center with equipment and exercise sessions
Sports: Freshwater swimming pool; 2 lighted tennis courts (night-play charge); windsurfing, kayaks; putting green, table tennis; diving, waterskiing, sailing trips, deep-sea fishing, Sunfish, fishing dock; golf, horseback riding, biking, hiking
Electricity: 220 volts/110 volts
Dress Code: Casual
Children: All ages; cribs; babysitters; one child under 12 years old can stay in garden room with parents free
Meetings: Up to 50 people
Day Visitors: Yes

Handicapped Facilities: No
Packages: Summer, spa, romance, others
Rates: Per room, single or double, daily,
FAB. *High Season* (Dec 17–Mar 11):
€450–€850 ($607–$1,147). *Shoulder*

Season (Mar 12–May 7): €410–€850
($553–$1,147). *Low Season* (May 8–
Dec): €380–€850 ($513–$1,147).
Service Charge: Included
Government Tax: Included

LE CAP EST LAGOON RESORT AND SPA

Francois, Martinique

One of the best kept secrets in the Caribbean is a resort in Martinique that opened several years ago to very little fanfare. Yet, it not only set a new standard for Martinique but is on par with the leading contenders in the Caribbean.

Located on the east coast of Martinique between the towns of Francois and Vauclin, Le Cap Est Lagoon Resort and Spa is an elegant, all-suite resort situated on its own peninsula about a 30-minute drive from the

International Airport in Lamentin. The seaside member of Relais & Chateaux overlooks a lagoon created by protective coral reefs that turn Atlantic waves into gentle waters. In 2010, the resort won a coveted fifth star, judged anonymously by an independent inspection agency overseen by Le Comité Français d'Accréditation, or The French Accreditation Committee (COFRAC)

The long driveway into the resort, bordered by sugar cane and stately palms, is a comely invitation to what lies ahead. At the open-air reception, you are greeted by one of the hostesses (rather than a concierge) elegantly clad in long beige tunics, who serves you a cool refreshment and a soothing cold towel, completes your registration and accompanies you to your suite. The resort's 50 suites are housed in 18 villas designed to resemble a Creole-style cottage with gingerbread trim and set in a profusion of tropical gardens along the seafront and aside the large swimming pool at the center and walkways leading to the boat dock and the beach.

Cap Est has three types of suites: garden; de luxe oceanview with private pool and outdoor shower; and ocean view executive suites with private pool. All are very large, measuring 2,400 feet or more. All suites are air-conditioned with overhead fans and have a bathroom with bathtub, separate shower and toilet, and a terrace.

The de luxe and executive suite bedrooms are furnished with king-size bed, desk, telephone, and have a shower outside in a small enclosed garden. The bathrooms have dual sinks, hair dryer, mirror, scales, and telephone. Executive suites have a dressing room. The living room is furnished with a sofa and loveseat, a plasma-screen television with satellite access, DVD player, cordless phone, safe, Internet access, and fax machine. Its maxibar is equipped with a fridge and espresso machine.

Guests at Cap Est have a choice of 2 restaurants—the casual, beachside Le Campeche for light fare, fresh grilled fish, and lobster, fresh from the lobster tank on site; and Le Belem, which serves a buffet breakfast and offers elegant gourmet dining in the evening. At the center of the room is the wine cellar contained in a huge drum meant to represent the tanks used for aging rum, Martinique's century-old industry. It holds 8,000 bottles of more than 120 varieties of wines from France. Guests also have the option of room service from 6:30 a.m. to 11 p.m. with a charge.

Le Cohi-bar, near the lobby and Le Belém restaurant, is the evening's rendezvous spot before dinner for cocktails and after dinner for entertainment when it features performances by one of the local music groups several times during the week. The bar also has a large choice of rums (more than 100 brands) including old rums from Martinique and a cigar cellar. The resort's has an executive meeting room.

The interior decor throughout the resort is colorful but quiet, and emphasizes natural materials, textures, and exotic woods, with a touch of Asian influence and sense of tranquillity.

The Spa, built with fine marble, is operated in collaboration with Guerlain, the famous French cosmetic and perfume company. The facility has two massage rooms, steam room, and offers seaweed treatments, mud therapy, and hydrotherapy as well as manicures, pedicures, and facials. Cap Est's other amenities include a library of books and DVDs, a well-equipped fitness room, 1 lighted tennis court, and a swimming pool; its private beach provides beach service. Windsurfing, sea kayaking, snorkeling, and kite surfing (with qualified instructor) are available, as is a small catamaran and a motorboat for lagoon and sea outings. The resort can arrange for deep-sea fishing, excursions to nearby islets, golf at the 18-hole Robert Trent Jones golf course in Trois Ilets; car or 4x4 rental are available from Hertz. Cap Est will appeal to anyone who appreciates a refined, sophisticated setting of tropical elegance, sumptuous yet understated accommodations, fine food, and service in a European ambience.

LE CAP EST LAGOON RESORT AND SPA ★ ★ ★ ★

La Prairie 97240, LeFrancois, Martinique, F.W.I.
Phone: +0596 (596) 54-80-80; **Fax:** +0596 (596) 54-96-00; www.capest.com
Owner: Société Hôtelière du Lagon
General Manager: Anthony Torkington
Open: Year-round except from Sept 1 to Oct 15
US Reservations: Relais & Chateaux, (800) 735-2478, or direct to the hotel
Deposit: 50 percent of total stay; 100 percent during the peak season
Cancellation Fees: See website
Minimum Stay: None except Christmas/New Year's minimum 7 nights
Arrival/Departure: Inquire from hotel regarding meeting service at airport
Distance from Airport: Aimé Césaire Martinique International, 10 miles; Private Airport transfer and return: €110

($148) for 1 to 3 persons; €160 ($216) 4 to 6 persons
Distance from Fort-de-France: 16 miles
Accommodations: 50 suites (19 garden, 24 deluxe, and 7 Executive) in 1- and 2-story villa, all with balconies or patios; king-size or twin beds
Amenities: Air-conditioning; direct-dial telephone, cable television, DVD, VCR, radio; safe; bath with tub and shower, radio, basket of toiletries; maxibar; room service; concierge; boutique
Fitness Facilities/Spa Services: Fitness center, spa with 6 treatment rooms
Sports: Freshwater swimming pool; 1 lighted tennis court; windsurfing, kayaks; diving, sailing trips, deep-sea fishing, golf arranged
Electricity: 220 volts
Dress Code: Casual during day; resort elegant for evening
Children: All ages; cribs; babysitters
Meetings: Up to 45 people
Day Visitors: Yes
Handicapped Facilities: Two suites
Packages: Yes
Rates: Per room, single or double, daily, including breakfast buffet. *High Season* (Jan 3–Apr 6): €600 ($810), €800 ($1,080) or €1,000 ($1,350). *Low Season* (Apr 7–Aug 31; Oct 13–Dec 14): €400 ($540), €600 ($810) or €800 ($1,080).
Service Charge: Included
Government Tax: Included

NEVIS

The lovely island of Nevis still typifies the Caribbean as many would like it to remain: gracious, innocent, and charming. Separated from St. Kitts by a 2-mile channel, Nevis rises in almost perfect symmetry from the sea to a dark green cone more than 3,000 feet high at its cloud-capped peak. Stretches of golden beach protected by coral reefs outline the coast.

Nevis was discovered by Christopher Columbus in 1493, and the first settlers came here from St. Kitts in 1628. Tobacco was their first export. By the 18th century sugar had replaced tobacco as the main crop, bringing with it large plantations and great wealth. Soon Nevis became the social hub of the Caribbean and developed an international reputation as the "Queen of the Caribbees."

Charlestown, on the western side of the island, is a West Indian colonial village lined with a medley of colorful old buildings so perfectly caught in time that the place could almost be a movie set. The Hamilton Museum was the home of Nevis's most famous native son, Alexander Hamilton, the first US secretary of the treasury, who was born here in 1755.

North of Charlestown, Pinney's Beach is a 4-mile stretch of palm-fringed sands, where the Four Seasons Resort—the island's first large modern hotel and golf course—is located. Nevis and its sister island of St. Kitts have something of a monopoly on charming historic inns set in old sugar plantations, much as the plantations themselves cornered the market on sugar in their heyday. Morning Star, known locally as Gingerland, has several plantation inns located at about 1,000 feet in elevation on the southern slopes of Mount Nevis. Lanes and footpaths, ideal for hikers, run from one estate to the other.

Information

Nevis Tourism Authority, Main St., Charlestown, Nevis; (869) 469-7550, (866) 55-NEVIS; Fax: (869) 469-7551; e-mail: info@nevisisland.com; www.nevis island.com

FOUR SEASONS RESORT NEVIS

Charlestown, Nevis, W.I.

For the people of Nevis the reopening of the Four Seasons Resort Nevis in December 2010 was like a phoenix rising from the ashes—not once but twice since it first opened 20 years ago. As the largest employer on this island of only about 9,500 people, the hotel's two-year closing after being badly damaged by a hurricane had been a major blow. Now fresh from top to bottom after $80 million spent in reconstruction and $40 million in upgrades and enhancements, the resort is better than ever.

Located on Nevis's leeward coast, Four Seasons enjoys a glorious setting along a 2,000-foot stretch of Pinney's Beach, where hundreds of stately palms grace the property from the sand to the foothills of lofty Nevis Peak. Arriving by boat from St. Kitts, you see the resort in the distance after 20 minutes at sea.

The resort maintains the high standards for which Four Seasons is known, and its facilities are outstanding. Others think so, too: The resort was the first in the Caribbean to receive the highly coveted AAA Five Diamond rating. The resort's commitment to hire and train local people is another plus.

The modern Great House with lounges, bars, and restaurants anchors the complex. Its lobby rises high to a mahogany-beamed ceiling and opens onto flower-filled terraces that lead down to the swimming pools and beach. To one side is a mahogany-paneled library-bar; on the other side is the reception center.

Four restaurants offer a choice of casual or elegant dining. They highlight local fresh fruits, vegetables, and seafood, including lobster. The casual Neve, specializing in Italian cuisine for dinner, is a large, indoor/outdoor restaurant with an open kitchen and a wraparound, screened porch for outdoor eating. Beyond, the Coral Grill, with indoor/outdoor seating and a separate entrance, offers charcoal grilled meats and local fish. A children's menu is available.

The poolside Cabana restaurant is open for lunch, cocktails, and dinner, and there's a separate beach bar. Mango, a casual seaside restaurant serving grilled specialties and West Indian cuisine, is located on the north side of the resort, just past the 18th green, from where diners can enjoy a great view of St. Kitts across the narrows.

The large, luxurious guest rooms are actually junior suites. Their decor is enhanced with stone tiles and soft colors. But the huge bathrooms (with telephones)—marbled from top to bottom—are the real showstoppers. All rooms have large verandas furnished with two wicker lounge chairs, side table and 2 arm chairs. Some of the nice touches include genuine down pillows, individual reading lights that clip onto books, and free laundry room facilities in each building. Dual-line phones are available in all guest rooms.

The resort also has a group of 43 luxury 2- to 6-bedroom villas (some with private swimming pools) available for rent. All are equipped with a kitchen, washer and dryer, multiple televisions, DVD and CD players. These villas enjoy panoramic views of the sea, golf course, and nearby islands; they have fully equipped kitchens and spacious living and dining areas, along with full access to the resort and its services.

Four Seasons' spectacular 18-hole championship course designed by Robert Trent Jones II, put Nevis on the map as a golf destination. The 6,682-yard, par 71 course climbs from sea level up the volcanic slopes of Mount Nevis to an altitude of about 400 feet at the signature 15th hole: an awesome 240-yard carry across a deep ravine.

The resort has 3 infinity-edge swimming pools, including one for adults only, and a large tennis complex. Five courts are lit; 4 are clay, and 6 are hard courts. The resort offers extensive water sports (use of nonmotorized equipment is free) and a fully equipped health club with locker rooms, steam room, weight training, studio classes, and trainers. Exercise, aqua-aerobics, walks, and other fitness activities are offered daily.

There's a variety of hiking tours as well as diving excursions. Several dive programs with a local dive master including a Dive and Dine with the Chef that starts with breakfast, includes a two-tank dive, and a picnic lunch. Participants are challenged to lasso their own lobsters and upon return to the resort, they have dinner on the catch prepared by a Four Seasons chef.

By the beach, 4 free-standing, 200-square-foot cabanas are available for rent on a first-come, first-served basis. The cost begins at $325 per day per cabana in low season, $850 in high season and provides an attendant and array of amenities.

The resort's spa is one of the most attractive in the Caribbean. It has 12 treatment rooms, most found in small West Indian–style gingerbread cottages, set in gardens around a large hot, rock-bound bath to one side and a long, cold-water pool on the far side of an outdoor lounge.

"Kids for All Seasons" is Four Seasons's program (free year-round) for children ages 3 to 9; it has a playroom with supervised activities and an outdoor playground. The resort provides children's beach toys, a bottle- and food-warming service, and supervised lunch, which is optional, as is an early dinner. The program operates from 8:30 a.m. to 5:30 p.m. Several times weekly there are beach activities and a snorkeling and sailing school program for children ages 8 and up. An entertainment center for teens and preteens has video games, billiards, and other activities.

A sea turtle education program developed in conjunction with the nonprofit Sea Turtle Conservancy (formerly Caribbean Conservation Corporation) teaches children about Nevis's three species of endangered turtles. The Adopt-a-Turtle program involves a group of turtles that have been satellite-tagged with transmitters for scientific research purposes, and which can be followed through an Internet-based program at home or at school. The program operates from July to October.

Reminiscent of a Florida golf resort, the hotel is designed to attract groups: small meetings, golfers, families, and honeymooners. Guests, mainly from North

America, range from tots to seniors, but most are active couples eager to enjoy the resort's spa and sporting facilities.

FOUR SEASONS RESORT NEVIS ★ ★ ★ ★

Box 565, Piney's Beach, Charlestown, Nevis, W.I.
Phone: (869) 469-1111; Fax: (869) 469-1040; www.fourseasons.com
Owner: S.K.Nevis Resort Llc.
General Manager/Regional Vice President: Andrew Humphries
Open: Year-round
US Reservations: Four Seasons Resort Nevis, (800) 332-3442, (869) 469-6234
Deposit: 3 nights; 30 days cancellation
Minimum Stay: 8 nights during Christmas
Arrival/Departure: American Eagle has nonstop service from San Juan directly to Nevis where guests are met and escorted to the resort. Alternatively, guests arrive by air in St. Kitts, where Four Seasons representatives meet and drive them to dockside lounge in Basse-Terre to board deluxe launch for 30-minute zoom across channel to hotel. En route, staff completes check-in.
Distance from Airport: (Vance Amory International Airport) 6 miles; $70 per room round-trip transfer. From St. Kitts airport, transfer via 25-minute boat ride, $125 round-trip for adults; $60 children (ages 5 to 11)
Distance from Charlestown: 1 mile; taxi one-way, $15
Accommodations: 196 rooms and suites (41 with 2 double beds, 138 with king-size beds; 17 suites) all with verandas; 43 villas with 2- to 6-bedroom, some with pools

Amenities: Air-conditioning, ceiling fan; telephone, clock-radio, television, VCR; baths with tub and shower, hair dryer, bathrobes, scales, lavish toiletries; stocked minibar; coffeemaker, icemaker; safe; no-smoking rooms; room service; hair salon
Fitness Facilities/Spa Services: Health club and spa (see text)
Sports: Golf (see text); 10 tennis courts (5 lighted), racquet rental; jogging, hiking, volleyball, croquet; 3 freshwater pools; snorkeling gear; abundant complimentary nonmotorized water sports; dive excursions
Electricity: 110 volts
Dress Code: Casual by day; cover-up and footwear in Great House but no swimwear after sunset. For dining room, collared shirts, trousers, closed footwear for men; jacket and tie not required. Dress shorts permitted elsewhere.
Children: See text. Children's pool; babysitting; no charge for children under 18 years old in same room with parents
Meetings: Up to 200 people
Day Visitors: Welcome with reservations
Handicapped Facilities: Yes
Packages: Romance, golf, honeymoon, wedding, villa
Rates: Two people, daily, EP. *High Season* (Jan–mid-Apr): $595–$4,000. *Shoulder Season* (mid-Apr–May 31; Nov 1–mid-Dec): $490–$3,200. *Low Season* (May–Oct): $335–$2,830. Prices include nonmotorized water sports. Villas, inquire.
Service Charge: 10 percent
Government Tax: 10 percent, plus $15 per day Coastal Protection Levy

GOLDEN ROCK INN

St. Georges Parish, Nevis, W.I.

High on the side of Mount Nevis, in an area known as Gingerland, is an unusual, small inn 1,000 feet above the sea. It's on the grounds of an 18th-century sugar plantation set in 25 acres of flower-filled gardens and surrounded by another 75 acres of tropical beauty. Golden Rock was built in the early 1800s by Edward Huggins, whose stone buildings have stood up well to time.

As soon as you start up the narrow lane from the main road to the inn, you know you've arrived at a special place. Rooms with walls of century-old stone masonry, barely visible under curtains of brightly colored tropical flowers, have been converted into the living and dining spaces, with practical additions made where needed.

In 2011 the inn was purchased by New York artists Helen and Brice Marden, whose abstract works are in the Museum of Modern Art in New York. The couple has refurbished the inn, made extensive renovations, and added new facilities throughout the property. The Long House, formerly the old estate's kitchen and storeroom, houses the dining rooms and the bar, the center of social activity in the evening. The rustic bar has a vaulted ceiling exposing the building's old walls. From it hang 2 large wicker baskets—lobster traps used by local fishermen—woven in a typical West Indian design that originated with the Carib Indians, who once inhabited the island. The congenial atmosphere at cocktails and after dinner makes it easy

to be part of the family of new friends. The Courtyard, a flower-graced terrace with the bougainvillea-laden stone walls, is the setting for lunch, afternoon tea, and cocktails, enjoyed to the musical accompaniment of birds and crickets. The old carriage house, recently rebuilt, was transformed into the library whose collection covers a wide range of subjects and authors from around the world. It is enlived with a newly acquired 30-year-old orchid collection.

The Sugar Mill, the original stone windmill tower pictured in the hotel's literature, was built in 1815 to supply power to the plantation. Today, it houses the honeymoon suite but is large enough for a family of 4 or 5. It has 2 floors connected by a winding wooden stairway and is furnished upstairs with a larger-than-king antique four-poster mahogany bed for romantics, and 3 beds downstairs. The rooms have wide window seats for reading or enjoying distance ocean views over the treetop.

Other accommodations are in 7 brightly colored cottages on the mountainside above the Long House, the vivid colors coming from some of Mardens' paintings. Inside, the cottages are serene with white walls and white ceramic tile floors covered with colorful antique Moroccan rugs. Each has a private bathroom and a front porch with a grandstand view. All amenities, such as shampoo, are organic. Hair dryer, coffee and tea maker, ice bucket, and ceiling fan are found in all rooms.

The rooms are basic but comfortable, with island-made furnishings. The most noteworthy are the canopied four-poster bamboo and mahogany beds made by the multitalented operations manager Rolston, who is also acclaimed for his rum punches.

Rolston, Sarah at the front office, and David, the head gardener (whose old-time string band plays on Saturday night) are typical of Golden Rock's gracious, friendly staff, most of whom come from the area and have been with the inn for a decade or more.

Dinner is served from 6 p.m. to 9 p.m. on the deck behind the Long House. The deck has a glass roof and is open on three sides. Weather permitting, you can dine under the stars or, in a new pavilion whose roof is designed to resemble an upside down copper pot, once used to boil sugar. The restaurant's menu offers 10 choices for starters and 8 choices for entrees. The hotel kitchen bakes its own bread daily and makes its own desserts. You will dine on homemade soups and other specialties prepared with herbs grown in the inn's gardens, fresh produce from village farmers, organically grown chickens and eggs, and fresh seafood from local fishermen. Golden Rock, known for its great cuisine, is one of the most popular restaurants in Nevis.

In the gardens between the Long House and the cottages is a large, 50-foot spring-fed pool with a shaded terrace and comfortable chaise longues from which you'll find wonderful views across the southern part of the island and the sea. The inn has a strand of sand on the windward side at Windward Beach for its guests' use. It is a wild, natural beach, and wonderful with good snorkeling (gear provided) and excellent beachcombing; there is no restaurant or bar.

The innkeepers take guests here and to several other beaches from 11 a.m. to 3 p.m. If you prefer to go off on your own, they can arrange a car rental at a good rate, and the hotel will pack you a picnic lunch. Conservationists will appreciate the owners' strong commitment to protecting the local environment. Golden Rock is a natural for nature lovers, with trails and unpaved roads in the immediate area for hiking. The Rain Forest Trail, beginning from Golden Rock, leads up the mountain past several hamlets to the rain forest on the side of Mount Nevis. The inn has a complimentary map for its guests to use. The trail is an easy hike. Keep a watchful eye and you are likely to see some wild monkeys observing you from behind the trees. The inn also organizes garden walks, hikes, and tours for guests, as well as keeping them abreast of interesting activities around the island.

A stay at Golden Rock is an unusual experience. The inn has a loyal clientele: an intellectually curious, well-traveled, eclectic group as likely to come from Europe as the US and Canada. Its historic setting is relished by romantics and history buffs. Its cozy, homey atmosphere makes everyone feel welcome, particularly someone traveling alone. Now, the artist/owners have brought a new dimension to the Rock, including an artist studio, so many artists also find their way to this little Caribbean oasis.

GOLDEN ROCK INN ★ ★ ∾

Box 493, St. Georges Parish, Nevis, W.I.
Phone: (869) 469-3346; Fax: (869)
469-2113; e-mail: goldenrockhotel@
sisterisles.kn; www.golden-rock.com
Owners: Helen and Bruce Marden
Manager: To be announced as of press
time
Open: Year-round except mid-Aug to
mid-Oct
US Reservations: Direct to hotel or the
resort's website
Deposit: 3 nights; 21 days cancellation
in winter; 2 nights deposit, 14 days cancellation in off season
Minimum Stay: None except
Christmas/New Year's holidays
Arrival/Departure: Transfer from St.
Kitts via ferry boat costs $10 per person
and takes 30 to 45 minutes. Contact
hotel for schedule. American Eagle usu-
ally offers daily service from San Juan.
Distance from Airport: 7 miles; taxi
one-way, $25
Distance from Charlestown: 5 miles;
taxi one-way, $18

Accommodations: 7 hillside bedroom
cottages with porches; all rooms with
twin or king-size beds; Sugar Mill tower
for up to 5 people
Amenities: Bath with shower, organic
toiletries, hair dryer; coffee and tea
makers, ice bucket; ceiling fan; no
air-conditioning
Sports: Freshwater pool, transport to
beaches; mountain bikes, mountain hiking; tennis nearby. Waterskiing, scuba
diving, sailing, windsurfing, sport fishing, kayaking, golf, horseback riding
arranged
Electricity: 110 volts
Dress Code: Smart casual at night;
informal in day
Children: All ages; babysitters available
Meetings: Small groups and wedding
parties, up to 26 people
Day Visitors: Welcome
Handicapped Facilities: No
Packages: Honeymoon, wedding
Rates: Per room, double, daily, EP. *High
Season* (mid-Dec–mid-Apr): $260–
$325. *Low Season:* $200–$235.
Service Charge: 10 percent
Government Tax: 10 percent

MONTPELIER PLANTATION
AND BEACH RESORT

Nevis, W.I.

Nestled in lovely gardens and surrounded by 30 acres of rolling terrain, Montpelier Plantation and Beach Resort has an air of timeless grandeur that gives the impression it has been there for three centuries, rather than a mere four decades.

Well, it has, and it hasn't.

The Montpelier Estate, in the interior hills at 750 feet above sea level on the southern side of Mount Nevis, was a prominent sugar plantation in the 18th century, belonging to the governor of the Leeward Islands. Here in 1787 the governor's niece, Frances Nisbet, wed Lord Nelson, the famous British admiral.

By the time James Gaskell, the hotel's previous owner, acquired the property in 1964, the original great house was long gone, but remnants of the mill and other structures were enough to provide foundations to build a small inn. By reusing the original stones and retaining the traditional architecture, the hotel's authentic appearance—at least in the main buildings—was achieved.

In the summer of 2001, Montpelier Plantation was acquired by the Hoffman family, who immediately set about upgrading, refurbishing, and updating the entire resort to make it more relevant to today's travelers. The owners have continued to add new facilities, amenities, and accommodations and to modernize old ones with an eye to appealing to a broader, younger, and more active vacationer. An emphasis on its beach facilities and the resort's new name reflect the effort. An imposing brimstone structure that appears to be a great house was actually the old sugar boiling room, which was rebuilt into a large lounge where evening activities take place. The attractive room's decor is contemporary enlivened with art by local artists on the wall.

The lounge opens onto the courtyard where breakfast is served. It overlooks pretty gardens heavily laced with tropical foliage around a huge 18th-century windmill that once powered the sugar factory. The mill has been converted into a specialty restaurant, dubbed the Mill Restaurant, where nightly guests can dine on an elegant 5-course fixed menu, dining by candlelight with a view of the stars through the Mill's vaulted windows. The gourmet dinner includes a glass of champagne and an intermezzo sorbet. The menu, which changes nightly, can be enhanced with wine pairings or tastings from the Montpelier's extensive wine cellar. Beyond the mill is a modern spring-fed swimming pool bordered by a terrace and bar where lunch is served. Indigo, the pool bar, is a casual dining option offering a tapas-inspired menu and is open Thurs, Fri, and Sat from 6 p.m. to 9 p.m.

The hotel's guest rooms are in cottages beyond the main hall, all with verandas overlooking Nevis's southern landscape and the sea. Many of the cottage rooms have hardwood floors and bathrooms renovated from top to bottom. All have high, beamed ceilings with ceiling fans, making them all the more spacious and airy. They are furnished in a modified minimalist style enlivened with floral arrangements. All guest rooms have air-conditioning and are furnished with fresh fruit and flowers daily. The resort's newest addition is a cottage suite, dubbed "The Little House." Actually, it's a century-old Nevisian cottage, completely renovated and modernized. It has 2 air-conditioned bedrooms, 2 baths, and a full kitchen and is equipped with a MP3 player, television, and DVD player. Incidentally, there is power redundancy for water and electricity, thus helping to ensure self-sufficiency in both.

Another change saw the transformation of a junior suite into the more open, airy garden suite, also with minimalist decor. The entrance, relocated to accommodate a sunken living room, provides panoramic views out to the sea and to Saddle Hill, and steps down to a landscaped private garden and gazebo. The remodeled bathroom has a rainhead shower and a large window looking out on a secluded garden.

Another 4 new villas with unobstructed views have a private gated entrance, plunge pool, and a sitting room with flat-screen television and Nespresso coffeemaker.

Montpelier has a long-established reputation for good cuisine. The kitchen purchases much of its food products from local sources—from vegetables grown by neighboring farmers to the town fishermen's catch of the day. Al fresco breakfast is a treat of local fruits, fresh-squeezed orange juice, and honey and homemade brown bread and johnnycakes. Lunch—a la carte—and tea are served outdoors as well. A continental breakfast can be taken in your room, and the hotel will pack you an early bird travel box. In the Court-yard Terrace, a demonstration kitchen is used alternately for Indigo and for cooking demonstrations.

In the evening before dinner guests gather in the lounge for cocktails and canapés in a weekend-in-the-country atmosphere; new and returning British and other European guests balance out the American ones. The Hoffmans often join their guests for cocktails. Dinner, served in The Terrace, the resort's AAA Four-Diamond restaurant, is a candlelight affair with a set menu offering a choice of entrees; menus are changed nightly. You can dine at tables for two, or you may join others. The dining terrace offers views past the floodlit palm trees to the sea and the lights of St. Kitts. Montpelier sponsors entertainment by a local band during the winter season. The hotel's charming historic setting attracts guests from other hotels for lunch or dinner. It is also a lovely and popular setting for weddings.

The hotel provides free transportation to and from its beach club, Montpelier Beach, on the northern end of Pinney's Beach, about 20 minutes away. Recently, the 2-acre beach site was upgraded and enhanced and its facilities expanded. The gazebos have been enclosed creating 6 private cabanas to offer shelter from wind and rain and to provide more privacy. The main pavilion was redesigned to include lounge seating and full bar service as well as a lunch deck Ocean kayaks and Trek 4300 mountain bikes have also been added. In

the winter season, there's a weekly beach barbecue lunch.

The Sugar Shop, a gift shop, has been relocated and refurbished. It has a guest computer with free Internet access. Wi-Fi Internet access is available at several hot spots and is free for guests. There is also a recreation room with television. The resort's spa is housed in a new private treatment room and offers a selection of spa treatments.

A member of the prestigious Relais Châteaux, the informal retreat with a AAA Four-Diamond rating has a wonderful staff who number nearly three times as many as the guests and who have been with the inn for years. Upon your arrival they will greet you with a rum punch and cool towel. The resort's timeless, unspoiled quality attracts nature lovers and couples of all ages as well as those traveling alone who appreciate its friendly atmosphere. The guests are likely to be college educated, well-traveled, and in their 40s or 50s, younger in the summer.

Montpelier is like a gracious private house—private enough that when Princess Diana needed to escape from the public eye and the British press, this was the place she chose.

MONTPELIER PLANTATION AND BEACH RESORT ★ ★ ★
Box 474, Montpelier Estate, Nevis, W.I.
Phone: (869) 469-3462; **Fax:** (869) 469-2932; **e-mail:** info@montpelier nevis.com; www.montpeliernevis.com
Owners: Hoffman family
General Managers: Tim and Meredith Hoffman

Open: Year-round except mid-Aug–early Oct

US Reservations: Direct to hotel

Deposit: 50 percent; 28 days cancellation for a refund of deposit less 5 percent

Minimum Stay: 10 nights during Christmas/New Year's

Arrival/Departure: Transfer service can be arranged

Distance from Airport: 12 miles; taxi one-way, $23

Distance from Charlestown: 4 miles; daily free transport to town and private beach; taxi, $15

Accommodations: 17 rooms in cottages (all with king-size beds; twins available on request), all with inside sitting area and outside verandas; garden suite (can be combined with an adjacent "plantation" room to create a 2 bedroom suite); 1 two-bedroom Little House.

Amenities: Ceiling fans; telephone with international direct dial; safe; tea and coffeemaker; bath with tub and shower, hair dryer; room service for continental breakfast; no radio, television; all with air-conditioning; free Wi-Fi

Fitness Facilities/Spa Services: Arranged on request

Sports: Tennis, racquets and balls free, professional for extra charge; snorkeling equipment loaned; waterskiing, deep-sea fishing, windsurfing, golf, horseback riding, hiking, eco-rambles arranged; free transportation once daily to/from its beach club on Pinney's Beach

Electricity: 220/240 volts; 110-volt shavers

Dress Code: Informal but with style; men wear long trousers in evening; jackets and ties not required

Children: 8 years and older

Meetings: Small executive groups

Day Visitors: Welcome with reservations

Handicapped Facilities: Limited; property has many stairs

Packages: Honeymoon, wedding, others

Rates: Two people, daily, AP. *High Season* (mid-Dec–Apr 30): $490. *Shoulder Season* (May–early June and Nov–mid-Dec): $390. *Low Season:* $290.

Service Charge: 11 percent

Government Tax: 9 percent

NISBET PLANTATION BEACH CLUB

St. James Parish, Nevis, W.I.

The keystone of the Great House indicates that Josiah Nisbet began building the great house of his sugar plantation on the northern shore of Nevis for his young bride, Frances, in 1778. Nisbet died a few years later; soon after, the wealthy widow attracted the attention of the famous British admiral Lord Nelson—and, as they say, the rest is history.

Today Nisbet Plantation, which has an idyllic location at the foot of Mount Nevis on its own beach (most Nevis plantations were on the mountainside), is a charming plantation inn with a magnificent lawn that flows to the water's edge between double rows of stately palms and flowering gardens. With a little imagination you can easily picture the opulent life here in bygone days.

Nisbet continued as a sugar and coconut plantation until the 1950s, changing hands several times. In 1989 David Dodwell, a well-known Bermuda hotelier, acquired the inn and made extensive renovations, adding deluxe cottages and a handsome beach complex with a freshwater pool, 2 restaurants, and a bar.

An aura of the past continues to permeate the gracious inn, particularly its 18th-century Great House in classic West Indian architecture of gray volcanic stone. The resort's centerpiece, it houses the air-conditioned main dining room furnished with attractive antiques, the lounge with a television, DVD, VCR, Internet access, a library, a bar, and a veranda stylishly furnished with rattan sofas and chairs. It makes an inviting setting for afternoon tea and cocktails, when guests gather to socialize before dinner and to listen to a variety of musical entertainment.Complimentary Wi-Fi is available throughout the hotel and in all rooms and there's a guest computer with Internet access in the lobby.

Next to the Great House is an open pavilion joining the reception area and the fitness center, a small gingerbread-trimmed cottage.

Accommodations are in pretty, pale yellow Nevis-style cottages generously spaced in the ¼-mile palm grove between the Great House and the beach, assuring ample privacy. The cottages, with louvered windows providing cross ventilation from the ever-present trade winds, are actually duplex suites, some with furnished screened patios serving as sitting rooms.

Other accommodations—3 two-story villas near the beach—have 4 premier units each, more spacious and luxurious than those in the duplexes. Each unit has a king-size bed, a step-down living room, a wet bar and refrigerator, and an open patio. Bathrooms have a tub as well as a shower. All guest rooms are furnished and painted in soft colors with stylish fabrics accented with local paintings, terra-cotta pottery, and fresh flowers. Nisbet's beautiful palm-studded beach is protected by reefs, but it can be windy, because it faces the Atlantic Ocean. It was the wind, however, that enabled Josiah Nisbet to put the plantation here in the first place. Now, as then, the wind keeps the air cool and relatively insect-free—and gently rocks the hammocks strung between the palm trees. The resort has a croquet

lawn, a large swimming pool with a hot tub, and a tennis court. The Palms Spa has a full menu of massages, body treatments, facials, manicures, and pedicures using Epicuren, La Natura, and Collective Skin Care products. Among the unusual amenities the resort offers guests is a digital video Flip camera to use, GPS units to navigate the hiking trails on Mount Nevis, and Nisbet's motor scooters to use around the island.

Breakfast is served in an informal setting at Coconuts, the restaurant in the attractive beach pavilion, while lunch is available at Sea Breeze, a beach bar. This is also the venue for the manager's weekly rum punch party and the beach buffet featuring fresh seafood and steak.

Dinner at the Great House, looking out across the avenue of coconut palms to the sea, is the evening's highlight. The romantic candlelit setting in the antiques-filled room, with its original mahogany floors, is ideal for the leisurely dinners of sophisticated European and Caribbean cuisine. During a full moon, when the light shines through the palm trees and reflects on the water, the scene is magical. The upper floor of the Great House has a screened-in veranda with dining tables, giving guests the option to dine indoors in the air-conditioning or outdoors. The Great House also has an outdoor patio on the first floor where afternoon tea is served.

Nisbet is the Caribbean as it used to be, appealing to those who appreciate the island's serenity and want their space. In this relaxing setting you can choose privacy or the company of others, who are likely to be an even mix of Americans and British with a sprinkling of Europeans. Families with children are welcome. Brides will not find a lovelier wedding setting. When couples get married at the inn, they can plant a coconut palm tree and the resort puts up a plaque with their names; on return visits, it's fun for them to see how much their tree has grown.

Some people say Nisbet's atmosphere is formal in an English manner, but I find the inn delightful. It's a bit tony, yes, but not stuffy.

NISBET PLANTATION BEACH CLUB ★ ★ ★

St. James Parish, Nevis, W.I.
Phone: (869) 469-9325; **Fax:** (869) 469-9864; **e-mail:** info@nisbetplantation.com; www.nisbetplantation.com
Owner: David Dodwell
General Managers: Jamie Holmes
Open: Year-round, except for one month, usually Sept
US Reservations: Island Resort Reservations, (800) 742-6008
Deposit: 3 nights; 28 days cancellation in high season; 14 days in low season
Minimum Stay: None, except during Christmas
Arrival/Departure: Airport transfer from St. Kitts or Nevis complimentary to guest staying 5 nights or longer; transfer package from St. Kitts, $70 per person
Distance from Airport: 1 mile; taxi one-way, $22
Distance from Charlestown: 8 miles; taxi one-way, $15
Accommodations: 36 units with king-size beds in 16 duplex cottages with patios; deluxe units have separate living room with convertible queen-size couch; 12 junior suites have living room, terrace, king-size beds, and couch that converts to queen; twin beds available on request
Amenities: Air-conditioning, ceiling fans; telephone; minibar, tea and coffeemaker; bath with tub in deluxe and premier rooms, shower only in superior rooms, hair dryer, bathrobes, basket of toiletries; nightly turndown service, daily ice service, laundry service, iron and ironing board, room service for continental breakfast; free Wi-Fi, hiker GPS, and Flip digital video cameras
Fitness Facilities/Spa Services: Fitness center; spa with full menu
Sports: Freshwater pool; free snorkeling gear, kayaks, tennis; lawn croquet; golf, fishing, windsurfing, scuba, horseback riding, and hiking arranged
Electricity: 110 volts
Dress Code: Informal by day; no beach attire in Great House and no jeans, shorts, or T-shirts after 6 p.m.; casually elegant in evening; jackets and ties not required
Children: All ages; children under 12 years old served dinner at 6 p.m. or by special arrangement; cribs, high chairs; babysitters
Meetings: Small meetings
Day Visitors: Welcome with reservations
Handicapped Facilities: No
Packages: Honeymoon, anniversary, wedding, adventure, all-inclusive, spa
Rates: Per room, double, daily, MAP. *High Season* (Jan–Mar): $670–$895. *Shoulder Season* (Apr–May; Nov–Dec): $445–$670. *Low Season:* $391–$611.
Service Charge: 11 percent
Government Tax: 12 percent

PUERTO RICO

American in tempo, Latin at heart, Puerto Rico is the gateway to the Caribbean. It has big-city action in San Juan and tranquillity in the countryside; glamorous resorts and friendly inns; golf, tennis, fishing, diving, horse racing, and baseball; and more history and scenic wonders than places many times its size.

Puerto Rico's two-year celebration of its 500 years of history in 1992 was centered around the exquisite restoration of Old San Juan, the oldest city under the US flag. Along cobblestone streets, magnificent old mansions are alive with the city's smartest restaurants, shops, art galleries, and museums.

Only 30 minutes from San Juan, the Caribbean National Forest, commonly known as El Yunque, is the only tropical rain forest managed by the US Forest Service. It has recreation areas and trails—and that's only the beginning. Across the center of Puerto Rico, a spine of tall green mountains divides the northern and southern coasts. The 165-mile Panoramic Route winds through the mountains and provides spectacular lookouts, hiking trails, swimming holes, and picnic areas.

Ponce, an architectural gem on the southern coast, is Puerto Rico's second largest town. It undertook a citywide restoration to mark the 300th anniversary of its founding in 1692. West of Ponce on the Caribbean coast, near La Parguera, is one of Puerto Rico's two bioluminescent bays, where microorganisms in the water light up like shooting stars with any movement.

Rio Camuy Caves Park near Hatillo is part of the Camuy River, the world's third largest underground river; you can see caverns as high as a 20-story building. These are but a few of the attractions that enable Puerto Rico to claim it is the "Complete Island."

Information
Puerto Rico Tourism Company, 135 W. 50th St., 22nd Floor, New York, NY 10020; (800) 866-7828; www.seepuertorico.com

EL CONQUISTADOR RESORT & GOLDEN DOOR SPA AND LAS CASITAS VILLAGE

A Waldorf Astoria Resort

Las Croabas, PR

"Hi, there!" the big, muscular waiter with a smile as broad as his shoulders exclaimed, greeting a couple of breakfast patrons, pencil and order pad at the ready. So startled by the robust friendliness were these jaded New Yorkers that it took them a moment to recover their composure. As though on cue, they lifted their shoulders, straightened their travel-weary backs, and responded with smiling faces, "Good morning, buenos dias." Neither could remember when they had been greeted with such enthusiasm by a waiter in the Caribbean, not to mention New York.

Service with a smile is only one of El Conquistador's assets. El Conquistador is a destination in itself. It offers options in accommodations—five separate clusters, each with a different appeal, due to its location and layout; in dining and entertainment—11 restaurants, several lounges and bars, and a casino; and in diversions—an 18-hole golf course, 7 tennis courts, 6 swimming pools, a Golden Door Spa and fitness center, a shopping arcade, marina, water park, an offshore beach-fringed island with water sports, and one of the most beautiful and complete convention centers in the Caribbean. And all of this in a dramatic setting with stunning decor and a multimillion-dollar art collection.

Spread over 500 acres overlooking the fishing village of Las Croabas and Las Cabezas de San Juan National Park on the northeastern tip of Puerto Rico where the Atlantic meets the Caribbean, Puerto Rico's first true megaresort opened in October 1993. It is located 31 miles east of San Juan, about an hour's drive from San Juan International Airport.

Set at the edge of a 300-foot-high bluff and cascading down a heavily wooded cliffside to the shore, the multimillion-dollar resort is a reincarnation of a hotel of the same name built on the site 30 years earlier. El Conquistador, a Waldorf Astoria Resort, was so thoroughly remodeled and expanded that only those with exceedingly keen memories are likely to recognize anything of its forerunner.

To avoid the often sterile, homogenized character of megaresorts and to overcome their huge size, interior decorator Jorge Rosello, a master at space planning best known for his renovation of El Convento and La Concha hotels, drew on Puerto Rico's Spanish heritage to give El Conquistador a distinctive local ambience.

Lounges, lobbies, patios, and plazas lead you from one space to another. Everywhere the eye is greeted with pleasing settings, dramatic vistas, or surprises. Around a corner or by an elevator where most hotels might have a table and mirror, Rosello created a conversation nook; in lounges where guests might idly gaze up to a blank ceiling, he occasionally added an interesting but unobtrusive fresco.

Standard guest rooms, most with terraces, are as large as the minisuites of most hotels. They have the minimalist white walls, furniture, and bedcovers with sunburst yellow and red pillows and throws. Some have 2 double beds, but most are furnished with a king-size one. Rooms also have a sofa that opens into a bed, handsome rattan chairs, a desk, and 3 phones, including one in the bathroom, plus a 2-line cordless phone with dataport and safe. All are air-conditioned and have ceiling fans.

The entertainment unit has a flat-screen television (there's also a small one in the bathroom), DVD, and CD player, iHome stereo/alarm/MP3 docking stations. All guest rooms have high-speed Internet access. The bathrooms are a triumph. Unusually large, the dressing rooms—separate from the bathtub or shower and toilet—have a long marble counter with a sink and a large mirror surrounded by theater lights, plus a separate vanity and chair and a small refrigerator.

In the bathroom you will find a hair dryer, bathrobes, and plush towels. The walk-in closet has a safe and an iron and ironing board. Wall-mounted bedside lamps can be turned up brightly for reading or down low for—well, you decide.

El Conquistador's impressive entrance, reminiscent of the courtyard of a grand palazzo, sets the style for the resort. The large, inviting terrace sits under a high ceiling of staggered, peaked red tile roofs, suggesting houses in an Andalusian village. The tile and marble patio with conversation corners tucked in between the lush foliage has as its focus one of the resort's 5 large bronze sculptures by Angel Botello, the late Spanish-born artist who made Puerto Rico his home for almost 40 years. From the sculpture at the edge of the patio, there is an expansive view of the sea, with Palomino Island and other islets in the foreground and Culebra and Vieques in the distance. Below are bougainvillea-bedecked terraces, fountains, waterfalls, and 3 swimming pools that connect the main building wings.

Las Brisas, the northern wing, and La Vista, on the south, crown the crest of the bluff, providing most rooms with wonderful ocean views.

The lobby bar near the casino is the late-night hot spot with live entertainment by island bands. Club 21 is a sports bar by the casino. Off the main lobby is the nightspot with nightly entertainment; there are also the shops, a Starbucks, and an Internet center for guests to use without charge. The resort also has Wi-Fi. Beyond the casino is an ice cream bar and the coffee shop and family restaurant, Cafe Caribe, offering sandwiches, traditional American dishes, and Caribbean specialties; and on the second level, accessible by an escalator, are 3 restaurants: La Piccola Fontana, Italian; Blossoms, Pan-Asian; and Strip House, the New York City steakhouse. The resort offers a Caribbean meal plan package starting at $259 per night per person that includes accommodations, along with breakfast and dinner options at seven restaurants on property. To one side, the main lobby is connected via a plaza to the convention center—gorgeous and glamorous with its handsome carpets,

glittering crystal chandeliers, and fine furnishings enhanced by original art and antiques, marble, and rich woods. It is the largest, most beautiful convention facility in Puerto Rico, if not the Caribbean, with 4 elegant ballrooms, 37 meeting rooms, terraces, and gardens. The center has a separate entrance and its own activities desk. A helicopter pad is located to its west side.

On the north side the lobby leads to a V-shaped building with 5 floors of guest rooms. The main floor is actually the fifth floor; guest-room floors are built down the hillside.

Las Brisas Restaurant, with casual indoor and outdoor dining terraces, open from breakfast through late evening, offers continental and American fare, including "fitness first" menus and Domino's pizza. Cafe Bella Vista, another casual open-air spot overlooking the swimming pool complex, offers sandwiches and salads and is open for lunch and dinner. Along with 3 pools—one with a swim-up bar—there are 5 whirlpools, lanais, lounge chairs with small red flags to signal an attendant, and the Gazebo, an outdoor bar.

La Vista, the hotel's southern wing, is near the golf and tennis facilities. Rooms on the eastern side overlook the pool complex and spectacular sea views; those on the west look out over the golf course.

Additional accommodations are found in three distinct "villages." Each cluster has its own manager. Las Olas, midway down the cliff, has a private setting intended mainly for honeymooners. Built in a half moon around a large swimming pool, the units have large balconies overlooking the marina and coast. Las Olas and La Marina by the shore are reached from the hilltop Las Brisas via a funicular that runs regularly throughout the day and evening.

La Marina, meant to resemble a Mediterranean fishing village with a boat-filled harbor and waterfront shops, offers accommodations in town houses. It is designed for families and those who want to be near water sports and the water park. Its restaurants include the Sting Ray Cafe, serving seafood specialties, and the casual Ballyhoo Bar and Grill with pizza, salads, sandwiches, and a raw bar.

From La Marina, where sailing and deep-sea fishing can be arranged, water taxis ferry guests in 15 minutes to Palomino, the resort's 100-acre tropical island rimmed with white-sand beaches. The island offers swimming, sunning, snorkeling, sailing, windsurfing, kayaking, horseback riding, and more. All equipment is nonmotorized. Scuba diving can be arranged, and there is a hiking trail. Next to La Marina is the most exciting addition in El Conquistador's recent $120 million renovation: the 2.4-acre Coqui Water Park, the island's first, with something for every member of the family. It's high-tech meets nature in an action-packed 253-foot double innertube slide; high-speed, 40-foot vertical drop; 26-foot serpentine flume body slide; and innertube water rides along an 8,000-square-foot lazy river with wave technology that pushes riders through the river. There is a huge sunbathing deck, a 8,500-square-foot infinity-edge pool, a kids' pool area with a kids slide, the Oasis Bar & Grill, and an area for

events. Park tickets for resort guests cost from $14.95 for children to $19.95 for adults and include tubes, pool chairs, and towels.

Camp Coqui, named for Puerto Rico's indigenous tree frog, the coqui, is the resort's daily supervised activities for children and costs $95 per day. The kids are separated into two groups: ages 4 to 9 and 10 to 13. Camp Coqui offers a wide range of educational and fun-filled diversions, from Spanish lessons and nature hikes to a marine biology session before snorkeling. There's specially designed kid-size equipment, such as mini-windsurfers, tennis, and golf gear. Activities are held at Camp Coqui's facilities on Palomino Island daily from 9 a.m. to 3 p.m. and include snack (for half-day), lunch (if full day), and a signature T-shirt. Babysitting services are available.

LAS CASITAS

On the bluff beyond La Vista is Las Casitas, a resort-within-a-resort where exclusivity is the keynote. It combines the privacy and personalized service of a small hotel with the facilities of a large resort. Designed to resemble a colonial village complete with cobblestone streets, a bell tower, fountains, a public plaza, and villas in the style of Old San Juan, it is the most luxurious part of El Conquistador, offering lovely villa accommodations and personal service—enough to win a AAA Four Diamond rating. The 90 pastel-colored villas, intended for affluent travelers who want privacy and a tony ambience, have

1 to 3 bedrooms, a living room, and a fully equipped kitchen. Those poised on the edge of the cliff have balconies that embrace spectacular views.

Concierge service and private butlers are on hand to pamper guests and fill their every request. They will unpack bags, make reservations, arrange parties, and even cook special meals if asked. The service begins before you leave home with a pre-arrival call to determine your preferred drinks, meals, and other details so that your casita can be stocked accordingly. The royal treatment continues on arrival, when each guest is met at the airport by a resort representative who assists with baggage and transfers. At the resort, Las Casitas guests are personally welcomed by a village host and escorted to their villa, which are fitted with casually elegant, comfortable furniture specially designed for Las Casitas and accented by textured fabrics. All units have entertainment centers in both the living room and bedroom with television, DVD, and CD player and high-speed Internet access. You'll also find a stocked bar, multiline telephones, safe, hair dryer, and an iron with ironing board. The kitchen has an oven, microwave, and coffeemaker, and it's stocked with dishes and cutlery. Las Casitas guests enjoy housekeeping service twice daily and exclusive use of the village swimming pool, Jacuzzi, terrace, and library lounge.

Las Casitas village is convenient to the golf course and tennis facilities, and is next to the resort's fabulous Golden Door Spa with 25 treatment rooms. You can begin with a personal trainer who will analyze your needs, discuss your goals, and design a fitness program that you can take home. Then you have a range of treatments—from massage to aromatherapy and hot stones—from which to select. A fitness center with a full range of equipment will help you keep in shape. The spa has outdoor cabanas for treatments in 3 locations—at the Marina, Palomino Island, and the tai chi lawn.

El Conquistador's 18-hole golf course (6,700 yards, par 72), designed by award-winning architect Arthur Hills, is a beautiful spread across hills and valleys with four small lakes, one with a waterfall. Rain-forest-clad El Yunque is in the background; views of the Atlantic are to the north and of the Caribbean to the east. Six holes with water hazards and tight greens of Bermuda grass challenge a player's accuracy rather than strength. There's a practice putting green and free golf clinic daily. El Conquistador is operated by Troon Golf. The tennis complex has 4 lighted courts, including a stadium court. A daily clinic is conducted by one of the pros. The clubhouse for the golf and tennis complex has a pro shop, locker rooms, and the Grill, an outdoor terrace where breakfast, lunch, and cocktails are served. Golf Grill is a snack bar on the golf course; a refreshment wagon circles the course. Make no mistake, El Conquistador is large—very large. You will sense its dimensions upon arrival and when you first walk through the various lounges and levels to your room. But you will quickly forget about its size when you begin to see the details—and that's the beauty of it.

EL CONQUISTADOR RESORT & GOLDEN DOOR SPA AND LAS CASITAS VILLAGE ★ ★ ★ ★

1000 El Conquistador Ave., PO Box 70001, Las Croabas, PR 00738
Phone: (787) 863-1000; **Fax:** (787) 863-6500
Las Casitas: (787) 863-6746; **Fax:** (787) 863-6758; www.elconresort.com, www.lascasitasvillage.com
Owner: Hilton Worldwide
General Manager/El Conquistador: Dermot Connoley
Open: Year-round
US Reservations: (800) 468-8365; **Las Casitas:** (800) 452-2274
Deposit: 1 night; 3 days prior cancellation
Minimum Stay: None
Arrival/Departure: El Conquistador has a fleet of vehicles to transport guests between San Juan International Airport and the resort. Cost is $74 round-trip per adult and $54 round-trip per child 12 years and under, billed to your hotel account. For Las Casitas, see text.
Distance from Airport: (San Juan International Airport) 31 miles
Distance from Fajardo: 2 miles
Accommodations: 983 rooms, suites, and villas with terraces in 5 locations; 750 guest rooms; 17 suites; **Las Casitas:** 155 casitas (1-, 2-, 3-bedroom villas); either 2 double beds or one king
Amenities: Air-conditioning, ceiling fans; safe; bath with tub and shower, hair dryer, his and hers robes, iron and ironing board; 2 televisions with movie channels, DVD and CD player, iHome dock, 3 multiline phones; small refrigerator; desk; nightly turndown service, room service; casino; spa; shopping arcade; **Las Casitas:** see text
Fitness Facilities/Spa Services: See text
Sports: 8 swimming pools; 7 lighted tennis courts, pro; golf course, clubhouse, pro shop, locker room, bar; 32-slip marina, sailboats, catamarans, yacht charters; deep-sea fishing arranged; Palomino Island with snorkeling, diving, hiking, volleyball, kayaking, windsurfing, horseback riding, new water park, and more
Electricity: 110 volts
Dress Code: Casual by day; casually elegant in evening
Children: Camp Coqui with supervised activities; cribs, high chairs; babysitters
Meetings: Large convention center with 4 ballrooms and 37 meeting rooms, Internet, Wi-Fi
Day Visitors: Yes
Handicapped Facilities: Limited
Packages: Adventure, golf, tennis, honeymoon, family, waterpark; summer, Caribbean meal plan package
Rates: $459–$769; rates vary by season, inquire
Service Charge: 14 percent
Government Tax: 11 percent

THE GALLERY INN/GALERIA SAN JUAN

Old San Juan, PR

Artists don't usually have the temperament for managing a hotel, but for Jan D'Esopo, it's only one of several things on her plate—or palette, in this case. This is an art-gallery-cum-inn, as the name implies, and there is nothing quite like it in the Caribbean. But what really sets the Gallery Inn apart is that it occupies 6 of the oldest buildings in Old San Juan. The last one was added after extensive renovations in 2007.

La Cueva del Indio, as one of the rambling old buildings was known, faces north to the Atlantic Ocean from the topmost crest of the Old City. Strategically located between the two large forts, the structure is the oldest military residence (built about 1750) on the northern side of the old walled city. Historians believe it served as the captain's quarters for the Spanish Artillery.

New York–born Jan and her husband, Manuco Gandia, a native of Puerto Rico, acquired their first building in 1961; its restoration took two years. Today, the complex of adjacent buildings has more than 50 spaces: a maze of rooms, passageways, courtyards, balconies, and gardens on 7 levels. You need a map to find your way around.

The art gallery and its exhibit rooms occupy most of the ground floor and double as the inn's lobby. The entrance is marked only by a street-number sign, but you will know you are in the right place when you see a row of sculpted heads on the windowsill of the silk-screening studio at the front of the house. The gate leads into a small bricked courtyard filled with plants and more sculpture. You may be surprised by the exotic birds—macaws, Moluccan cockatoos, and an Amazon parrot peeping down from trees and perches. The guest rooms are situated in every nook of the 3-story white stucco buildings, and you make your way along narrow steps, around tight corners, and under broad arches. You will discover that the old stone, brick, and wood floors are seldom even, and steps go up and back down to reach some rooms. The handsome, beamed ceilings of ausubo wood (a termite-resistant native tree) are high in most places, but occasionally you might need to bend slightly to make your way. And everywhere plants and flowers overflow their bases.

Every wall and surface, bookshelf and ledge, is enlivened with sculpture and paintings, either by Jan or a young artist she is helping to get established, or by acclaimed artists who come to give seminars or simply to visit. Special rates are extended to artists—who are often seen painting in a courtyard—and musicians, who may exchange a few days' stay for a concert. Pianists Frederic Chu, Jose Ramos Santana, and Michael Lewin are a few of the world artists who vacation and play in the Gallery's handsome Music Room with a 9-foot grand concert Steinway piano. Candlelight chamber music and other concerts, free of charge for the inn's guests, are held frequently throughout the year (schedules available on the inn's website). August is its Music Festival Month. The Gallery is equipped with 7 studios: painting, sculpture, mold making, cold casting, silk screening, and even a micro foundry

for bronze casting. (Inquire in advance if you qualify.)

No two guest rooms are alike in size, decor, or amenities, but all have received a makeover that renovated, refurbished, and upgraded them—some to a deluxe level—with unusual rich fabrics, mahogany four-poster beds, or canopies and Tempur-Pedic mattresses—an unusual extravagance for a small, modest inn. Jan has painted *trompe l'oeil* in most of the rooms. Artists' rooms are nice and cozy but will not necessarily have a view; those without windows might have a painted balcony with a view. Some have terraces; all guest rooms have air-conditioning, telephone, and their own bath with shower.

Basically, the rooms are furnished in Spanish colonial decor, but the artist in Jan has enabled her to mix contemporary pieces, art, and antiques in an eclectic way without being funky. Well, maybe not too funky. To be honest, the entire house, from workshops to the sundeck on top, has a chaotic order to it, which is not surprising given all that happens here—the sculpting, painting, and music practicing—and that, of course, defines a great deal of its charm. One could say that the Gallery Inn is itself a work of art.

The Gallery offers a continental breakfast with fresh tropical fruit, which is included in the rate. Occasionally, Jan creates one of her famous dinners. (In addition to being an artist and innkeeper, she is an accomplished chef and caters elegant dinner parties for local businesses and visiting VIPs. She says she can seat as many as 90 people for dinner, but I haven't figured out where.)

With the addition of more restored buildings, a brand-new large kitchen was installed—and that, apparently, inspired Jan to acquire a full-time chef, a graduate of the Culinary Institute of America in San Francisco. The kitchen serves appetizers and dinner daily. Guests seem to prefer the Alamanda gardens with tables and seating for 30 people for dining. In case of rain or more formal requests, The Cannon Club, the name of the dining rooms below which occupies the entire ground floor of the fifth house, is used; it can sit groups of up to 80 persons. When dining in the garden, guests are surrounded by towers of home grown hydroponic lettuces, tomatoes arugula, and other vegetables and herbs, which land in the mojito making and salad seasoning, an amenity begun only recently. Menus are posted in the website, where more than 100 photos of the rooms and gardens will give you a good idea of The Gallery Inn before and after restoration.

Even more exciting, the newly acquired and restored building made possible the creation of a swimming pool with ancient brick walls as its backdrop and dubbed Sunken Wedding Gardens. In the evening, the pool's indirect lighting creates a magical setting.

The Gallery Inn has a refreshment bar in the main gallery that works on the honor system. You keep tabs and pay upon checkout. The Wine Deck on top boasts being the highest point in Old San Juan with views from San Juan Bay to the Atlantic Ocean and is a great perch for sunsets. Jan often joins guests for wine and tapas in the evening.

The guests who come here—as many from Europe as from the US—are an interesting group, well traveled, looking for the unusual, and as eclectic as the house. If you are exacting or need orderly surroundings to feel comfortable, pass up this one. On the other hand, if being amid art and artists is stimulating for you and you are flexible, undemanding, and willing to forgo some of the usual amenities of a hotel, or might enjoy a heated political discussion with Manuco, the man of the house, or want his opinionated restaurant recommendations–some of San Juan's best restaurants are within walking distance of the inn—you will enjoy a stay here immensely.

The inn is homey as well as historic, but there's no one to pamper you. The owners and their staff will try to accommodate you, but essentially, you fend for yourself. You are welcome as part of the family and encouraged to explore the 7 levels of the old houses, enjoy the paintings and sculpture, ask questions—even pick up a paintbrush if you feel so inspired.

THE GALLERY INN/ GALERIA SAN JUAN ($) ❧
204 Calle Norzagaray, Old San Juan, PR 00901
Phone: (787) 722-1808, 723-6515; **Fax:** (787) 977-3929; **e-mail:** reservations@thegalleryinn.com; www.thegalleryinn.com
Owner/Manager: Jan D'Esopo
Open: Year-round
US Reservations: Direct to hotel
Deposit: 1 night, payable by credit card
Minimum Stay: 2 nights during high season weekends (Nov–Apr)
Arrival/Departure: No transfer service

Distance from Airport: 10 miles; taxi one-way, $20

Distance from Condado Beach Area: 3 miles; taxi one-way, $10

Accommodations: 22 rooms and suites, all with air-conditioning, telephone, and private bath. There are 5 categories: Artist (1 double or queen bed, located in the interior with windows onto gardens and patios); Colonial (larger size, 1 queen or king, opening to interior gardens, patios, or balcony; Family (suite with parlor area, sleeps up to 4, balcony with partial view); Vista (more spacious, 1 queen or king, terrace or balcony overlooking sea or bay); and Top Side Suites (large garden balcony or terrace and Jacuzzi overlooking Atlantic Ocean)

Amenities: Honor bar; room service on request; air-conditioning, swimming pool, private bath, hair dryer, Internet access—computer use available, common area and in-room Wi-Fi access, fax (for guests), photocopy service; no television

Sports: Horseback riding, tennis, boating, snorkeling, scuba, windsurfing, deep-sea fishing, hiking arranged

Electricity: 110 volts

Dress Code: Informal

Children: All ages; cribs available

Meetings: Up to 40 people for meetings, 90 for dinner; 250 for receptions; conference room, banquet room

Day Visitors: Yes, by appointment

Handicapped Facilities: No

Packages: Several 3-day and off-season packages

Rates: Two people, daily, CP. *High Season* (Jan 2–Apr 8): $175–$325. *Shoulder Season* (Apr 9–June 9; Oct–Dec 13): $140–$310. *Low Season* (June 10–Oct 11): $120–$270; for off-season specials and AAA/AARP rates, inquire.

Service Charge: 9 percent

Government Tax: 9 percent

HOTEL EL CONVENTO

Old San Juan, Puerto Rico

This 16th-century convent in the heart of Old San Juan was transformed into a lovely, small hotel, with its historic architecture maintained throughout while the facilities behind its imposing facade have been modernized. By the time the present owners acquired the building, it had had so many incarnations, the fact that they could complete the renovations successfully was nothing short of a miracle.

Originally built in 1651 to house the first Carmelite convent in the New World and occupied by them until 1903, the building stood vacant for a decade until it was finally bought by the Church from the Carmelite sisters for $151. Subsequently, the building was rented as a dance hall and a flophouse without electricity, running water, or sanitary facilities. By 1953 it had become a parking lot for garbage trucks.

To save the historic building from the wrecking ball, Robert F. Woolworth (of the Woolworth family) bought it in 1959 from the Catholic Church for $250,000 and, after three years of renovations and restoration, opened it in 1962 as the elegant, hundred-room El Convento Hotel.

The hotel was a triumph socially but couldn't earn back what had been spent on it, and in 1971 the owner gave El Convento as a gift to the Puerto Rican government in lieu of back taxes. Over the next 25 years, the hotel deteriorated as a succession of management companies operated it. Finally in 1995 it was sold to a group of San Juan business interests that spent two years and more than $15 million (about $275,000 per room) to create a 57-room hotel. Several more millions were spent in 2003 to add 10 rooms on the second floor.

The renovations, which kept the architectural integrity of the original convent, were done by Jorge Rosello, an enormously talented Puerto Rican interior designer and space planner best known for the handsome interiors he created for El San Juan Hotel.

Partially covered during previous renovations, the spacious interior courtyard of the former convent—its arches and balconies hidden for centuries behind its 30-foot-thick walls—is again open to the sky.

The courtyard has three different street entrances. The lower floors of the building house meeting and banquet rooms, along with informal cafes: Patio Del Nispero, which takes its name from a huge tree whose spreading arms shade the courtyard, and offers breakfast and Nuevo-Latino lunch menus and also handles the catering functions. Cafe Caña at the Cristo Street entrance, was said to be Puerto Rico's first rum bar when it opened in 2008. It offers 38 local and 8 international rums and in addition to mojitos, it offers a "Rum Lab," where, by appointment, patrons can learn all about rum. The trendy eatery is open for lunch and dinner and late-night entertaining, serving traditional Puerto Rican fare.

El Picoteo offers a tapas menu and extensive wine list; and Pizza e Birra, the newest addition, offers over 20 different craft beers from around the world, live entertainment, television, and light bites. At Il Perugino, an award-winning Italian restaurant across the way on Cristo Street, guests who dine here can charge the fare to their room.

The hotel occupies the second to fifth floors and is reached by a private entrance and keyed elevator. Guests enter via the former convent entrance and check in at the ground floor concierge and reception desk. The wide corridors and rooms, decorated with handcrafted furniture from Spain, have retained their ancient tile floors (previously covered by carpeting), and their mahogany ceiling beams.

All rooms are air-conditioned and have a multiline telephone with dataport, flat-screen LCD television, Bose stereo radios, complimentary Wi-Fi throughout the hotel, iron and ironing board, coffeemaker, refrigerator with bottled water, safe, hair dryer, and robes. The hotel has a junior suite (Room 404), which is an ideal family suite with 2 double beds in the main bedroom and a pull-out couch in the living room.

Located adjacent to the pool terrace, it enjoys great views, too.

The grandest accommodations are the Vanderbilt suite, named for Gloria Vanderbilt, who stayed there, with a large bedroom and sitting room, elegantly furnished with antiques and rich fabrics; and the Casals Suite, named for Pablo Casals, the famous Spanish cellist who made Puerto Rico his home for four decades.

Hotel guests enjoy a complimentary early evening wine and hors d'oeuvres reception on La Veranda Terrace on the third level where the library is also located, offering guests use of computer and Internet access. The rooftop Mirador Terrace, with wonderful day and night views overlooking Old San Juan and San Juan Bay, has a small swimming pool and a Jacuzzi, and recently, a terrace garden where fruits, vegetables, and spices are grown and used in the kitchen and at the bar.

An indoor fitness center with massage facilities is located on the lower level of the hotel. Through a special arrangement, guests also have access to the beach at its sister hotel in Isla Verde. The hotel offers a business and conference center for up to 300 people.

El Convento, an Old San Juan landmark, is located on historic Cristo Street across from San Juan Cathedral, where Ponce de Leon is entombed, and within easy walking distance of the important historic sights, museums, art galleries, shopping, and some of the top restaurants in the city. It is 5 minutes from the cruise piers, making it convenient for pre- and post-cruise stays.

HOTEL EL CONVENTO ★ ★ ★
100 Cristo St., PO Box 1048, Old San Juan, PR 00902
Phone: (787) 723-9020; (800) 468-2779; **Fax:** (787) 721-2877; **e-mail:** info@elconvento.com; www.elconvento.com
Managing Company: International Hospitality Enterprises
General Manager: Efrain Rosa
Open: Year-round
US Reservations: (800) 468-2779
Deposit: 1 night; 3 days cancellation prior to arrival, otherwise 1-night penalty will apply
Minimum Stay: 3 nights Dec 27–Jan 1
Arrival/Departure: No transfer service
Distance from Airport: (San Juan International Airport) 5½ miles
Accommodations: 58 rooms and suites
Amenities: Air-conditioning, flat-screen LCD television, Bose stereo radio, CD player; refrigerator; multiline telephones with dataport; complimentary high-speed Internet access; hair dryer; bathrobes, coffeemaker, iron and ironing board; safe; nightly turndown service
Fitness Facilities/Spa Services: Fitness center
Sports: Plunge pool, Jacuzzi; tennis, golf, water sports arranged; walking tours
Electricity: 110 volts
Dress Code: Casual by day; smartly casual in evening
Children: All ages; babysitting available; no charge for crib in room; children under 13 free in room with parents
Meetings: 6 meeting rooms; up to 300 people
Day Visitors: Yes
Handicapped Facilities: Yes

Packages: Romance, Pre-/Postcruise; Town and Country; Sun, Fun & History; and others
Rates: Per room, single/double, **EP.** *High Season* (Dec 1–May 12): from

$235; suites, $625. *Low Season:* from $165; suites, $495.
Service Charge: 11 percent
Government Tax: 12 percent

LA CONCHA

A Renaissance Resort

Condado, San Juan, PR

Condado, San Juan's prime resort area, which, after almost a decade of decline, has made a comeback thanks to major hotel renovations, the addition of high-end boutiques—Ferragamo, Chanel, Gucci, among others—and most important, the rebirth of La Concha after being an empty eyesore for 10 years.

The hotel's opening in December 2007 marked, almost to the day, 49 years from when the original hotel opened and was hailed as the masterpiece of the "Tropical Modernism" architectural movement in the Caribbean. Today's La Concha, set on 6 tropical oceanfront acres, has maintained many of the original design elements, while redefining them for the 21st-century traveler. Responsible for the interior decor is Puerto Rican master designer, Jorge Rosselló, whose genius is seen in Hotel El Convento, and other hotels in Puerto Rico.

Now marketed under Marriott's Renaissance brand—the first in Puerto Rico, La Concha was only the first phase of a huge $220 million project that saw the addition of a hotel tower on La Concha's east flank added in 2010 and to the west, the restoration of the Vanderbilt mansion as the centerpiece of another hotel/condo complex.

Already a mecca of urban, seaside Latino chic for hotel guests, visitors, and Condado residents, La Concha boasts 6 restaurants and an elegant open-air plaza with cascading waters, fountains, and pools on one side of the expansive, open lobby.

Perla Restaurant, specializing in seafood and refined contemporary American cuisine, has an unusual and dramatic and setting—under the enormous concha shell, after which the hotel is named—and surrounded by a reflecting pool. The interior design by Jorge Rosselló is elegant with luxurious furnishings and exotic materials including eight hand-blown Murano glass light fixtures that illuminate the shell-shaped ceiling. Its wine cellar holds more than 3,000 bottles with over 800 labels. Open for dinner daily, Perla also offers 30 wines by the glass, all under a special climate-control apparatus on display.

Voga, an Italian Grill overlooking the Atlantic Ocean, serves Italian-American dishes based on old family recipes in a modern ambience. Fresh pastas made daily by Chef Luis Castillo can be enjoyed for dinner. Solera, an open-air, multilevel terrace poolside restaurant, serves light lunches, dinner, and at cocktail time, pitchers of sangría and flavored mojito accompanied by tapas by Chef Janette Berríos. In the lobby, Komakai, a 13-seat sushi bar open nightly, serves sushi, sashimi, traditional rolls, and several signature options. The casual Sidewalk Cafe, a bistro, highlights fresh seafood salads, prepared daily, roast vegetable salads, soups, wraps, smoothies, and pastries. The cafe has entrances from inside the casino, as well as from street level. Aroma, the lobby bar offers continental breakfast, coffee, and cocktails. A full breakfast buffet is also served every morning on the mezzanine level.

La Concha has 248 spacious guest rooms, including 16 suites, in the first building and 235 suites and poolside cabanas in the Suite Tower. Throughout, contemporary design and minimalist decor are brightened with chartreuse, raspberry, and orange pillows and throws. The ocean-view rooms and junior suites are furnished with a king bed and a pull-out couch.

All guestrooms are furnished with 37-inch LCD flat-screen television, DVD player, iPod dock, and video games; premium cable and movie channels; hair dryer; robes and slipper; spa-style showers, mini-refrigerator; work desk with convenient electrical outlets and ergonomic chairs.

The Suite Tower at La Concha Resort has 235 suites, available for long- or short-term stays. There are three room types: one bedroom, two bedroom, and studio suites, all with European-style kitchenettes, entertainment center, custom carpets, turndown service, and panoramic ocean views. The Spa suites have a Jacuzzi on the balcony. The Tower's centrally located Ocean Lounge has a private adults-only pool, valet parking services, and a dedicated concierge.

In addition to a multilevel infinity swimming pool and Jacuzzi, La Concha's oceanfront fitness center enables guests to work out while enjoying expansive views of the sea. A spa is planned.

The state-of-the-art Casino Del Mar, open 24/7, features a VIP high-limit slot parlor with a private cage window and an honor bar stocked with wine, champagne, and hors d' oeuvres.

La Concha's extensive meetings and banquet facilities can accommodate 80 to 800 people in an array of locations, most with panoramic ocean views. These include Las Nereidas, the grand ballroom; Salon del Mar, a compact room with optional outdoor terrace space; 12-person boardroom; Atlantiko, situated under the Perla seashell, accommodating up to 800 people; Mirador, a rooftop space with city views; Indigo, accessible by a glass-enclosed bridge over water; Sereno pool area and Sereno Sand, an "adult sandbox" for team-building activities or cocktails. All are equipped with audio-visual systems, free Wi-Fi, and business center support. The resort has a qualified staff for planning and support for high-tech conferences, events, and for weddings, even with a wedding blog.

La Concha offers complimentary Wi-Fi throughout the hotel, laptops free-of-charge in the lobby, and live music in the lobby bar, a Puerto Rico hotel tradition.

LA CONCHA, A RENAISSANCE RESORT ★ ★ ★
1077 Ashford Ave., San Juan, PR 00907

Phone: (787) 721–7500, (800) 999-2252; **Fax:** (787) 724-1949; **e-mail:** info@laconcharesort.com; www.laconcharesort.com
Managing Company: International Hospitality Enterprises
General Manager: Luis R. Rivera
Open: Year-round
US Reservations: (877) 524-7778
Deposit: By credit card
Minimum Stay: None
Arrival/Departure: None
Distance from Airport: 5 miles
Distance from Capital: 5 miles
Accommodations: 483 rooms and suites. Suite Tower: 1- and 2-bedroom, studio suites; Spa suites with Jacuzzi on balcony
Amenities: Air-conditioning, 37-inch LCD flat-screen television, DVD player, iPod dock, and video games; premium cable and movie channels; hair dryer; robes and slipper; spa-style showers, mini-refrigerator; work desk and ergonomic chairs. Lobby laptops free of charge; live music in lobby bar. Suite Tower: kitchenettes, entertainment center, custom carpets, turndown service; adults-only pool, valet parking, concierge
Fitness Facilities/Spa Services: Fully-equipped gym
Sports: 4 outdoor pools; snorkeling, scuba, golf, boating, fishing, horseback riding, hiking arranged
Electricity: 120 volts
Dress Code: Casual by day; elegantly casual in evening
Children: Yes
Meetings: See text
Day Visitors: Yes
Handicapped: Limited wheelchair-accessibility; dedicated rooms

Packages: PR Experience, romance, wedding, others

Rates: Per room, EP, year-round: from $219 for king, $359 suite

Service Charge: 11 percent

Government Tax: 12 percent

EL SAN JUAN HOTEL & CASINO

A Waldorf Astoria Resort

Isla Verde, Carolina (San Juan), PR

Stylish, luxurious, and fun, the El San Juan lets you have your cake and eat it, too. It's a complete beachside resort only a few miles from the airport but within easy reach of the city center. It's large enough to offer all the facilities you could possibly want but not so large that it loses its personality.

Indeed, the El San Juan is so distinctive you could never confuse it with another hotel. Walk through its lavish lobby, brimming with art and activity, or stroll over to the poolside veranda and gardens, and you'll know immediately that this is like no other place.

The El San Juan does have its quiet corners, but this hotel is really for people who want to be in the center of the action, day or night. It has seven restaurants (each with a different cuisine), 12 bars and lounges, a casino, a disco, three swimming pools, three tennis courts, water sports, a health club and spa, a daily children's program, an arcade of chic boutiques, and a staff of more than

1,000 who make sure it hums around the clock.

Set in 15 acres of tropical gardens on the Atlantic northern coast, the El San Juan is located on the eastern edge of the city. The landmark hotel reigned as the grande dame of Caribbean hotels in the 1960s, but by the decade's end, when Puerto Rico's fortunes had tumbled, the El San Juan closed and the Isla Verde area deteriorated. Williams Hospitality bought the hotel in 1984 and reopened it one year and $50 million later, launching Puerto Rico's tourism renaissance. It's now a Waldorf Astoria Resort, owned by LXR Luxury Resorts, which spent $52 million to redesign, renovate, and refurbish the lobby, guest rooms, meeting spaces, pool and beach areas, and add new restaurants and trendy nightspots.

The El San Juan has actually undergone three transformations by three interior designers, with completely different ideas, working more than a decade apart but resulting in remarkable harmony.

In the 1960s New York designer Alan Lanigan traveled through Africa, Asia, and Europe collecting artwork, relics, and decorative and architectural elements to embellish the hotel. He acquired storefronts to design a shopping arcade, and shipped heavy, centuries-old wooden doors from North Africa; oil paintings and art deco lamps from Europe. In the 1980s Puerto Rican interior designer Jorge Rosello recognized the uniqueness of Lanigan's work and built on it. He enlivened the interior with a more cheerful tropical environment.

The top to bottom renovation brought new restaurants and shops and a new beachfront wing with 21 deluxe suites and a private pool at the edge of the beach and surrounded by tropical gardens. The suites—as large as some New York apartments—are furnished in mahogany pieces with colorful fabrics and pillows and a convertible sofa. Each has a minibar, a safe, three multiline telephones, voice mail, fax-modem outlet, high-speed Wi-Fi Internet access, flat-screen TV, iHome station, and an iron and ironing board. The huge bathrooms have a double-sink vanity, separate shower, and 6-foot-long whirlpool bathtub. In the latest transformation, the most dramatic new settings are the guest rooms and the gardens. Created by Barry Design Associates, who was responsible for all interior renovations, the guest rooms have a total new look. Bathed in white with splashes of fuchsia and chartreuse in pillows, throws, and artwork on the walls, one's eye is immediately drawn to the soft and sensual sheers covering the window and door to the veranda with a hint of orange and a tropical pattern that picks up the colors in the room. Classic lines are mixed with modern materials in the acrylic desk chair and lamp that are replicas of an antique lamp and chair.

The hotel offers a great variety of guest rooms: poolside, ocean, and garden suites, and moderate, standard, and superior rooms and suites in the tower. A few suites have kitchenettes.

For its outdoor transformation, El San Juan called on New York–based nightlife designer Stephane Dupoux who designed the seductive Encanto

Beach Club, meant to create the ultimate outdoor party scene in San Juan's sultry tropical environment. The redesigned deck and poolside areas have an open-air lounge with 24 canopied, double daybeds, 3 private cabanas, 25 retro-circular lounging pods, overstuffed chaise lounges and cocoon chairs, hammocks, swings, a swim-up bar, and outside showers. The sexy ambience goes a step further with subtle scents and a state-of-the-art sound system.

Early birds can be served "breakfast in bed" poolside that can be ordered the night before, and start their Encanto Beach Club mornings with water chi, an aqua version of tai chi, or yoga classes on the beach. The latest addition, the Burger Bar, offers specialty burgers, salads, appetizers, and a variety of cocktails.

For an extra level of luxury, one of the three private tiki hut cabanas is yours for $700 for the day where you'll have Wi-Fi, flat-screen television, minibar and safe. The famous, fabulous, action-center lobby, with new decor including a lovely blue-glass sculpture (the famous oval chandelier is still there) is the hub of the hotel and the best people-watching spot in San Juan. To one side is the Silver Bar, in handsome silver and red. It's the only Cruvinet wine bar in the Caribbean and offers 22 champagnes and wines by the glass. To the other side is the Gold Bar and the casino.

Live entertainment is in the lobby bars and the new Rose Ultra Lounge, which as the name suggests, is designed to appeal to romantics with soft rose tones and candle-lit decor to set the mood. Said to be a first in San Juan entertainment, it stages an original, burlesque-style floor show, "Ran Can Can," complete with fabulous costumes, vibrant music, and beautiful dancers. A contemporary bar with a lounge feel, The Rose caters to a sophisticated crowd. It has two bars, a VIP area, table and bottle service, live music, and controlled access. Club Brava, one of San Juan's "hot" discos, is a mecca for the under-23 crowd. On the roof Brother Jimmy's, the first and largest Brother Jimmy's outside of New York City, boasts a Backyard Movie House, bar, mechanical bull, 22 LCD flat-screen televisions, and more.

The variety of dining choices include Las Terranzas, a casual outdoor terrace cafe overlooking the pool and gardens; The Palm, a replica of the famous Manhattan steakhouse; La Piccola Fontana, for northern Italian dishes; Yamato, a Japanese restaurant with a sushi bar; Starbucks; and Galleria Pizza and Trattoria, serving open-hearth pizzas, located off the lobby.

KOCO, a modern Caribbean restaurant, rum bar, and lounge blends cuisine, as well as decor of Caribbean, Asian, and Latin elements in fun, tropical and relaxed ways. The culinary team is headed by Executive Chef Hector Crespo, who has worked with such great chefs as Sam Choy and Wolfgang Puck; and Chef Sylva Senat who studied under Daniel Boulud and worked at Jean Georges and Buddakan in New York City. With its large space situated off the main lobby, Koco easily accommodates private parties and corporate groups. The Edouard de Paris Day Spa, on the 10th floor, is a full-service spa with five private treatment rooms; a couples' nook for couples massages; "Vapeur," for a wet steam experience; separate men's and women's locker rooms; and a relaxation lounge.

In 2009, El San Juan Hotel's sister hotel, the Condado Plaza and Casino in Condado, completed a multimillion-dollar contemporary redesign of all rooms, meeting, and public spaces, including an impressive new lobby designed by David Rockwell, and the addition of Strip House steakhouse.

EL SAN JUAN HOTEL & CASINO ★ ★ ★ ★ ★

6063 Isla Verde Ave., #187, Carolina (San Juan), PR 00979
Phone: (787) 791-1000; **Fax:** (787) 791-6985; www.elsanjuanhotel.com
Owner: Hilton Worldwide
General Manager: Jorge Garcia
Open: Year-round
US Reservations: (866) 317-8935; **Fax:** (787) 791-6985
Deposit: 1 night; 3 days cancellation
Minimum Stay: None
Arrival/Departure: No transfer service
Distance from Airport: (Luis Marin Muñoz International Airport) 5 miles; taxi one-way, $15
Distance from Old San Juan: 10 miles; taxi one-way, about $20
Accommodations: 382 rooms and suites, most with verandas (261 in main building, 128 in gardens and on beach)
Amenities: Air-conditioning, ceiling fan; cable flat-screen television, DVD, clock-radio, CD player; 3 telephones; iHome dock, Wi-Fi, safe; iron and ironing board; bath with tub, shower, vanity, bathrobes, toiletry basket, 5-inch television, hair dryer; nightly turndown service on request; ice service, stocked minibar; 24-hour concierge, room service; business services
Fitness Facilities/Spa Services: Fully equipped fitness center and spa on 10th floor of main building
Sports: Beach, 3 freshwater swimming pools, 3 Jacuzzis, 3 lighted tennis courts, equipment, daily clinics free; snorkeling, scuba, windsurfing for fee; golf, boating, fishing, horseback riding, hiking arranged
Electricity: 110 volts
Dress Code: Casual by day; elegantly casual in evening
Children: All ages; Kids' Klub, supervised activities; game room; cribs, high chairs; babysitters
Meetings: 14 meeting rooms, up to 1,200 people
Day Visitors: Welcome
Handicapped Facilities: Limited; wheelchair-accessible; dedicated rooms
Packages: Honeymoon; Caribbean Magic
Rates: Two people, daily, EP. *High Season* (Dec 23–Apr 30): $239–$2,500. *Low Season:* $159–$2,500.
Service Charge: 14 percent
Government Tax: 11 percent

THE RITZ-CARLTON, SAN JUAN

Isla Verde, Carolina (San Juan), PR

Located in Isla Verde on 8 beachfront acres less than 10 minutes from the international airport, this hotel is a Ritz-Carlton inside and out, with signature architecture and design. But check the details and you will see that it has a style and character all its own.

First, there is the lobby, whose windows span the first and second floors and look out on the gardens to the swimming pool and the sea. It's very impressive. Here, in the pleasant surroundings of the lobby lounge, a continental breakfast, tea, and cocktails are served, usually with background music. It sets the tone for the hotel. And does this hotel have tone!

From the moment you step into the rosy beige marbled lobby, you see and sense a refinement that no other hotel in San Juan can match. To the right is the front desk—it's marble; to the left is the concierge's desk—it's marble, too. And the floors, here and throughout the hotel, are covered with the most handsome hotel carpets ever to grace a hallway. Wonderful works of art by Puerto Rican artists enliven the walls.

The building is in the shape of a U around a swimming pool and gardens that stretch to a wide beach and the sea. To one side of the pool is a large Jacuzzi under a pretty gazebo; to the other, the Ocean Bar and Grill (which serves lunch and daytime snacks), a spa and fitness center, and 2 lighted tennis courts.

Across the gardens in the west wing are the restaurants on the ground level; upstairs is a huge, elegant ballroom that extends to an outdoor terrace overlooking the gardens and the pool. Around the corner from the lobby and tucked out of sight is a large casino—the first for a Ritz-Carlton—with its own separate entrance. Over the last several years, The Ritz-Carlton San Juan has made big and small changes, including the addition of 40 more balconies. The contemporary-style balconies, designed by a Puerto Rican architectural/engineering firm, are 15 feet long by 3.5 feet wide with terra-cotta-tiled floors and a wrought-iron frame. Large enough for two chairs and a small table, they overlook the hotel's beautiful gardens and the ocean beyond. The balcony rooms carry a higher premium of $110 to $115 per night, depending on the season.

The guest rooms seem a bit small by Ritz-Carlton standards, but they are tastefully appointed and have large marble bathrooms with separate toilets. All guest rooms and suites were refurbished recently with more contemporary decor, Internet access, flat-screen television, Bulgari toiletries, and the addition of a new, almost revolutionary (for Ritz-Carlton, that is) amenity—a coffeemaker. But in true Ritz-Carlton style, it's no ordinary coffee pot. Rather, a sleek, pod-type coffeemaker and an equally stylish pot for brewing tea are encased in a fine mahogany box, reminiscent of a colonial campaign chest. It has compartments for china cups, stirrers, as well as coffee pods (regular and decaf), a selection of teas, small containers of real cream, and packets of sugar. The air-conditioned rooms have stocked minibars, 3 telephones with dual lines and dataport, a clock-radio, a safe, a

hair dryer, scales, and signature bathrobes. There is twice-daily maid service and 24-hour room service. Nonsmoking floors are available.

The Ritz-Carlton Club floor, accessible only by a key-activated elevator, has deluxe rooms, a private lounge, and gracious, truly helpful concierge staff. Complimentary continental breakfast, light lunch, afternoon tea, hors d'oeuvres, cordials, and truffles are offered.

Mares, the main restaurant, has indoor and outdoor seating by the gardens. It seems to have won a big vote of approval from San Juan residents, judging from the crowds at Sunday brunch. By the swimming pool and near the beach is the Ocean Bar and Grill, a moderately priced, open-air eatery, popular for lunch.

In 2007, the BLT Steak restaurants of French chef Laurent Tourondel opened BLT Steak at the Ritz-Carlton, its first one in the Caribbean. BLT (which stands for Bistro Laurent Tourondel) Steak, is open for dinner only. It has a raw bar and a selection of seafood entries, but the specialty is steak, particularly Kobe beef and Wagyu Skirt, the American version. Both are expensive. There is also a selection of 15 desserts and a small kid's menu. The Italian restaurant, II Molino New York, Tiffany & Company, and Little Switzerland boutiques are other amenities added. The hotel's 20,000-square-foot spa and fitness center, housed in an elegant marble and stone bilevel building, has 11 treatment rooms for facials, massages, manicures, pedicures, hydrotherapy, and body wraps. The fitness center offers yoga, aerobics, and other strength and fitness activities.

The Ritz Kids Club, for ages 5 to 12, operates Sun to Thurs from 9 a.m. to 4 p.m., Fri and Sat from 9 a.m. to 9 p.m. This was the first Ritz-Carlton to offer a Ritz Kids Day at the Spa.

THE RITZ-CARLTON, SAN JUAN ★ ★ ★ ★

6961 Avenue of the Governors, Isla Verde, Carolina, PR 00979
Phone: (787) 253-1700, (800) 241-3333; **Fax:** (787) 253-0700
Owner: Caribbean Property Group
Management: The Ritz-Carlton Hotel Company, LLC.
General Manager: Steve Redkoles
Open: Year-round
US Reservations: Direct to hotel, (800) 241-3333
Deposit: 1 night, 14 days after booking; 3 to 7 days cancellation in high season, depending on week
Minimum Stay: 4 to 7 nights in winter
Arrival/Departure: Transfer arranged for fee
Distance from Airport: 1½ miles; taxi one-way, $10
Distance from Old San Juan: 3 miles

Accommodations: 416 guest rooms, 6 executive suites, 40 pool-view kings, 4 garden suites
Amenities: Air-conditioning; safe; cable television, 3 telephones with dual lines and dataport, clock-radio; baths with tubs and showers, hair dryers, bathrobes, scales, deluxe toiletries; honor bar; twice-daily maid service, 24-hour room service; nonsmoking floors available
Fitness Facilities/Spa Services: Full-service spa
Sports: Swimming pool, water sports; golf, diving, deep-sea fishing, horse racing, sailing, horseback riding arranged
Electricity: 110 volts
Dress Code: Casual chic; trousers for men at dinner
Children: All ages
Meetings: Up to 1,300 people
Day Visitors: Yes
Handicapped Facilities: Yes
Packages: Spa, summer, honeymoon
Rates: Per room, EP. *High Season* (Dec 21–Apr 30): $369–$1,669. *Low Season:* $219–$899. For presidential or 2-bedroom suites, inquire.
Service Charge: 14 percent
Government Tax: 11 percent on room

ST. BARTS

Tiny St. Barts is an Eden of 8 square miles with green hills and rolling terrain edged with pretty white-sand beaches and ringed by shallow reefs ideal for snorkeling. The darling of sophisticates and others who can afford it, this haven was discovered four decades ago by the Rockefellers and the Rothschilds, who wisely kept it a secret as long as they could.

A 10-minute flight from St. Martin, St.-Barthélémy (as it is properly named) is one of the French West Indies. The language is French, the currency is the euro, and the boutiques are stocked with famous French designer perfumes and accessories. It is also the gastronomic capital of the Caribbean, with 60 gourmet restaurants at last count.

Arawak Indians, Christopher Columbus (who named the island for his brother's patron saint), French settlers from St. Kitts, the Knights of Malta, Carib Indians, Frenchmen from Normandy and Brittany, the British, and the Swedes all were here. Those who left a permanent mark were the Swedes, who named the tiny harbor and capital, Gustavia; and the French from Normandy, from whom most of the population are descended.

At Corossol, the most traditional of the tiny fishing villages, shy elderly women still don the calèche, a stiff-brimmed bonnet derived from a 17th-century Breton style, and make handwoven straw hats and other products from the supple straw of latania palms' fan-shaped fronds.

The tiny island is a beguiling beauty on which every turn in the road—and there are many—reveals striking panoramas. It is easy to tour by car on its roller-coaster roads.

Gustavia, the miniature port on the western coast, is a yachting mecca. On the north St. Jean Bay is the center of resort and water-sports activity. Grand Cul-de-Sac, a large reef-protected bay on the northeast, is another resort center. On the northwestern end, Colombier is a pretty cove accessible by foot or boat.

Anse des Flamands to the north is one of the island's most beautiful beaches; Governor's Cove and Anse de Grande Saline, to the south, are the most secluded. Signs banning nude bathing abound but are not always obeyed: Teeny monokinis are the fashion.

Information

French West Indies Tourist Board, 825 3rd Ave., 29th Floor, New York, NY 10022; (212) 745-0950, (800) 391-4909; Fax: (212) 838-7855; www.st barthonline.com, www.st-barths.com

EDEN ROCK

St.-Barthelémy, F.W.I.

Perched on a great crag of quartzite splitting the splendid beach of St. Jean Bay, the historic Eden Rock was St. Barts's first hotel—a diamond in the rough now polished and returned to stardom.

Designed and built in 1953 by pioneer-aviator-turned-longtime-mayor Remy de Haenen, who first landed his tiny plane on a grassy field nearby, the stone structure where he made his home sprouts dramatically from a rock base that has long been an island landmark. The property gradually became run-down on an island increasingly chic, until it was sold in 1995 to a British couple armed with the resources and sense of style to set the jewel properly. And did they ever! David and Jane Matthews completely restored and upgraded the inn, adding new rooms, a pool, water-sports center, and three restaurants.

They acquired their next-door neighbor, Filao Beach, and replaced its cottages with one-bedroom suites and four deluxe cottages. Now Eden Rock has 33 accommodations "on the rock" and along the beach. Among them are a three-bedroom Big Beach House with a private swimming pool, Jacuzzi, two bathrooms, and terrace; and two beach-front villas—the two bedroom ultra-luxe Villa Nina with an art gallery, a private butler, pool, use of a Mini Cooper and more; and Rockstar with four bedrooms on three levels with spectacular views.

On "top of the rock" the Howard Hughes Loft Suite, the hotel's signature suite, has 360-degree views of the bay, three terraces, and two bathrooms; and Waterlily, a one-bedroom beach bungalow with nice stone and woodwork, a private infinity pool, Jacuzzi, and terrace. Michael's Suite on the beach has a private swimming pool and Philippe Starck bathroom. A group of contemporary rooms are found in the split-level Plantation houses on the beach. All have terraces with beach views; the ground floor suites have direct access onto the beach. All are furnished with a king bed; two ground floor suites have disabled access and facilities.

Eden Rock's original clifftop rooms, with names such as the Greta Garbo Suite, are the breezy best choices, although every room is different. Some have four-poster beds, mosquito netting, antiques, and panoramic terraces; some are awash in tropical colors with watercolors and gouaches by Jane and her children; others are old-fashioned with whimsical touches such as steamer trunks and family heirlooms from the owners' Surrey estate.

Harbour House has a large balcony overlooking the bay, a private courtyard garden, a plunge pool, a kitchenette, a bath and shower, a sitting area, and a separate children's quarters. The bedroom, decorated in white and gold, is furnished with a handcarved king-size bed, antiques, and original oil paintings.

All rooms have been individually decorated by Jane Matthews, an artist in her own right. All have air-conditioning, direct-dial phone, safe, tea and coffeemaker, bathrobes, Bulgari amenities, hair dryer, minibar, flat-screen satellite television, DVD, high-speed Internet access, nightly turndown service, and 24-hour room service. Concierge and night butler services are available, as are iPods and daily newspapers.

The Sand Bar, directly on the beach, is open for breakfast and lunch and busy all day with casual, a la carte dining. Adjacent to it is The Pub, which serves drinks and offers board games for guests. On-The-Rocks, open for breakfast and dinner, is literally perched "on the rock." The restaurant has an open kitchen, tables on two dining levels, a bar, and spectacular views over St. Jean Bay. It serves traditional French-based cuisine with the freshest, local catch (and expensive).

Eden Rock has a small, open-air spa at the water's edge with seawater pools carved from the rock and an outdoor treatment room; the services of a physiotherapist are available, based on your needs. In-room massage is also available. Eden Rock's beach area is fully serviced with teak beach loungers, umbrellas, bar service, beach towels, and iPods for guests' use. Snorkeling is superb thanks to the coral reef that surrounds the rock. Snorkel gear, rafts, and kayaks are available for guests. Hobie Cats and windsurfing equipment are available for rental. The resort's 65-foot yacht that accommodates up to 16 people, is available for excursions. She has three double cabins and three bathrooms and carries a Jet Ski on its stern. Diving and fishing trips can also be arranged.

Jane's Gallery is the art gallery of Eden Rock's owner Jane Spencer Matthews, who studied fine art at Rhodes University South Africa and the Slade Art School in London. It is both a commercial art gallery and a studio where guests can try their hand at painting in any medium. The Rockshop boutique has fashions from around the world and sells Eden Rock signature label.

The Eden Rock manages to combine elegance and just plain funky fun into a small package on one of St. Barts's prime locations.

EDEN ROCK ★ ★ ★ ★

Baie de Saint-Jean, 97133 St.-Barthelémy, F.W.I.
Phone: (590) 590-29-79-99; **Fax:** (590) 590-27-88-37; **e-mail:** info@edenrock hotel.com; www.edenrockhotel.com
Owners: David and Jane Matthews
General Manager: To be announced as of press time
Open: Year-round except Sept 1–Oct 17
US Reservations: Karen Bull Associates, (888) 576-6677; (877) 563-7105
Deposit: *High season,* 3 nights, 45 days cancellation. Christmas holidays, 10 nights, full prepayment, 60 days cancellation. *Low season,* 1 night, 30 days cancellation
Minimum Stay: 10 days, Christmas; 5 days, Feb; 3 days, off-season
Arrival/Departure: Complimentary transfers included in St. Barts. Direct transfers from St. Maarten or Anguilla to St. Barts on Eden Rock's 65-foot yacht arranged.
Distance from Airport: 1 mile; taxi one-way, €10 ($13)

Accommodations: 33 units (beachfront suites, deluxe rooms, beach cottages) with king, queen, or 2 singles; some with four-posters
Amenities: Air-conditioning, ceiling fan; direct-dial telephones; safe; minibar; flat-screen satellite TV, DVD, high-speed Internet; Bulgari amenities, tea and coffeemaker, bathrobes, nightly turndown service; room service 24/7; concierge.
Fitness Facilities/Spa Services: Outdoor mini-spa with seawater rock pools; exercise machines on beach
Sports: Swimming pool, water sports
Electricity: 220 volts/60 cycles
Dress Code: Casual
Children: All ages
Meetings: No
Day Visitors: Yes
Handicapped Facilities: No
Packages: Summer, honeymoon
Rates: Per room, daily: *High Season* (Jan 4–mid-Apr): cottages from €695 ($938); beach room from €1,050 ($1,417); classic suites €1,325 ($1,788); premium suites from €1,675 ($2,261); beach houses from €2,125 ($2,868). *Low Season:* from €505 ($681); €665 ($897); €805 ($1,086); €1,195 ($1,613); €1,450 ($1,957), respectively. Rates include airport transfer, buffet breakfast, and service charge.
Service Charge: Included
Government Tax: 5 percent

HÔTEL GUANAHANI AND SPA
St.-Barthelémy, F.W.I.

Gingerbread-trimmed Creole cottages in Easter-egg colors sit in baskets of flowering gardens on 16 hillside acres sloping down to inviting beaches. Overlooking Grand Cul de Sac to the east and Marigot Bay to the west, Guanahani is a deluxe oasis of refined simplicity.

But this stylish haven has more to it than simply a touch of class. It's *très sympathique*—classy and cozy at the same time. Since it opened in 1986, Guanahani has been a hit among an international array of celebrities and well-heeled sophisticates in search of privacy and comfort in a quiet tropical setting.

Guest rooms and suites are situated in colorful 1- and 2-story cottages, each with one, two, or three units, at various levels of the hillside. Due to their location, some afford a greater sense of privacy and better views than others. They also differ in size, layout, and decor.

For all the exuberant colors of the exterior, Guanahani's guest rooms are marked by the elegance of simplicity: a soft, light, fresh decor in white with pastel accents rendered in fine fabrics and linens. All rooms face the sea and have their own covered wooden veranda secluded in a garden.

Most have the high, beamed ceilings typical of Creole architecture, which make them seem spacious, and are furnished with a king-size bed (some four-poster) or twins, a sitting area with a desk, a stocked minibar, and a large tiled bathroom. Some suites have Nespresso coffee machines, some have whirlpools, others splash pools. The landscaping is impeccable and the housekeeping immaculate. Guest room decor incorporates Zen-inspired design with rich woods and clean lines giving them a trendy elegant look.

In late 2010, Hôtel Guanahani & Spa closed for three months for renovations, refurbishings, and upgrades and to add a new posh suite. Located in a remote setting on the beach, the two-bedroom Admiral Suite resembles a villa and has exclusive access to a small private beach. Named after the title of admiral that Christopher Columbus received from the King of Spain, the suite features custom-designed furniture incorporating leather and wood elements and in tribute to its namesake, has such navigation tools as a spyglass and a sextant.

The Serenity Suite, a premiere oceanview suite at the top of the hill, has been revamped and turned into a luxury two-bedroom butler unit, each with bathroom with a Turkish bath and a Jacuzzi. The peaceful haven pays tribute to its name in its decor, with elements evolving around the theme of water and boasts a waterfall and olive tree at the private entrance. It has a pool and gardens plus exclusive use around the resort of an electric car.

These two suites bring to six the number of Butler or Prestige Suites, each with private pools and terraces that open onto the sea and its own full-time butler. Among the services, he can unpack the guests' suitcases upon arrival, iron their clothes before their first evening, or draw a bath with essential oils from the spa and fresh flowers.

The loftlike oceanview Wellness suite, which has an outside covered bathroom with shower and a private terrace, is located on the spa's upper level with a 180-degree view of the ocean and hotel grounds. It comes with private access to the spa and unlimited after-hours use of the spa area. The Marigot Suite, built adjacent to the spa, offers guests four spa treatments, which can be received in the private treatment room next to the suite's garden. It also has a private pool and garden.

The two-bedroom Pelican Suite, overlooking Grand Cul de Sac Bay, has a master bedroom with king-size bed and second room with king or twin beds—both rooms have bathroom with shower. There is a living room with convertible sofa bed and a private garden with a Jacuzzi. The similar style two-bedroom Beach House, set directly on the beach, has a private garden terrace and an outdoor Jacuzzi. The Garden House and La Villa are the resort's only three-bedroom suites. The Garden House offers tranquility in a plush garden setting while La Villa has a large secluded outdoor terrace and large swimming pool. Both have private parking.

Many standard rooms and suites were repainted in soothing white, off-white, pearl, sand and light grey tones, with rare wood elements and soft cotton fabrics with touches of lavender, yellow, orange, and blue. Some bathrooms were remodeled, opening them onto private outdoor gardens. The terraces and outside decks of more than 20 rooms were enlarged and have new outdoor furniture of lounge chairs with plush pillows and elegant coffee tables.

Early on, Guanahani established a reputation for fine, albeit expensive, cuisine in both of its restaurants. L'Indigo, the informal open-air restaurant, has a delightful setting beside one of the Caribbean's prettiest swimming pools, with a wide wooden deck overlooking the grove of palm trees that lines the beach. Like everything else about Guanahani, it has style. Breakfast is served here, or you can dine on tropical fruit and freshly baked croissants on your terrace. L'Indigo also serves lunch and dinner.

Bartolomeo is a more formal (but only slightly) restaurant serving gourmet French cuisine and Mediterranean specialties at dinner. Actually, the only "formal" elements are the crystal and china glowing in the candlelight and the five-star service.

The resort has a good way of taking care of children. Breakfast and lunch are offered daily with a special menu for children age 6 and under at Indigo at specific hours. The kindergarten for ages 2 to 6 recently moved to the beach and operates from 9 a.m. to 5 p.m., offering a taste of French culture and language through various interactive activities and games. There is a €100 supplement for a third person in a double room; children under 6 years old are free of charge. Guanahani has two beaches (neither as inviting for swimming as the pretty freshwater pool or Jacuzzi) and tennis courts, as well as a tennis pro for private instruction. A wide range of water sports is available. Horseback riding and trips by private planes or yachts can be arranged.

You can get your exercise walking between the upper sections and the beach pavilion, reception area, tennis courts, restaurants, boutique; a road barely wide enough for a car winds through the property, connecting the facilities. The new and improved and well-equipped fitness center was relocated across from the beach and the boutique moved into its place.

The Guanahani Spa by Clarins has a total of 11 rooms. The full-service spa has an open-air design featuring rich woods and natural stone. Cascading water in the entry, gardens, and a lily pond add to the tropical ambience. There is a swimming pool, hammam, herbal tea room, beauty salon, and boutique. Among Paris-based Clarins' signature treatments are safflower or lavender fruit salt body scrub and detoxifying hydrotherapy jet bath. Spa packages with two treatments per day (including a three-day package for couples) are available. Although it's the island's largest hotel, Guanahani doesn't seem big, but that's the secret of St. Barts. Its hotels are on the same scale as the island, the ambience low-key. Gracious and romantic, Guanahani is glamorous in an understated way.

HÔTEL GUANAHANI ★ ★ ★ ★
Anse de Grand Cul de Sac, 97133 St.-Barthelémy, F.W.I.
Phone: (590) 590-27-66-60; **Fax:** (590) 590-27-70-70; **e-mail:** guanahani@ wanadoo.fr; www.leguanahani.com
Owner: Société Hotelière des Antilles Françaises, a subsidiary of Colony Capital
General Manager: Marc Thézé

Open: Year-round

US Reservations: Leading Hotels of the World, (800) 223-6800, (212) 515-5600; **Fax:** (212) 515-5840

Deposit: None; only credit card number; 30 days cancellation in winter, 14 days in summer

Minimum Stay: 10 nights during Christmas; 5 nights in February; 3 nights balance of year

Arrival/Departure: Airport transfers included

Distance from Airport: 3 miles; taxi one-way, €20 ($27). The hotel provides free airport transfers for its guests.

Distance from Gustavia: 5 miles; taxi one-way, €25 ($34)

Accommodations: 68 units (33 rooms and 35 suites of which 14 have pools); all suites have sitting room, terrace

Amenities: Air-conditioning, ceiling fans; telephone, cable television; bath with shower, hair dryer, deluxe toiletries, bathrobe; safe; stocked minibar; nightly turndown service, 24-hour room service; boutique, hairdresser; car rental service

Fitness Facilities/Spa Services: Fitness center with exercise equipment; full-service spa by Clarins

Sports: 2 freshwater swimming pools; private plunge pools; 2 lighted tennis courts and equipment; free use of snorkeling gear and nonmotorized water-sports equipment; scuba for fee; boating, fishing, horseback riding arranged; 2 beaches

Electricity: 220 volts

Dress Code: Casual but chic at all times; no shorts, tank tops, swimsuits, T-shirts, or similar attire in dining room after dark

Children: See text; cribs, high chairs; babysitters

Meetings: Up to 22 people

Day Visitors: Welcome

Handicapped Facilities: No

Packages: 5- and 7-nights

Rates: Per room, daily, CP. *High Season* (mid-Jan–mid-Apr; Nov–mid-Dec): €996–€2,606 ($1,344–$3,518). *Low Season* (mid-Apr–Oct 31): €390–€1,186 ($526–$1,601). For 2 and 3 bedroom villas, inquire.

Service Charge: Included

Government Tax: Included

HOTEL SAINT-BARTH ISLE DE FRANCE

St.-Barthelémy, F.W.I.

Flanking Anse des Flamands, a wide strand of fine white sand described by *Paris Match* as "la plus belle" of St. Barts's 14 beaches, and sprawling into a magnificent latania palm grove across the way, the Isle de France (as it is locally known) is a prime beach retreat.

Opened in 1991, the resort was extensively redesigned when new owners acquired it over the last decade resulting in a more contemporary, romantic ambience. The property is divided into two separate areas, each with a large pool and its own charm. On the beach side are a dozen rooms in a large, two-story building: six upstairs, six down, all facing the water and the beautiful beach, and unusually spacious by St. Barts's standards.

The enormous ground-floor junior suites have French doors opening onto

patios facing the pool and beach. Huge marble bathrooms have separate shower and tub and dual sinks. Upstairs rooms come with seafront terraces.

The furnishings follow the contemporary minimalist decor with white from floor to ceiling with touches of color in the pillows and throws, lamp shades, draperies, and chairs. Some have splendid handcarved four-poster beds with romantic mosquito netting.

All units have a minifridge, tea and coffeemaker, cable television, and safe. Large, elegant marble baths sport huge tubs (some with whirlpools), separate showers, bidets, double vanities, hair dryers, bathrobes, and other amenities.

The main building has a small reception area, a charming veranda with conversation areas, and a marble breezeway leading to the pool, beach, and restaurant.

On the other side of the road are 16 woodsy cottages etched into the palm grove in a secluded retreat, quite unlike any other resort on the island. A few latania bungalows are designed for family use: Some are suites; some have one entrance to two separate bedrooms, each with its own bath.

Others are intended for couples, particularly those with large oval bathtubs for two beside a blooming planter and a tinted picture window with miniblinds. Some units face the pool directly, but on hot days, the tendency is to close up and turn on the air-conditioning.

The resort has a one-bedroom hillside bungalow, featuring a kitchenette, terrace, and private swimming pool overlooking a spectacular sea view; a two-bedroom Fisherman's cottage with a small sitting area, kitchenette, exterior garden, and courtyard; and a two-bedroom beach suite located directly on Baie des Flamands beach has a private sundeck, living room, and Jacuzzi.

The hillside bungalow, with the best view of the sea and a private plunge pool, is less expensive than a beach room. It offers lots of privacy. Ah, but there are 50 stairs up or down, no room service, and housekeeping only once a day in the morning—all elements that might deter some people. The room is furnished with a king-size bed and has a bathroom and a terrace with a kitchenette.

In 2011, the resort added two Flamands Villas with direct access to beach. Boasting nearly 4,300 square feet of living space, the three-bedroom villas were designed by Penny Morrison of Morrison Interiors, London, who gave them a beach-house ambience blending contemporary design with the rustic sophistication for which the hotel is known. For example, the color and style of the antique driftwood coffee tables complement the distressed wooden floors and mix with modern artwork. Each villa boasts a spacious living room, fitness room, home cinema, fully equipped kitchen with high-end appliances, complimentary mini-bar, iPod dock and wireless Internet, and an infinity plunge pool. Each bedroom has its own bathroom with a handmade stone bath, double vanity, separate dressing area, and oversized windows to let in natural light.

The resort's spa, housed in its own separate cottage and an al fresco pavilion, offers a wide range of treatments andrecently entered a partnership with Natura Bissé, a skincare company from Barcelona, Spain. Also tucked among the palms are two lighted tennis courts and an exercise room with treadmill, Stairmaster, Lifecycle, rowing machine, and free weights. The resort's beautiful beach has a beach bar and lounging chairs under big white canvas umbrellas.

La Case de l'Isle, the hotel's beachfront open-air restaurant and one of the best hotels restaurants in St. Barts, is designed after a traditional island house or case and serves breakfast, lunch, and dinner by candlelight, with light French and island fare.

Service and style both come with smiles under general manager Evelyn Weber, who brings reassurance in English to the hotel's North American patrons and her truly Gallic flair and savoir-faire to the European guests.

HOTEL SAINT-BARTH ISLE DE FRANCE ★ ★ ★ ★
PO Box 612, Baie des Flamands, 97098 St.-Barthelémy, F.W.I.
Phone: (800) 810-4691, (590) 590-27-61–81; Fax: (590) 590-27-86-83; e-mail: hotel@isle-de-france.com; www .isle-de-france.com
Owner: Charles Vere Nicoll
General Manager: Evelyn Weber
Open: Year-round except Sept–mid-Oct
US Reservations: Direct to hotel, (800) 810-4691
Deposit: 3 nights; 30 days cancellation; 60 days Dec–May
Minimum Stay: None
Arrival/Departure: Round-trip transfers included in room rate
Distance from Airport: 3 miles; taxi one-way, €20 ($27)
Distance from Gustavia: 3 miles; taxi one-way, €20 ($27)
Accommodations: 39 rooms and suites with terraces or patios (beach, garden, or hillside), all with king or twins, 7 with four-poster king, 3 garden rooms with shower only, 2 villas with 3 bedrooms
Amenities: Air-conditioning; telephone, DVD, flat-screen cable TV; safe; tea and coffeemaker, stocked minifridge; marble bathroom with tub (some with Jacuzzi), separate shower, bidet, double vanities, bathrobes, basket of toiletries; room service, nightly turndown service; boutique; free Wi-Fi, iPod dock
Fitness Facilities/Spa Services: Fitness room with exercise equipment; full-service spa
Sports: 2 freshwater pools; snorkeling, sailing, windsurfing (fee); deep-sea fishing, boating, scuba, arranged
Electricity: 220 volts
Dress Code: Casual chic
Children: All ages; cribs; babysitters
Meetings: No
Day Visitors: Yes
Handicapped Facilities: No
Packages: Honeymoon; spa, summer; 2- and 3-week packages May 1–Oct 31
Rates: Per room, double, daily, CP. *High Season* (Jan 5–mid-Apr): €695–€1,760 ($938–$2,376). *Low Season* (mid-Apr–Aug 31; mid-Oct–mid-Dec): €479–€1,140 ($646–$1,539). For hillside bungalow, Fisherman's cottage, and 2- and 3-bedroom beach suite rates, inquire.
Service Charge: At discretion of guests
Government Tax: Included

LE SERENO

Grand Cul de Sac, St.-Barthelémy, F.W.I.

Shortly after it opened, Le Sereno quickly appeared on top-10 lists, A-lists, the "hot" lists of fashion and travel magazines, newspapers, and the Internet. Divinely simple and simply divine sums up typical descriptions. What brought all this attention was the resort's designer—the ultra-cool French interior designer Christian Liaigre, who has been called the hautest of haute designers.

Actually, Le Sereno is a reincarnation of Hotel Le Sereno, a St. Barts stalwart for more than three decades, but the similarity is in the name only. The new resort has 37 completely new, spacious beachfront suites and villas of very clean modern design inside and out. They overlook the sheltered, 600-foot palm-shaded, reef-protected beach of Grand Cul de Sac on the east end of St. Barts, and as its name implies, it is a haven of serenity. The beachfront gem has been well described as being like St. Barts itself—a contradiction of luxury and simplicity.

All the stylish suites and villas have ocean views, private terraces, and landscape gardens by Venezuelan landscape architect Fernando Tabora, known in the Caribbean for his beautiful gardens of several Barbados hotels. Liaigre's minimalist, custom furnishings conform to his signature white against dark wood furniture and trim, with taupe and cream accents. They are complemented by signature robes and linens made for Le Sereno by D. Porthault. All units are air-conditioned and provide complimentary wireless high-speed Internet access, cordless phones, flat-screen satellite television, iPod dock, safe, hair dryer, deluxe toiletries, and twice-daily housekeeping service.

Le Sereno's Beach Club has a beachfront, freshwater infinity swimming pool, and equipment for snorkeling, kayaking, and others water sports. The Fitness Center offers equipment and can supply fitness trainers. In-room spa treatments are provided by Ligne St. Barth, the long-established local company that makes skin-care products from natural ingredients. A stand-alone spa is scheduled to open in 2012.

Le Restaurant des Pêcheurs with an eclectic mix of Liaigre-designed furniture, captures an outdoors feeling in a stylish yet relaxed setting for breakfast, lunch, and dinner. As the name implies, its specialty is fish supplied daily by local fishermen. The resort also offers a "Beach and Pool" menu of light fare, available from noon until sundown. The Lounge, next to the restaurant, and Martini Bar are opened throughout the day and evening.

In addition to its much praised accommodations, Le Sereno receives good marks for its high quality service by a well-trained staff.

LE SERENO ★ ★ ★ ★
B.P. 19, Grand-Cul-de-Sac, 97133 St.-Barthélemy, F.W.I.
Phone: (590) 590-298-300; Fax: (590) 590-277-54; e-mail: info@lesereno .com; www.lesereno.com
Owners: Ignacio Contreras and Ricardo Dunin
General Manager: Jacques Roy
Open: Year-round, except Sept and Oct

US Reservations: (888) 537-3736; reservations@lesereno.com
Deposit: 3 nights; 30 days cancellation; for Holiday season, 50 percent at time of reservation and balance 3 months prior to arrival
Minimum Stay: 3 nights; Holiday season, 10 nights
Arrival/Departure: Round-trip airport transfers included in rates
Distance from Airport: 4 miles; taxi one-way, €25 ($34)
Distance from Gustavia: 6 miles; taxi one-way, €30 ($40)
Accommodations: 37 beachfront suites and villas
Amenities: Air-conditioning, Porthault linens, free wireless high-speed Internet access, cordless phones, flat-screen satellite television, iPod dock, safe, hair dryer, signature robes, deluxe toiletries, and twice-daily housekeeping service
Fitness Facilities/Spa Services: Fully-equipped fitness center; trainers available; in-room spa treatments by Ligne St. Barth (spa scheduled to open in 2012)
Sports: Freshwater infinity swimming pool, equipment for snorkeling, kayaking, kitesurfing and others water sports
Electricity: 220v; 110 available
Dress Code: Chic casual
Children: Yes
Meetings: No
Day Visitors: To restaurant; swimming pool €15 ($20) fee for lounge chair (priority goes to hotel guests during Holiday season)
Handicapped Facilities: Public and common areas wheelchair accessible; 2 equipped suites
Packages: Honeymoon; 3 to 12 nights

Rates: Per room, double, per night, with continental breakfast, tax and service charges, round-trip airport transfers. *High Season:* from €680 ($918) suite to €2,330 ($3,145) villa; *Low Season:* €480 ($648) to €1,930 ($2,605). Holidays have special rates and 5 night minimum stay requirement; inquire.
Service Charge: Included
Government Tax: Included

LE TOINY

St.-Barthelémy, F.W.I.

If you like grand vistas, privacy, and exclusivity; appreciate planning and detail; don't give a whit about beaches; and can handle steep hills and steeper prices—then you are probably a good candidate for Le Toiny, a Relais & Chateaux member.

Perched on a hillside on the windy, rocky southeastern region of St. Barts, the tony cottage complex is the only upscale resort in this corner of the island; in which, heretofore, tourism development had not been seen.

Designed in the style of Creole houses, each cottage is a large self-contained deluxe suite with a living room, kitchen, large bedroom, walk-in closet, furnished covered terra-cotta terrace, and 20-by-10-foot private heated pool overlooking the sea, all designed with exquisite attention to detail. The villa suites are staggered along the hillside in tropical flora so as to ensure maximum privacy. Each villa suite has its own gated entrance and a red mailbox flag that serves as a "Do Not Disturb" sign, emphasizing privacy.

Although the decor evokes the colonial era with mahogany furniture, including four-poster beds, the kitchens have the latest high-tech equipment. The gleaming white tile bathrooms—among the largest in the French West Indies—are ultraposh, with separate tub and shower, double sink, hair dryer, bathrobe, and designer soaps and toiletries. The cottages also have CD and DVD players, wireless Internet, and daily international newspapers.

A main building holds the elegantly decorated reception and a bar-lounge. It opens onto the restaurant, La Gaiac, set on an open-air terrace, which embraces a large swimming pool and overlooks extensive sea views. The restaurant is considered one of the best on the island. Menus can be reviewed on the hotel's website. Chef Stephane Mazieres was recently honored with the much-coveted Relais & Chateaux Grand Chefs award. The resort has its own organic greenhouse cultivated on a former pineapple field. It grows 20 different vegetables and herbs used in the restaurant. The hotel's new gym has Technogym treadmills, fitness bike, elliptical machine, and more. Private fitness coaching as well as yoga and Pilates lessons can be organized on request. A footpath leads down to the shore, but the sea here is generally too rough for swimming; water sports can be arranged.

The Serenity Spa Cottage, surrounded by lush vegetation with panoramic views, offers a wide range of treatments featuring products by Ligne St. Barth, a popular line of locally made oils, fragrances, and skin products derived from the extracts of papaya,

pineapple, and passionfruit, to name a few of the tropical fruits and herbs used. The spa offers facials, wraps, massages, and more in air-conditioned comfort or outdoors on a deck with spectacular views of the sea. The spa also accommodates couples. Spa treatments are available in-suite. A list of treatments with prices is on the website. In early 2008, Le Toiny acquired new owners, ES Development Company, an American investment group. Until now, they have keep Le Toiny more or less as returning guests will remember it, making only additions that have made the resort even better.

LE TOINY ★ ★ ★

Anse de Toiny, 97133 St.-Barthelémy, F.W.I.
Phone: (590) 590-27-88-88; **Fax:** (590) 590-27-89-30; **e-mail:** contact@letoiny .com; www.letoiny.com
Owner: ES Development
General Managers: Guy and Dagmar Lombard
Open: Year-round, except from Aug 30–Oct 28
US Reservations: reservations@letoiny .com
Deposit: 3 nights; 30 days cancellation; full prepayment with package
Minimum Stay: 10 nights during Christmas/New Year's
Arrival/Departure: Airport transfers included
Distance from Airport: 4 miles (15 to 20 minutes); taxi one-way, €30 ($40)
Distance from Gustavia: 5 miles (15 to 20 minutes); taxi one-way, €25 ($34)
Accommodations: 14 villas with 1-bedroom and private heated pools (with central living room/dining room/

kitchenette, large bathroom, terrace); 1 villa with 3 bedrooms

Amenities: Air-conditioning, ceiling fans; 3 direct-dial telephones, 2 flat-screen satellite TVs with CD and DVD players, wireless Internet, daily newspapers; exercise equipment; hair dryer, bathrobe; safe; stocked minibar; nightly turndown service, concierge, 24-hour room service; boutique; car rental service

Fitness Facilities/Spa Services: New gym with Technogym equipment; new air-conditioned spa, outdoor or in-room treatments

Sports: Freshwater swimming pool; 15 private pools; water sports, boating, fishing, diving, windsurfing, kite surfing arranged; hiking path; tennis nearby

Electricity: 110 and 220 volts

Dress Code: Casual but chic at all times

Children: Yes

Meetings: No

Day Visitors: Welcome

Handicapped Facilities: 1 cottage

Packages: Summer (Apr–Aug 31); romance, escape

Rates: Per villa, double, daily, CP. *High Season* (Jan 5–Mar 31): €1,250–€1,680 ($1,687–$2,268). *Shoulder Season* (Apr 1–May 31; Nov 21–Dec 19): €820–€960 ($1,107–$1,296). *Low Season* (June 1–Aug 31; Oct 28–Nov 20): €550-€750 ($742–$1,012). For 2- and 3-bedroom suites rates, inquire. Airport transfers included.

Service Charge: Included

Government Tax: 5 percent on hotel charge

LE VILLAGE ST. JEAN HOTEL

St.-Barthelémy, F.W.I.

This cluster of hillside cottages is the best-kept secret on St. Barts. And now, after almost two years of renovations and upgrading, it's also the best value. Set high on the side of a steep hill overlooking St. Jean Bay at the heart of St. Barts, Le Village St. Jean combines quiet villa living with hotel facilities and amenities. It's all within walking distance of popular restaurants, shops, and the island's liveliest beach.

For years this unpretentious resort has attracted an impressive list of distinguished guests, including the Zabars of New York deli fame; the late well-known food critic Craig Claiborne, who came annually at Christmas, and who kept a set of pots and pans here; an occasional French or American movie star; and an array of smart people from 18 to 80 who know a good value when they see it.

But even with its great location, grand views, sensible accommodations, and moderate prices, its biggest assets, many *habitués* will tell you, are the friendliness and care that its savvy family owners convey.

Created in 1970 by André and Gaby Charneau, who came to St. Barts from Guadeloupe, the resort is now operated by their daughter Catherine and son Bertrand. Their energy and commitment add that extra sparkle to this hilltop gem. One or all will greet you upon arrival with a warm welcome.

The white stucco cottages trimmed with wood and native stone are designed to resemble a hillside village with a variety of styles and accommodations: hotel rooms, one- and two-bedroom suites with covered sundecks in two-story cottages, a three-bedroom house, and a deluxe villa with a private pool. The units are large for this island, and comfortably furnished with twin or king-size beds and tile floors and baths and fitted with flat-screen television with cable. All rooms have sea views, some better than others.

The 4 hotel rooms are high-ceiling bedrooms with a balcony overlooking the sea and furnished with twin beds and shower, hair dryer, Roger Gallet toiletries, and minifridge. All rooms and suites are air-conditioned and some also have ceiling fan, telephone, free Wi-fi access, radio, and safe. Hotel rooms and a few cottages have flat-screen satellite television. Continental breakfast is included in the rate.

Standard cottages have fully equipped kitchenettes that open onto a terrace serving as an open-air living room/dining room and have views of St. Jean Bay; garden cottages have partial views of the sea. Superior cottages are larger with more spacious terraces. All have been redecorated and upgraded, resulting in a fresh, light, and joyful look overall. Some rooms have walls of light tangerine or lemon or blue and white bedcovers and bright colored pillows and throws, others have white walls with vivid colored spreads. Five units have second bedrooms suitable for children.

One suite with a Jacuzzi and kitchenette is actually a tiny villa with a wrap-around terrace in a secluded garden with an outdoor shower. It is equipped with a CD/DVD player, iPod dock, and stereo system as well as the amenities in rooms and cottages. La Case, a new cottage resembling the traditional homes on the island, is set at the highest point of the village. It has a large wooden deck with a Jacuzzi, as well as a garden patio. Also new are the Junior Terrace Suites with a bedroom, salon with sofa bed, and two bathrooms and terrace, ideal for families with children; and the two-story Family Cottages, which can house up to six people.

Villa Iguana, a two-bedroom, two-bath cottage with a private swimming pool, has a magnificent view of the bay. Designed in contemporary style by Jinnie Kim, a noted Korean-American designer, the deluxe Villa Iguana is a combination of luxury and simplicity as well as practicality with such conveniences as a modern stainless steel kitchen—all at a reasonable price.

The resort's new restaurant, Le Bar du Village the indoor-outdoor terrace restaurant and bar, serves light fare in a fun ambience. Just down the hill is Kiki-é Mo, an Italian gourmet food market offering meals throughout the day in a casual setting as well as takeout and catering.

One level up from the restaurant is the attractive, freshwater swimming pool newly retiled in blue mosaic with a larger deck. On the base of the former boutique is a stunning new two-level building of glass and ipe, a tropical wood, housing the hotel's small, modest spa on the first floor and a gym with exercise equipment on the second floor. Private yoga and stretching classes are available on request. Further diversions include a reading library, bocce alley, and free wireless connection.

It's about a three-minute spill down the hill to the beach (though a 10-minute steep climb on the return), with restaurants, shops, other hotels, and water-sports centers along St. Jean Bay. You don't need a car, but you might want one for exploring the island, checking out the other beaches, and sampling some of the expensive temples of haute cuisine (with the money you save staying at Le Village).

HOTEL LE VILLAGE ST. JEAN ★ ★

PO Box 623, 97098 St.-Barthelémy, F.W.I.
Phone: (590) 590-27-61-39, (800) 651-8366; **Fax:** (590) 590-27-77-96; **e-mail:** reservations@villagestjeanhotel; www .villagestjeanhotel.com
Owners: The Charneau family
General Manager: Catherine Charneau
Open: Year-round
US Reservations: Direct to hotel, (800) 651-8366
Deposit: 3 nights, 5 nights in Feb; 45 days cancellation; 60 days for Feb, 30 days in summer
Cancellation Fees: €100 ($135) penalty for cancellation in winter; €60 ($81) in summer; €150 ($202) penalty for Feb cancellation
Minimum Stay: 12 nights during Christmas
Arrival/Departure: Complimentary airport transfer (upon request in advance)
Distance from Airport: 1 mile; taxi one-way, €15 ($20)
Distance from Gustavia: 3 miles; taxi one-way, €15 ($20)
Accommodations: 28 units in 19 cottages and 3 villas (6 hotel rooms, 16

one-bedroom units, 2 Jacuzzi suites, 5 one-bedroom suites with small guest bed, 2 two-bedroom villas, and 1 three-bedroom villa); with twin, queen-size, or king-size beds; all suites with kitchenette or full kitchens

Amenities: Air-conditioning, ceiling fans; direct-dial telephone with voice mail, stereo with CD player; bath with shower only, hair dryer; refrigerator; flat-screen cable television in hotel rooms, some suites; room service for breakfast; free Wi-Fi, library

Fitness Facilities/Spa Services: New fitness center with exercise equipment; yoga and stretching classes on request

Sports: Freshwater swimming pool, Jacuzzi; bocce, gym, tennis, boating, snorkeling, scuba, windsurfing, deep-sea fishing, horseback riding arranged for charge

Electricity: 220 volts/60 cycles

Dress Code: Casual

Children: All ages; cribs, high chairs; babysitters

Meetings: None

Day Visitors: Only by advance request

Handicapped Facilities: Jacuzzi suite

Packages: Summer, honeymoon

Rates: Per room, 2 people, CP or cottage, daily. *High Season* (Jan 8–mid-Apr): €225–€660 ($304–$891). *Low Season:* €135–€460 ($182–$621).

Service Charge: Included

Government Tax: 5 percent on room only

ST. KITTS

Located in the heart of the Leeward Islands, St. Kitts has a beauty and grace that enchants visitors, taking them back to another era when life was more genteel. From all the Caribbean islands he saw, Christopher Columbus selected St. Kitts to name for his patron saint, St. Christopher.

It's something of a newcomer to Caribbean tourism, but St. Kitts was the first island settled by the English in 1623, giving England great wealth from the land that produced the highest-yielding sugar crop in the world. From their base in St. Kitts, the English settled Nevis, Antigua, and Montserrat, but not before battling the French, who arrived in 1624 to stake out their claim. St. Kitts remained a British possession until 1983, when full independence was established.

Shaped like a paddle with an area of 65 square miles, St. Kitts rises from intensively cultivated lowlands and foothills to a central spine of mountains covered with rain forests. The northern part of the island is dominated by Mount Liamuiga, known in colonial times as Mount Misery, a dormant volcano that rises to almost 4,000 feet. A coastal road makes it easy to drive—or bike—around the island and provides access to the splendid hiking of the mountainous interior. There are no cross-island roads through the central mountains, but there are footpaths.

The Southeastern Peninsula, a hilly tongue of land different in climate and terrain from the main body of St. Kitts, is covered with dry woodland and salt ponds and scalloped with the island's best white-sand beaches. It has a new magnificently engineered highway of about 7 miles that has made this part of the island accessible by land for the first time.

St. Kitts and its sister island of Nevis are separated on the surface of the sea by a 2-mile-wide strait known as the Narrows, but they're joined below the surface by a subterranean rock base on which their volcanic mountains were formed eons ago. Daily ferry service connects the two islands.

Information

St. Kitts Tourism Authority, 414 E. 75th St., New York, NY 10021; (212) 535-1234, (800) 582-6208; Fax: (212) 734-6511; e-mail: info@stkittstourim.kn; www.stkittstourism.kn

OTTLEY'S PLANTATION INN

Basseterre, St. Kitts, W.I.

Fashion magazines from California to the Champs Elysées have been using this gorgeous Caribbean "Tara" as a backdrop almost from the day it opened. Perched on a hillside overlooking St. Kitts's eastern coast, the elegant inn is built into the historic ruins of a sugar plantation. It is set in 15 magnificent acres of manicured lawns and gardens, with rolling fields edged by palm trees in the front and a mango grove and rain-forested mountains to the rear.

Established about 1703 after the Ottley family came to the island, it continued to operate as a plantation—under different owners—until the 1960s. In 1988 Americans Art and Ruth Keusch bought Ottley's with their daughter and son-in-law, Martin and Nancy Lowell and later joined by a sister, Karen Keusch.

After making extensive renovations and adding a second floor to the great house, they opened the inn in 1990.

The drive from the main eastern coast road climbs through cane fields and along columns of royal palms to lawns so well tended you'll think they are the fairways of a swank golf course. Upon arrival you will be greeted by a member of the family—all hands-on managers. Marty, a congenial host whose horticultural training is evident everywhere, will offer you a welcome drink and show you to your room.

The great house, dating from 1832, is a majestic brimstone structure with two tiers of wraparound balconies trimmed with white railings, yellow shutters, and Brazilian hardwood doors. The ground floor has a formal living room, beautifully appointed with antiques and period furniture, and a mahogany bar. It provides an elegant setting for afternoon tea, cocktails, and evening socializing. A small side room has the library, with a television set and DVD player.

The first floor has 2 guest rooms, and upstairs are 6 wonderfully spacious ones with high, beamed ceilings—Scarlett O'Hara would have loved them. Each room is different, but all are delightfully furnished with antiques and mahogany and wicker furniture. Plush bedspreads are set against pastel walls and wooden floors. The spacious bathrooms have separate dressing areas, well-lit vanities, tubs, and showers.

Large bedroom windows with dark wood louvers let in the breezes and open onto views of the exquisite gardens and surrounding countryside flowing to the sea. You can enjoy breakfast and take in the view. And everywhere there are enormous bouquets of fresh tropical flowers.

Near the entrance the English Cottage, once a cotton storehouse, has a large bedroom and a separate sitting room that can be converted into a bedroom; each has its own patio and bathroom—one with a Jacuzzi bath and a plunge pool.

Below the great house are five luxury cottages, four with two large guest rooms and one with three guest rooms. These spacious cottages have elegant Italian tile baths, minibars, hardwood doors, and louvered shutters; they are handsomely decorated in Caribbean colonial style. The larger of the two rooms has a king-size bed, a Jacuzzi tub in the bathroom, and a private plunge pool on the patio. The slightly smaller second room, furnished with either a king or twin beds, has a romantic corner tub in the bathroom; it can also be furnished with a sofa and used as a sitting room. Thus, as a private cottage, it has a bedroom and sitting room, two bathrooms, two private patios (one with a plunge pool), and magnificent views.

To one side of the great house is an official-size croquet court and at the back, a tennis court. On the other side is the Mango Orchard Spa, housed in a small attractive West Indian–style cottage at the forest's edge. It offers a wide array of treatments ranging from a basic manicure to an aromatherapy massage and a Shiatsu massage. Treatments need to be booked at least 24 hours in advance.

On the southern side of the great house, steps lead down to garden terraces and the beautiful stone ruins of the boiling house, now converted into a spring-fed swimming pool with a bar and stone terrace at the far end. One wall of the boiling house, with arched windows opening onto the swimming pool, forms a backdrop for the Royal Palm, the inn's open-air restaurant featuring contemporary Caribbean cuisine, popular with Kittitians and guests from other hotels as well. The Sunday champagne brunch is a particular favorite. Special, too, are the elegant candlelight dinners under balmy, star-filled Kittitian skies.

Next to the great house is the remnant base of the windmill, landscaped with flowers and flowering trees. It is a popular setting for outdoor weddings—a more romantic spot would be hard to imagine. Behind the great house is a mango orchard with wonderful old trees. Ottley's fruit- and flower-filled gardens attract birds by the dozens.

Farther on, a bridge leads to footpaths along a gully and stone walls to trails through the property's rain forest. The vegetation is fabulous, with enormous mahogany trees, gigantic elephant ears, and other rain-forest species. Self-guided tours are available, but Marty is a wonderful guide, too.

Ottley's historic, romantic setting, coupled with its informal, friendly atmosphere, will appeal both to singles and couples who seek a quiet vacation in gracious surroundings. The numbers—24 rooms for 48 guests, on 35 acres, attended by a staff of 45—all but guarantee space, grace, and peace.

OTTLEY'S PLANTATION INN

★ ★ ★ 🐌

Box 345, Basseterre, St. Kitts, W.I.
Phone: (869) 465-7234, (800) 772-3039; Fax: (869) 465-4760; e-mail: info@ottleys.com; www.ottleys.com
Owners/Managers: Art Keusch, Martin and Nancy Lowell Karen Keusch
Open: Year-round
US Reservations: Direct to hotel, e-mail: reservations@ottleys.com
Deposit: Full prepayment; 30 days cancellation, except 45 days for Christmas/New Year's
Minimum Stay: 7 nights during Christmas/New Year's
Arrival/Departure: Airport transfer included for stays of 7 paid nights and longer
Distance from Airport: 6 miles (15 minutes); taxi one-way, $20
Distance from Basseterre: 10 miles; taxi one-way, $25; daily free shuttle to town, 2 beaches, and golf course

Accommodations: 23 rooms (8 in great house; 6 two-room cottages; 1 three-room villa), all with verandas; king-or queen-size beds (4 with twin or king-size beds, 2 with two queens); 9 with Jacuzzi and plunge pool; villa with full kitchen can accommodate up to 8 people
Amenities: Air-conditioning, ceiling fans; telephone; safe; umbrella, flashlight; bath with tub and shower, hair dryers, basket of toiletries; coffeemaker; iron and ironing board; room service on request; minibar; television in some Supreme rooms, if available, by advance request
Sports: Tennis court; croquet; daily free shuttle to beach with water sports; hiking on trails adjacent to property; golf, fishing, boating, snorkeling, scuba, windsurfing, horseback riding arranged
Electricity: 110 volts
Dress Code: Informal; smart casual at dinnertime
Children: Year-round in royal suites and grand villa
Meetings: Up to 35 people
Day Visitors: Yes, restaurant; reservations required for dinner and recommended for Sunday brunch
Handicapped Facilities: No
Packages: Honeymoon, wedding, golf, diving, 5 to 10 days or longer custom-tailored
Rates: Per room, double, daily, EP. *High Season* (mid-Dec–mid-Apr): $244–389. *Shoulder Season:* $194–$289. *Low Season:* $179–$259. Rates also available for 2-room suites and 3-room Grand Villa, inquire.
Service Charge: 10 percent
Government Tax: 10 percent VAT and 2 percent Island Enhancement tax

ST. LUCIA

Lush, mountainous St. Lucia, the second largest island in the Windwards, is a nature lover's dream with scenic wonders on a grand scale. Every turn in the road—and there are many—reveals spectacular landscapes of rain-forested mountains and valleys covered with fruit and flowering trees. Mostly volcanic in origin and slightly pear shaped, St. Lucia is only 27 miles in length, but its mountainous terrain rising to more than 3,000 feet makes it seem much larger.

On the northwestern coast Castries, the capital, overlooks a deep natural harbor sheltered by an amphitheater of green hills. On the northern tip Pigeon Point, an island connected to the mainland by a causeway, has been made into a national park. It has a historic fort and museum and is the venue for St. Lucia's annual international jazz festival.

Soufrière, south of the capital, is the oldest settlement on St. Lucia. At its prime in the late 18th century, there were as many as one hundred sugar and coffee plantations in the vicinity. The quaint little port has a striking setting at the foot of the magnificent Pitons, sugarloaf twins that rise dramatically at the island's edge.

Soufrière lies amid a wonderland of steep mountain ridges and lush valleys, and it is the gateway to some of St. Lucia's most celebrated natural attractions: a drive-in volcano with gurgling mud and hot springs, pretty waterfalls, sulfur baths with curative powers that were tested by the soldiers of Louis XVI, and a rain forest with a trail across the heart of the island.

St. Lucia has some of the best and the worst roads in the Caribbean. None encircles the island completely, but you can make a loop around the southern half, which has the main sightseeing attractions. A new road along the western coast from Castries to Soufrière has made one of the most scenic drives in the Caribbean a joy to travel again. An alternative is a 45-minute motorboat trip available daily between Castries and Soufrière.

Information

Saint Lucia Tourist Board, 800 2nd Ave., 9th Floor, New York, NY 10017; (212) 867-2950, (212) 867-2794, (888) 4-STLUCIA; e-mail: stluciatouridm@aol.com; www.stlucianow.com

ALMOND MORGAN BAY

Choc Bay, St. Lucia, W.I.

Set on a cove amid 22 acres of landscaped gardens, the Almond Morgan Bay is a member of Barbados-based Almond Beach International Resorts. Opened in November 2005 on St. Lucia's northwest coast, it is a family-oriented, all-inclusive resort and a cut above the usual.

Formerly the St. James Club Morgan Bay, Almond spent $55 million renovating and redesigning the property beyond recognition of its previous life and added another 100 rooms. From the entrance off the main road, through the open-air lobby to two free-form pools, Almond Morgan Bay has the look of a country club. Its 345 rooms, housed in three-story units, are spread along the beachfront and climb to the hillside. The rooms come in five categories,

some have ocean views, some garden, some both. Four categories accommodate three adults or two adults and two children under age 17. The fifth—one-bedroom oceanview suites—have a spacious bedroom and living area and accommodate four adults or two adults and three children. Superior deluxe beachfront rooms are popular for their location and with families because they frequently have connecting rooms.

All rooms are in light tones for the furniture and decor. Full-length windows brighten the rooms and broadened the view; glass doors open to small private balconies. The one-bedroom suites have larger balconies accessible from the bedroom and living room. All rooms are air-conditioned and have king or two double beds, satellite television, safe, tea/coffeemaker, hair dryer, and modern bathrooms. In-room spa treatments are available.

Almond Morgan Bay has four restaurants. Two casual open-air, seafront restaurants offer a full buffet breakfast, afternoon tea, and a la carte lunch and dinner daily. Two others require reservations and serve dinner only: Morgan's Pier, a rustic over-the-water restaurant for fresh seafood specialties; and Le Jardin, an adults-only, gourmet restaurant featuring French Creole cuisine. The latter becomes a piano bar after dinner. Room service is available for lunch and dinner.

This family resort has a good children's program. The Kids Club, an activity and play center with an experienced staff, supervises four age-specific programs: a nursery for infants; a Mini Kids Club for ages 2 to 4; Kids Club for ages 4 to 7 and 8 to 12; and Teen Center for youngsters 13 and older. The facilities are housed in colorful cottages near the resort's four tennis courts and next to the poolside Plum Tree Bar and Grill where hot dogs, pizza, and salads are available. All but the very youngest children have a variety of outdoor activities and gather in the Slush Hut where machines dispense popcorn, smoothies, drinks, and ice cream—all included in the all-inclusive price.

Almond Morgan Bay has four freshwater swimming pools (two in the Kids Club area) and a variety of water sports. The Fitness Center is fitted with a full line of exercise equipment and offers aerobics, West Indian dance, and other classes. A personal trainer is available.

Tennis comes with free group instruction. Almond Morgan Bay is a very good value for anyone, but particularly for families who appreciate its range and variety of facilities, activities, and services in the all-inclusive price.

ALMOND MORGAN BAY ★ ★ ★
Choc Bay, Castries, St. Lucia, W.I.
Phone: (758) 451-2500; e-mail: info@almondresorts.com; www.almondresorts.com
Owner: Almond Resorts Inc.
General Manager: Frank King
Open: Year-round
US Reservations: (800) 4-ALMOND
Deposit: Prepay in full
Minimum Stay: None
Distance from Airport: (Hewanorra International Airport): 25 miles (90 minutes); (Castries & George Charles Airport): 3 miles (15 minutes)
Accommodations: 345 rooms and suites
Amenities: Air-conditioning, phone/voice mail, minifridge, safe, hair dryer, iron/board, alarm clock, tea/coffeemaker, satellite television; private bath/shower; guest computer in the business center costs $10; free Wi-Fi in lobby; golf cart on call for transport around resort
Fitness Facilities/Spa Services: Fitness center; spa treatments available in rooms
Sports: See text
Electricity: 110 and 220 volts
Dress Code: Strictly maintained in all restaurants: cover-up over swim wear; shoes must be worn; and at dinner, men, shirts with sleeves; no shorts except barbecue nights
Children: Kids Club (see text)

Meetings: Small meetings/groups; private check-in with welcome drink, dedicated hospitality desk, 1 complimentary room for every 20 rooms booked; conference center use complimentary, including coffee breaks and use of audio/visuals; open bars at private dinners and cocktail parties

Day Visitors: *Day Pass:* 7:30 a.m.–2 a.m., for breakfast, lunch, snacks, drinks, afternoon tea, dinner, use of facilities and entertainment, $120 per adult, $65 per child 5 to 12 years old; $30 per child from 1 to 4 years old. *Lunch Pass:* noon–3 p.m., for lunch, drinks, use of facilities $60 adult; $25 child 5 to 12 years old, $12 child 1 to 4 years old. *Dinner Pass:* 6 p.m.–2 a.m. for drinks, dinner, entertainment $75 adult, $30 child 5 to 12 years old, $15 child from 1 to 4 years old

Handicapped Facilities: 2 ground floor rooms; golf carts available for guest transfer to rooms

Packages: Wedding, honeymoon, renewal of vows

Rates: Per person double daily, All-Inclusive, from $270 (Jan 6–Apr 15) and from $220 (Apr 16–Dec 20). For special promotions, see www.almond resorts.com

Service Charge: Included

Government Tax: Included

ANSE CHASTANET RESORT AND JADE MOUNTAIN

Soufrière, St. Lucia, W.I.

On the northern side of Soufrière, facing the twin peaks of the Pitons, is one of the Caribbean's most enchanting resorts. Anse Chastanet, built along a steep hillside of tropical splendor overlooking a secluded cove, has a setting so idyllic that you will forgive (if not forget) the atrocious road leading there. If you prefer, you can also reach this hideaway by boat, arriving directly on Anse Chastanet's golden beach.

There are hillside rooms in octagonal, gazebo-type cottages, all with grandstand views of the Pitons or the sea and the unforgettable St. Lucian sunsets. The rooms are comfortable but not fancy—why compete with nature? They have wood-beamed ceilings and walls of louvered windows and doors leading to wraparound verandas draped in brilliant bougainvillea and hiding under some of the flowering trees for which the cottages are named. Near the beach are three two-story villas, housing 12 deluxe suites and harmonize so well with their natural settingthey can hardly be seen. All Anse Chastanet's rooms have furnishings of tropical hardwood—mahogany, wild breadfruit, and purple heart—designed by owner Nick Troubetzkoy, an architect, and crafted by local woodcarvers. Woven grass rugs (a St. Lucian specialty) are on the earthen tile floors; original art by local and international artists decorates the walls; and bright plaid madras cotton is used for the bed and cushion covers. (Madras is used by St. Lucian women for traditional dress.)

Troubetzkoy's dazzling creations—eleven huge suites of bold, sensational design—put Anse Chastanet in a league of its own when they were added in 1993. These handsome architectural wonders, perched high above the first cottages, offer luxury and space. Some rooms have atrium gardens; others are built around trees, much like a tree house. Each suite has a different arrangement, and all have breathtaking views. But don't expect them to look like an *Architectural Digest* spread. Rather, they are rustic and sparsely furnished. Six premium suites in Cottage 7 have the Pitons as their centerpiece. The enormous bedroom/sitting room extends to a terrace with no walls.

Then in 2005, Troubetzkoy went himself one better with Jade Mountain, a group of suites not only more spectacular than his previous ones, but just about the most spectacular accommodations in the Caribbean. Built on the highest point of the Anse Chastanet mountainside in harmony with nature, these suites were grouped together to create a resort within a resort. The name, Jade Mountain, reflects Troubetzkoy's love for the Pitons, which led him to become an avid collector of carved antique jade "mountains," some of which are on display in the club room.

The bedroom and living areas with 15-foot-high ceilings, bathroom, and infinity-edge pool flow into one another. There is no formal separation between the sleeping and living spaces. The rooms have ceiling fans, king-size beds, refrigerators, coffeemakers, irons and ironing boards. The large, spacious suites are open with a fourth wall missing entirely, creating the perfect platform from which to embrace the gorgeous Pitons, sea, and sunset.

Given the much-coveted AAA Five Diamond rating for 2011, Jade Mountain has three room-rate categories reflecting the square footage of the Jade Mountain suites, pool size, and the scope of the view that changes somewhat with the elevation and location. "Star" suites range from 1,400 to 1,800 square feet with 450-square-foot pools; "Moon" suites are 1,600 to 1,950 square feet with 650-square-foot pools. "Sun" suites, the top category, with the most commanding 270-degree panoramic view, have more than 2,000 square feet and pools up to 900 square feet. They also have a small wine cabinet.

All pools have shallow water lounging areas and a swimming area 4½ feet deep. At night they are illuminated with fiber optic lights, the color of which guests can personally control. The pools are surfaced in one-of-a-kind glass tiles, custom crafted and specifically designed for Jade Mountain. These tiles have a sophisticated, textured iridescent surface on one side and a smooth but undulating surface on the other. The pools are lined with the iridescent side facing out, while the suite's bathroom is faced with the smooth, undulating surface. Each pool has its own designed glass tile color scheme that extends to the bathroom, adding to each suite's unique personality.

Bathrooms have tropical hardwood vanities with fine brushed stainless steel European fixtures, polished mirrors, custom light fixtures, and porcelain washbowls, makeup mirrors, and hair dryers. The smooth, cool, coral tile flooring contrasts with the shimmering handmade glass tile shower walls and high-tech stainless steel shower units

with powerful massage jets and a gentle rainfall showerhead. Each bathroom has a large whirlpool tub for two on a raised platform overlooking the room, pool, and the view. Oh, that view! Jade Mountain has its own reception area and concierge service. Like the rest of Anse Chastanet, the suites are tech-free: no phones, radio, or television in the rooms. Internet access is available at reception. Each suite has a call button to summon room service and housekeeping 24 hours a day. There are also five Sky Jacuzzi suites at the lower level of the building that share the same view and Jade Mountain resort privileges but do not have a pool.

A small spa, Kai en Ciel, with two treatment suites and a small fitness room is for the exclusive use of the Jade Mountain guests, who also enjoy all the restaurants and facilities of the Anse Chastanet Resort below. But exclusive to them is the Jade Mountain Club where they can dine on Jade Cuisine, created by Chef Allen Susser of Chef Allen's Restaurant in Miami, who is known for his originality in using fresh fish and locally grown, seasonal fruits, vegetables, and herbs. Throughout the year, the resort has a series of culinary festivals designed by consulting Chef Allen Susser, and his team and highlighting local fruits, vegetables, and herbs often grown in the resort's own gardens. In 2011, the resort launched of the first of a series of Celebrity Guest Chef, which has included such noted chefs as Thomas Buckley, executive chef at Nobu Miami Beach, among others. These events are only for Jade Mountain guests. The scheduled can be found on the resort's website.

Anse Chastanet requires you to be something of a mountain goat. Nothing but your legs gets you up and down the 100 or more stone steps that climb from the beach to the topmost rooms (Jade Mountain guests have shuttle service). But it's worth every heart-pounding breath for the magnificent scenery. There is also an easier way, at least for part of the climb: If you rent a car (as some guests do), you can drive on the service road to the beach. There's also shuttle service, available on request.

Anse Chastanet's main reception pavilion contains an open-air bar, a library, the Treehouse Restaurant and terrace where breakfast and dinner are served. You'll dine in the magical, romantic setting of the Treehouse on cuisine that also makes generous use of fresh seafood, vegetables, and other local ingredients. Trou-au-Diable, the beach restaurant, serves breakfast and features Creole specialties at lunch; the beach bar is open all day. You can also have lunch under your thatched umbrella on the more secluded northern end of the beach. Five or six nights each week the restaurant is transformed into the very popular Apsara, specializing in fine Indian cuisine.

By the beach, Anse Chastanet has a tennis court and a spa with several massage therapists who provide an extensive variety of facials, therapeutic massages including reflexology and aromatherapy, and other treatments in the privacy of your room or in the beachside spa center with six treatment rooms. It is open daily from 9 a.m. to 8 p.m. On the second floor is an art gallery. There are also two boutiques and a water-sports center.

Anse Chastanet fronts some of St. Lucia's best reefs, which are protected as a marine park. They are close enough for snorkelers to reach directly from the beach. Some divers call the stretch between Anse Chastanet and the Pitons the best diving in the Caribbean.

Scuba St. Lucia is the resort's PADI Gold Palm/National Geographic Dive Centre/SSI (Scuba Schools International) training facility, directed by a 10-member professional team. Also open to nonhotel guests, it offers beach and boat dives four times daily, night dives, and courses for beginners, certification, and underwater photography. The resort's 37-foot O-Day sailing vessel is available for half- and full-day trips, as well as for introductory lessons.

A more secluded strand of sand is a 10-minute walk (or a few minutes' motorboat ride) north of Anse Chastanet at Anse Mamin, a fully serviced beach with shelter. Here you can also explore the extensive 18th-century ruins of Anse Mamin, one of the earliest sugar plantations on St. Lucia, or if you prefer something less taxing, the resort has palapas on the beach where spa services are available.

Anse Chastanet is close to some of St. Lucia's main natural attractions and offers guided hikes on the property at no charge to guests. Off-property hikes start at $65 per person and include a guide, transportation, and sometimes a picnic lunch. The resort has also developed nature, bird-watching, and botanical tours.

Bike St. Lucia is the resort's mountain-biking facility offering guided excursions on custom-designed rain forest trails, clearly marked for levels of difficulty and patrolled by Bike St. Lucia staffers. Each rider is issued a Bell helmet, souvenir water bottle, and trail map. Bike rentals cost half day $39, and full day $69.

The manager's cocktail party starts the week's evening activities. There is live music nightly and a beach barbecue with a reggae band at least twice weekly. But Anse Chastanet is not a place for nightlife; most guests are back in their "tree houses" by 10 p.m.

That Anse Chastanet, with its romantic ambience, attracts honeymooners comes as no surprise. It is also the setting for about eight weddings per month. But you don't have to fall into either category to fall in love with this corner of paradise. And yet, Anse Chastanet isn't for everyone. But if you are a sporting enthusiast or something of an escapist, yearn for tranquillity, relish beauty, and are refreshed by remarkable tropical landscapes, you will love every minute at this friendly, unpretentious resort.

ANSE CHASTANET RESORT AND JADE MOUNTAIN ★ ★ ★ ★ ★ 🐚

PO Box 7000, Soufrière, St. Lucia, W.I.
Phone: (758) 459-7000, (800) 223-1108; Fax: (758) 459-7700; e-mail: ansechastanet@candw.lc; www.ansechastanet.com, www.bikestlucia.com, www.scubastlucia.com, www.jademountainstlucia.com
Owners/Managing Directors: Nick and Karolin Troubetzkoy
Open: Year-round
US Reservations: Ralph Locke Islands, Inc., (800) 223-1108; Fax: (310) 440-4220

Deposit: 3 nights in winter, 2 nights in low season; 30 days cancellation
Minimum Stay: 3 nights in winter, 5 nights during Christmas/New Year's
Arrival/Departure: Airport transfer arranged for fee; hotel runs scheduled boat to Castries
Distance from Airport: Hewanorra International Airport: 18 miles (45 minutes); taxi one-way, $65; George F. L. Charles Airport: 20 miles (2 hours); taxi one-way, $85
Distance from Castries: 20 miles; taxi one-way, $75; private water taxi, $120
Distance from Soufrière: 1½ miles; taxi one-way, $10
Accommodations: *Anse Chastanet:* 49 units with twin or king-size beds (3 standard, 4 premium, 12 deluxe beachside, and 29 hillside gazebo-cottages; 1- and 2-bedroom suites), all with verandas. *Jade Mountain:* 5 Jacuzzi suites; 24 suites with private infinity pools.
Amenities: Ceiling fans; bath with shower only, hair dryers, basket of toiletries; tea and coffeemakers, minibars with optional provisioning plans; room service for breakfast. No radios, telephones, televisions, air-conditioning. *Jade Mountain,* see text.
Fitness Facilities/Spa Services: See text
Sports: Tennis court (no lights); free snorkeling, Sunfish, windsurfing; no pool; superior dive facilities with full range of equipment, 3 dive boats and 36-foot trihull flattop for up to 24 divers, film lab for underwater photography; changing rooms, freshwater showers
Electricity: 220 volts/50 cycles

Dress Code: Casual; men wear slacks or long-cut Bermuda shorts and shirts in evening

Children: None under 10 years of age; babysitters on request

Meetings: Up to 75 people

Day Visitors: Individuals with advance notice

Handicapped Facilities: No

Packages: Honeymoon, scuba diving, wedding, spa

Rates: Per room for two people, daily. *High Season:* EP (Jan 3–mid-Apr) $495–$915. *Shoulder Season:* EP (mid-Apr–May 31; Nov 1–mid-Dec): $385–$785. *Low Season* (June–Oct 31): $330–$695. Single and triple rates available, inquire. *Jade Mountain:* EP; *High Season:* $1,380–$2,680. *Shoulder Season:* $1050–$2,250. *Low Season* (June–Oct): $950–$2,050.

Service Charge: 10 percent

Government Tax: 8 percent

THE BODY HOLIDAY

Cariblue Beach, St. Lucia, W.I.

One of the first of its kind in the Caribbean, The Body Holiday is a health and well-being resort offering an organized but unregimented vacation. It is designed for today's professionals, striking a middle ground between the rigorous regime of a health spa and a typical beach vacation. For active and fitness-minded people, it's the best buy in the Caribbean and has been recognized with a myriad of awards.

The Body Holiday is the ultimate all-inclusive resort. For one price you get all meals, English tea, and snacks; use of the extensive spa with one treatment per day and an extensive range of sports and fitness facilities with expert instruction; all drinks and beverages; nightly entertainment; and all gratuities and taxes.

Set on secluded Cariblue beach on the northwestern tip of St. Lucia, The Body Holiday spreads over 15 hillside acres of tropical gardens. It has guest rooms in two-, three-, and four-story buildings. Except for 29 standard rooms with garden views, all have terraces or patios looking west to the sea—and what a treat. Sunsets are magnificent.

In summer of 2011, The Body Holiday undertook an extensive $20 million transformation, renovation, and upgrading to make it a five-star. The renovations have resulted in significant updates to the public area and dining venues, the addition of a new infinity-edge swimming pool and boardwalk, and expansion of the water-sports and diving centers. The standard garden-view rooms were renovated while the grand luxury ocean front room and junior suites were enhanced.

The redesigned lobby is more open and inviting; a new structure in the main restaurant has put the buffet in a new air-conditioned building and a new grill was added to the Clubhouse. Tao, its gourmet restaurant, was enlarged and the deli's deck now extends from the Clubhouse to the beach where there are new trendy daybeds. Between the Clubhouse and Tao is a new, three-level infinity pool. The resort's gym has been doubled in size and a walking/jogging trail created.

In 2008, the oceanfront and oceanview rooms were upgraded with marble floors and furnished with four-poster, king or two queen beds, mini-fridge, iPod stations, and bathrooms with double-sink marble vanities. All rooms, except the standard garden, have refridgerators. The Grand Luxury oceanfront suites, the most desirable for their size, have large marbled bathrooms with bath and shower, separate marble makeup and double-sink vanities, and generous balconies overlooking the ocean. Those on the top floor of a 2-story building by the sea have a separate bedroom and living room, divided by double doors; they adjoin another guest room, providing the option of a two-bedroom suite. The resort has standard rooms priced as singles with no supplement; it is one of the very few hotels in the Caribbean with accommodations for singles. Each is a generous 280 square feet.

The Oasis, designed in the Moorish style of Spain's Alhambra Palace, is one of the most comprehensive health and well-being centers in the Americas and now with 36 treatment rooms, is probably the largest. A range of sophisticated "ritual" treatments includes a program for pregnant women, a program of Ayurvedic treatments, and a specialist skin clinic. Treatments can be booked in advance on the resort's website. What's more, you can customize your entire Body Holiday experience before you come. The Oasis includes a team from Kerala, India, the original source of the art of Ayurveda, who provides lifestyle counseling and nutritional advice, as well. The Oasis can pamper you with exotic wraps, Balinese massage, facials, as well as acupuncture techniques and Suikodo Chinese Bodywork.

All meals include a wide choice of dishes and are served in a choice of four venues. Cariblue is an open-air, beachside restaurant encased in tropical gardens serving breakfast and lunch with lavish buffets. Dinners in Cariblue are served a la carte, except for a Caribbean buffet one evening each week. Wines at lunch and dinner and all other beverages are included. The Clubhouse is open every evening for an informal barbecue, and the Deli is open throughout the day for snacks and lunch, specializing in smoothies.

Tao, the resort's award-winning, gourmet restaurant, immediately gained a well-deserved reputation for extraordinarily fine East-West fusion dishes. Tao's decor, which blends Asia and the New World, is as handsome as the cuisine is remarkable. And best of all, dining here is included in the resort's basic rates, except for a few signature dishes which carry a small supplement.

The air-conditioned piano bar, the gathering spot for cocktails and after-dinner socializing, features music by the resort's pianist nightly from 7 p.m. until the last guest retires.

Sports facilities are fabulous. Topping the list of water sports are trips for certified divers. You can also dive and snorkel directly off the beach. Windsurfing, water skiing, and Sunfish and Hobie Cat sailing, including instruction are offered daily. The resort has three pools—one for water volleyball and excercise, one for swimming, and the Oasis spa lap and exercise pool—as well as bicycles, aerobics, yoga, fencing, archery, and weight training, all with instruction.

The fitness instructor will adapt a program to your needs and you then get personal, individualized training for the duration of your stay. The Body Holiday has daily tai chi and yoga classes, and a popular "Master Class" program year-round. It varies from classes by highly skilled professionals in various physical, mental health, and fitness disciplines, all covered by the resort's all-inclusive rate.

Golf is available at a nearby 18-hole layout at a special rate including golf cart. The resort has a golf academy with four practice holes, putting green, and two resident professionals; an archery range; and a tennis pavilion with two courts and a club house. Tennis attire is required. Turtle-watching, which might include overnight camping on the beach, is often available from about March through June when the females come ashore to lay their eggs in the sand.

Finally, if all of this wasn't enough, more intrepid guests can opt to "Walk on the Wild Side," an exclusive The Body Holiday adventure program that explores St. Lucia's rain forest, climbs the famous Pitons, and more.

THE BODY HOLIDAY
★ ★ ★ ★ ⛵

PO Box 437, Cariblue Beach, St. Lucia, W.I.
Phone: (758) 457-7800, (800) 544-2883; **Fax:** (758) 450-0368; **e-mail:** reservations@thebodyholiday.com; www .thebodyholiday.com

Owner: Sunswept Resorts, St. Lucia
General Manager: Andrew Barnard
Open: Year-round
US Reservations: Direct to hotel or (800) 544-2883; **e-mail:** thebodyholi day@sunsweptresorts.com
Deposit: 3 days minimum prior to reservation, balance within 21 days
Minimum Stay: None
Arrival/Departure: Transfer not included
Distance from Airport: (George F. L. Charles Airport) 7 miles (20 minutes); Hewanorra International Airport: 28 miles (90 minutes), taxi one-way $90.
Distance from Castries: 8 miles; taxi one-way, $40
Accommodations: 154 rooms including 29 singles (all with four-poster canopy king-size beds, terraces, and ocean or garden views)
Amenities: Air-conditioning; bathroom with shower, marble vanity with 2 sinks in oceanfront rooms; hair dryer, bathrobe, basket of toiletries; mini-fridge (except single rooms); coffee/tea maker telephones, Internet access ($20 per stay); room service for continental breakfast; boutique; gift shop; no television; iPod dock in all rooms
Fitness Facilities/Spa Services: See text
Sports: See text

Electricity: 220/110 volts
Dress Code: Sports and beachwear during day; cover-up in dining rooms; only slightly dressier in evening
Children: Minimum age 12 years old during June 16–Sept 6 and 16 years at other times
Meetings: None
Day Visitors: Welcome with reservations; packages range from $35 from 12:30–3 p.m. with lunch and drinks to $150 full day with lunch, dinner, and drinks; treatments subject to availability and priced separately
Handicapped Facilities: Limited, inquire
Packages: Honeymoon, wedding, occasional yoga and other specialties; special priced ones
Rates: Per person double, daily, All-Inclusive. *High Season* (Jan 6–19): $547–$772; (Jan 20–Mar 31) $581–$806; (Dec 21–Jan 5) $776–$1,001. *Shoulder Season* (Apr 1–June 16): $545–$770; (Oct 7–Dec 6) $556–$781; (Dec 7–20) $450–$675. *Low Season* (June 17–Oct 6): $450–$675. Single rates available, inquire.
Service Charge: Included
Government Tax: Included

CAP MAISON

Gros Islet, St. Lucia

Set on a 4-acre, cliff-top corner of St. Lucia's north end overlooking the Caribbean Sea and a short drive from Rodney Bay, Cap Maison offers the best of two worlds: Seclusion and tranquility within the upscale Cap Estate area, and only minutes from the island's most popular restaurants, shopping, nightlife, plus a host of diversions: golf, snorkeling, diving, kite surfing, horseback riding, hiking, tennis, and the Friday night Jump-up in the village of Gros Islet.

The hotel's architecture and design reflect the Spanish Caribbean of yesteryear with brick-lined walkways, multi-tiered balconies, terracotta roof tiles, a central courtyard and fountain amid a profusion of ornamental tropical gardens. Interiors with lots of wood, natural materials, handmade textiles and furnishings, jalousie doors and windows; hand painted tiles, brick barrel-vaulted ceilings, wrought iron chandeliers and copper filigree wall lamps showcase the high quality craftsmanship and attention to detail.

Fifty fashionably-appointed rooms, junior suites, and exceptionally spacious one-, two-, and three-bedroom villa suites enjoy scenic views due to the hotel's position on the bluff. All have large bathrooms and the villa suites are equipped with professional-grade kitchens, spacious living and dining areas, online fridge packages and a private chef option, indoor/outdoor showers and private pools, located either on the ground floor or on a private roof top terrace.

All rooms and suites have an air-conditioned bedroom with king-size beds, except for garden-view rooms that have twin beds (which can be made into doubles). Some suites have a sofa bed in living room. Bedrooms lead to spacious, nicely furnished verandas. All accommodations have ceiling fan, iPod dock, BOSE music center, DVD, flat-screen television, handsome bathrooms with showers and hand-painted tiles, deluxe Italian amenities, tea/coffee maker, and mini-bar. Internet access is available in all rooms and suites plus Wi-Fi hotspots in some public areas. Villa suites have an automatic washing machine. A garden room and one- or two-bedroom villa suite can be combined to create a two- or three-bedroom accommodations. Guest rooms are serviced by private butlers.

The resort has an air-conditioned sports lounge and a sunset bar by the water, which are available for private occasions. A walk-in wine cellar stocked with over 185 different old and new world wines, doubles as a private dining room where guests can enjoy exclusive wine tastings with the sommelier and rum samplings.

The Cliff at Cap, the main restaurant open for breakfast, lunch, and dinner, is directed by executive chef Craig Jones, a former St. Lucian Chef of the Year. Its menu offers French-West Indian–inspired contemporary fare based on fresh local products and fresh seafood. The restaurant, named for its dramatic location, is perched at the edge of a cliff that is literally the island's end. Multilevel decks and sitting areas provide unobstructed views to Pigeon Point on the south and yachts and cruise ships sailing by where the Caribbean meets the Atlantic.

The Cliff Bar, one of the resort's three bars, serves light meals and snacks for lunch and tapas in the evenings. The Beach Bar at Smugglers Cove operates during the day to 5 p.m. Theo's, an indoor honor bar with flat-screen television, is popular for pre-dinner cocktails and late night socializing. Rock Maison, a wooden deck atop a rock out to sea, is a romantic sunset perch where champagne is delivered by zip line. It's also perfect for yoga, tai chi, spa treatments, weddings, and afternoon tea.

Spa Maison offers a full menu of spa services using products from Sothys, a French company with over 60 years experience in the beauty industry and by therapists, trained by it. The spa has two treatment rooms with outdoor terraces as well as a treatment room for couples, and a salon for manicures, pedicures, and hair styling. Massages can also be enjoyed in one's room or in a quiet area of the resort. At the après treatment veranda guests enjoy brews made with infusions based on fresh-cut flowers and herbs from the resort's garden.

An air-conditioned lounge with library and large-screen television can be used for meetings up to 50 people; equipment can be provided.

Cap Maison I, the resort-owned and operated 46-foot yacht, is available for the exclusive use of the resort's guests for sunset cruises, wedding parties, special events, and day or overnight excursions to a neighboring island. The air-conditioned yacht, which sleeps 4 passengers comfortably, has 2 private cabins, 2 bathrooms—1 with a separate glassed-in shower. It is finished with polished teak interiors, a full galley, soft beige leather banquettes, and an expansive forward deck for sunbathers. A skipper and private chef prepare all meals, including line-caught fish reeled in from the deck. Rates, plus 18 percent for service and tax, range from $600 for a Sunset Cruise to $2,000 for a full day excursion and include skipper, crew, mooring/docking charges, fuel, and drinks for a maximum of 12 passengers.

Starting in January 2012, Cap Maison will introduce a great package "Peak to Beach" with Ladera (also in this chapter), a very different style hotel overlooking the Pitons in southern St. Lucia. You spend three nights at each resort plus enjoy a host of goodies like a spa treatment, meals, wine, transfers between the resorts, and more. Check it out.

Cap Maison prides itself on being green. During its building hotel and facilities construction, it incorporated products based on sustainable resources and minimal use of synthetic products, such as plastics. The hotel relies on solar energy for its hot water, and the rooms and windows were designed to optimize the trade winds off the sea to reduce the need for air-conditioning. Recycled water is used to irrigate the grounds, and organic food suppliers provision the hotel. Diversions are many, beginning with golf at the nearby 18-hole St. Lucia Golf & Country Club.

CAP MAISON ★ ★ ★ ★ 🥄

Cap Maison, PO Box 2188, Gros Islet, St Lucia, W.I.
Phone: 001-758-457-8670; **Fax:** 001-758-450-8847; www.capmaison.com
Owner: The Gobat family
General Manager: Ross Stevenson

Open: Year-round
US Reservations: Direct to hotel: reservations@capmaison.com or 001-758 457 8691
Deposit: Secured with credit card
Minimum Stay: 1 night; 7 nights Christmas/New Year's
Arrival/Departure: One-way, air-conditioned car transfer to resort from George FL Charles Airport (Castries), $35 one way; from Hewanorra International $85–$150 per couple; helicopter transfer from Hewanorra to GFL Charles plus car to resort, $320 per couple
Distance from Airport: From Hewanorra International, 1½ to 2 hours by car; from GFL Charles Airport, 30 minutes by car. (See above for prices)
Distance from capital: 8 miles; taxi one-way, $40
Accommodations: 49 units in 9 buildings (15 garden, 12 junior suites with furnished terrace; 3 villa suites in courtyard with 1 bedroom. One-bedroom split level villa suites: 4 with Jacuzzi on first floor; 5 with pool on ground floor; 9 with pool and swim-up counter on roof terrace; mini bar; deluxe bathroom; 1 two-bedroom split-level villa suite with roof terrace pool. Villa suites have kitchen, separate sitting room/dining area, and sofa bed in living room.
Amenities: BOSE systems, stereos, cable television, iPod stations, deluxe Italian bathroom amenities, Internet access in rooms and suites, Wi-Fi hotspots in some public areas. Room service, in-room dining in villas; private chef option; boutique
Fitness Facilities/Spa Services: Gym with cross-trainer, exercise bike,

treadmills, resistance machines, yoga classes. Spa/hairdresser

Sports: Cliff-top infinity pool and Jacuzzi, courtyard pool, nonmotorized water sports, snorkeling at Smugglers Cove, windsurfing, hobie cats, boggie boards, and kayaking. Nearby tennis at St Lucia Racket Club; kite surfing on request; golf at 18-hole championship St Lucia Golf & Country Club, 5 minutes away

Electricity: 210 volts/3-prong plug; 110 volts/2-prong plug.

Dress Code: Casual by day, elegantly casual for dinner.

Children: All ages, year-round. No children under 12 years in upper-floor suites. Cots for infants under 2 years, free. Babysitting on request.

Meetings: Small meetings up to 100 persons can be accommodated but without dedicated meeting space, resort does not actively promote them

Day Visitors: Yes, restaurant, with reservations

Handicapped: Limited facilities

Packages: Weddings, Honeymoon, Peak to Beach (combination with Ladera)

Rates: Per room, double, *High Season* (Jan 3–Apr 30): $435–$935; villa suite with pool, $1,040–$1,255. *Low Season* (May 1 to Dec 19): $403–$705 and $850–$1,050. *Christmas Season* (Dec 20 to Jan 2): $495–$950 and $1,135–$1,380.

Service Charge: 10 percent

Government Tax: 8 percent

COCO PALM

Rodney Bay, St. Lucia

St. Lucia's first boutique hotel, Coco Palm, is truly one of the best values in the Caribbean, offering services and facilities found in four-star hotels but at moderate prices.

Located in St. Lucia's hip Rodney Bay Village, that is being called St. Lucia's answer to South Beach, the hotel's design is a combination of contemporary and Creole tradition set in gardens overlooking the swimming pool.

Coco Palm's guest rooms and suites are situated in either the modern four-story Palm building or Kreole Village next door (formerly Coco Kreolo, a former home renovated into an inexpensive small hotel). Recently, the upgraded Kreole Rooms were integrated into Coco Palm and provided the same amenities.

Each room is dressed in island colors of blue, green, and yellow with mahogany furniture reflecting a French Creole style and St. Lucian art on the walls. Bathrooms have glass-walled, walk-in shower stalls with rain showerheads and a built-in seating area in the shower and granite vanity tops. All rooms are air-conditioned and have ceiling fans, cable television/DVD, cordless phone, international direct dialing, free Wi-Fi, minifridge, safe, coffee/tea maker, hair dryer, iron/ironing board, and dual-voltage outlets.

The 30 Pool View rooms overlook Coco Palm's free-form swimming pool and have sliding glass doors that open up to a tiny terrace. The most popular rooms are six ground-level Swim-Up rooms where guests can literally open the bedroom sliding glass doors and step into the swimming pool. The suites are located on the top floor of the Palm building, some with pool view, some with garden view. All have a separate bedroom and living room with a window seat, two bathrooms (one with shower and one with double-sink vanity, bathtub, and walk-in shower). They also have iPod/MP3 interface, flat-screen television, and a living room sofa that opens up to a bed. Children under 12 stay for free.

Included among the suites are four Family Suites (600 square feet) comprised of a master bedroom with both a shower and Victorian roll-top tub, as well as flat-screen television, iPod docking station, and cordless phones. The adjoining room offers two twin beds, cable television, DVD player, and its own bathroom and can accommodate two children, 16 years and under. One of the suites has been converted to a premium suite with 50-inch television and named the Darren Sammy for the current West Indies cricket captain and St Lucian hero who patronizes Coco Palm.

Coco Palm has an innovative "host" system that eliminates the traditional check-in desk. Instead, each floor has an assigned host who serves as a personal guide to assist guests throughout their stay, providing much of the same service as a concierge. To avoid the check-in ordeal, guests upon arrival are taken directly to their rooms; check-in can be done at the guest's leisure. Also each of the floors has two housekeepers who service the rooms on their floor.

The hotel's restaurant, Ti Bananne, is an open-air eatery offering Caribbean Creole fare and on most nights, entertainment. Easily accessible to folks in Rodney Bay village, it has its own entrance from the street and is popular with local residents. Coco Palm recently added a second eatery with lighter fare at Kreole. Also new are poolside showers and bathroom facilities.

Adjacent to the Kreole Rooms is a newly built conference center, in the style of a traditional chattel house. It can accommodate from 40 to 90 people in its conference room and and 18 to 30 persons in its boardroom, depending on these rooms configuration. It is fully fitted with wireless Internet access and can provide secretarial services. A second boardroom is also available. Inquire from Coco Palm for details.

Coco Palm is a five-minute walk from Reduit Beach, one of St. Lucia's nicest beaches, with water sports, beach restaurants, and local bars.

The hotel offers spa treatments at Coco Beauty Clinic, a chattel-house-style cottage adjacent to the Palm building. Treatments are available by appointment only.

Coco Palm's CYS (Customize Your Stay) program is intended to handle guests' needs—airport transfers, flowers in the room, restaurant reservations, tours, excursions, spa treatments—in advance of their arrival.

COCO PALM ★★
Reduit Beach Avenue, Rodney Bay Village, Gros Islet, St. Lucia, W.I.
Phone: (758) 456-2800; **Fax:** (758) 452-0713; **e-mail:** reservations@coco-resorts.com; www.coco-resorts.com
Owners: Allen and Feolla Chastanet
Managing Director: Feolla Chastanet
General Manager: Jean St. Rose
Open: Year-round

US Reservations: (866) 588-5980 or **e-mail:** usreservations@coco-resorts.com
Deposit: Secured with credit card
Minimum Stay: 3 nights peak seasons
Arrival/Departure: Arrange for fee
Distance from Airport: George FL Charles Airport 6 miles; Hewanorra International Airport 27 miles. Taxi service (with water and cold towels) from Hewanorra, $90 for up to 3 persons; GFL Charles, $30 up to 3; executive taxi: $120 and $40; luxury transfers (with drinks, snacks, and cold towels): $150 and $60 respectively
Distance from Castries: 7 miles
Accommodations: 108 rooms (12 patio pool, 35 pool view and garden view; 18 garden patio; 6 swim-up; 8 one-bedroom suites; 4 family suites, 20 Kreole)
Amenities: Air-conditioning, ceiling fan, cable television, DVD player on request; cordless phone, international direct dialing, free Wi-Fi, coffee/tea maker, minifridge, hair dryer, iron/ironing board, dual-voltage outlets, safe; walk-in shower stall with rain showerheads and built-in seat. Suites have additional shower en-suite with roll-top bathtub and walk-in shower; and room service; iPod in top rooms/suites
Fitness Facilities/Spa Services: Spa treatments in hotel room, near pool, or roof deck
Sports: Swimming pool; short walk to beach with water sports; golf, sailing, waterskiing, diving (for certified divers), snorkeling, kayaking, rain forest hiking, mountain biking arranged
Electricity: 220/110 volts
Dress Code: Resort casual

Children: Day-care and babysitting services available; under 12 years free when sharing with parents
Meetings: Top floor private room for small meetings, audiovisual equipment, and business services
Day Visitors: In the restaurants; day rooms on request
Handicapped Facilities: Yes

Packages: Wedding, honeymoon, getaway, family, and others
Rates: Per room, CP: *High Season* (Feb 1–Mar 31): $170–$435. *Low Season* (Jan 3–31 and Apr 1–May 9; May 14–Dec 22): $145–$343. *Jazz Festival* (May 10–13): $180–$445.
Service Charge: 10 percent
Government Tax: 8 percent

LADERA

Soufrière, St. Lucia, W.I.

Crowning a ridge directly above the Pitons, the award-winning Ladera is a small resort at 1,100 feet above sea level with unusual accommodations often described as deluxe tree houses. Over the years the privacy and heavenly setting of this enchanting resort have charmed celebrities, such as Oprah Winfrey and Matt Dillon, who have spent almost a week there, and just plain folks—enough apparently that in 2005, readers of a leading travel magazine voted Ladera the "Best Resort in the World."

In the world? That's a tall order, but what is indisputable is Ladera's unique location and the unusual way the resort is designed to take full advantage of the location and its natural surroundings.

All of Ladera's six villas and 26 suites have no wall on their west side. They are completely open and front an incredible view of the Pitons and the Caribbean Sea, yet provide complete privacy. Each unit also has a small pool equally as private. With its wooded hillside setting at such height, no one but the birds can see into your room.

Although each of the suites and villas is different in layout and decor, they have many similar features. All are constructed of tropical hardwoods and stone and have wooden beam ceilings. They are furnished with netting-draped mahogany four-poster beds and other furniture made by Ladera's own craftsmen and decorated with colorful prints and local paintings and sculpture.

The Petit Piton, or one-bedroom suites, have grotto-style plunge pools, and two-bedroom villas have slightly larger pools with waterfalls. A one-bedroom suite has an open-air master bedroom with a queen-size bed and a plunge pool. The Gros Piton, or deluxe one-bedroom suite, has a larger open-air master bedroom, a large plunge pool fed by a waterfall, and extensive views.

All accommodations have private bathrooms, refrigerators with a complimentary "welcome stock," and coffee/tea makers, but no telephones or televisions. (Telephone, fax, and computer station in the resort's office are available for guests to use.) Rooms are not air-conditioned and don't need to be due to Ladera's elevation. It's always cooler here than at lower levels in St. Lucia, and trade winds provide constant natural air-conditioning. Flowers from Ladera's beautiful gardens, cut fresh daily, are displayed in guest rooms and throughout the resort. Ladera is a "green" resort; your hot water is solar heated.

The dreamiest of these love nests are the five Hilltop Dream Suites located at the end of the forested ridge at the farthest point from the public areas. These suites have an open bedroom and living area, four-poster king bed, and bathroom. Each suite has a private pool with a waterfall, and fabulous views. Given the resort's dreamy setting, it's no wonder that it has long been a popular wedding and honeymoon destination. Now, there's a new open-air Paradise Pavilion in the rain forest setting for ceremonies and receptions of up to 80 guests. And with it has come a group of wedding packages starting from $995 for legal arrangements, witnesses, and a simple ceremony by Ladera's infinity pool to $1,600 that upgrades the basic package with a private ceremony in Paradise Pavilion, flowers, champagne reception, and a wedding cake. Ladera's wedding planner: (866) 290-0978; weddings@ladera.com.

Ladera's restaurant, Dasheene, is as famous as the resort with the same fabulous views from three levels. Headed by award-winning Chef Orlando Satchell from Jamaica and St. Lucian Chef Nigel Mitchel, Dasheene offers an eclectic, innovative cuisine blending Caribbean, Asian, and European traditions and stresses fresh fish and local fruits and vegetables. The no-smoking restaurant serves three meals, afternoon tea, and cocktails. Reservations are recommended. On Saturday the chefs conduct a market tour, followed by a cooking class for hotel guests. The resort also keeps menus from nearby restaurants when guests want to try other places.

Next to the restaurant with full view of the Pitons and the sea is an infinity pool (seen in the movie *Superman II* and rumored to be the first ever built) and deck area where cocktails and snacks are served poolside.

Ladera's Ti Kai Posé Spa (meaning "the little house of rest") has four treatment rooms (in-room massages are also available) and offers a variety of massages, scrubs, wraps, and facials. The most unusual treatment, called Sulphur Mud Wrap, includes both a body scrub and a body wrap. Therapists take spa guests to the nearby Sulphur Springs, where the mineral mud that originates from St. Lucia's famous "drive-in" volcano is used in the treatment. A complimentary shuttle takes guests to/from nearby beaches and provides snorkeling equipment. Ladera can arrange hiking/rain forest walks with local guides, horseback riding, scuba diving, deep-sea fishing, whale watching (seasonal), or a private yacht for a day sail out along the Pitons and St. Lucia's beautiful Caribbean coast.

In January 2012, Ladera will introduce a neat package "Peak to Beach" with Cap Maison (also in this chapter), a very different style hotel at the north end of St. Lucia. You spend three nights at each resort plus enjoy lots of goodies included like a spa treatment, meals, wine, transfers between the resorts, and more. Check it out. Ladera is an adult resort and does not accept children under the age 15 except during the Christmas season when families with children 4 years and older are welcome.

LADERA ★★
PO Box 2225, Soufrière, St. Lucia, W.I.
Phone: (758) 459-7323; **Fax:** (758) 459-5156; (866) 290-0978; **e-mail:** reservations@ladera.com; www.ladera.com
Owner: Tiara Consulting, Inc.
General Manager: To be announced as of press time
Open: Year-round except mid-Sept/early Oct
US Reservations: Direct to hotel, (866) 290-0978 or Karen Bull Associates, (800) 738-4752; **Fax:** (404) 237-1841
Deposit: 2 nights; cancellation 21 days to avoid forfeiting deposit
Minimum Stay: 7 nights Christmas; 4 nights New Year's; 3 nights, winter to mid-Apr
Arrival/Departure: Airport transfer arranged for GFL Charles Airport (SLU) $100 or Hewanorra Airport (UVF) $80 per couple, one way. Transfer included for some packages, inquire. UVF airport allows private jets. Daylight Water Taxi transfer from GFL Charles Airport, $240 per couple one way.
Distance from Airports: GFL Charles 25 miles; Hewanorra, 18 miles
Distance from Castries: 22 miles
Accommodations: 25 units (9 villas, 18 suites) with villa swimming pool or plunge pool
Amenities: Private pool, minibar, coffee/tea maker; hair dryer, iron/ironing board, bathrooms, beach towels; no telephones or television; safe available; charge for room service for meals and snacks; computer/Internet, phone and fax at reception
Fitness Facilities/Spa Services: Ti Kai Pose Spa offers facials, massages, body scrubs, wraps, waxing, manicures, and

pedicures; Botanic Gardens mineral baths arranged

Sports: Main pool, private plunge pools; rain forest hiking, bird-watching tours, horseback riding, sailing, diving, snorkeling, sport fishing, and whale-watching (in season) arranged

Electricity: 220 volts, 50 cycles (square, 3-prong plug), adapters available

Dress Code: No official dress code for Dasheene; during day, shorts, T-shirts, dresses, dry bathing suits with cover-ups accepted. For dinner, smart casual to elegant; gentlemen requested to wear sleeved, collared shirts, long pants, and footwear; jackets are not required. No shorts, tank tops, beach footwear, or bare feet.

Children: None under age 15, except at Christmas/New Year's when families with children ages 4 and older welcome

Meetings: Only when entire resort is booked

Day Visitors: At Dasheene with reservations

Handicapped Facilities: No

Packages: Wedding, renewal vows, all-inclusive

Rates: Per night, single/double. *High Season* (Jan 3–Apr 9): one-bedroom suite or villa, with pool, $665–$875; *Shoulder Season* (Apr 10–June 30; Oct 1–Dec 21): $525–$750. *Low Season* (July–Sept 30): $400–$595. Hilltop Dream Suite, $1,005, $875, $825 respectively. For 2-bedroom option, inquire. Rates include breakfast, afternoon tea, beach shuttle, snorkel gear.

Service Charge: 10 percent

Government Tax: 8 percent

ST. MAARTEN/ST. MARTIN

This small island in the heart of the Caribbean is Dutch on one side and French on the other. How an island of only 37 square miles became divided hardly seems to matter anymore except to history buffs and tax collectors.

Columbus discovered the island in 1493 and claimed it for Spain; several centuries later a young Dutchman, Peter Stuyvesant, lost a limb wresting the island from Spain. Still later the French got into the fray, and somewhere along the way, the Dutch and the French agreed to stop fighting and to divide the island instead.

Today there are no border formalities, because there are no real boundaries. The only way you can tell you are crossing from one country to the other is a welcome sign at the side of the road. A short 20-minute drive separates Philipsburg, the capital of Dutch St. Maarten, and Marigot, the capital of French St. Martin. The two flags nonetheless give the island an unusual international flair.

Philipsburg is the main port for cruise ships and the commercial center. The international airport is also on the Dutch side. Until recently Marigot was a village, but with new development it has become as busy as its Dutch counterpart. Yet it is unmistakably Gallic.

St. Maarten is intensively developed for tourists. Still, it remains one of the Caribbean's most popular islands: It has something for everyone, whatever the style, and offers as much to do as places 10 times its size.

The island has excellent sports facilities for tennis, golf, horseback riding, sailing, diving, windsurfing, and sport fishing. There's nightlife at discos and casinos. You can shop in trendy boutiques or air-conditioned malls for goods from around the world.

St. Maarten has a well-deserved reputation as a food lover's haven, and you can find restaurants serving Italian, Mexican, Vietnamese, Indonesian, Chinese, French, Dutch, and West Indian cuisine. The truly gourmet ones are in the village of Grand Case, near Marigot, but be prepared when the bill comes.

St. Maarten is a transportation hub for the northeastern Caribbean. Its location makes it an ideal base for exploring nearby Anguilla, Saba, Statia, St. Barts, and St. Kitts/Nevis.

Information

St. Maarten Tourist Office, Vineyard Office Park, W.G. Buncamper Road, 33 Philipsburg, St. Maarten, N.A.; (599) 542-2337; Fax: 599-542-2734; www .vacationstmaarten.com, www.stmaarten.com
St. Martin Tourist Office, 825 3rd Ave., 29th floor, New York, NY 10017; (212)745-0945; Fax: (212) 260-8481; www.stmartinisland.org

LA SAMANNA
St. Martin, F.W.I.

Snow-white villas draped in brilliant magenta bougainvillea sit between sea and sky on 55 tropical hillside acres stretching along one of the Caribbean's most gorgeous beaches.

Small and exclusive, La Samanna was designed with the international sophisticate in mind, to provide unpretentious luxury far from the real world. Set on the crest of a hill overlooking a 3,500-foot arc of deep white sand on Long Bay, the resort combines striking Mediterranean-Moorish architecture and colorful decor with a sophisticated Riviera ambience. When it opened in 1974, it set a new style in casual elegance in the Caribbean.

La Samanna was conceived by the late James Frankel, a New York businessman who was inspired to bring the flavor of the Mediterranean to the Caribbean. He equated luxury with privacy and asked noted Caribbean architect Robertson "Happy" Ward to design a private oasis of villas like a secluded estate rather than a hotel. La Samanna was named for Frankel's three daughters—Samantha (who's married to tennis great Ivan Lendl), Anouk, and Nathalie.

Today, in contrast to St. Martin's unbridled growth, La Samanna, now owned by Orient-Express, is an oasis of untrammeled beauty, appreciated even more now than when it first burst onto the scene. Upon entering the gardens, walled from the outside world, you find classic white stucco structures recalling a Greek island village. Stone steps wind down a multilevel sweep of balconies, arches, terraced gardens, and shaded walkways to the beach.

At the entrance to the main building, you will find a reception desk, a concierge, and a small lounge. They open onto the Le Reserve Restaurant to one side and on the other, step down to La Samanna's signature Baie Longue Bar with its colorful Indian wedding-tent canopy and Moorish-style furniture. Below the bar, a flower-encased terrace overlooks a pretty swimming pool smothered in gardens.

In 2007 La Samanna completed a multimillion-dollar renovation with major enhancements that included an infinity-edge freshwater pool by the sea, along with a new beach bar and deck, an expanded fitness center, a special seaview site for weddings, a business center for Internet access and office services, new guest rooms and villas.

For its size, La Samanna has a surprising variety of accommodations— seven categories of guest rooms plus villas. Deluxe ocean-view guest rooms are located in the three-story main building and along the beach. Rooms and suites open onto balconies that have low balcony walls with ironwork railings to capture the fabulous view of Long Bay. Every guest room, suite, and villa has modernized living spaces, expanded bathrooms, new upholstery, bedding, and bath linens. Atop the main building is a 1,200-square-foot Romance suite with a large outdoor terrace and plunge pool with grandstand views of the Caribbean and the beach. The suite has an al fresco dining area and lounging cabana. The outdoor space flows into the interior where the white decor

is brightened with the colorful paintings of well-known local artist Roland Richardson. The suite's entertainment center has a plasma television and a DVD collection of romantic films and CDs. Among the mood-setting amenities are a personalized bottle of wine and a pantry stocked with candles and bath salts. Flowers, fruit, and champagne are refreshed daily.

The resort's main accommodations are two-story units and villas with one- to three-bedroom suites that dot the hillsides and spill down to the beach. Most guest rooms and villas have individual entrances and private terraces or patios and are separated by a jungle of flowering hedges and trees that provide maximum privacy. Deluxe suites with bedroom, living room, terrace, and small kitchen also have a rooftop terrace with plunge pool, bistro table and chairs for dining, chaise longues, and outdoor showers.

The addition of eight palatial villas perched on the bluff to the west of the main building, brought an ultra-deluxe level to the resort. Keeping with La Samanna's graceful Mediterranean architecture, the villas boast over 4,600 square feet of living space with three or four master bedrooms and oversized private terraces, luxuriously furnished with great attention to detail. The villas are air-conditioned and have a sunken living room, wraparound terrace and infinity-edge pool, outdoor shower, indoor/outdoor dining, an office area, large, fully equipped open kitchens with stainless steel appliances, a second-floor terrace with breathtaking views of Long Bay, and independent entrances for each floor. Bedrooms are furnished with television, DVD player, large bathrooms, bathrobes, hair dryers, L'Occitane bath amenities, and fresh flowers.

At the beach are the six circular beach cabanas with wood flooring. Each is equipped with two iPods with a selection of music, CD/stereo/radio system, DVD player, chilled champagne, sunning products, lounge chairs, and a cabana attendant who brings fresh towels, lunch, and arranges for spa treatments in the privacy of the cabana. Cost per day is $350 in summer, $500 in winter. The "Midnight Cabana" offers a telescope for stargazing and private dining by the beach.

Beach attendants provide complimentary chilled water, fruit and sorbets, and cold towels during midday. Once weekly, guests can take in a movie under the stars. The resort's array of water sports include sailboats, kayaks, waterskiing, snorkeling, and diving trips, and its own fleet of luxury yachts and cruisers.

Le Reserve restaurant, an open-air terrace with an eagle's-nest view of Long Bay, has an additional terrace for alfresco dining, providing a more relaxed, inviting atmosphere. The restaurant has long had a reputation as one of the Caribbean's best and most original—and very expensive. It is headed by French Chef Vincent Wallez who has retained the resort's tradition of combining innovative French cuisine with Caribbean influences. From time to time the resort offers a celebrity guest chef program.

The restaurant has an extensive wine list with 12,000 bottles from 13 countries—a collection begun by Frankel, who was a connoisseur. La Cave, the wine cellar, has a private dining room that can handle 15 guests for private wine tasting and dinners. The Beach Bar features light lunch selections daily.

La Samanna's fitness center, doubled in space, has a dedicated area for cardio equipment and a wing for free weights and weight training equipment. There also is a Pilates and yoga studio, a certified fitness trainer, and morning aerobics classes. The La Samanna Spa with its indoor/outdoor tropical garden treatment rooms proved to be so popular it had to be expanded in its first year.

Other facilities include three tennis courts with night lights; a meeting pavilion with state-of-the-art audiovisual equipment and lounge. The resort offers wedding packages designed by professional planners. La Samanna has several boutiques that stock designer jewelry, perfume, fine clothing, and the resort's signature line. The boutiques and a helicopter landing pad are built into a coral knoll across from the resort's main building.

La Samanna caters to a sophisticated, affluent clientele. Through the years the privacy and elegant informality have pleased a roster of stars, celebrities, and captains of industry, most from North America, some from Europe. The romantic resort is an ideal honeymoon spot, but its seclusion and villa facilities also make it desirable for couples and families with young children.

LA SAMANNA ★ ★ ★ ★
PO Box 4077, Marigot 97064, St. Martin, F.W.I.

Phone: (590) 590-87-64-00; **Fax:** (590) 590-87-87-86; www.lasamanna.com
Owner: Orient Express
General Manager: Pascal Deyrolle
Open: Year-round except Sept–Oct
US Reservations: La Samanna, (800) 854-2252; **Fax:** (212) 575-7039; **e-mail:** reservations@lasamanna.com
Deposit: 3 nights; 30 days cancellation, winter; 15 days Apr 15–Aug 31
Minimum Stay: 10 nights during Christmas holidays; 5 nights over high-season weekends and some holidays
Arrival/Departure: Airport meet-and-assist service (see text)
Distance from Airport: 1½ miles; taxi one-way, $20
Distance from Philipsburg: 2½ miles; taxi one-way, $40
Distance from Marigot: 5 miles; taxi one-way, $18
Accommodations: 83 rooms and suites; 8 villas with 3- and 4-bedrooms—all with kings or twins, and all with terrance or patio
Amenities: Air-conditioning in bedroom, ceiling fan; telephone; bath with tub and shower, bathrobe, hair dryer, deluxe toiletries; safe, television, DVD; nightly turndown service; refrigerator (stocked on request), 24-hour room service; boutiques; for the new villas, see text
Fitness Facilities/Spa Services: Fitness center; full-service La Samanna Spa
Sports: 2 freshwater swimming pools; 3 lighted tennis courts, tennis pro; water-skiing, windsurfing, Sunfish, free snorkel gear; waterskiing lessons available; golf, horseback riding, fishing, sailing charters arranged
Electricity: 220 volts
Dress Code: Casual; no jacket or tie required at dinner
Children: All ages; cribs; babysitters; children under age 12 free in room with parents
Meetings: Up to 60 people
Day Visitors: With reservations for lunch or dinner
Handicapped Facilities: No
Packages: Honeymoon; spa; stay 7 days/pay for 5
Rates: Per room, daily, FAB. *High Season* (mid-Dec–mid-Apr): $995–$2,995. *Low Season:* $495–$1,650. Villas per night from $2,000 summer; to $6,500 winter; and to $9,000 holidays
Service Charge: Included
Government Tax: 5 percent
Resort Fee: 10 percent

ST. VINCENT & THE GRENADINES

Nature's awesome power and exquisite beauty live side by side in this chain of idyllic islands. Mountainous and magnificent, St. Vincent is the largest of the multi-island group. Its lush terrain, thick with tropical forests and banana plantations, rises quickly from the sea to more than 4,000 feet in the smoldering volcanic peaks of La Soufrière in the north.

The Botanic Gardens in Kingstown, the capital, are the oldest in the Western Hemisphere. Among their prized species is a breadfruit tree from the original plant brought from Tahiti by Captain Bligh of the Bounty.

St. Vincent has a series of mountain ranges up the center of the island. The Buccament Forest Nature Trail is a signposted loop through the fabulous rain forest where gigantic gommier and other hardwoods make up the thick canopy towering more than 100 feet.

La Soufrière has erupted five times since 1718, most recently in 1979. The crater, about a mile across, smolders and emits clouds of steam and sulfur fumes. The Falls of Baleine tumble 70 feet in one dramatic stage through a steep-sided gorge of volcanic rock at the foot of the Soufrière Mountains. From Kingstown the falls are accessible only by sea; excursions depart almost daily.

The Grenadines, stretching south from St. Vincent more than 65 miles to Grenada, are a chain of three dozen islands and cays often called by yachtsmen the most beautiful sailing waters in the world. Only eight are populated.

Bequia, the largest and most developed of the Grenadines, is known for its skilled sailors and boatbuilders. The island's laid-back lifestyle has made it a favorite of artists, writers, and old salts who never found their way back home.

Young, Palm, and Petit St. Vincent are private island resorts; Mustique is a celebrity mecca. Other islands with resorts are Mayreau, Canouan, and Union, all with remarkable beaches and small resorts with facilities for sailing, diving, fishing, and other water sports. Tobago Cays are four uninhabited islets scalloped with seemingly untouched white-sand beaches and beckoning aquamarine waters.

Dive aficionados call St. Vincent the sleeper of Caribbean diving; reef life normally found at 80 feet in other locations grows here at depths of only 25 feet and includes an extraordinary abundance and variety of tropical reef fish.

Information

St. Vincent and the Grenadines Tourist Office, 801 2nd Ave., 21st Floor, New York, NY 10017; (212) 687-4981, (800) 729-1726; Fax: (212) 949-5946; www.discoversvg.com

YOUNG ISLAND

St. Vincent, W.I.

If painter Paul Gauguin had stopped here after leaving Martinique, he might not have pressed on to the South Seas in his search for the totally exotic. The lush, volcanic terrain of undeveloped St. Vincent is a dead ringer for Tahiti 50 years ago, and it's still teeming with mystery.

But there's no mystery about Young Island. This 35-acre private-island resort only 200 yards off St. Vincent's southern shore is luxury amid tropical profusion, a fantasy version of Polynesia in miniature. Your adventure begins when you board a Grenadine version of the *African Queen* for the 5-minute ride across the narrow channel to Young Island.

One of Young Island's longtime staff members meets guests at the dock, usually preceded by a waiter carrying a tray of hibiscus-decorated rum punch. (You'll need a drink after the daylong journey—two plane rides, taxi, and boat—it takes to reach Young's tropical shores.)

From the dock you will be led along stone paths through a maze of greenery to your island quarters—one of 29 thatched bungalows of Brazilian hardwood and volcanic stone tucked away on the beach or hidden on a hillside. What they lack in television and DVDs, they more than make up for in comfort and lush surroundings.

Guests partial to bird's-eye views and aerobic hikes always choose the hillside aeries. These feel like tree houses but offer great comfort and enchanting island decor as well as unexpected amenities: a huge bowl of local fruits in all cottages and, for guests on a return visit (often couples who honeymooned here), a bottle of wine. Two of the beachside cottages have plunge pools and CD players.

Inside the bungalow you feel as if you are outside. Vertical wooden louvers let in the outdoors, and sliding glass doors open onto a huge balcony suspended above the bush. A seductive hammock for two awaits, along with a splendid view of the mountainous mainland or the Grenadines, dribbling south toward Grenada. Even the shower, cleverly appended to the dressing quarter with its jungle canopy and shoulder-high wooden "curtain," is alfresco. The three original luxury hillside suites (#28, #29, and #30) have plunge pools and CD player and the largest accommodation, Duvernette Suite (#26), has a small infinity edge swimming pool. All cottages have a refrigerator, safe, and private patio. Superior cottages are those nearest the beach and on the shoreline or low on the hillside. Luxury suites are beachside and hillside.

Cottage #15 has been converted into a treatment room of the Spa Kalina, a full-service facility. Guests may prebook massages, facials, manicures, pedicures, scrubs, reflexology, and waxing. It uses products from Earth Mother Botanicals of Barbados, which are made from natural ingredients and include a Bajan cane sugar body scrub, sea salt body scrub, ylang-ylang hydrating cream, and guava seed foot scrub, among others.

Somewhere down below is a free-form freshwater pool enveloped in a forest of tropical foliage. A tennis court hides amid the breadfruit and banana trees. Water spirits head for the dock to go snorkeling, windsurfing, or sailing. Dive St. Vincent is headquartered directly across Young Island Cut. Young also keeps a yacht along with a captain and chef, for day or overnight sailing trips; it offers a package that combines a stay at the resort with a two- or three-day cruise of the Grenadines.

But most guests tend to plop on the beach in hammocks under one of the *bohios,* the thatched-roof gazebos that enhance the island's South Pacific appearance. Occasional thirst may propel some to paddle a few strokes from shore to the Coconut Bar, a swim-up bar in a thatched hut that seems to float atop the Caribbean waters. Breakfast, lunch, and dinner are served in shaded garden nooks, some bounded by a moat, overlooking the beach. In the office nearby, guests can also check out their e-mail free for 15 minutes at a time.

By night guests gather in the wood-beamed bar and enjoy a variety of local entertainment several times a week. A cocktail party is held by the pool on Friday night.

Young offers a proper wine list, and the menu changes daily. The results might be such tempting choices as papaya soup laced with garlic or an island-grown avocado brimming with caviar, perhaps followed by just-caught lobster or a fillet of red snapper in cream-and-pepper sauce.

It's only when you hike back into the bush and up the hill that you might regret the many-course dinner, nurtured with spirits of cane and grape.

YOUNG ISLAND ★ ★ ★

Young Island Crossing, PO Box 211, St. Vincent, W.I.

Phone: (784) 458-4826; **Fax:** (784) 457-4567; **e-mail:** frontdesk@young island.com; youngisland@vincysurf .com; www.youngisland.com

Owners: Dr. Frederick Ballantyne and Vidal Browne

General Manager: Bianca Porter

Open: Year-round, except Sept 7–Oct 1

US Reservations: Ralph Locke Islands, Inc., (800) 223-1108; **Fax:** (310) 440-4220

Deposit: 3 nights in winter, 2 nights in summer; $1,500 for packages

Minimum Stay: 7 nights required during Christmas

Arrival/Departure: Transfer service arranged for fee

Distance from Airport: (St. Vincent Airport) 1½ miles; taxi one-way, $10

Distance from Kingstown: 3 miles; taxi one-way, $12

Accommodations: 29 cottages, all with patio (19 superior, king bed, beachside, shoreline, or low on hillside; 4 deluxe, larger king bed, with sitting area in bedroom, or large patio; 5 luxury full suites with bedroom, separate sitting room, plunge pool, coffeemaker and CD player; 2 beachside suites with king bed, 3 hillside with 2 queen beds. Hillside Duvernette suite with spacious separate living and dining areas, small infinity-edge pool, furnished deck with chairs, umbrella, hammock, coffeemaker, CD player

Amenities: Ceiling fans; garden shower, hair dryer, basket of toiletries, ice bucket, small refrigerator; coffeemaker/ tea; safe; nightly turndown service, room service for breakfast; 17 cottages have the option of air-conditioning, which must be requested with booking

Fitness Facilities/Spa Services: Spa Kalina, a full-service facility

Sports: Freshwater swimming pool; 1 lighted Har-Tru tennis court; free use of pedal boats, snorkeling gear, windsurfing equipment, and kayaks; sailing, deep-sea fishing, diving arranged at additional cost

Electricity: 220 volts/60 cycles; some cottages also have 110 volts/50 cycles

Dress Code: Casual

Children: All ages; cribs, high chairs; babysitters available at prevailing rates

Meetings: Up to 40 people; no equipment

Day Visitors: For meals

Handicapped Facilities: Limited

Packages: Honeymoon; Sailaway, dive, summer family

Rates: Per room, double, daily, MAP. *High Season* (mid-Dec–Mar 31): $532–$1,222. *Shoulder Season* (Apr 1–Aug; Nov–mid-Dec): $472–$934. *Low Season* (Sept–Oct): $448–$892.

Service Charge: Included

Government Tax: Included

THE FRANGIPANI HOTEL

Bequia, St. Vincent & the Grenadines, W.I.

You've heard it said that if you stand long enough in Times Square, sooner or later you'll see the whole world go by. In its own (decidedly more laid-back) way, the beach bar at the Frangipani Hotel can make a similar claim. Okay, maybe not the whole world—but surely a good slice of its more interesting and eccentric citizens.

Bequia's Admiralty Bay is one of the finest deepwater harbors in the Caribbean, and often the first landfall for yachts cruising from the Mediterranean to these warm waters. The Frangi, as it is known to habitués, is smack in the heart of the waterfront, surrounded by flowering bushes and trees.

Once the family home of the former prime minister of St. Vincent and the Grenadines, Sir James "Son" Mitchell,

it has been welcoming yachties and tourists for so many years that it has achieved legendary status.

The Frangi has never tried to be anything other than what it is—a comfortable inn—and there, in its utter lack of pretension, lies its charm. Mere steps from the yacht-filled bay, the hotel has been described in a novel this way: "Like the white hunter bars in Kenya, it's a pickup place, social headquarters, news central, information booth, post office and telegraph [and now phone, fax, and Wi-Fi] office, in short, the nerve center of the permanently-in-transit charter-boat trade."

Here you can gossip or flirt with serious salts who have circumnavigated the globe often, with boat bums and beach bunnies, Washington lawyers on bare-boat charters, college professors and freelance backpackers, couples with unpublishable biographies, locals and winter residents, dreadlocked Rastafarians, billionaire Arabs on zillion-dollar yachts, minor celebrities, older men with younger women, younger men with older women, and trios and combos of every age, nationality, and color imaginable.

On Thursday night the Frangi holds its weekly jump-up (barbecue and steel band), so called because the music does make it difficult not to jump up and dance. Around the bar, people are generally so chatty (and, as sundown turns the sky mauve, full of rum) that Attila the Hun could make friends here. Needless to say, solo travelers love it, though most guests are couples.

Breakfast, lunch, and dinner are served in an open-air dining room by the lobby. The food has been upgraded in the last few years and is very good, mostly West Indian fare with international touches cooked in quantities by local women who obviously enjoy their work. A Saturday morning buffet breakfast in the winter months has been added. The drinks along with a new cocktail menu, are good, too. The extensive wine list offers fine imported wines

Rooms at the Frangipani also have been updated and upgraded. The rooms are airy and comfortable and have phones and television, and wireless Internet access is available for a fee. The garden and deluxe units are equipped with a safe, fridge, coffeemaker, and the usual amenities such as shampoo. Rooms in the old house that face the water are simple—bed, tabletop fan,

cold-water hand basin, mosquito netting. Shared hot-water bathroom facilities are at the end of the corridor, and all share the one balcony overlooking the bay. The view—and the people-watching—make up for it.

The nicer stone units with balconies, two of which now have air-conditioning, are in the back of the main house. The smaller and less expensive garden units overlook the garden, and are furnished with twin or queen-size bed, private bath, separate dressing room, fans, fridge, coffeemaker, and safe. The deluxe units on the hillside have a large, spacious room with a choice of twin or a king-size bed, private bath, separate dressing room, fans, fridge, coffeemaker, safe, and balcony with lounge chairs. Some rooms have a desk and television/DVD. The air-conditioned rooms are furnished with four-poster king-size bed, private bath, separate dressing room, balcony with lounge chairs, fridge, coffeemaker, safe, desk, flat-screen television with DVD player and have a wonderful view of the bay. Room service breakfast is available in these accommodations.

The marble-tile-floor lobby is small but has maps and a take-one-leave-one paperback library. Anything you need, if it's humanly possible to obtain, will be provided cheerfully by the friendly staff. (In return, satisfied repeat guests happily run a supply train from New York bagels to hard-to-find plumbing supplies.)

Not much happens past 9 p.m. on the island, and dinner is nearly impossible to find after 7 p.m. But on Thursday, the barbecue, jump-up revelry, and the band (playing the same five amplified songs nearly every night at a different hotel) assault the eardrums till midnight or later.

Pack light; dress is very casual, but swimsuits are frowned upon by the local people except on the beach. Serious resort wear and high heels will cause muffled giggles (if not a sprained ankle). The island offers no glitz, gambling, or Gucci.

The Frangi has a tennis court and water sports (diving, snorkeling, wind-surfing) are available at two dive shops close by; two gorgeous beaches are a half-hour stroll or a short ride away.

People stay here for what can honestly be called one of the last few "true Caribbean experiences" still available. If you're looking for professionally deco-rated, five-star polish, don't give this one even a thought.

THE FRANGIPANI HOTEL ★

Box 1 BQ, Bequia, St. Vincent & the Grenadines, W.I
Phone: (784) 458-3255; Fax: (784) 458-3824; e-mail: frangi@vincysurf .com; www.frangipanibequia.com
Owner: Sir James "Son" Mitchell
General Manager: Sabrina Mitchell
Open: Year-round except Sept–mid-Oct
US Reservations: Direct to hotel; reser-vations@frangipanibequia.com
Deposit: 2 nights; 21 days cancellation less 10 percent
Minimum Stay: None

Arrival/Departure: No transfer service. If arriving by yacht, tie your dinghy to Frangi's dock; if by air, land at airstrip—however, landing could be chancy due to winds on eastern side of island. Try the scenic 20-minute roller-coaster drive across southern Bequia to hotel. Ferry daily between St. Vincent's Kingstown and Bequia, one-way, about $8
Distance from Airport: (Bequia) 3 miles; taxi one-way, $15
Accommodations: 15 rooms (5 original rooms in main building, 10 in garden units, all with balcony; air-conditioned Deluxe with king-size four-poster bed)
Amenities: Ceiling fans; bath with shower only; breakfast service in garden units; 2 units with air-conditioning and television; Wi-Fi access
Sports: Tennis free; boating, snorkeling, diving, windsurfing instruction for fee; hiking, birding; sunset cruises; no pool
Electricity: 220 volts
Dress Code: Very casual
Children: All ages; cribs; babysitters
Meetings: No
Day Visitors: Welcome
Handicapped Facilities: No
Packages: Dive
Rates: Per room, double, daily, EP, including 10 percent VAT. *High Season* (mid-Dec–mid-Apr): $75–$250. *Low Season:* $60–$180 (air-conditioned deluxe). Single rates are available.
Service Charge: 10 percent
Government Tax: Included

THE COTTON HOUSE

Mustique Island, St. Vincent, W.I.

Despite its role as snooty Mustique's only hotel of note, the Cotton House is more charming than grand, neither intimidating nor formal. Rather, it has the appeal of an English country inn set on manicured shores.

Opened in 1977, almost two decades after Colin Tennant bought Mustique and began developing it as a private tropical paradise for his royal and ritzy pals, the Cotton House was created out of the ruins of the stone and coral buildings of an 18th-century sugar and cotton plantation. The lovely two-story stone main house, originally the warehouse, was the brainchild of the famous British theater designer Oliver Messel, whose genius created many of the posh houses on Mustique.

The main house, with its refined proportions, is highlighted by cedar shutters and arched louvered doors. It's ringed with wide, breezy verandas where afternoon tea and candlelit dinners are served. A handsome horseshoe-shaped wooden bar is at the entrance to the large salon with high-peaked, wood-beamed ceilings; the salon, or Great Room, is lavished with painstakingly preserved antiques and amusing accoutrements. The original fabric designs by Oliver Messel was copied and freshened. It serves as the resort's focal point, where guests meet, mingle, and relax. Afternoon tea is served on the veranda that overlooks the lily pond.

The resort has a pool and a pool bar in the original sugar mill and private plunge pools in eight suites. Cotton Hill

Residence, a lovely two-bedroom villa with a large sitting room and dining room, has its own staff and butler, and outdoor gazebo. Situated on a hilltop with panoramic views of Mustique, the Atlantic Ocean and the resort's gardens, it boasts a new private swimming pool. Each of the well-appointed bedrooms is large and furnished with king beds draped in netting. The spacious bathrooms offer extra large soaking tubs; one has a private outside shower overlooking the gardens. One of the bedrooms is set apart from the main living space providing greater privacy.

The Cotton House's venue for fine dining is The Veranda Restaurant, which serves breakfast and dinner with a menu of Italian and eclectic international cuisine with Caribbean flavors. For casual lunch, the Beach Cafe and Bar offers alfresco dining at the water's edge with a menu that stresses local produce and freshly caught fish, lobster, salads, pizzas, and grill items. A picnic lunch or in-room dining can be choices from the chef's menu or yours and is meant to be more than plain room service.

Accommodations are in several Georgian-style buildings. The Grenadine Suites, with two upper and two garden-level deluxe accommodations with private verandas, look out at the ocean and the gardens colored with hibiscus and bougainvillea. They are connected by French doors from the bedroom and living room. The two lower Grenadine suites have private plunge pools. Battowia and Baliccau Houses, both with duplex suites, are ideal for families because each has two bathrooms and lots of outdoor space.

Most of the rooms and suites are furnished with a king-size bed draped in mosquito netting and have large marble bathrooms, usually with tub and shower. The attractive and understated interior decor is varied with white and blue, peach and beige and other combinations and white pickled-wood furniture. All guest rooms are equipped with air-conditioning and ceiling fans, flat-screen television and DVD/CD player, espresso machine, PC connection, minibars, and a pillow menu of ten selections. All have a terrace or patio. In the Great Room, a dedicated computer with broadband Internet access is free for hotel guests' use. Free Wi-Fi service is available anywhere on the hotel property.

A short way from the main house on the west side and only steps from the Caribbean Sea is the restored Coutinot House with five rooms and suites, adding more variety to the resort's accommodations. The three Seafront rooms (two with plunge pools), and the Seafront Master room and Seafront suite (both with plunge pools), offer the ultimate in privacy and panoramic sea views. They are furnished with writing desks, armoires, full dressing rooms, and wrought-iron, four-poster beds. Their large bathrooms have separate tubs and showers; the landscaped gardens directly outside add privacy and an indoor-outdoor effect. Tubs are strategically positioned for great views of the Caribbean and Grenadine Islands beyond. Each guest room has a wraparound terrace, ideal for watching the fabulous sunsets.

Coutinot House has a private path leading to a secluded beach. You can book rooms in Coutinot House individually or book the entire house. Prices include all meals, beverages (including wine, champagne, beer, and house cocktails), afternoon tea, water sports, tennis, and Cotton House amenities and services. The Cotton House has two tennis courts and is set between two of the white-sand beaches that scallop the island. It has Sunfish, windsurfers, and other water-sports equipment, and the dive shop offers a resort course and PADI certification. Snorkeling within swimming distance from shore at Endeavor Bay Beach is terrific. Deep-sea fishing and sailing excursions to nearby islands can be arranged. Only a short walk from the main house is a bird sanctuary; hiking almost anywhere on Mustique rewards you with outstanding views.

The Cotton House Spa, located only steps from the beach, has four treatment rooms and a relaxation room and offers facials and massage and a selection of body treatments. Treatments can be booked online. The ground floor of the bi-level facility houses a fitness center with exercise equipment. A boutique with Cotton House label selections is located on the second floor, along with the spa.

Cotton House guests are greeted by a resort representative in Barbados for their air transfer to Mustique. Upon arrival on the island, they are welcomed by the resort's director of guest relations, who escorts them to the resort and to their rooms. The housekeeping staff will unpack and press all clothing on your day of arrival at no charge. For those traveling with children, nanny service and babysitting are available.

THE COTTON HOUSE ★ ★ ★
Box 349, Mustique Island, St. Vincent, W.I.
Phone: (784) 456-4777; **Fax:** (784) 456-5887; **e-mail:** reservations@cotton house.net; www.cottonhouse.net
Owner: The Mustique Company
General Manager: Eleonore Petin
Open: Year-round, except Sept to mid-Oct
US Reservations: Direct to hotel, (877) 240-9945; reservations@cotton house.net
Deposit: 3 nights winter, 2 nights shoulder/summer; cancellation varies by days and season, inquire
Minimum Stay: 7 nights during Christmas with 50 percent deposit upon reservation confirmation; 5 nights in Feb
Arrival/Departure: Airport meet/ transfer in Barbados to Mustique for a 45-minute flight; or via St. Vincent with transfer to Mustique by air. In 2011, The Mustique Company added new nonstop transfers between St. Lucia (Hewanorra Airport) and Mustique. Private air transfers also available. All transfers are booked by the resort.
Distance from Airport: 1 mile; transfer included in hotel rate
Accommodations: 17 rooms and suites, and cottages (11 with private plunge pools), and including a 2-bedroom residence with a large swimming pool, butler, and vehicle
Amenities: Air-conditioning, ceiling fans; telephone; bath with tub and shower, hair dryer, bathrobes, basket of toiletries; ice service, minibar; nightly turndown service, room service, 7 a.m.– 11 p.m.; pillow menu; flat-screen television, DVD player, CD/stereo; safe; free

Wi-Fi Internet connection, iPod docking station; unpacking/pressing service upon arrival; twice daily maid service. Concierge service; daily international newspapers, CD/DVD library, boutique **Fitness Facilities/Spa Services:** Spa with 4 treatment room; fitness center with cardiovascular equipment **Sports:** Freshwater swimming pool, hammocks on beach, free use of 2 tennis courts and nonmotorized water sports, snorkeling gear, windsurfing, kayaks, biking, hiking, bird-watching; deep-sea fishing, horseback riding, diving arranged for charge. **Electricity:** 220 volts **Dress Code:** Casual by day; casually elegant in evening

Children: All ages; children's menus; nanny service available on request **Meetings:** None **Day Visitors:** No **Handicapped Facilities:** No **Packages:** 5 nights pay for 4; 7 nights pay for 6 **Rates:** Per room, double, daily, MAP including a la carte breakfast and VAT. *High Season* (mid-Dec–Apr 27): $1,030–$1,550. *Shoulder Season* (Oct 27–mid-Dec): $830–$1,400. *Low Season* (Apr 28–Sept 1): $720–$1,200. For Cotton Hill Residence rates, inquire. **Service Charge:** 10 percent **Government Tax:** Included

PALM ISLAND BEACH CLUB
Palm Island, St. Vincent, W.I.

The 135-acre private island scalloped with five white-sand beaches, is located at the southern end of the Grenadines. It has a free-form freshwater swimming pool with waterfalls, two restaurants, two bars, a boutique, air-conditioned fitness room, and two wedding gazebos.

The island was originally turned into a resort by the late John Caldwell, dubbed the Johnny Appleseed of the Caribbean. When he came upon the island, it was an uninhabited, mosquito-infested swamp that Caldwell remade as his own private paradise. But then probably anything seemed easy after he had sailed 8,500 miles alone in a small boat from Panama to Australia to find and marry his Mary, separated from him by World War II—a story described in his book *Desperate Voyage*.

Caldwell obtained the island from the government of St. Vincent for a $1 annual fee and a 99-year lease and promptly changed the name from Prune (who would believe an island called Prune was paradise?). Over the course of several decades, he planted thousands of coconut palms all over the island (and neighboring islands), earning himself the title of Coconut Johnny. The palms grew into the magnificent specimens that sway in everyone's daydreams and dot the resort's pure white beaches and undulating interior. Caldwell also planted every species of Caribbean tree that blossoms or bears fruit—all attracting an enormous variety of birds and turning Palm Island into a nature preserve and wildlife refuge.

In 1999, Palm Island was purchased by Rob Barrett, whose company manages Galley Bay Resort and Spa in Antigua and owns several other Caribbean hotels, and who made extensive renovations, upgrades, and expansion, adding more accommodations, facilities, and amenities and practically transforming Palm Island into a new resort.

The resort has several types of rooms, with over half of them directly on the beach and the others only steps away. Palm View rooms, located a few yards from the beach, overlook the tropical gardens. They have a sitting area, king-size bed (four have canopy beds) and a large bathroom with a deep-soaking tub and separate shower. Four suites are in a two-story building with wraparound balcony (two upstairs and two down). Each has a separate sitting area, a bathroom with a double shower (no bathtub), and is furnished with two queen-size beds plus a pullout couch. These rooms are particularly suited for a small family.

The spacious Beach Front rooms have king-size bed, bathroom with shower only, and are only steps from the clearest, purest aqua stretch of Caribbean water ever to lap a beach; mountainous Union Island and other nearby islands float on the horizon. Five Island lofts and four one-bedroom have air-conditioned rooms and large baths with shower and tub.

There are also two villas: The three-bedroom Seafeathers sleeps up to 6 adults and has a patio and a private pool; and Southern Cross sleeps four adults and has its own 10-foot-by-20-foot infinity edge swimming pool and use of golf cart for duration of stay. The bedrooms have marble bathrooms with large showers. Both villas are surrounded by 4 decks and are stocked with snacks, coffee, fruit, cereal, and beverages. All accommodations have balconies or patios, air-conditioning, ceiling fans, louvered windows, and are outfitted with custom-designed rattan and bamboo furniture and original artwork created by a resident Palm Island artist. The amenities include a safe, minifridge, basket of toiletries, bathrobes, nightly turndown service, and afternoon tea.

The upgraded public areas have contemporary furniture in the dining rooms and reception area, library, and the television/Internet room. (There is no charge for the Internet.) The air-conditioned fitness room has exercise equipment and a massage room for spa treatments.

The Royal Palms Restaurant serves breakfast, lunch, and dinner, while the smaller Sunset Grill and Bar offers grills and light fare in a casual beachside setting. Palm Island has long been a popular stop for yachties, who enliven the social scene at the bar and often stay for dinner.

Topping the list of activities is the superb snorkeling for which the island is known. It is surrounded by reefs, most within wading distance or a short swim from shore. A day trip to the nearby Tobago Cays National Marine Park is an absolute must. These uninhabited islets, surrounded by water so brightly turquoise it almost hurts your eyes, offer some of the best snorkeling in the Western Hemisphere. Palm Island also offers hiking on three nature trails, windsurfing, kayaking, Hobie-style catamarans, reef fishing, tennis court (including balls and rackets), table tennis, bike, and pitch and putt golf course.

Palm Island operates as an all-inclusive resort, one of the few on its own private island in the Caribbean. Breakfast, lunch, dinner, afternoon tea, and all drinks by the glass are included in the rates, as is the use of sports facilities, equipment, and instruction; tips and taxes. Scuba excursions, deep-sea fishing, and boat charters can be arranged for an additional charge.

Although Palm Island Beach Club is a pristine island in a spectacularly beautiful setting, ideal for a honeymoon or wedding and for travelers who truly want to get away from it all.

PALM ISLAND BEACH CLUB
★ ★ ★

1601 30th Ave., Deerfield Beach, FL 33442
Phone: (784) 458-8824, (866) 237-2157; **Fax:** (784) 458-8804; **e-mail:** palm@eliteislandresorts.com; www.palmislandresortgrenadines.com, www.eliteislandresorts.com
Owner: Rob Barrett/Elite Island Resorts
General Manager: Chris Ghita
Open: Year-round
US Reservations: (800) 858-4618, (954) 949-2132; reservations@eliteislands.com
Deposit: 3 nights; 30 days cancellation; for holiday periods, inquire
Minimum Stay: 3 nights, except holidays; inquire
Arrival/Departure: 50-minute flight (daily) from Barbados to Union Island ($200); there guests met by Palm Island representative and transferred by golf cart to dock to board Lady Palm for 10-minute boat ride to island. Air reservations handled by Palm Island's reservation office.

Distance from Airport: (Union Airport) 1 mile

Accommodations: 43 units (32 rooms, 4 suites, 5 lofts) with balconies or patios and king-size beds; 2 villas

Amenities: Air-conditioning, ceiling fans; radio; safe, minifridge, coffee-maker; bath with shower only, some with tubs; bathrobes, hair dryer, toiletries; no television in guest rooms; television/library room with satellite television and Internet access

Sports: 5 beaches, free-form freshwater swimming pool, tennis, nature trails, nonmotorized water sports; minigolf, cycling, croquet

Fitness/Spa facilities: Air-conditioned room with exercise equipment; massage room for spa treatment and services

Electricity: 110 volts

Dress Code: Smartly casual. After 6:30 p.m. long pants, short- or long-sleeved shirts, jeans, dresses, skirts and dress shorts; no flip flops, tennis shoes, T-shirts or tank top/sleeveless shirts in dining room.

Children: Summer only; all ages

Meetings: None

Day Visitors: No

Handicapped Facilities: No

Packages: Honeymoon, wedding, spa, adventure

Rates: Per room, two people, daily, **All-Inclusive.** *High Season* (mid-Dec–mid-Apr): $910–$1,165. *Low Season* (mid-Apr–mid-Dec): $795–$1,030. For Villa, single, triple, and quads rates, inquire.

Service Charge: Included

Government Tax: Included

PETIT ST. VINCENT RESORT

Petit St. Vincent, St. Vincent, W.I.

If you've ever fantasized about owning your own private tropical island—complete with invisible elves to cook, clean, and bring you drinks in your ultracomfy abode—start packing.

The late Haze Richardson was one of those rare individuals who did more than fantasize: He reclaimed what was basically an uninhabited 113-acre speck of land in the middle of nowhere and over 20 years turned it into one of the premier private-isle resorts in the Caribbean. Other resorts may be more stylish and manicured, prettier, and more lush, but only on Petit St. Vincent (pronounced PET-ty St. Vincent, or just PSV to cognoscenti) can you live out your dream of being all alone, in casual luxury, beyond the reach of time and care in the middle of an aqua sea. You and your significant other can easily spend a week on PSV without ever having to see another human being. You can even miss the manager's cocktail party and no one will bat an eye. But you might not want to miss the local string band from Petit Martinique, or the little band from Carriacou that comes with fiddle, guitars, quatro, and steel pans, or the steel band from Union on Saturday nights.

Then, too, what is paradise to some could drive others to the brink within 24 hours. PSV has no town, there's no local bar to repair to, and your fellow guests—while nothing if not well bred and polite—won't be around to socialize. You'll spot other houses, but only in the distance. So be sure you can handle it. PSV is a haven for honeymooners and harried tycoons who expect superior service, security, peace, and privacy—and

private beaches outside their widely spaced stone cottages.

Now marking its 43rd anniversary, the resort has embarked on a multi-million dollar investment program, keeping what is best, improving what is needed, and adding what its loyal guest have recommended. For starters, all 22 cottages have been remodeled. These accommodations are actually full-size houses, built of bluebitch stone with wood-beamed roofs and large windows.

Each has a spacious living room with 2 daybeds; an oversize bathroom with large vanities, dressing room, and rock showers; big bedroom with a king-size bed; terra-cotta floors; and patio with hammock. Large windows and sliding doors look out on foliage and sea views. The cottages are furnished with tasteful, very comfortable couches and chairs, upholstered in neutral tones and attractive entryways with patterned brick. Six on the beach, suited to families or groups of friends, were made into two-bedroom/two-bath cottages with outdoor covered living and dining areas.

All cottages now have quiet air-conditioning units, minibars stocked with free non-alcoholic beverages, remodeled bathrooms, new furniture and fabrics. Still, however, the cottages have no television, phone, or Internet. There are small gardens, with flowering plants by every cottage. Small, secluded beaches are only steps from the door of most cottages, but be warned: Windy Point is aptly named—the wind gusts can be enough to awaken even heavy sleepers. There are definite variations in room types between those on hills and promontories, which are more secluded and offer the grandest views, and those on the beach, which are closer together but still private.

PSV has long had a reputation for serving some of the best food in the Caribbean, continental with West Indian flavors. The resort grows fruits and vegetables, raises chickens, and imports supplies almost daily from the States (filet mignon, duck, wines, fresh produce), and the chef does wonderful things with them. Meals are served in the Pavilion, the open-air dining and bar area overlooking the dock, where the deck was extended to provide for more outdoor seating. A wine cellar with a tasting table has been added in the area behind the bar and both guest and staff kitchen equipment have been upgraded. A new outdoor beach restaurant and bar, under the trees near the beach BBQ is open daily from 11 a.m. to sunset

Yet, many guests prefer room service—and it is room service like no other. You signal your needs by raising the yellow flag outside your door; staff members, who putt-putt continuously around the island in minimokes, take your written or spoken order for food, drink, or whatever else you fancy. Guests are the only ones on Caribbean time; service is swift (there is a ratio of two staff members per guest), assuming you haven't raised your red flag mistakenly in the interim. Red flags mean "leave me alone," and PSV personnel have strict orders not to bother you for any reason when they see one.

Should you care to venture beyond your own patch of paradise, there is a lighted tennis court with Astroturf, and a jogging and fitness trail that winds around the island. When that becomes too tiring, you'll find hammocks under thatched canopies thoughtfully placed every 100 yards or so along the beach. A day by the beach is so popular with guests that they can order lunch, drinks, and a thermos of cold water to be brought to them. Each of the thatched palapas on the west beach have a dining table, two chairs, two chaise longues, a small cocktail table, and new fresh water showers.

Further to the west on the hillside looking south is the new, open-air spa with four treatment rooms. The resort's boutique has been moved down near the new beach bar and has been replaced by a proper reception and concierge desk. Behind the scene, PSV has significantly upgraded its electrical generation, water desalination, and waste disposal facilities to be both more efficient and less polluting.

PSV is raising turtles, which are kept in a temporary turtle pond. The aim is to increase the turtle population in these waters and the number of females that come to the island beaches to lay their eggs.

Most water sports—windsurfers, ocean kayaks, "spyaks" for reef viewing, Hobie or Sunfish sailing lessons—are included in the rates. Scuba diving is extra. If island living has gotten into your blood and even a house seems too civilized, you can live out your shipwreck fantasies in style. PSV will arrange a boat to drop you on a tiny island of blinding white sand, in turquoise water even more blinding. It looks unreal, with nothing on it but a thatched umbrella for shade. The islet's official name is Mopion; guests prefer to call it Petit St. Richardson.

Evening entertainment is limited to music on the resident piano, local string band from a neighboring island, Scrabble, an after-dinner brandy, and conversation. A moke will drive you home or you can stroll your way there, flashlight in hand, then enjoy a moonlight swim—and don't forget to hoist the red flag, darling, while I open the champagne.

PETIT ST. VINCENT RESORT ★ ★ ★

Petit St. Vincent, St. Vincent, W.I.
Phone: (784) 458-8801; Fax: (784) 458-8428; e-mail: info@psvresirt,com; www.psvresort.com
Owner/Manager: Phil Stephenson and Robin Paterson
Open: Year-round except Sept–Oct
US Reservations: Petit St. Vincent, PO Box 841338, Pembroke Pines, FL 33084; (954) 963–7401, (800) 654-9326; Fax: (954) 963-7402; e-mail: info@psvresort.com
Deposit: 3 nights; 30 days cancellation
Minimum Stay: None
Arrival/Departure: Complimentary transfer arranged by boat only; on Union Island PSV picks up guests who arrive by Grenadine Airways from Barbados or St. Vincent or private charter. In Barbados, PSV representative meets and assists with transfers.
Distance from Airport: (Union Airport) 4 miles
Accommodations: 22 in villas with patios; doubles with king-size beds plus 2 queens

Amenities: Air-conditioning, ceiling fans; shower, hair dryer, basket of toiletries, bathrobe; CD player, safe, minibar; beach bags, umbrellas; flashlights; ice service, nightly turndown service, room service 7:30 a.m.–9:30 p.m.; no telephone or television
Fitness Facilities/Spa Services: Masseuse from nearby Carriacou by appointment for fee, who also gives yoga classes
Sports: 1 tennis court; Sunfish and Hobie Cat sailing, snorkeling gear, ocean kayaks, spyaks, windsurfing free; diving, waterskiing, deep-sea fishing, charter boat sailing for charge
Electricity: 110 volts
Dress Code: Casual by day; island casual in evening
Children: All ages; cribs; high chairs; babysitters
Meetings: No
Day Visitors: Yes
Handicapped Facilities: Limited
Packages: Summer
Rates: Per 1-bedroom, two people, daily, **FAP**. *High Season* (Nov 1–Apr 30): $1,350. *Low Season* (May 1–Aug 31): $1,050; 2 bedroom, $1,850 and $1,550, respectively. Children (14 years and younger) $150 extra per child, per night, high season; $100 low season. Rates include 3 meals daily, non-alcoholic beverages, and use of water sports as noted in text above.
Service Charge: 10 percent
Government Tax: 10 percent

TRINIDAD & TOBAGO

Different yet similar, this island duet is the ultimate Caribbean kaleidoscope: A mélange of Europeans, Africans, and Asians has woven intricate cultural patterns into a tapestry of fabulous flora and fauna.

The birthplace of calypso and steel bands, Trinidad is the country's banking and trading center; its visitors are more interested in business than beaches. Twenty-two miles to the northeast lies tiny Tobago, an island so lavishly beautiful and serene that it makes even the most severe Caribbean cynic smile.

The mating of Trinidad and Tobago is a bit of a historical irony. Columbus discovered Trinidad on his third voyage and named it for three southern mountain peaks symbolizing to him the Holy Trinity. The Spaniards held the island for three centuries until they were unseated by the British in 1797. But Tobago, because of its strategic location, was so prized by Europeans that it changed hands 14 times. Finally, in 1889, Tobago asked to become a part of Trinidad; they became independent in 1962.

Trinidad has gone through the oil boom and bust. At the heart of Port-of-Spain, the capital, Victorian architectural relics give it a distinctive character. It has an interesting zoo, botanic gardens, and restaurants featuring local cuisine that reflects the country's West Indian, East Indian, and Chinese components.

Trinidad explodes once a year in Carnival, the granddaddy of all Caribbean Carnivals. The balance of the year, it offers tennis, golf, art galleries, and museums in historic buildings, antiques in offbeat shops, and a music- and dance-filled nightlife.

The most southerly of the Caribbean island states, Trinidad is 7 miles off the Venezuela coast and was originally part of the South American mainland. Its flora and fauna include many South American species not seen elsewhere in the Caribbean. But of all its natural wonders, the most spectacular is the bird life. More than 425 species from North and South America and the Caribbean meet here in the forested mountains and mangroves. Of special note is the nightly sunset arrival of hundreds of scarlet ibises, the national bird, to roost in a sanctuary of the Caroni Swamp only 7 miles south of the capital. Guided boat trips through the swamp end where the birds return daily.

Information
Trinidad and Tobago Tourism Development Company; PO Box 222, Level 1, Maritime Centre, 29 10th Ave., Trinidad, W.I.; (868) 675-7034, (800) 816-7541; Fax: (868) 675–7432; e-mail: info@tdc.co.tt; www.goTrinidadand Tobago.com

ASA WRIGHT NATURE CENTRE

Port-of-Spain, Trinidad, W.I.

Deep in a rain forest on the slopes of the Northern Range at 1,200 feet overlooking the Arima Valley is the Asa Wright Nature Centre, a bird sanctuary and wildlife reserve with an inn. Built about 1906, the inn is in the Victorian estate house of the former coffee, citrus, and cocoa plantation, now mostly returned to the wild. It is surrounded by dense tropical vegetation; sitting on its veranda is like being in an aviary, except that the birds come and go freely from the surrounding rain forest.

The centre, a private institution unique in the Caribbean, was established in 1967 on the Spring Hill Estate by its owner, Asa Wright, an Icelandic-born Englishwoman whose rugged manner may have helped give rise to many tall tales about her. She acquired the 197-acre property upon the death of her husband and was persuaded by naturalist friends to create a nonprofit trust to preserve the area and make it a study and recreation center.

The inn is rustic but comfortable; services are minimal. Most of the rooms are in bungalows, furnished with a bureau, desk, chair, and reading lamp and have attractive bedcovers and curtains; all have private bath and international phone service. The rooms also have screened porches or outside areas where you can enjoy the birds and the great outdoors in privacy. Free Wi-Fi service is available throughout the manor house and veranda, but the signal is spotty in some of the guest rooms.

At the entrance to the manor house, beyond the office where useful nature books can be purchased, are the main house's two bedrooms. Directly on, a hallway leads into the parlor and, to one side, the dining room. Both rooms are comfortably furnished in a traditional, homey manner as they might have been in their plantation days. On the veranda outside the parlor, guests gather for afternoon tea and at other times to watch birds, as well as nightly before dinner for the inn's complimentary rum punch. Full bar service is available throughout the day and at meals, including a selection of fine wines.

All meals, fresh and hearty, are served in the dining room buffet style. The kitchen will prepare picnic baskets if you want to spend the day hiking and birding or drive to the beach on Trinidad's Caribbean northern coast.

Natural history programs with slides, lectures, and videos are usually scheduled in the evening. But by evening, after an active and exhilarating day with nature, you will probably be happy to go quietly off to bed.

The centre has its own guides and five hiking trails, which day visitors may also use for a small fee. (E-mail dayvisit@asawright.org for information; reservations for lunch are required.) The trails, ranging from half-hour strolls to difficult three-hour hikes, are designed to maximize viewing of particular species. Maps are available for self-guided forays into the rain forest.

With ease you will see tanagers, thrushes, trogons, blue-crowned motmots, many species of hummingbirds, the beautiful crested oropendola, and dozens of other bird species. The trails pass through magnificent rain forest; the upper-story canopy is often more than 100 feet above you. North of the centre are other trails at 1,800 feet, where you can spot species that prefer high elevations. Generally the best weather, and thus most favorable time, to see the greatest variety of birds is from December to March, although a variety of tropical birds can be seen year-round.

The most celebrated species at Asa Wright is a nesting colony of oilbirds, which make their home in a cave located on the property. This rare bird is found only in Trinidad and in northern South America. The site can be visited only with a guide. A guided tour of the centre grounds and visit to the oilbird cave is included only on stays of three or more nights to control visitation to the oilbird colony. While the inn accommodates guests on an individual basis, most people here are likely to be part of a natural history or birding group from the US, Canada, or Britain.

The Asa Wright Nature Centre is unique, though obviously not for everyone. For bird-watchers, naturalists, and hikers, it's nirvana. And I believe this quiet, friendly inn should also appeal to anyone—age 8 to 98—who is a true nature lover.

ASA WRIGHT NATURE CENTRE (S) 🦤

Blanchissuese Road, Arima, Trinidad & Tobago, W.I.
Phone: (868) 667-4655 (for voice messages only); **Fax:** (868) 667-0540; **e-mail:** asawright@caligo.com; www .asawright.org
Owner: Asa Wright Nature Centre, a nonprofit trust

General Manager: Ann Sealey
Open: Year-round, except for a month in summer, which varies year to year, inquire
US Reservations: Caligo Ventures, 513 Fleming St., #11, PO Box 6356, Key West, FL 33041-6356; (800) 426-7781; US/Canada; (305) 292-0708; **Fax:** (305) 292-0706; www.caligo.com/trini dad/index.html
Deposit: $100 per person
Minimum Stay: None
Arrival/Departure: Transfer service arranged for fee
Distance from Airport: 1½-hour drive; taxi one-way, $35
Distance from Port-of-Spain: 2-hour drive. From Arima: 7¾ miles (30 minutes); taxi one-way, approximately $25
Accommodations: 25 rooms, most with terraces (2 in main building, 21 in bungalows; 19 with twins, 2 with kings, 3 singles with air-conditioning)

Amenities: Ceiling fans; bath with shower only; phones in rooms; no television, radios, air-conditioning (except in singles), or room service
Sports: No facilities; natural pool for wading; Caribbean coastal beaches less than an hour drive
Electricity: 110 volts
Dress Code: Very casual
Children: Over 8 years of age
Meetings: Up to 50 people
Day Visitors: Yes
Handicapped Facilities: Very limited
Packages: Natural history and birding tours
Rates: Per person, daily, **AP.** *High Season* (mid-Dec–Mar 31): $215 (double), $295 (single). *Shoulder Season* (Apr 1–30 and Nov 1–Dec 15): $170 (double), $225 (single). *Low Season:* $150 and $180, respectively
Service Charge: Included
Government Tax: Included

TURKS & CAICOS ISLANDS

A diver's paradise lying at the end of the Bahamas chain, the Turks and Caicos (pronounced KAY-kos) have been dubbed the Caribbean's Last Frontier. A British Crown Colony made up of eight islands and several dozen cays, the islands stretch across 90 miles in two groups separated by the Turks Island Passage, a deep-water channel of 22 miles.

To the east is the Turks group, which has Grand Turk, the capital with about half of the colony's population of 20,000; and neighboring Salt Cay, an old settlement with windmills and salt ponds, declared a Heritage Site under UNESCO's World Heritage program.

To the west are the Caicos Islands—South, Middle, North—which form an arch on the northern side of Caicos Bank. The small archipelago is surrounded by virgin reefs, most uncharted. Provo, as Providenciales is known, is the commercial center and the site of most of the resort and commercial development. North of Provo is Pine Cay, home of the Meridian Club and Parrot Cay.

The islands are not richly blessed with tropical vegetation, but they do have a surprising variety of flora. Coconut palms, casuarinas, sea grapes, and palmettos give them a rugged, windswept beauty. Middle Caicos and North Caicos have fertile soil with lush patches of citrus and fruit trees.

The islands have some exceptional natural attractions: almost 200 miles of untouched beaches, acres of tropical wilderness and wetlands, and magnificent seas with some of the most spectacular marine life in the world. Several locations are national parks and bird sanctuaries (two islets in the Turks and eight locations in the Caicos), and a nature lover's paradise.

Grand Turk, the capital, is a long, skinny island of 9 square miles along the Turks Island Passage. The sleepy island burst on the scene after an elaborate cruise facility was built, attracting many cruise ships on Caribbean itineraries. Grand Turks and its neighbor Salt Cay are great places for whale-watching in spring and autumn, when the passage becomes a thoroughfare for migratory humpback whales and giant manta rays.

Information

Turks and Caicos Islands Tourist Board; 5 Applewood Dr., Swiftwater, PA 18370; (800) 241-0824; e-mail: pewing@tcigny.com; www.turksandcaicos tourism.com

AMANYARA

Northwest Point, Providenciales, Turks and Caicos Islands, B.W.I.

Opened in March 2006, the first member of the aesthetically sensitive Amanresorts group to be built in the Caribbean, Amanyara is set in an isolated coastal area on the northwest end of Providenciales (better known as Provo), far removed from major development on the eastern part of the island. The resort is reached by an unpaved road through a remote area covered with native bush and stunted trees. Its pavilions and private villas can barely be seen in the woods surrounding them. Its small, secluded beaches hidden in rocky ironshore coves overlook the 4,168-acre Northwest Point Marine National Park with some of the world's best wall and reef diving. But there is nothing about this Amanresort that would have you thinking "dive resort."

Amanyara is exquisitely beautiful. Its name, meaning "peaceful place," derives from *aman,* the Sanskrit word for peace, and *yara,* the word for place in the Arawak language. It is well named, but perhaps, too peaceful for most people.

Upon arrival, you enter the resort through a large, very high ceiling reception pavilion that opens onto a formal reflecting pool landscaped with trees. The setting is so serene, so perfectly symmetrical and harmonious, it's like walking through the gates of a Shinto shrine.

The reflecting pool is framed on one side by the library and a boutique, and on the other, by the restaurant and bar. As your eyes lead you through these rooms, you are awestruck by the rich, intricately laid wood that dominates the space and is the singular important element in the simple but elegant decor. Everywhere, Amanyara is open to the elements—the sun, reflections from the pond, the breeze, and the sounds and sights of the ocean.

All the lines are straight until you reach the bar—what drama! The circular room sits under a soaring roof that is a magnificent work of art for its intricately assembled slates of beautiful wood. Surrounding the bar at the center are oversize lounging daybeds.

The restaurant provides a choice of dining settings: The first part is open to the breezes; the second, air-conditioned. The open setting leads down onto a terrace with outdoor seating beneath two large trees. Both areas have views to the ocean. The air-conditioned section also opens to an outdoor balcony that enjoys views across the reflecting pool. The menu offers a selection of Asian and Mediterranean fare with an emphasis on local seafood, served in portions almost as sparse as the decor. The staff, you will notice, is mostly Asian.

Beyond the restaurant and bar is another drama. A long, narrow black stone swimming pool (164 feet by 26 feet) with a terrace alongside a long sundeck looks out over the sea. On either end of the pool are two lounge pavilions from which shallow entries to the pool also provide for water lounging. There's a third lounge pavilion closer to the ocean and an outdoor shower.

On a dune above the white-sand beach is the Beach Club, an informal lunch dining venue open throughout the day for grills, sandwiches, salads, and occasional informal beach barbecues in the evenings. The interior is terraced

with a bar in front, or lower terrace that leads to a large wooden deck. At the beach, equipment for snorkeling, sailing, kayaking, and other sports is available.

Beyond is a grassed courtyard and Amanyara's Dive Centre, operated by Ocean Vibes, whose instructors offer scuba diving for beginners to advanced and specialty courses. A 5-mile-long fringing reef parallels the coastline. Rays, dolphins, and hammerhead, reef, and lemon sharks have been sighted; humpback whales pass through during their winter migrations.

The library, with its reading terrace overlooking the reflecting pool, has books on the Turks and Caicos, along with novels, magazines, newspapers, CDs, DVDs, board games, and Wi-Fi, which is also available in all accommodations. Next door is the boutique, with a small selection of resort wear, jewelry, gifts, and sundries. A 30-seat multimedia screening room is fully equipped with a DVD and VHS player, cable television, high-speed Internet and video/data projection capabilities; movies are shown regularly.

Amanyara's accommodations are found in 40 wood-shingled pavilions, each measuring 1,250 square feet and identical in layout and design. They best capture the Aman aesthetic with a simple palette of colors and materials, the finely finished wood of the furniture, and floors of polished sand-colored terrazzo with teak inlays.

The pavilion sits on a platform either at the edge of a tranquil pond with a wooden sundeck extending over the water, or atop the ironshore in dry-wood vegetation with the ocean peeking through, here and there. Three sides of the pavilion are mostly glass, bringing the outdoors inside, and an overhanging roofline shades its three outdoor terraces. Glass doors slide open to catch the sea breezes, when that's preferred to the air-conditioning. Rocky paths lead to an occasional sandy cove hidden in the ironshore by the sea.

The room interior (about half of the pavilion overall) has a king-size bed at the center; behind it sits a writing desk and chair. To one side is a cabinet with a minibar. One corner of the room has a reading chair with a footstool and an entertainment console housing a flat-screen television with a Bose DVD/CD player and sound system. The bathroom, separated from the bedroom by a decorative wooden screen, has a free-standing bathtub. Twin vanities, hair dryer, umbrella, makeup mirror, shower, and separate toilet are found on either side of the bathroom, as is a dressing area and closet with a safe, bathrobes, slippers, and beach bag. The bedroom/living room opens onto the 3 outdoor wooden decks: One has twin banquettes for lounging or dining; another, 2 daybeds; and the third has a sunken table with cushions (sunken so as not to obstruct the view from the bed). Recently, 40-by-14-foot private pools, flanked by a 1,000-square-foot private deck and garden area, were added to 6 pavilions.

On the south side of the property, Amanyara has three-, four-, and five-bedroom villas, each sitting on about an acre and a half of land in dry tropical vegetation, either along the oceanfront or by a pond; some have internal reflecting ponds. The villas are centered around a rectangular or square infinity-edged swimming pool in black volcanic rock surrounded by hardwood decking. The free-standing bedroom pavilions are similar to those of the resort with some having an outdoor bathtub and shower. All villas have a large living and dining pavilion, outdoor dining area, fully-equipped kitchen, cook, and housekeeper. Each villa also comes with two, four-seat golf cars, and guests have access to the resort's facilities and services. Some villas have an additional bedroom suitable for up to four children and a nanny.

The Fitness Centre has exercise equipment—treadmills, bikes, elliptical trainers, rowing machines, a range of resistance training machines, dumbbell set, incline bench, body bars, and mats, and offers aerobic workouts. A personal trainer is available upon request. Racquets and balls are available for use on the two floodlit, Har-Tru clay tennis courts.

The Serenity Villa, Amanyara's spa and wellness facility, is spread over an acre and a half of lush landscaping and bordering a tranquil pond. It has four double treatment pavilions built around a 10-square meter swimming pool lined with lounging chairs, a reception and relaxation pavilion with a spa boutique, an outdoor yoga sala and a Pilates studio. Guests can choose from a variety of massages, wraps, scrubs, facials, and beauty treatments, all of which may also be enjoyed in the privacy of their individual pavilion or villa. A master-in-residence guides guests through the latest holistic healing practices. Complimentary morning yoga classes are held regularly and private yoga, Pilates, meditation, or personal training sessions can be arranged.

Snorkeling from the beach at Amanyara is super. The sandy bottom declines gradually until the reef wall falls away dramatically into a sheer vertical drop. Additionally, the rock formations surrounding the resort are home to many small fish; excellent snorkeling is found in there. The Turks and Caicos Islands have some of the finest deep-sea fishing grounds in the world. Both light tackle and game fishing charters can be arranged.

A nature discovery centre, adjacent to Amanyara's beach, is an indoor and outdoor camp with a full-time naturalist in residence and provides regular daily activities to explore the island's natural wonders to educate guests of all ages. Visiting marine and natural history educators conduct programs as well. The centre also has a shallow pool for young children.

Amanyara is so beautiful aesthetically, don't pass up an opportunity to see it. But this resort is clearly not for everyone. Amanresort habituées (who like to call themselves Aman-junkies) relish it. But such serenity can be intimidating and barely talking above a whisper tiring. You may want peace and quiet, but 24/7 for a week or two? Think about it.

AMANYARA ★ ★ ★ ★
Northwest Point, Providenciales, Turks and Caicos Islands, B.W.I.
Phone: (649) 941-8133; Fax: (649) 941-8132; e-mail: amanyara@amanresorts.com; www.amanresorts.com
Owner: Caicos Resorts Ltd.

Management: Amanresorts
General Managers: Marco Franck
Open: Year-round
US Reservations: (866) 941-8133 or amanyarares@amanresorts.com
Deposit: 3 nights (2 nights May 1–Oct 31)
Minimum Stay: Pavilions, Thanksgiving Week (Nov 23–27) 4 nights, villas 2 nights. Christmas/New Year's (Dec 22–Jan 7) 8 nights; no arrival/departure Dec 3; 5 nights over President's Weekend (Feb 17–25) and Easter (Mar 30–Apr 14) 5 nights.
Arrival/Departure: Private transfer included in rate
Distance from Airport: 20-minute drive
Distance from business center: 30-minute drive
Accommodations: 40 pavilions, 6 with private pools; 15 villas with 3-, 4-, and 5 bedrooms (to be increased to 33 villas)
Amenities: See text
Fitness Facilities/Spa Services: Gym, tennis; spa villa and in-room treatments
Sports: See text
Electricity: 110 volts/60 cycles
Dress Code: None
Children: All ages but some pavilions not suitable for toddlers; no charge for child under age 12 years sharing a pavilion with their parents.
Meetings: Theater style for 30
Day Visitors: Lunch and dinner reservations, subject to space
Handicapped Facilities: No handicap-modified rooms; one bathroom in public area
Packages: 5-night Wellness; 7-night Romance

Rates: Per pavilion/villa, per night: *Christmas/New Year's* (Dec 18–Jan 2): $1,980–$2,550. *High Season* (Jan 3–May 31): $1,550–$2,150; villas, $7,000–$15,250 and $5,600–$13,950. *Low Season:* inquire. Rates include airport transfers, minibar, nonalcoholic drinks, local and long-distance phone calls, wireless in-room Internet access, yoga classes, nonmotorized water sports, daily snorkel trips, tennis courts/equipment/hitting partners, afternoon tea, and all coffee, tea, and soft drinks served in the villa

Service Charge: 10 percent

Government Tax: 11 percent

GRACE BAY CLUB

Providenciales, Turks and Caicos Islands, B.W.I.

Situated on one of the most beautiful beaches in the world—12 uninterrupted miles of powdery porcelain sands washed by gorgeous, reef-filled turquoise waters, fronting 1,100 feet of the pristine shore—the 11-acre Grace Bay Club is a hideaway that is elegant yet casual, sumptuous yet understated and refined.

The Grace Bay Club is designed for affluent, sophisticated international travelers who appreciate quality along with tranquillity. It was the first luxury resort to open on Provo (Providenciales on the map), and although many others have popped up over the last decade, there's little likelihood that any of them will surpass this impeccably designed and superbly maintained beauty by the bay.

Set in gardens on the beach, the Grace Bay Club suggests a gracious

Spanish village in stucco the color of the late-afternoon sun. Red tile roofs at staggered levels, terra-cotta or marble floors, stone balustrades, wrought-iron balconies, and shaded terraces are interlaced with lush courtyards, splashing fountains, and arched pathways framed in bright bougainvillea.

Grace Bay offers accommodations in three different sections. Grace Bay Club Hotel (the original buildings which have had major renovations) is the adults-only section. Here, no two suites are alike, and range from ocean-view 850 to 1,700-square-foot one- and two-bedrooms with terrace or patio. Ground-floor units boast patios with private solariums and paths leading to the beach, all hidden from view in tropical landscaping. Bathrooms in these units were made much larger and have dual vanities, marbled tub and shower. The suites are self-contained retreats with oceanfront terrace or patio, kitchenette refrigerator. The larger units have dishwasher.

As part of the resort's recent million-dollar upgrade, the adults-only pool was transformed into a glass-edge, infinity pool and bar with cutting-edge design. More than twice the size of the original pool, the new one is anchored by a 12-foot glass wall facing the luminous turquoise water of Grace Bay, creating an almost aquarium-type experience. Connection to the Infiniti Bar was also improved, providing more oceanfront outdoor space for weddings and group events.

Another section of the resort called The Villas at Grace Bay Club, is the family area with four five-story buildings,

each with nine large, luxurious condominiums that are either junior, one-, two-, or three-bedroom suites and the penthouse, a four-bedroom suite covering the entire floor. All accommodations have air-conditioning and a ceiling fan, a direct-dial phone, flat-screen television, DVD, and CD player.

The third and newest section is The Estate at Grace Bay, 2 six-story buildings with 22 ultra-elegant, pricey condominium suites. They range from oceanfront junior suites (800 square feet) with bed/living room, terrace, minibar, bathroom, and outdoor rain shower encased in glass and stone to a 7,000-square-foot penthouse with four bedrooms with living room, dining room, media room (or optional bedroom) and private study with terrace; Jacuzzi tub, grill, and rain shower on terrace, and private elevator access.

Most suites measure about 3,700 to 4,700 square feet with three or four bedrooms; some are anchored by an infinity-edge plunge pool. They have a Bose speaker system, wireless Internet, and kitchen fitted with Wolf & Sub Zero appliances, custom Italian cabinetry, wine chiller, elegant minibar, and Grohe faucets, among other fine features. The Estate suites are part of Grace Bay's inventory for rent. A limited number of private beach cabanas, spacious enough for spa treatments and dining are available to Estate guests for $200 day.

When you enter the main, air-conditioned reception, furnished like the living room of a home, you will be greeted by the concierge or an attendant with a refreshing cool drink and a cold hand cloth while you check in. You will be assigned a "personal concierge" who is a combination butler and concierge, able to take care of your needs from unpacking to arranging a party or sightseeing, who will accompany you to your suite. He will give you a cell phone and number to call anytime you need his services.

A design masterpiece, the Anacaona Restaurant, named for the Lucayan Indian goddess (her name means "flower of gold"), consists of palapas strung along the beach. In the evening tiki torches cast a romantic glow, enhanced by flickering candlelight from each table. The main palapa's thatched roof (built by Seminole Indians from Florida) is supported by a ring of classic white columns, and arranged on four levels, so that diners on each have front-row views of the tranquil turquoise-turned-lavender-turned-silver waters of Grace Bay, framed by floodlit palm trees and smoke from the flaming torches. The restaurant's menu was created by executive chef Wolfgang von Weiser with contributions from celebrated chefs from around the world. It also offers "Private Island" dining—a service, available only for one group or couple each evening, that comes with a private butler, chef, and customized menu. Beachfront tables are decorated in fine-dining style and adorned with tiki torches.

A black marble bar, dubbed The Infiniti Bar, that stretches 90 feet across the beach from the restaurant to the water's edge, is probably the longest bar in the Caribbean. Designed by Keith Hobbs of United Designers, noted for his work with Nobu and the London W

Hotels, the black marble creates the illusion of water with the structure floating above the beach into the ocean. During the day, the bar is shaded by canopies, but in the evening, it is open to the sky and offers full restaurant service and a special cocktail menu.

The Lounge is a contemporary beach oasis at the water's edge with lounge chairs, sailcloth canopies, and evening sunsets to watch by flickering torches and glowing fire pits. The open-air space has a martini menu and serves tapas, accompanied with live music from local musicians during the week.

The Grace Bay Club layout stretching along its long beachfront made it easy to provide all the villa accommodations with ocean views, and the addition of an on-the-beach family swimming pool and the outdoor, casual-dining waterfront grill cleverly helped separate the two areas: the villas, the new section, is active with children and their families, while the hotel, the original section and its freshwater swimming pool, form an adult area for those who prefer tranquillity.

The resort's Kid's Town offers a variety of outdoor activities for kids ages 5 to 12, such as hikes, snorkeling, semi-submarine treks, kayaking, horseback riding, and sailboat and other excursions. Prices range from $39–$135. Family adventures can also be arranged with a local ecotour company. The Kid's Town "V.I.K." Club (Very Important Kids Club) costs $130 to $230 per child and includes a personal greeting by a Kids Coordinator, fruit punch upon arrival, a Kids Town programs, nightly turndown service, unlimited use of the Kid's Town playroom, water sport, a gift pack and other features.

Grace Bay's other amenities include a Jacuzzi overlooking the beach and two lighted tennis courts. There is a small video and book library as well as backgammon, chess, and other games. The former reception area is used for groups. It houses a small business center with two computers with free Internet access for guests. The resort's boutique is there, too.

Also expanded and upgraded in the most recent renovations were the Anani Spa, Fitness Center and boutique. The Anani Spa was given a contemporary, fresh redesign plus two new treatment rooms, one including an outdoor soaking tub for specialized treatments, fronted by a contemporary new fountain. The relaxation and manicure/pedicure rooms were also renovated and expanded and locker rooms redesign. White-washed wood tile, white lacquer wood finishes, contemporary white Corian vanities, translucent lobby walls, and elegant linen curtains provide a soft ambience, as does the design of the new spa boutique.

The spa offers a wide variety of services, including aromatherapy, massage, reflexology, facials, wraps, pregnancy massage, waxing manicures and pedicures, as well as special treatments for men. The spa uses Elemis products.

The Fitness Center was also renovated with new flooring, bright colors, and four new Life Fitness treadmills. It offers a full daily schedule of classes from yoga and Pilates to children's ballet and karate.

Complimentary windsurfing, Sunfish sailing, and snorkeling gear, along with a full range of water sports and bone-, bottom-, and deep-sea fishing are available. Day sails and small-boat excursions to nearby uninhabited islands are popular. Scuba diving—some of the best in the Tropics—and golf just across the road can be arranged.

GRACE BAY CLUB ★ ★ ★ ★

Grace Bay Circle Road, PO Box 128, Providenciales, Turks and Caicos Islands, B.W.I.

Phone: (649) 946-5050; Toll-free (+1) 800-946-5757; **Fax:** (649) 946-5758; **e-mail:** info@gracebayclub.com; www .gracebayclub.com

Owners: Mark Durliat and Partners
Managing Director: Nikheel Advani
General Manager: Thierry Grandsire
Open: Year-round
US Reservations: (800) 946-5757
Deposit: 3 nights, Dec 16–Jan 1, cancellation must be received before Nov 1
Minimum Stay: 10 nights during Christmas/New Year's; 5 nights, winter
Distance from Airport: 10 miles
Distance from Provo Center: 3 miles
Accommodations: 59 oceanfront suites (junior and 1 to 4 bedrooms), all with one or more private terraces or balconies, all with king-size beds (convertible to twins) and some with queen-size pullout sofa beds; 22 estate suites (junior to 4 bedrooms, combinable to 5- and 6-bedroom suites)
Amenities: Air-conditioning, ceiling fans; direct-dial telephone, flat-screen cable television including DVD/CD players, complimentary high-speed wireless Internet access; iPod docking stations; safe; refrigerator (some with ice maker); bath with tub and shower, bathrobes and slippers, hair dryers, Elemis

bath amenities; room service 7 a.m.–10 p.m.; daily maid service, nightly turn-down service; daily *New York Times*
Fitness Facilities/Spa Services: Full-service spa and fitness center
Sports: 2 swimming pools and Jacuzzi; 2 soft-surface, lighted tennis courts; complimentary water sports including windsurfers, Hobie cats, kayaks, bicycles, snorkeling; scuba diving, and sailing arranged for additional charge; free shuttle to Provo Golf Club, where guests receive reduced green fees and priority tee times
Electricity: 110 volts
Dress Code: Casual sportswear by day; elegantly casual in restaurant for dinner; long pants, collared shirts

Children: All ages; Kid's Club, see text
Meetings: Small meetings up to 20 persons
Day Visitors: Welcome
Handicapped Facilities: No
Packages: Honeymoon, wedding, golf, and spa
Rates: Per room, double, daily, CP. *High Season* (Jan 8–Apr 14): $995–$1,850. *Shoulder Season* (Apr 15–May 27; Nov 1–Dec 13): $750–$1,375. *Low Season:* $575–$1,095. Airport transfer included. MAP available. Rates for 2 to 4 bed-rooms, villas and estate suites, inquire.
Service Charge: 10 percent
Government Tax: 11 percent

THE MERIDIAN CLUB ON PINE CAY

Pine Cay, Turks and Caicos Islands, B.W.I.

Because the only way to reach Pine Cay is by boat or private plane, you could say the Meridian Club is remote and exclusive. But what really sets the resort apart and makes it one of the truly great hideaways is its refreshing simplicity and its wild natural setting along one of the world's most gorgeous beaches.

The small, unpretentious resort belongs to the homeowners of an exclusive residential development on Pine Cay, a privately owned 800-acre island—about the size of New York's Central Park—floating on spectacularly beautiful aquamarine water between Provo and North Caicos.

Set on 2 uninterrupted miles of pristine white sand washed by clear, languid water, the club is comprised of a clubhouse and clusters of cottages less than a stone's throw from the beach. Some of the private homes also are available for rent. No cars are allowed on the island; you get around on leg power by walking or biking or, when available, by golf cart.

The clubhouse is the reception and social center, with an indoor-outdoor dining room on the first floor and an attractive upstairs lounge with a bar, corner library, and veranda. Guests and homeowners—a well-traveled, well-heeled, and somewhat intellectual group—mingle here nightly for cocktails hosted by the manager and for after-dinner socializing.

The clubhouse opens onto the pool, which has a wide terrace used for breakfast, lunch, and tea, and for barbecues on Wednesday and Saturday night. Dinner is an informal affair in the dining room. The food is good, not gourmet.

The resort has a visiting chef program during the season.

The beachfront cottages are connected by a walkway lined with local flora. Most guest rooms are large junior suites, tastefully furnished. They have a king-size or twin beds, a separate sitting area, a large bathroom with shower, and screened porches facing the beach. There is also an outside shower with hot and cold water and each suite has its own thatched beach hut with lounge chairs for two.

At the end, a bit separate from the group, is Sand Dollar, a hexagonal cottage that honeymooners like for its privacy. The rustic cottage has stone floors and a tiled bath with an enclosed outdoor shower. It has its own thatched beach hut just large enough to shade two.

Recently, the resort was given a complete renovation and upgrade that included freshening the 12 guest rooms, Sand Dollar Cottage, and common areas with new decor inside and out; the reconstruction of the lobby and the gift shop; new furnishings of the bar and outdoor lounge and dining areas; and the installation of a new pool filtration system. By the time you see it, the pool and deck and the resort's walkways will have been given a face-lift with new surfaces and a new pump for the pool. Behind the grill there is a new guest bathroom area for pool guests to use and an outdoor shower, convenient for late departures.

The resort has seven boats for guest transport, fishing, snorkeling, ecursions, and other activities. Use of water-sports equipment and daily excursions to nearby cays for snorkeling are included in the room rate. The snorkeling, with the reefs rich in marine life, is some of the best you will ever find. Bonefishing, which is said to be outstanding in May, is also available, as is deep-sea fishing. The resort also arranges for golfers to play at the Provo Golf Club on Provo.

But of all the changes, perhaps the most important has been moving reservations to ring directly at the Club, enabling the resort to provide more personalized service and a quick response to inquiries with greater knowledge regarding the resort and the island.

Several features set the Meridian Club apart from other retreats. The untamed appearance of Pine Cay is the most apparent and the one the homeowners are determined to maintain. Strong-willed environmentalists, they have resisted the temptation to expand and, instead, have converted about two-thirds of the island into a national park. They are equally vigilant about the coral reefs protecting the island.

Covered mostly with dry scrub, Pine Cay has freshwater lakes and gets its name from a type of tree that covers vast areas of the Caicos. It has a nature trail, and any dirt road can be used by birders to spot some of the 120 bird species found here.

The camaraderie between owners and guests is unusual, too. (In most resort developments the residents and resort guests seldom see one another.) The congeniality and high number of repeat visitors are also reflected in the warm relationships between guests and staff members, who, if not polished to Savoy shine, are attentive and caring.

Although the Meridian Club is barefoot living most of the time, it maintains a certain gracious style and civility. Its small size makes it easy for guests to feel at home quickly. In addition to homeowners and their affluent friends, your companions are likely to be professionals, business executives, eastern establishment types, and a titled European or two. Times may be changing, but not on Pine Cay; there are still no cars, no television, and cellular phone use is discouraged. If you find it necessary to use your cell phone, you will be asked to make your phone calls by the tennis court—away from everyone—and not in your room or on the beach as a courtesy to other guests.

THE MERIDIAN CLUB ON PINE CAY ★ ★ 🐚
Pine Cay, Turks and Caicos Islands, B.W.I.
Phone: (866) PINE CAY, (746-3229); (649) 941-7011; e-mail: reservations@ meridianclub.com; www.meridianclub .com
Owner: The Meridian Club
General Managers: Beverly and Walter Plachta
Open: Nov 1–July 31
US Reservations: (866) PINE CAY (746-3229), (649) 946-7758; or reservations@meridianclub.com
Deposit: 3 nights; 45 days cancellation, subject to a 4 percent service fee; policy may vary during holiday periods
Minimum Stay: 7 nights during Christmas
Arrival/Departure: For stays of 7 nights or more, the club provides either boat- or air-taxi transfer at its discretion

between Provo and Pine Cay. Inquire from reservations.

Distance from Airport: (Provo Airport) 10 miles; taxi to boat dock one-way, $36 for 2 persons, $16 each additional; resort has 2,500-foot airstrip used by private planes, small charters, and inter-island carriers

Distance from Provo Center: 15 miles

Accommodations: 12 suites in beach-front bungalows, all with terrace or patio; twin beds or king; private home rentals available

Amenities: Ceiling fans; bath with shower, refrigerator, standing fan, hair dryer, bath robes, in-room safe, toiletries; ice service, nightly turndown service, room service for breakfast; afternoon tea; no air-conditioning, telephone, television, VCR, radio, clock

Sports: Freshwater pool; tennis and equipment, bikes, boating, snorkeling and equipment, sailboats included; wilderness trails and birding; deep-sea fishing, bonefishing, tarpon fishing, reef fishing, scuba, and golf on Provo arranged

Electricity: 110 volts/60 cycles

Dress Code: Always casual, no tank tops; evening, chic casual for women, slacks and collared shirts for men

Children: No children under 12 years of age except during Christmas/New Year's Week and Family Months of June and July when children 6 years old and up are permitted. Those under 18 not allowed in bar after 6 p.m. unless accompanied by an adult family member

Meetings: Up to 26 people

Day Visitors: Day Pass available with prior arrangements. $85 per person including lunch, plus tax and service; transfers not included

Handicapped Facilities: No

Packages: Hideaway, Shell Seeker

Rates: Two people, daily, **AP,** for week's stay (1–3 or 4–6 nights are slightly higher). *High Season* (late Dec–Mar 31): $1,085–$1,310. *Shoulder Season* (Nov 1–Dec 23): $790–$1,015. *Low Season* (Apr–July 31): $800–$1,025. Rates include transfers from Provo airport to Pine Cay via taxi and boat. For information on cottages and rates and hotel packages, see website.

Service Charge: 10 percent

Government Tax: 11 percent

PARROT CAY

Providenciales, Turks and Caicos Islands, B.W.I.

This secluded, exclusive, private-island hideaway zoomed to the top of the charts as the place to see and be seen almost from its first day, thanks to its well-known, well-heeled owners, who have a loyal, and often royal, following, and prices likely to make everyone take notice.

Parrot Cay actually began in the late 1980s, when a wealthy Kuwaiti constructed the resort on the uninhabited islet. By 1991, the resort was completed and scheduled to open, but before the first guests were to arrive, the Gulf War erupted.

Parrot Cay remained shuttered and desolate for the next seven years, when it was purchased by an unlikely twosome, Singaporian Christina Ong—owner of London's Metropolitan and Halkin, as well as prestigious hotels in Asia—and British entrepreneur and founder of the Hard Rock Cafe and Planet Hollywood restaurant, Robert Earl, who no longer is an owner but maintains a home at Parrot Cay.

They realized the potential and lure of this abandoned getaway rapidly approaching a state of decay, with a 3.2-mile-long ribbon of powdery white-sand beach, bordered by crystalline azure waters. The infrastructure was already there; all that was needed was some imagination and an infusion of millions.

And did they ever. When the word got out, the beautiful people and celebrities came running. On a single day in its first spring, Bruce Willis, the Saatchi family of advertising fame, and noted fashion designer Jean Galliano were all in residence in their respective beach suites.

Located on an almost inaccessible 1,000-acre island in the Turks and Caicos, Parrot Cay is elegant in its simplicity. It is designed for those who demand anonymity, yet want to be in the company of trendsetters who must be the first to discover the newest playground.

Aside from the privacy, the lure—especially when you're luxuriating in a beach suite or being indulged by the largely Indonesian staff—is the aura of casual elegance achieved by British interior designer Keith Hobbs of London's United Designers.

Hobbs took the elements of traditional colonial decor and artfully blended them with Asian simplicity—four-poster beds and a lavish use of white fabrics, especially gossamer-thin netting around the beds and as curtains. The effect is romantic and soothing, not to mention sensuous. Teak furniture with woven reed seats and backs in the simplest of Asian lines is everywhere.

The main building, where designer Rolf Rothermel was in charge, is an updated version of Caribbean colonial architecture, set high on a hill overlooking the Atlantic on one side and the inlet that separates the cay from the larger island of North Caicos on the other. Rothermel gave the original dark-wood building a lighter look by painting the railings of its multilevel terraces white, set off by the blues and aquas of the water.

From the main building, sited at the top of a 50-foot rise (the highest point of the island), the rooms and

suites in two-story, red-tile-roof buildings cascade down the hill toward the sea. Along the beach are the newer cottages, all with one- and two-bedroom suites and by far the most desirable—and expensive—of Parrot Cay's 60 accommodations.

The original swimming pool was covered over and serves as a gigantic flowerpot with 5 palm trees shading the zero-entry pool. Alongside is Lotus, the poolside restaurant and bar—only steps from the water's edge—serving a light-fare at lunch and Asian cuisine for dinner. The Terrace restaurant is another option for breakfast and dinner when serving Mediterranean cuisine is on the menu. A few steps away near the beachside suites is the fitness center, with a full complement of weights and exercise equipment.

Beyond lie the one- and two-bedroom beach suites, each with direct access to the beach. The two-bedroom units have private pools. The most private are the three-bedroom villas, which have their own pools.

In 2008, The Sanctuary, an eight-bedroom rental property with two infinity pools and Jacuzzi, opened. It is actually two, four-bedroom villas with one common area called the pavilion, but the two houses must be rented together. Situated on the most private part of island, farthest from the hotel, The Sanctuary has an eclectic decor with elements from Bali to Africa in East meets West harmony.

If you must stay in touch with the outside world, multiple international direct-dial phones are strategically placed in each room and suite, free Wi-Fi and high-speed Internet access is available in all rooms, library, and Terrace Bar, while the daily *New York Times* fax is presented at breakfast. Televisions and DVDs are in all rooms.

Wending your way to Parrot Cay, has become easier in recent years as scheduled, direct air service is available from Miami, New York, and other major gateways to Providenciales, or Provo, as it's known by aficionados. After being met by the resort's greeter and assisted into a waiting van, you'll have a 15-minute cab ride to the Parrot Cay's private dock, where at the welcome center you will be greeted with a chilled face towel and cold drink until one of the resort's cruisers will whisk you over smooth, translucent, inside-the-reef waters to Parrot Cay in about 35 minutes.

At the dock you're greeted by the staff and driven in Parrot Cay's version of a stretch limo—an elongated golf cart (there are no cars on the island)—to the main building, where a chilled face towel and cold drink await you. You'll immediately sense that you've chosen well. From here it's on to your suite or room, where your luggage is already in place.

Life on Parrot Cay is as you please. There are two lighted tennis courts, an armada of small watercraft, a well-stocked library and lounge, and a large, circular bar to enjoy before and after dinner—which, by the way, is served in the dining room one floor below.

Diving for all levels, snorkeling, waterskiing, Hobby Cats and catamaran sailing, windsurfing, kayaking, deep-sea fishing, and island tours can be arranged.

Parrot Cay's Asian-style spa, the COMO Shambhala Retreat with nine treatment rooms, will pamper you with Asian-inspired body treatments of imported herbs, spices, and flowers and massage techniques and other spa rituals to induce deep relaxation and promote revitalization. Along with these are such Eastern-inspired therapies as Thai and Shiatsu massage, body realignment, and yoga. The spa has an infinity pool and sun deck with outdoor shower, a yoga studio and yoga pavilion, a Pilates hut, and a private Pilates studio, separate male/female steam rooms, sauna, and outdoor Jacuzzis, and a gym with weights and cardio equipment—and all this less than two hours from Miami.

PARROT CAY ★ ★ ★ ★
PO Box 164, Providenciales, Turks and Caicos Islands, B.W.I.
Phone: (649) 946-7788, (877) 754-0726; **Fax:** (649) 946-7789; **e-mail:** res@parrotcay.como.bz; www.parrotcay.como.bz
Owner: COMO Hotels and Resorts
General Manager: Grant Noble
Open: Year-round
US Reservations: Direct to hotel, (649) 946-7788; toll free: (877) 754 0726; **Fax:** (649) 946-7789; or **e-mail:** res@parrotcay.como.bz.
Deposit: 3 nights; 14 days cancellation; 110 days prior to arrival Jan 4, 2012
Minimum Stay: 10 nights during Christmas/New Year's holidays; 5 nights during certain holiday; 3 at other times
Arrival/Departure: Transfer from Providenciales Airport included (see text)

Distance from Airport: (Providenciales Airport) 20 minutes to dock by car and a 35-minute sea journey to the resort

Accommodations: 70 rooms and villas (31 garden-view rooms, 11 ocean-facing rooms, 4 one-bedroom COMO suites, 9 one-bedroom beach houses/villas with plunge pools, 2 two-bedroom beach villas with private pools, 1 three-bedroom COMO villa with pool. Rooms furnished with four-poster kings). *Separate from main resort:* Parrot Cay Estates, 3 privately owned, three-bedroom villas in resort's rental pool; The Residence, a complex of five-bedroom house along side 2 three-bedoom villas can be taken individually or as a complex; and The Sanctuary, 2 four-bedroom villas with one common pavilion, must be rented together; and Tamarind, the newest estate, with a three-bedroom and a two-bedroom villa, which can be rented together or separately.

Amenities: Hotel rooms: air-conditioning, ceiling fan; direct-dial telephone with voice mail; safe; bath with tub and shower, quality toiletries, hair dryer; robes, mini-bar, tea and coffeemaker; umbrella, room service; satellite television, radio, CD player, DVD; library, free Wi-Fi and high-speed Internet access, also in library and Terrace Bar; yoga mat on request; concierge, in-room dining; butler service in larger villas

Fitness Facilities/Spa Services: See text

Sports: Hobie Cats; lighted tennis courts; air-conditioned gym; nature trail; snorkeling, windsurfing, waterskiing, diving; golf in Provo at additional cost

Electricity: 110 volts

Dress Code: Smartly casual

Children: All ages; babysitting

Meetings: No

Day Visitors: No

Handicapped Facilities: No

Packages: Romantic getaways and others (see website)

Rates: Per room, per night, FAB. *High Season* (early Jan–mid Apr): Rates start at $847. *Shoulder Season* (late Apr–May 31 and Nov–Dec 20): $726. *Low Season* (June 1–mid-Oct): from $605. For 2- to 8-bedroom villas; inquire.

Service Charge: 10 percent

Government Tax: 11 percent

THE REGENT PALMS

Providenciales, Turks and Caicos Islands, B.W.I.

The multimillion-dollar luxury resort, which opened in early 2005 on Grace Bay Beach, combines classical design incorporating elements from the islands' colonial British connection in the architecture, building materials, and interiors, and modern amenities with a fine attention to detail.

You enter The Regent Palms through a coral stone gateway, leading down a tree-shaded drive to the reception, a formal Palladian edifice styled after a plantation manor house. The reception opens onto the prettiest setting of the resort—an interior courtyard and formal sunken garden with a fountain in the middle. In perfect symmetry along the sides of the garden are tree-shaded, colonnaded walkways under lattice trellises covered in vivid bougainvillea and fronting small stone cottages housing upscale boutiques.

At the far end of the garden is the graceful two-story Mansion, classic in symmetry and detail. Open-air and terraced on the first floor, the coral stone building houses the main restaurant, Parallel23, and bar on the ground floor and a 2,000-square-foot ballroom with balconies on the second floor. On the back side of the building are the business center and an Internet room with computers and printer for guests' use. High-speed Internet access is also available in the suites and there is wireless Internet access poolside and at the beach.

The 12-acre site, which was little more than sand when building began, is now graced with hundreds of palm trees and gardens of flowering shrubs, orange trees, and perennial flowers.

From the Mansion, foliage-lined walkways lead to the large, irregularly shaped infinity pool with big round, cushioned pods for sunning at the center and wooden decks for people-watching at the front. A large Jacuzzi sits in the middle of the pool and is reached by a bridge; to one side is a swim-up bar, four concrete banquettes and tables in the water for lunching without leaving the pool.

Next to the pool, the sunken terrace of Plunge restaurant provides for barefoot snacking on Caribbean-flavored dishes, salads, and pizzas. In the afternoon pool attendants circulate with fresh fruit kebabs, aromatherapy spritzing, cold water, and chilled towels. The pool is crowded when the resort is full, especially with families and kids.

Five large, coral stone five-story buildings with one-, two-, and three-bedrooms and penthouse suites form a tight U around the pool. The suites, some more than 1,500 square feet, have truly elegant appointments and sumptuous baths. Carved four-poster beds with hand-tufted mattresses and custom-made linens of 488-thread-count Egyptian cotton are the sort of details that signal the luxurious nature of these suites.

Throughout, the architecture reflects the classical elegance of British colonial buildings of the Caribbean. Creamy, textured coral stone quarried on Barbados is the dominant building material. White stepped Bermuda roofs top the residence structures; other buildings have native cedar shingle roofs, open verandas, and wraparound porches—characteristics of Great House designs. Unseen is an underground network of tunnels for services and personnel.

Interior design and furnishings, art and accessories, such as traveling chests, campaign chairs, and blue Chinese vases, reflect the eclectic mix found in colonial estates across the British Empire, including the Caribbean. White and neutral colors, including the crown moldings, walls, curtains, and vaulted ceilings, lend a refined touch. Floors are a mix of pale limestone and travertine marble. In contrast, bed frames and other custom-made furniture are dark mahogany, intricately carved and inlaid with exotic veneers.

Rooms have private balconies with outdoor seating and are furnished with flat-panel LCD television, DVD/CD player, a microwave, refrigerator, and coffee machine. Some have full kitchens, others kitchenettes, and all are equipped with Viking appliances.

The eight penthouse suites with great views of the sea and offshore islands come with vaulted ceilings, keyed elevator access, a study (or extra bedroom) with high-speed Internet access, large travertine terraces with a pergola, an interior "water room" with waterfall shower, and an adjacent SunSuite with an outdoor shower, garden, and Jacuzzi. Butler service is available for an extra charge. Large suites and penthouses have full-size chef's kitchens so guests can retain a personal chef for meals and entertaining.

The Mansion, the centerpiece and social hub of the resort, houses the resort's (very expensive) restaurant,

Parallel23, open for breakfast and dinner year-round. Its continental buffet breakfast is included in the room rate. The restaurant offers tropical fusion cuisine and an extensive wine list in a casually elegant setting, indoor and alfresco on the terrace overlooking the gardens. It also has a display kitchen with a wood-burning oven. The Green Flamingo bar next to Parallel23 has indoor/outdoor seating and is a popular pre-dinner or late-evening meeting venue.

The scent of burning incense mixed with the fragrance of flowers and the soothing sound of fountains and waterfalls greet you when you enter the Regent Spa. Housed in a separate building covering an acre near the resort's entrance, the spa is an oasis of serene gardens, reflecting pools, and unusual treatment rooms in coral stone structures surrounded by water.

The reception area, fitness center, yoga pavilion, beauty salon, and spa boutique face a quiet courtyard and a formal Japanese garden beside a large reflecting pool. The men's and women's changing rooms flanking either side of the yoga pavilion have secluded sunning terraces. On the other side of the changing rooms is the inner sanctum of the spa. A lovely central palm-lined promenade with three treatment cottages on each side are reflected in the dark pool waters with such perfect symmetry it seems to be a mirage.

The cottages are architectural gems: The back wall of each treatment room slides open revealing a reflecting pool that is surrounded by a privacy wall and fountain. After sunset, lit oil lamps in the fountain add another exotic element.

At the end of the promenade are two larger private spa suites where couples can be pampered for a half or full day. The suites have a shower, treatment area, and private garden terrace for sunning or dining under the stars. Sliding window walls open onto the reflecting pool on one side and the garden on the other. The spa has 4 Zareeba cabanas providing the most exotic treatments of all. Forming the backdrop of the spa is an 8-foot-tall/80-foot-long wall with cascading water.

The spa menu offers Sonya Dakar products and treatments, such as Mother of Pearl Body Exfoliation, the signature treatment. It incorporates native elements such as hand-crushed local queen conch shells mixed with an aromatherapy oil to polish and soften. There's a new men's treatment room and a menu of treatments, including a classic razor shave and a line of men's care by Art of Shaving.

The yoga, Pilates, and meditation pavilion offers daily classes. Other facilities include a beauty salon and a fitness center with state-of-the-art equipment and daily classes. Private classes and personal trainers are available.

While you are being pampered in the spa, your kids can have a great time in the Conch Kritters Club, with a kids' playroom and scheduled activities for ages 4 to 12 years. The playroom has board games, computer and video games, and toys. The trained staff also offers yoga and Pilates for club members. The club is open on demand as needed from 7:30 a.m. to 10 p.m. Full-day sessions cost $90 per child; half day, 9 a.m. to noon, $45; and evenings, which include kids-only dinner and a movie, $70 per child. Babysitting services are also available.

The resort has a tennis court for day or night play and Hobie Cats, snorkel gear, kayaks, windsurfs, floats, and children's toys available for use. Golf at nearby Provo Golf & Country Club course is only a few minutes away and diving can be arranged.

Upon arrival you'll find chocolate chip cookies and two bottles of water in your suite. Upon departure, your farewell bag will have bottled water and a granola bar for the trip home.

THE REGENT PALMS ★ ★ ★ ★
Providenciales, Turks and Caicos Islands, B.W.I.

Phone: (649) 946-8666; **Fax:** (649) 946-5188; **e-mail:** info@thepalmstc.com; www.theregentturksandcaicos.com
Owner: Stan Hartling.
General Manager: Karen Whitt
Open: Year-round
US Reservations: (866) 877-7256
Canada: (800) 567-5327
Deposit: 3 days; 21 days cancellation. Christmas/New Year's reservations require 50 percent credit card deposit at booking and full payment by Nov 1
Cancellation Fees: Cancellations after Oct 1 and no-shows will not be refunded
Minimum Stay: 3 days at Thanksgiving; 7 days at Christmas/New Year's
Arrival/Departure: Meet/assist service and transfers included in rate
Distance from Airport: 8 miles
Distance from business center: 4 miles

Accommodations: 72 one-, two-, three-bedroom, and 8 penthouse suites
Amenities: Hand-tufted king bedding; fine linens, bath sheets; minibar, flat-panel television; safe; high-speed Internet; complimentary water, nightly turndown. Master bath: hydro-massage bathtub, separate marble shower. Penthouse: full kitchen with Viking appliances
Fitness Facilities/Spa Services: See text
Sports: Swimming pool, tennis court lit for night play, croquet lawn. Nonmotorized water sports: Hobie Cats, snorkel equipment, kayaks, clear canoes, windsurfers, floats; children's beach toys; diving, sailing, golf arranged
Electricity: 110 volts
Dress Code: Smart casual
Children: All ages; Conch Kritters Club playroom and supervised program for ages 4 to 12
Meetings: Up to 160 people
Day Visitors: Spa and dinner with reservations
Handicapped Facilities: No
Packages: Spa, honeymoon, wedding
Rates: Per room, per night, double. *High Season* (Jan 3–Apr 10): $850–$990; suites $1,250–$3,700. *Low Season* (Apr 11–Dec 18): $625–$725; suites $950–$2,800. *Christmas Season* (Dec 20–Jan 2): $1,030–$1,600; suites $2,060–$5,830. Rates include continental buffet breakfast in restaurant and nonmotorized water sports.
Service Charge: 10 percent
Government Tax: 10 percent

US VIRGIN ISLANDS

Topside or below, few places under the American flag are more beautiful than our corner of the Caribbean. Volcanic in origin, the Virgin Islands are made up of 50 green gems floating in a sapphire sea; only three are developed. They are only a short distance apart, yet no islands in the Caribbean are more different from one another.

St. Croix, the easternmost point of the United States, is the largest. A low-lying island of rolling hills, it was once an important sugar-producing center. Many plantation homes and sugar mills have been restored as hotels, restaurants, and museums; Christiansted and Frederiksted, the main towns, are on the National Register of Historic Places.

St. Croix offers an impressive variety of activities, from hiking in a rain forest to turtle-watching, but its most popular sports are snorkeling and scuba diving. The island is surrounded by coral reefs; off the northeastern coast is Buck Island Reef National Monument, the only underwater park in our national park system.

St. John, the smallest of the trio, is truly America the Beautiful. Almost three-quarters of the mountainous island is covered by the Virgin Islands National Park. Around its edges lovely little coves hide some of the most alluring porcelain-white beaches and aquamarine waters in the Caribbean.

The National Park Service Visitor Center in Cruz Bay schedules ranger-led tours, hikes, and wildlife lectures and publishes a brochure outlining 21 trails. Cruz Bay, the island's main town, is booming from new popularity and rapidly losing its tiny-village charm to traffic. The ferry from St. Thomas takes 20 minutes.

St. Thomas floats on a deep turquoise sea with green mountains and an irregular coastline of fingers and coves sheltering idyllic bays and pretty white-sand beaches. Only 13 miles long, it seems larger because of its dense population and development. Its capital, Charlotte Amalie, is the busiest cruise port in the Caribbean.

St. Thomas offers good facilities for water sports and for tennis and golf, but it is best known for its smart boutiques with clothing, accessories, perfumes, and jewelry from world-famous designers.

The Virgin Islands, as US territories, have a special tax status that gives returning US residents a $1,200 exemption from customs duty rather than the $600 applied to visitors from other places.

Information

US Virgin Islands Division of Tourism, (800) 372-8784, (212) 502-5300; Fax: (212) 332-2223; www.visitusvi.com; www.stjohnusvi.com

THE BUCCANEER

Christiansted, St. Croix, U.S.V.I.

At The Buccaneer you could roll out of bed to play golf or take a swim at one of the two pools before breakfast, explore some of the Caribbean's best reefs fronting three white-sand beaches before lunch, and then enjoy a game of tennis before dinner—all within eye-shot of the pink palazzo whose history stretches back 340 years.

Spread over 340 tropical acres near Gallows Bay on St. Croix's northern coast, The Buccaneer was opened in 1948 as an 11-room inn in a 17th-century estate house by a family whose origins on the island date from the same period. The building's thick walls and graceful bonnet arches are still visible in the French Wing; the Cotton House serves as administration space; and the 18th-century sugar mill is the venue for

the manager's weekly cocktail party and weddings.

Now greatly enlarged and developed into a complete resort, the main building sits on a rise with commanding views. The roadside entrance passes along a drive lined with royal palms and well-kept gardens bright with bougainvillea and a great variety of tropical trees. Never ones to rest on their laurels, The Buccaneer recently completed a two-year $5 million renovation to every aspect of the resort, including the makeover of its 138 guest rooms and bathrooms updated with new glassed enclosed bathtubs; upgrading and expansion of its spa and its services, and refurbishing of the dining areas and lobby.

Some of the resort's accommodations are in the main building, while others are housed in a variety of cottages and bungalows near the fairways and tennis courts and in terraced gardens cascading from the main building to the sea. All have terraces. If you are a beach body, you may prefer the rooms that snake along the seashore. They have high, cedar-beamed ceilings and stone terraces overlooking the sea and pretty sunsets. Oceanfront rooms have marble floors and bathrooms. Three deluxe one-bedroom suites, Ficus (two bedrooms) and Frigate (one bedroom), are furnished with four-poster beds, two baths, and a living room.

The five family cottages, reserved exclusively for families of up to five members, are designed to appeal to both kids and parents. They have kids' rooms with two twin beds plus a trundle bed and walls hand-painted with fish and mermaids by St. Croix muralist Isabel Picard. Both parents' and kids' rooms have flat-screen television with DVDs. The master bedroom has spacious window seats that double as beds and reading nooks. Each cottage has large picture windows framing views of the Caribbean Sea and a furnished patio and lawn.

The most luxurious accommodations are 12 beachside units, called Doubloons, in keeping with the resort's tradition of naming rooms for gold coins rumored to have been buried by the buccaneers who sailed these islands. The large rooms are housed in a marble-terraced villa that echoes the island's Danish colonial architecture. Each has king-size four-poster beds or two queen-size beds, wide terraces or balconies with beach and sea views, picture windows with window seats, walk-in closets, and spacious bathrooms with whirlpool tubs and double showers.

Thirty-two rooms on the second floor of the main building have marble floors, carved four-poster beds, and doors made of solid mahogany. Originally known as the Hamilton Wing—for Alexander Hamilton, who spent his childhood here when the property was called Estate Shoys—the second story follows the contour of the original 17th-century foundation, which results in a group of rooms that each have a different shape and size; all have great views.

Another historic group, the four Widow's Mite rooms—originally built in the 1700s and so named because their expansive sea views recall rooms used by a ship captain's wife awaiting her husband's return from a long voyage. Now they have marble floors, newly outfitted bathrooms, all-new furniture, and a window seat tucked into the panoramic bay window.

The Buccaneer's tennis complex is the largest on the island. The 18-hole golf course (5,810 yards, par 70) dips and dives from hilltops to the water's edge. For fitness folks a 2-mile, 18-station par course jogging and exercise path winds through the hilly terrain. Those with something less strenuous in mind can join the weekly art class or check their e-mail on a computer provided for guests.

At the new Hideaway Spa you can iron out the kinks while your kids participate in a free program that includes crafts, supervised snorkeling, sing-alongs, parties, and their own daily newsletter. Renovation of the spa created a new salon for body treatments and massages with fresh new decor of serene earth tones, soothing water features, and aromatherapy scents. The spa offers a broad menu of massages, wraps, and body polishes. Body treatments may be paired with manicures, pedicures, hair services, and facials in a variety of half-day and full-day spa packages.

The daily Kids Camp for 4 to 12 year olds offers an introduction to SCUBA, snorkel and kayak, free wireless Internet access, water toys at the beach, twice daily maid service, daily entertainment and activities, and more.

One of The Buccaneer's two pools is by the main building, set into 17th-century foundations. The second is a free-form pool on quiet Beauguard Beach next to the Grotto, where burgers and snacks are available.

The Beach Shack, the water-sports center, offers staff-led snorkel and kayak tours. Lunch is served daily at the Mermaid, a breezy beachside restaurant, which is also the setting for some evening meals, especially enjoyed by families and guests preferring a light meal.

At breakfast in the open-air Terrace in the main building, you'll enjoy views of the fairways and the sea; in the evening the lights of Christiansted twinkle in the distance. Dinner offers a continental menu with West Indian flair. The Brass Parrot is a separate air-conditioned restaurant adjacent to the Terrace, serving as the resort's banquet and meeting room. Nightly the Terrace bar hosts live musical entertainment by different combos.

The Armstrong family, now the third generation to operate the hotel, is a family of naturalists. General manager Elizabeth Armstrong leads free weekly nature walks. The golf course is a popular birding spot. The Buccaneer is a member of the Historic Hotels of America, so named by the National Trust for Historic Preservation.

A quiet, self-contained, family-owned and -operated resort with a casual and friendly ambience, The Buccaneer is suitable for all ages and all situations, from singles to families. It appeals most to travelers who want an active vacation with a wide range of sports. Many guests are repeaters; some are from families that, like the owners, are into the third generation.

THE BUCCANEER ★ ★ ★ ★
Box 25200, Gallows Bay, St. Croix, U.S.V.I. 00824-5200
Phone: (340) 712-2100, (800) 255-3881; Fax: (340) 712-2105; e-mail: mango@thebuccaneer.com; www.the buccaneer.com
Owners: The Armstrong family
General Manager: Elizabeth Armstrong
Open: Year-round
US Reservations: Direct to hotel, (800) 255-3881
Deposit: 3 nights winter; 1 night summer; 5 nights Christmas/New Year's
Minimum Stay: 1 night
Arrival/Departure: Transfer service included in honeymoon packages
Distance from Airport: 10 miles (30 minutes); taxi one-way, $20 for 2, $10 each additional passenger; private car, $42 for up to 4 people
Distance from Christiansted: 2 miles; taxi one-way, $7; hourly hotel shuttle to town, $3 per person, one-way, $5 round-trip
Accommodations: 138 rooms and suites, all with terraces (50 oceanfront, 34 Great House, 12 Doubloons, 12 ridge rooms, 12 tennis units, 8 family cottages, 5 suites, and 5 units in various locations); 54 with kings, 84 with 2 queens

Amenities: Air-conditioning, ceiling fan; safe; telephone, satellite television; refrigerator; dressing area; bath with tub and shower, basket of toiletries, hair dryer; ice service, nightly turndown service, room service at specific hours; boutiques

Fitness Facilities/Spa Services: Health club; spa treatments (see text)

Sports: 2 freshwater pools; parcourse exercise path; 8 Laykold tennis courts (2 lighted), pro shop, fee for courts, lessons, equipment; golf, green fees, charge for equipment, caddies, carts, lessons; snorkeling, kayaking, free lessons and equipment; day and evening cruises, fishing, horseback riding arranged

Electricity: 110 volts

Children: All ages; activities program; cribs; babysitters; during summer children 18 and under stay free in room with parents

Meetings: Up to 90 people

Day Visitors: Yes

Handicapped Facilities: Limited

Packages: Golf, tennis, honeymoon, wedding, family

Rates: Per person, double, daily, FAB. *High Season* (mid-Dec–Mar): $340–$1,045. *Low Season* (mid-Apr–mid-Dec): $295–$730. Weekly rates available in summer; inquire.

Energy Surcharge: 10 percent

Government Tax: 8 percent

CANEEL BAY

A Rosewood Resort

St. John, U.S.V.I.

Consider these numbers: 166 rooms on 170 acres and a staff of 400, and seven beaches. Not bad odds, you could say. But these are only some of the elements that have made Caneel a legend.

Opened in 1956 as the late Laurance Rockefeller's first Caribbean venture, Caneel was the first of the ecologically built hideaways of the original RockResort style where less is more. Caneel is built into the ruins of an old sugar plantation within the Virgin Islands National Park. It sprawls across a peninsula scalloped with seven flawless beaches protected by coral reefs that are also part of the national park. Indeed, the fact that Caneel is framed on all sides by the national park forever ensures its pristine quality.

The Caneel appeal is immediately apparent, with acres of carpetlike meadows, artfully arranged shrubbery, and gardens of tropical flowers. Guest rooms are clustered in cottages of natural rock and weathered wood. They're all but hidden in the vegetation and are widely scattered. Some rooms are in the hillside tennis gardens, but most are set directly on the beaches.

The Cottage Point area on a bluff facing the water is the most requested honeymoon spot for its seclusion. Paradise Beach is next to the famous Cottage 7, formerly the Rockefeller home and now luxury digs for visiting bigwigs. Scott Beach, where units are in single-story buildings, is popular for its afternoon sun and lengthy beach. And cozy Turtle Bay Beach boasts the best snorkeling.

Regardless of locale, Caneel's rooms are airy and spacious and remain no-nonsense affairs with walls of louvered and screened windows for cross ventilation, and private patios. They are furnished in a retro "beach house" design featuring handcrafted furniture and fabrics inspired by the Caribbean palette in refreshing sea-foam greens and blues.

Although there still are no telephones or television in the guest rooms, Caneel has made several nods to the 21st century. Air-conditioning was added to all units, and bathrooms were renovated and upgraded. There are outdoor phones with AT&T direct at each of the clusters of buildings, and you can now get a complimentary cellular phone from the front desk if you really must stay connected to the outside world. Wi-Fi is available throughout the resort and is offered on a complimentary basis. A business center in a private room by the front lobby has a computer, printer, Internet access, and telephone.

Breakfast and lunch buffets indulge guests with many choices. If you prefer a light lunch, the open-to-the-breezes bar by the central building is a delightful setting in the shade by day and popular for drinks in the evening. If you prefer quieter, air-conditioned comfort, Turtle Bay Estate House serves breakfast and a midday meal during the winter season. You can also return there daily for afternoon tea.

Caneel is at its most magical at night, when the grounds are aglow with low "mushroom" lamps, and Polynesian-style torches hidden in the thick foliage light the paths near the activities building. A laid-back combo completes the mood with light dance music.

Dinner is served in three locations, all with a view of the twinkling lights of St. Thomas in the distance. The casual Beach Terrace on Caneel Bay Beach has an open kitchen with a wood-burning stove and rotisserie. It serves a buffet breakfast and lunch and the Monday night grand buffet. Equator, in the flower-festooned ruins of an 18th-century sugar mill, offers a cornucopia of Caribbean and other specialties and a fun Caribbean carnival decor in which to enjoy it—but all, naturally, in the low-key style that is Caneel's trademark.

The third venue is the enormous 18th-century manor house, site of the more formal, romantic Turtle Bay Estate House, where it's time to dress up and sit down to a 5-course meal.

Caneel offers a host of water sports and a variety of sail excursions and charter cruises. Beach Hut staff members are trained to give lessons in the use of snorkeling equipment and in windsurfing, Sunfish sailing, kayaking, and aquafins.

The resort has 11 tennis courts and tennis pros who arrange round-robins, hold clinics, and are available for lessons. You'll find jogging paths (and hiking trails in the national park) and an air-conditioned fitness center with cardio-vascular training equipment. Caneel Bay offers two open-air cabanas for spa treatments such as massages, facials, and wraps with views overlooking the beach.

Caneel is able to handle the growing demand from guests who want to bring their children, and at the same time, accommodates those who come to Caneel to get away from children—theirs and anyone else's. The program selects beaches appropriate for families and those seeking tranquillity. There are also two beaches for those over 12 years of age. Also, the resort has created the Teen Center, which is equipped with Ping-Pong, a pool table, computer with Internet access, and a jukebox.

Turtle Town, a children's center at one end of the property, has a full-time director and a staff of one counselor to every five children. Each day's program has a theme with special stress on environmental appreciation of the resort and of St. John.

Whether you fall into the with-kids or no-kids group, contact the manager in advance and be specific about your needs. Fortunately, Caneel is large enough and so spread out that it can accommodate guests of all ages without anyone trampling on others, provided the resort is informed of guests' needs in advance.

CANEEL BAY, A ROSEWOOD RESORT ★ ★ ★ ★
PO Box 720, St. John, US V.I. 00831-0720
Phone: (340) 776-6111; **Fax:** (340) 693-8280; **e-mail:** caneel@rosewood hotels.com or www.caneelbay.com
Owner: CBI Acquisitions
General Manager: Nikolay Hotze
Open: Year-round
US Reservations: Rosewood Hotels and Resorts, (888) ROSEWOOD, (888) 767-3966; **Fax:** (340) 776-6111
Deposit: 3 nights; 28 days cancellation for Dec 17–Apr 8; and 21 days prior to arrival in Spring and Fall seasons; 14 days in summer

Minimum Stay: 10 nights during Christmas

Arrival/Departure: Transfer on Caneel Bay's cruiser from St. Thomas five times daily, $110 round-trip per person transfer fee adults, $55 round-trip for children ages 5 to 12. Distance from Airport: (St. Thomas Airport) 12 nautical miles (see Arrival/Departure, above)

Distance from Cruz Bay: 3 miles; taxi one-way, $5-$10 per person

Accommodations: 166 rooms in 1- and 2-story cottages with terrace (33 ocean view, 54 beachfront, 37 premium, 5 in Cottage 7, 10 courtside, 27 tennis/garden)

Amenities: Air-conditioning, ceiling fans; bath with shower (few with tub), hair dryer, toiletries, iron and ironing board; safe; coffeemaker, minibar, sodas and ice service; nightly turndown, room service with charge for breakfast; no telephone; television in Estate House Lounge and Beach Bar; nightly movies; business center, Internet

Fitness Facilities/Spa Services: Fitness center (see text); massage on request

Sports: Freshwater swimming pool; 11 tennis courts; tennis and nonconcession water sports included in rate; deep-sea fishing, boating, golf in St. Thomas arranged; dive shop offers resort course, certification; clinic; jogging path, hiking trails

Electricity: 110 volts

Dress Code: Casual by day; in evening men required to wear collared shirts and trousers

Children: Year-round (see text)

Meetings: Up to 250 people

Day Visitors: Welcome in certain areas only

Handicapped Facilities: Limited

Packages: 3- and 7-night for 2 people, honeymoon, wedding

Rates: Per room, daily, CP. *High Season* (Dec 17–Apr 8): $500–$1,400. *Shoulder Season* (Apr 9–May 31; Nov 1–mid-Dec): $450–$1,200. *Low Season:* $425–$875

Service Charge: 10 percent

Government Tax: 8 percent on room only

MAHO BAY CAMPS HARMONY AND ESTATE CONCORDIA PRESERVE

St. John, U.S.V.I.

Folks, we're talking camp here. Camp as in camping—no private baths, no hot water, not even running water, except in the communal bathhouses.

This escape to paradise means tented cabins, which you'll probably share with friendly little lizards, mosquitoes, and other bugs. Getting to this heavenly rest takes seven hours or more via plane, taxi, ferry, and another taxi. On the last stretch—a bone-cracking ride on the wooden seats of a converted flatbed truck—self-doubt may set in. At Maho's reception area you'll be checked in by a friendly attendant, who'll give you the dos and don'ts about Maho and about protecting paradise. Then you'll lug your luggage up (or down) the hill to your abode.

It's obvious that Maho Bay Camps is not for everyone. What may be less obvious is why I have included Maho in this book in the first place. But, you see, many people think Maho offers the greatest vacation in the Caribbean. They come from all over the US and all walks of life. Maho has one of the highest winter repeat rates—80 percent—in the Caribbean. The staff is made up mostly of folks who came as guests and decided to stay.

Maho Bay, a private campground in the Virgin Islands National Park, is unique in the Caribbean. It was created in 1976 by engineer-ecologist Stanley Selengut, who has been teaching the world that being an environmentalist can be good business. The camp enjoys a gorgeous setting on a wooded hillside that falls to a small beach and overlooks an exquisite bay of reef-protected turquoise waters and expansive scenery of mountainous green neighboring islands. Maho Bay has none of the amenities of a typical tropical retreat. On the other hand, true campers call it luxurious.

Accommodations are in tented cabins, all but hidden in the thick foliage that climbs the hillsides, and are connected by a network of boardwalks and wooden steps. The dense woods help ensure privacy but sometimes obscure the view. Each cabin, made out of a translucent water-repellent fabric, is built on a 16-by-16-foot wooden platform suspended above the ground on wooden pilings, like a tree house. It is surprisingly roomy and quite comfortable.

The tent has a sleeping area with twin beds; a sitting area just large enough for a trundle sleeping couch and a fold-out cot; a small kitchen unit with a two-burner propane stove, electrical outlets, cooler, dishes, and utensils; and an outside deck, which makes a great perch for watching the sunset or counting the stars.

There are five bathhouses with sinks, toilets, and showers at various locations around the property; a grocery store, which is neither nonprofit nor cheap;

a multipurpose outdoor community center for meetings, seminars, and weddings; barbecue areas; and a cafeteria-style restaurant and bar in an outdoor pavilion with spectacular vistas where breakfast and dinner are available.

If you are more of a beach person, you might prefer the camp's lower reaches, but if you don't mind the hike to heaven, the tents higher up are the most desirable, both for their wonderful views and because they have high ceilings with ceiling fans, which stir the air and help keep away mosquitoes.

Maho's greatest innovations are at Harmony—perfect for people who love the idea of camping but can't hack the inconvenience. Selengut, in conjunction with the US National Park Service, built six units, each with two large guest rooms, following the Guiding Principles of Sustainable Design. The units are built totally from recycled materials, partly to prove that it can be done and partly to test products in the school of hard knocks of the Caribbean.

If no one had told you, you probably would not realize that these units were anything other than attractively furnished hotel rooms with a kitchen and dining area, a bath, and a large terrace. The hot water in each unit is powered by sun; some of the original solar use has given way to standard electricity to provide consistency in guest comfort. If you go with the spirit of adventure and curiosity and if you truly care about the environment, you will enjoy your stay.

Maho has a craft center, focused principally on glassmaking as part of its Trash to Treasures recycling program, with demonstrations daily by artists-in-residence. Craft classes in pottery, glassblowing, painting, and fabric printmaking are offered each week. A list of classes/times being offered for the year is available from the website. Some works of art can be purchased at Maho and online.

Maho also has a program for children 6 years and older, offering classes in pottery, paper making, papier mâché art, and more, to teach children the potential for recycling in a fun and creative way. Nothing goes to waste at Maho, if it can be recycled. Nothing.

As St. John beaches go, Maho's isn't much, but there are two longer white-sand stretches a short walk or swim away. All three beaches are great for snorkeling. The resort offers scuba, sailing, windsurfing, and kayaking at an additional charge. But the highlight is hiking on any of the national park's 21 trails.

Maho protects the environment with missionary zeal—and with the national park's rules. Evening programs are usually eco-oriented and may feature presentations by staff from the national park service or a visiting expert. Maho also hosts conferences on ecology.

Maho's taxi service makes trips every two hours into Cruz Bay during the day, but if you want to take in the town's nightlife, transportation in the evening can be a problem unless you rent a vehicle. Jeeps are recommended.

The really sad news is that after 37 years of operations, 2011 could be Maho Bay Camps' last. Its lease expires July 31, 2012. The Trust for Public Land (www.tpl.org), a nonprofit land conservation organization, has been trying to buy the land from the current owners, but those negotiations were unsuccessful and the land is once again on the open market. Concordia Eco Resort, Maho's sister eco-resort, will continue without interruption because that property is not located on leased land. Stay tuned.

Always the innovator, Selengut developed Concordia Eco Resort, another tented resort, located on a hillside on the less traveled southeast corner of St. John near Coral Bay and abutting the Virgin Islands National Park's Salt Pond and Ram Head areas. It began as something of a combination of the first two—not as basic as Maho and not as deluxe as Harmony, but over time Concordia has become a deluxe tented resort.

Concordia began with 25 eco-tents with comforts that go beyond ordinary camping such as fully equipped kitchens, solar-powered refrigerators, solar-heated showers, and private composting toilets. Each unit is designed to accommodate a family of up to six. In addition to the eco-tents, there are nine Concordia studios that range from a single room to a two-floor duplex with kitchen, bathroom, and private deck.

Eight new Eco-Studios, each with queen-size bed plus a queen-size futon sofa/bed, accommodate four people. It also has kitchen facilities, bathroom with solar-heated shower and comfortable private deck. Each unit features glass and concrete countertops, tiles, and lampshades, and clay sconces fired at Maho's pallet-burning kiln. The location of the new studios allows guests access to Salt Pond beach trail and Cafe Concordia.

Cafe Concordia & Meeting Pavilion is a remarkably innovative, multiuse green building that has a well-stocked grocery store, cafe offering alfresco dining, events pavilion, and large open space with extensive panoramic views. The wheelchair-accessible structure is topped with a 1,500-square-foot greenhouse roof-covered deck. In winter and spring Cafe Concordia serves breakfast and dinner, plus great views of the hills and ocean. At day's end, Happy Hour starts at 5 p.m.

The pavilion and open spaces provide a stunning setting for functions from yoga classes to island weddings and can accommodate 50 for meetings and workshops.

St. John architect Glenn Speer used green building techniques throughout. To reuse existing materials, the pavilion deck was built entirely of rock filled gabion (large cage) baskets excavated from the site. Baskets are planted with native vines and hanging plants to blend into the natural landscape. Water is collected from the roof and processed to potable standards on site. Glass blocks admit natural light and lighting fixtures and decorative touches were made at Maho Bay Camps recycled arts center.

Estate Concordia was instrumental, with the help of volunteers with mobility disabilities, including wheelchair-users, in testing some newly designed accommodations that have walkways for convenient access and living quarters with wide doorways, large bathrooms with spacious shower stalls, and utilities within easy reach. Some volunteers using assistive/adaptive recreational equipment also had the chance to swim, snorkel, kayak, sail, and even scuba dive, fulfilling lifelong dreams. Details on facilities and prices are available from Maho Bay Camps.

If you understand that Maho is a campground, and that's the type of vacation you want, you will not find better facilities in a more beautiful setting in the Caribbean. Unfortunately, many people not suited for Maho—perhaps having a romanticized notion of what it is—go there anyway, attracted by the low price and the illusion that they can hack it.

MAHO BAY CAMPS, HARMONY AND ESTATE CONCORDIA PRESERVE (S)

Cruz Bay, St. John, U.S.V.I. 00830
Phone: (340) 776-6240; **Fax:** (340) 776-6504; **e-mail:** mahobay@maho.org; www.maho.org
Owner: Stanley Selengut
General Manager: Adrian Davis
Open: Year-round
US Reservations: Maho Bay Camps, Inc., (800) 392-9004, (340) 776-6240; **Fax:** (340) 715–2020
Deposit: Half of reserved stay; 14 days cancellation less 50 percent of room cost
Minimum Stay: 7 nights holiday weeks
Arrival/Departure: No transfer service; 20-minute ferry ride from Red Hook dock on St. Thomas to Cruz Bay, $6; 45-minute ferry from Charlotte Amalie to Cruz Bay, $12
Distance from Cruz Bay: Maho, 8 miles; taxi one-way, $14 for 1, $10 shared; Maho's service, $8. Concordia, 12 miles. Car rental advised; arriving guests are given detailed driving instructions.
Accommodations: Maho, 114 tent cabins, all with twin beds, sleeping couch and foldout cot; 12 guest rooms in 6 Harmony units. Concordia, 25 eco-tents; 9 studios, 8 eco studios
Amenities: Maho fan; showers in communal bathhouses. For Harmony and Concordia, see text.
Sports: Hiking in national park; boating, snorkeling, diving, windsurfing, kayaking, deep-sea fishing available
Electricity: 110 volts
Dress Code: Informal
Children: All ages welcome
Meetings: Up to 125 people
Day Visitors: Welcome
Handicapped Facilities: No facilities at Maho; one unit at Harmony. Facilities at Concordia, inquire
Packages: No
Rates: Two people, daily, EP. **Maho,** *High Season* (mid-Dec–Apr 30): $140; $15 each additional person. *Low Season* (May 1–mid-Dec): $80. **Harmony,** *High Season* (mid-Dec–Apr 30): $220–$250. *Low Season* (May 1–mid-Dec): $130–$155. **Concordia,** *High Season:* eco-tents $160–$190, $15 extra person. *Low Season:* $110, $15 extra person; studios, $165–$255, $25; $120–$165, $15, respectively
Service Charge: None
Government Tax: 10 percent

FRENCHMAN'S REEF AND MORNING STAR MARRIOTT BEACH CLUB

St. Thomas, U.S.V.I.

The pretty pink edifice with white trim and natural stone accents is set in landscaped, flowering gardens at the edge of a promontory overlooking the Caribbean Sea.

Frenchman's Reef and Morning Star Marriott Beach Club, its adjacent sister resort on the beach—Marriott franchises since 1992—closed in May 2011 for five months to complete a major $48 million renovation.

A palm-lined driveway leads to the entrance where you step into a beautiful lobby, open and airy with views that extend all the way out to the sea. In the latest refurbishing, the lobby has been refreshed with contemporary Caribbean furniture in pod-style seating arrangement, meant to encourage guests to take advantage of the lobby as a public space for socializing or conducting business.

A double stairway leads down to bars and restaurants on the first level, which overlooks a pool area that wraps all around the building's sea side. On the lower level the pool area with a waterfall and views to infinity at every turn has been transformed to create a more fully integrated, aquatic experience. Now, it has separate, diverse components: the main one is a free form infinity-edged pool with Jacuzzis and lounging sun shelves; a kids' pool has interactive water elements; and the third is a grand cascading natural pool. Border areas have

346

improved seating, new surfaces, deck lighting, and modern fiber-optic lighting displays. At the far side of one pool, another set of steps leads down to a third level with another waterfall and an extension of land along the rocky coast at the edge of the cliff.

To one side of the pool complex is the Sunset Bar and Grill, the Reef Health Club, and Reef Spa, which have been complete renovated, updated, and expanded with a brand-new fitness center in a more accessible location and an exclusive spa pool featuring bubble beds, massage jets, and plunge areas.

On the other side is the Rum Bar Terrace with a great view of Charlotte Amalie It's amusing to be here in the late afternoon, watching the cruise ships sail out of the harbor. The passengers on the ships are taking as many pictures of the resort as the hotel guests are of the ships. The terrace is also popular at night with the lights of St. Thomas in the background and the twinkling stars overhead.

A pretty gazebo on the southern side of the pools is used for weddings (the hotel does such a huge wedding business that it has a special department, Weddings in Paradise, to handle them). Here, too, steps lead down to Morning Star Beach Club; another swimming pool and jacuzzi; two lighted Omni-turf tennis courts; the 2- and 3-story Morning Star Villas, a beachfront snack bar and a small convenience store.

Windows on the Harbor, the main dining room has been completely renovated. It serves breakfast, lunch, and dinner, but the most popular event is the Friday-night seafood buffet.

The Reef's other eateries are the Presto Marketplace, a snack bar and convenience shop by the lobby and Havana Blue Restaurant, Coco Joe's Bar, Star Market Coffee House, and The Sand Bar at Morning Star Beach Club. The Pirates Den is a nightclub with live entertainment and a sports bar. Another wing of Frenchman's Reef houses a ballroom and meeting rooms with a separate area for group check-in and a business center.

When the resort was redesigned in the past, 22 rooms of the old hotel were eliminated to make way for 88 luxury suites and a new floor was added on the top of the hotel to create a group of bi-level suites with living rooms and loft bedrooms, and 17 royal suites with cathedral ceilings, Jacuzzis, and a spiral staircase that winds up to the bedroom. The first phase of the ambitious project was completed in December 2010 with the renovation of the Sea Cliff wing, which has 80 luxuriously appointed guestrooms.

In the latest renovation, all 302 guest rooms of Frenchman's Reef resort's main tower were given completely new interiors with fresh elegant decor in shades of sage, cream, and blue with timber finishes and contemporary furnishings. The redesigned rooms also have new tech features, Marriott's "Revive" bedding, down comforters, thicker mattresses with plush toppers and fluffier pillows, and rain style shower heads. All rooms have a hair dryer, coffeemaker, iron and ironing board, telephone with voice mail and data lines, safe, television, chaise longue, desk, balcony, and 24-hour room service. Frenchman's Reef's clifftop location affords most rooms spectacular views.

The water-sports center offers snorkeling, diving, kayaking, windsurfing, parasailing, sport fishing, night canoeing, and sailing excursions. Free clinics for tennis, snorkeling, and diving are offered, as are aerobics and jazzercise. A ferry shuttle departs from a special dock several times a day for Charlotte Amalie, eight minutes away by boat.

FRENCHMAN'S REEF AND MORNING STAR MARRIOTT BEACH RESORT ★ ★ ★

Marriott Beach Resorts, PO Box 7100, St. Thomas, U.S.V.I. 00801
Phone: (340) 776-8500; **Fax:** (340) 715-6191; 800-524-2000; **e-mail:** resorts@marriott.vi; www.frenchman sreefmarriott.com; www.morningstar beachclub.som
Owner: Marriott International
General Manager: Jose Gonzalez
Open: Year-round
US Reservations: (800) 223-6388; (800) 524-2000
Deposit: 2 nights; 7 to 15 days cancellation, depending on season
Minimum Stay: None
Arrival/Departure: Transfer arranged upon request
Distance from Airport: (Cyril E. King Airport) 6 miles; taxi one-way, $10 for one person, $8 each for more than one;

baggage fee, large bags $4 each, small bags $2 each
Distance from Charlotte Amalie: 3 miles; taxi one-way, $8 for 1 person, $6 each for more than 1
Accommodations: 382 rooms and suites at Frenchman's Reef; 96 villa units at Morning Star
Amenities: Air-conditioning; direct-dial telephone; safes; cable television, movies; refrigerator; 24-hour room service; bath with tub and shower, hair dryers, toiletries; iron and ironing board; shops; full-service business center; wedding service
Fitness Facilities/Spa Services: See text
Sports: 2 freshwater swimming pools; 2 tennis courts; water sports
Electricity: 110 volts
Dress Code: Casual
Children: All ages
Meetings: Up to 1,000 people; audiovisual facilities
Day Visitors: Yes, with reservations
Handicapped Facilities: Yes
Packages: Family, honeymoon, wedding
Rates: Per room, single or double, EP. *High Season* (late Dec–mid-Apr): from $628. *Shoulder Season* (mid-Apr–June 1): from $444. *Low Season:* from $221. **Morning Star Beach Club,** *High Season:* from $906; *Mid-Season:* from $672; *Low Season:* from $454.
Service Charge: 8 percent on room
Government Tax: 8 percent on room

THE RITZ-CARLTON, ST. THOMAS

St. Thomas, U.S.V.I.

Commanding a magnificent setting at the eastern end of St. Thomas with expansive views of the US and British Virgin Islands, the Ritz-Carlton with its Italian Renaissance style and hilltop location could easily have you imagining that you are somewhere on the Italian Riviera.

Terraced in 30 acres of lavish gardens, the elegant resort was designed by Barbadian architect Ian Morrison, whose signature is the adaptation of various Mediterranean architectural elements to Caribbean settings. The main building and centerpiece of the resort suggests a Venetian Renaissance palace outfitted with a prince's ransom of Italian marble. Its red tile roof and ochre stucco facade are reminders of the Mediterranean style.

From the hotel's impressive entrance reached by a long, flower-lined driveway, you arrive at an imposing valet-attended porte cochere and step into the palazzo and onto beautiful Portuguese marble mosaic floors. These lead you through graceful arched and columned hallways to the reception desk.

This, it turns out, is the upper level of the palazzo, with high-arched Palladian windows that open onto spectacular views of the resort and the islands dotting the turquoise Caribbean waters below. At the center of the building is a small inner courtyard; one of its walls has several lion-head fountains with water cascading gently from one to another.

This imposing structure holds the administrative offices, several fashionable boutiques, meeting and banquet space, a concierge desk on the top level, and the Ritz-Kids room on the lower. The rest of the resort spans the hillside in both directions and falls to the beach via a flower-festooned stone stairway and a magnificent vanishing-edge pool.

Rimming the southern side are six multilevel beige stucco buildings with flower-filled terraces, resembling large villas on the Italian Riviera; each is named for a tropical flower. They house large guest rooms with fresh decor and large balconies with fabulous views, air-conditioning, ceiling fans, coffeemakers, hair dryers, and room-enlarging mirrors.

Each room has marble floors and is furnished with a flat-panel television, high-speed Internet, stocked minibar, a desk and chair (some have one or two love seats with a coffee table), a Sealy Posturepedic® Plush bed designed for The Ritz-Carlton, with 400 thread-count linens and down feather pillows. There are three telephones—by the bed, on the desk, and in the bathroom. In the closet you will find an umbrella along with a digital safe. The marbled bathroom has a long, narrow shelf over two separate sinks along with toiletries, a pair of monogrammed seersucker bath-robes, and iron and ironing board.

The three buildings house 55 Club Level rooms, 15 executive one-bedroom suites; three,1,850-square-foot presidential suites, the opulent Ritz-Carlton Suite and the Club Lounge are in a 5-story villa connecting the three buildings. Ritz-Carlton Suite has two-bedrooms, a dining and living area, fitness room with treadmill, and bath with rain showers and soaking tubs. The large, private key-activated Club Lounge has a dedicated concierge and offers five food presentations daily.

On the northern side of the palazzo is a large spa with 11 treatment rooms and a beachside cabana, salon, and retail boutique. Treatments feature preparations of organic and pure ingredients. The fitness center has exercise and weight-training equipment and a personal trainer on request. The Motion Studio, located near the fitness center, is used for aerobics, yoga, Pilates, and other fitness classes.

Sail's, the oceanfront restaurant, has an extended roof cover and offers open-air dining during the day. In-room dining is available around the clock. Bleuwater, enhanced by floor-to-ceiling French doors that open onto a view of the bay, is the resort's sophisticated, signature restaurant, specializing in fresh local seafood choices created by Executive Chef Fabien Gnemmi. The vegetables it serves are delivered weekly from The Chef's Garden in Huron, Ohio, which practices sustainable agriculture, ensuring maximum flavor and nutrients. The restaurant is open daily for breakfast and dinner; reservations are required. The Great Bay Lounge, which has an outdoor deck for dining, serves sushi and an eclectic menu of small plates and cocktails. It has a billiards table and board games and features nightly live entertainment.

The hills rimming the Ritz-Carlton form something of an amphitheater cupping the beach. To the south is a mangrove pond with ducks and other birds and at the center is a gorgeous 125-foot-long free-form swimming pool with a vanishing edge on the side toward the sea, allowing the water to spill over the edge like a waterfall—when you look across the pool, the water seems to disappear into the sea.

Snorkeling, windsurfing, Sunfish and Hobie Cat sailing, as well as dive instruction, certification, and excursions are all available for an additional charge. The hotel's 53-foot catamaran, Lady Lynsey, offers day sails and cocktail cruises. Nine moorings are available for guests who want to arrive by boat. The tennis complex has lighted Astroturf courts. A horticulturist leads walking tours. For more sedate activity, a resident artist offers watercolor classes upon request, for $65 per person.

The Ritz-Kids Club, a children's program for ages 5 to 12, is available daily Mon to Fri, 10 a.m. to 4 p.m. On Tues it is also available 6:30 to 9:30 p.m., and on Thurs during the evening hours only. The program is supervised by trained counselors and offers a wide range of fun and educational activities. The cost is $95 for a full day including lunch. Babysitting services are also available.

The Ritz-Carlton should appeal to just about anyone who likes a stylish atmosphere and can afford the tab. Bear in mind that you will need to do quite a lot of walking. There are golf carts to fetch you from your room to the palazzo, but they tend to function on island time—which is to say, slow.

THE RITZ-CARLTON, ST. THOMAS ★ ★ ★ ★
6900 Great Bay, St. Thomas, U.S.V.I. 00802

Phone: (340) 775-3333; **Fax:** (340) 775-4444; **e-mail:** sttrz.leads@ritzcarlton.com; www.ritzcarlton.com/stthomas
Owner/Management: THC St. Thomas Corporation
General Manager: Bernd Khulen
Open: Year-round
US Reservations: (800) 241-3333
Deposit: 3 nights; 30 days cancellation
Minimum Stay: None, except during Christmas; inquire
Arrival/Departure: Transfers available
Distance from Airport: (Cyril E. King International Airport) 13 miles 30 (minutes); taxi one-way, $18 per person, plus charge for luggage
Distance from Charlotte Amalie: 6 miles (20 minutes); taxi one-way, $15
Accommodations: 180 rooms and suites (including 55 club rooms; 15 executive, 3 presidential, and Ritz-Carlton suites)
Amenities: Air-conditioning, ceiling fans; 3 international direct-dial telephones; marble bath with tub and shower, 2 sinks, separate toilet, hair dryer, toiletries, bathrobes; twice-daily maid service with nightly turndown service; stocked minibar; coffeemaker; iron and ironing board; clock, CD player, radio/cable television; safe; beauty salon; laundry and valet service; 24-hour room service
Fitness Facilities/Spa Services: See text
Sports: Freshwater swimming pool; snorkeling, windsurfing, Sunfish sailboats, Hobie Cats; scuba instruction, full certification, dive available for additional charge; lighted Astroturf tennis courts, equipment, lessons; golf at Mahogany Run and deep-sea fishing arranged

351

Electricity: 110 volts

Dress Code: Casual by day; casually elegant in evening

Children: All ages; RitzKids, ages 5 to 12; babysitters; Kids meal plan

Meetings: Up to 200 people

Day Visitors: No day passes

Handicapped Facilities: Entire property is wheelchair accessible. Rooms available, however, be aware that property is on hillside and very spread out.

Packages: Honeymoon, wedding, dive, family, others

Rates: Per room, daily, EP. *High Season* (mid-Dec–Apr 30): $619–$2,000. *Shoulder Season* (May–early July; Oct–mid-Dec): $350–$1,200. *Low Season:* $299–$750.

Government Tax: 8 percent room tax

Resort Fee: $58 per person, per day

ON THE HORIZON

This section features new resorts that hold the promise of being among the best.

Antigua
SUGAR RIDGE
Antigua, West Indies

Perched high on the forested hill-side after which it is named, Sugar Ridge overlooks the southwest coast of Antigua and commands extensive views from Jolly Beach on the west to Darkwood Beach on the south. Opened December 2009, the resort in contemporary design was created by the global architectural and design firm, OBMI, after more than four years and an investment of $30 millon, despite a sinking world economy that could have derailed it.

Once an island whose wealth came from sugar, the hotel's interior designer Antiguan Charmaine Benjamin-Werth of island-based d-Studio, used it as the focus of a simple design concept "that was all about sugar—in every possible incarnation," she has explained. The idea is reflected in her colors like caramel, vanilla, molasses, green, and orange and mixed with textures that recall sugar cubes, sugar cane stalk, citrus, honey-combs, and crystals. The result is warm and welcoming spaces, suggesting the pleasurable sensations evoked by sugar as well as the island's heritage.

Benjamin-Werth drew material from sources around the globe—and around the corner. Travertine tiles from Turkey, wood flooring from Guyana and custom-made Indonesian teakwood furniture are enlivened by the distinctive photographs of local artists Jennifer Meranto and Yensa Werth. Contemporary and comfortable, the designers hand can be seen and felt everywhere. All 60 of its rooms enjoy views of the green landscape rolling down to palm fringed beaches lining the Caribbean shores at their feet; neighboring Redonda, St. Kitts, and Nevis are in the distance. The guest rooms with dark wood doors and trim against cream-colored walls pick up color in the orange throws and pillows on white bedcovers. Rooms are grouped in sets of four, each with their own private entrance. Upper floor rooms have a large outdoor living area with a daybed and dark wood railings; they are comfortably furnished for outdoor dining and relaxing. The ground floor rooms are similar in their interiors but have a plunge pool in the outside area.

All accommodations are air-conditioned and have ceiling fan, an iPod dock, electronic safe, telephone, mini-fridge, tea/coffeemaker, complimentary wireless Internet throughout the property; LCD flat-screen cable television; radio frequency activated door lock, bathrobes, hairdryer, iron and ironing board.

Guest services can organize such water sports, fishing, sailing and diving. Beach facilities and a marina are only a few minutes away and accessed by the hotel's private shuttle. Play on the nearby golf course can be arranged. Sugar Ridge also has a retail area with a variety of boutiques.

The 6,000-square-foot Spa at Sugar Ridge was developed with Aveda, said to be the first such venture for this spa specialist in the Eastern Caribbean. The full-service spa with five treatment rooms and a gym occupy the entire ground floor of the main building. Its large collection of treatments feature the latest in holistic therapies as well as a hair salon with manicure and pedicure services. The air-conditioned gym has Cybex fitness equipment, including 13 cardiovascular machines. Adjacent to the gym is an air-conditioned studio for aerobics, Pilates, and yoga classes. Adjacent to the spa is an 82-feet-long lap pool plus a smaller leisure pool with cabanas and sun bathing areas.

Sugar Ridge's restaurants, Carmichael's and Sugar Club, the main one overlooking the central pool area, have garnered rave reviews since they opened. Their stunning decor and hilltop open-air setting with unending sea views are a fine match for the cuisine. Their chefs focus on what's fresh from Antigua's local market and offer Caribbean and Mediterranean cuisine with modern flair. Sugar Club is a pleasant, informal yet stylish restaurant open for breakfast, lunch, and dinner. Carmichael's also offers a list of American, European, and New World wines. Room service is available from 8 a.m. to 9 p.m. with $10 charge per tray.

Sugar Club Bar, adjacent to the restaurant, extends to a lounge area with colorful and comfortable contemporary furnishings and is popular for a pre-dinner cocktail or after-dinner cigar and aged rum. Open nightly until late in the evening, it offers live entertainment three times a week. Sugar Ridge is well suited for weddings, small meetings, and incentive groups, who can rent the entire resort.

SUGAR RIDGE
PO Box 153, Jolly Harbour, Antigua
Phone: (268) 562-7700; Fax: (268) 562-7701); e-mail: hotel@sugarridgeantigua .com; www.sugarridgeantigua.com
Owner: Mongoose Development
General Manager: Keith Martel
Open: Year-round
US Reservations: Direct to hotel, hotel@sugarridgeantigua.com; Toll Free US: (866) 591-3881

Distance from Airport: 35-minute drive from V.C. Bird International Airport
Distance from Capital: 25-minute drive from St. John's
Accommodations: 60 rooms and suites
Children: All ages. Up to age 2 are accommodated free in a room with parents. Four pairs of adjoining rooms with twin beds available at reduced rate for one or two children with one or two adults in connecting room.
Rates: Per room, per night, double with breakfast: *High Season* (Jan 5–Apr 14): $370–$450. *Low Season* (Apr 15–Dec 21): $260–$380. Meal plans and children's rates are available, inquire.
Service Charge: 10 percent
Government Tax: 10.5 percent

British Virgin Islands
SCRUB ISLAND RESORT, SPA & MARINA
British Virgin Islands

When you say something started from scratch or in this case scrub—it's no exaggeration to say it about Scrub Island Resort, a 230-acre private island development, a 10-minute motorboat ride north of Tortola and neighboring the island of Little Camanoe.

When the developers set out to design the initial master plan of the property, the island had nothing—no roads, no power, no electricity, no water—nothing but scrub, a "virgin" in the British Virgin Islands. The developers literally started from scratch to create a project that would produce financial results for the developers while at the same time preserve the natural character of the island.

An interesting side note that caused a great deal of early discussion was the name of the island. "Scrub" is not exactly an alluring name for a resort. But the name has history. And when you see the island, it's easy to understand how it got its name. When the British Virgin Islands was a pirates' haven 350 years ago, the seaman used to take their boats to low-lying Scrub Island all but hidden behind its mountainous neighbors—haul them out from the shallows, and scrub the barnacles off the bottoms of their boats. History has prevailed.

Another interesting note: Scrub Island development began as a real estate venture until it ran into the headwinds of the 2007–2008 housing market crash and the embattled economy. That's when the developers shifted gears and focused on creating a resort with a full-service hotel, a state-of-the-art marina, and the best stocked grocery shop and provisioning store this writer has seen in the Caribbean.

Scrub Island Resort is comprised of 26 deluxe guest rooms and 26 one-bedroom suites in several buildings of contemporary design—all with ocean views. On a hillside above the hotel are an additional 8 two- and three-bedroom villas.

The resort's main building has a reception lobby and meeting rooms on the first floor and an indoor air-conditioned restaurant with an outdoor terrace on the second level. The terrace overlooks the large lagoon-style, multi-tiered swimming pool with a waterfall and a swim-up bar to one side; the docks and marina in the other direction and neighboring islands in the distance.

A second building closer to the marina houses, in addition to the suites, the full-service Ixora Spa and fitness center, the grocery store, and a sundries shop. The resort has equipment for snorkeling and kayaking and an on-site dive shop.

The decor throughout the hotel combines the aura of the British colonial Caribbean with rich woods in overhead beamed ceilings, doors, and bedroom furniture and an understated modern luxury in its amenities that include island-wide Internet access. Air-conditioned guest rooms have bamboo ceiling fans, a king-size bed with soft down bedding and fine linens, 50-inch plasma television, bamboo ceiling fans;

bathroom with separate shower and bathtub, Bulgari toiletries, and iron and ironing board. The suites have a full kitchen with granite countertops and stainless steel appliances, including Wolf range and SubZero refrigerator. Caravela, the main restaurant, serves breakfast and dinner, while more casual fare is available at Aliseo, an open-air eatery adjacent to the main pool. Cocktails and wines by the glass are offered at the main bar, Tierra! Tierra!, and the Gourmet Market and Cafe has a wine bar and prepares coffee, sandwiches and snacks, daily from early morning. Each day of the week the resort has a different evening focus: Caribbean buffet on Monday, Tapas and Martinis on Tuesday, etc. Adjacent to Caravela is the Candle Room with enormous candles providing the glow for wine pairing dinners for up to 20 persons on Thursday.

Scrub Island's Marina, a short stroll from the resort, offers 53 deep-water slips including 5 for large mega-yachts, and available for lease or transient docking. Guests can rent boats or book half- or full-day fishing excursions with guide and equipment and head for the North Drop, the world-record hot spot for Blue Marlin.

Scrub Island is fringed by three pristine beaches one accessible only by kayak that shelve gently into the azure sea. The 1,000-foot-long North Beach on the north side of the island is the most beautiful of the three beaches where there has been virtually no development, except for One Shoe, a small beach bar. Protected coves, nature trails, and panoramic views invite exploration of other parts of the island. Birding and turtle-watching are other diversions. With fewer than 200 people likely to be on the island at any time, privacy is all but assured.

SCRUB ISLAND RESORT, SPA & MARINA

Scrub Island, British Virgin Islands
Phone: (281) 440-3440; Toll Free: (877) 890-744; Fax: (813) 269-4802; e-mail: reservations@mainsailbvi.com; www.scrubisland.com
Owner: Mainsail Lodging & Development
General Manager: Martin Smith
Open: Year-round
US Reservations: Toll Free: (877) 890-744
Arrival/Departure: Private launch to/from Trellis Bay (Tortola) and airport on Beef Island
Distance from Airport: Beef Island/Trellis Bay, just over 1-and-a-half miles, 5-minute taxi ride to Trellis Bay to board ferry for 10-minute ride to Scrub Island
Distance from Capital: 30-minute taxi ride from Roadtown, Tortola to Trellis Bay to board ferry for 10-minute ride to Scrub Island
Accommodations: 50 ocean-view units (25 rooms, 25 one-bedroom suites; two-, three-, and four-bedroom private villas.
Children: All ages; cribs available
Packages: Honeymoon, spa, dive, and others (see website)
Rates: Per room, per night, double: *High Season* (Jan 4–Apr): 10 Ocean View $750; 1-bedroom suite, $1050; 2-bedroom suite, $1,350. *Low Season* (Apr 11–Sept 30; Oct 1–Dec 21): $575–$625, $775–825, $975–$1,025. *Holiday* (Dec 21–Jan 3, 2013): $1,050, $1,750, $2,300, respectively
Service Charge: 10 percent
Government Tax: 7 percent

Curaçao
BAOASE LUXURY RESORT
Marie Pampoen, Curaçao

Opened in 2010, Baoase Luxury Resort fronting a 1,000-foot beach on the southeast shore of Curaçao, drew international attention from the first day. And rightly so. This one is a real beauty.

Baoase's residential-style accommodations reflect the quality of an elegant home. Refined Asian-influenced decor surrounded by meandering free-form pools, waterfalls, palm trees, and Caribbean flora creates an inviting ambience to wind down and soak in the serenity.

The experience can begin upon arrival at the Curaçao airport where for a fee, the hotel's chauffeur will meet you and transfer you in air-conditioned luxury to the resort. You can even book VIP airport service to be met at your airplane by a personal escort who guides you through customs, collects your luggage, and escorts you to the taxi/pick-up area; on departure you can wait in the VIP lounge and be guided through check-in.

Awaiting you at this small resort are the reception and welcome desk and a welcome drink and hors d'oeuvres, 15 beautifully decorated luxury rooms, suites, and villas, some with pools or Jacuzzi, some with both, some with kitchens and all in red tile roof cottages smothered in lavish tropical gardens; a beach bar and restaurant; a private beach, three plunge pools and two swimming pools, three Jacuzzis and five whirlpools, and a fitness center. To be added are deluxe beach suites and an indoor restaurant, spa, beachside sunset bar, and a super-yacht harbor in the future.

The villas are three types: Garden View with a private pool and a Jacuzzi in the garden, and Ocean Front and Ocean View open directly onto the infinity pool. Except for the number of bedrooms, their interiors are similar. There also is the Master Villa, which is rented only by special request.

The two- and four-bedroom Garden View villas have handsome contemporary interiors with Asian touches in the decor, a fully equipped kitchen, and an open terrace furnished for dining. Each bedroom has a luxury bathroom and an outdoor open-air shower/bath. The master suite has hardwood floors and shuttered doors under a high roof. They are furnished with a king-size bed dressed in white and topped with brightly colored silk runners and pillows. The recessed wall behind the bed has shelf with an orchard arrangement illuminated by a soft light overhead. A similar second bedroom on the top floor is furnished with a queen bed and equipped with reading lights, safe, desks, and chairs. It also has a balcony looking out at the pool or the garden. The kitchen with dark gray cabinets and shuttered windows is equipped with an electric stove/oven, a full size fridge, coffee machine, and other appliances.

The two Ocean Front and three Ocean View villas are similar to the Garden View villas in decor. The three-bedroom ones have two luxury bathrooms and one outdoor open-aired shower/bath. Bedrooms two and three are on the top floor, each with a balcony, which looks across the pool or garden to the ocean. In all villas, dining can be enjoyed inside in the air-conditioned dining area upstairs or on the open terrace.

The suites are either ocean view or ocean front; each has a terrace with a Jacuzzi and are furnished with a king-size bed. The Bunga Anggrek suite (named for an Indonesian flower, as are other accommodations) is on a second floor providing a panoramic view of the beach and turquoise sea. It also has access to one of the swimming pools. The Mawar Putih and Mira suites have inside and outside sitting areas with sea views. Their spacious bathrooms have a bathtub and a rain shower for two.

The deluxe Banyan Tree loft (592 square feet) tucked behind the resort's old Banyan tree, is suited for a family of four. The ground floor has a king-size bed and a roomy bathroom with shower; the loft bedroom is furnished with a queen-size bed. The loft also has an outside, fully equipped kitchen on its patio. The Banyan Tree Room, suitable for two, also behind the old tree, is furnished with a king-size bed and an outdoor open-aired shower/bath. The deluxe Colonial Room (376 square feet) with a terrace looking out at the gardens is suitable for two persons. All Baoase's accommodations are air-conditioned and have either a terrace or porch. They are fitted with free wireless Internet access, flat-screen television, DVD players/library access, Dolby surround system, safe, telephone, cellphone rental, tea/coffee maker, hair dryers, bathrobes, and slippers, Gilchrist & Soames bathroom amenities, daily maid, and nightly turndown service. The suites have a mini-bar, while the villas have well-equipped kitchens; butler service is available upon request for an extra charge.

Dining at Baoase offers the option of in-villa cooking with the resort's chef preparing a meal tailored to your taste or the Baoase Beach Bar & Restaurant, directly on the beach and open for breakfast, lunch, and dinner.

Baoase offers kayaks free-of-charge and can arrange diving and snorkeling on the wonderful coral reef in the waters fronting the resort, as well as fishing and boat trips and other water-sports and island excursions. Baoase's beach staff arranges loungers, towels, umbrellas, and provides bar service. Spa services are available in villas and suites or at the beach. The fitness center, opened daily from 7 a.m. to 11 p.m., has state-of-the-art equipment. Baoase offers several settings for weddings and can handle small meetings for up to 20 people.

If you are wondering about the resort's name, Baoase (pronounced Baw-o-ah-se), it is made up of the B and A initials of the owners' names, Bibi & Ad, and how they see their resort as their oasis.

BAOASE LUXURY RESORT
Winterswijkstraat 2, Willemstad, Curaçao
Phone: + 599-9-46-11-799 (Resort direct); Fax: + 599-9-46-12-799; Toll-Free US and Canada: (888) 409-3506; e-mail: info@baoase.com; www.baoase.com
Owner: Ad van der Valk
General Manager: Koen Appels
Open: Year-round
US Reservations: Direct to resort
Arrival/Departure: Round-trip transfer arranged for $120 for 4 persons; the VIP version $120 for 2 persons, additional person $40; guided from airplane by host $55 per person, per trip
Distance from airport: 13 miles, 25-minute drive from Curaçao International Airport
Distance from capital: About 2 miles
Children: All ages; request must be made prior to reservation confirmation. Babysitting arranged for extra fee.
Rates: Per room, per night, double, *High Season* (Jan 4–Apr 24): $375–$635. *Low Season* (Apr 25–Dec 17): $325–$550. All rates include daily breakfast. For 2-, 3-, 4-bedroom villas, inquire.
Service Charge: 12 percent resort fee
Government Tax: 7.84 percent

Puerto Rico

ST. REGIS BAHIA BEACH RESORT

Bahia Beach, Puerto Rico

The opening in November 2010 of the St. Regis Bahia Beach Resort on 483 beautiful acres east of San Juan marked the debut of St. Regis Hotels & Resorts in the Caribbean and brings to Puerto Rico one of the most storied luxury hotel legacy in travel. (The St. Regis brand was founded by John Jacob Astor IV over a century ago with the opening of the first St. Regis Hotel in New York City.)

Set on a former coconut plantation stretching between the El Yunque rain forest and the Espiritu Santo River to 2 miles of Atlantic beach, the resort boasts a signature restaurant by a famous chef, a 10,000-square-foot Remède Spa, an ocean-front championship golf course by Robert Trent Jones Jr., St. Regis butler service, and even its own bird sanctuary honored as the Caribbean's first certified Gold Audubon Signature Sanctuary.

Designed by Hill Glazier architectural firm, this resort of refined elegance has 139 luxuriously appointed guest rooms, including 35 suites with private terraces looking out to ocean views, and 25 private St. Regis Estate Homes. The accommodations have been designed as low-rise plantation style buildings that harmonize with the natural beauty of their surroundings. Their residential-style interiors have a beamed, recessed ceiling with rattan fan, custom-designed cherry-wood furniture with a carved headboard and oversized desk against a palette of neutral tones with moss green and terracotta accents.

Bedrooms have either one king or two queen pillowtop beds dressed in Pratesi linens, a duvet, and down or hypoallergenic pillows. They are fitted with a 40-inch LCD television and Samsung Sound Bar surround system, iPod dock, DVD/CD player, and free wireless high-speed Internet access, a wet bar, mini-refrigerator, safe, and a walk-in closet. The spacious marble bathroom has an oversize tub, separate rain shower, double vanity, Remède bath amenities, bathrobes and slippers, and a television imbedded into an oversized bathroom mirror.

As part of its commitment to sustainable development, the St. Regis Bahia Beach Resort created a 2.4-acre nursery and garden to supply plants and trees for landscaping and reforestation as well as fresh produce and herbs for its spa and restaurants. To ensure a minimal disruption of the building site's natural plant and wildlife, the resort had a "green team" composed of an ecologist, two agronomists, and a landscape architect and cultivated native and indigenous plants that protect the natural vegetation of the resort's coastal and forest areas. The resort's cuisine features fruits, vegetables, herbs, and spices grown from the dual-system hydroponic garden of the plant nursery that allows for pesticide-free, nutritionally rich production of diverse crops such as bananas, peppers, eggplant, arugula, radishes, chilies, fennel, ginger, and more.

The St. Regis Bahia Beach's signature restaurant, Fern, offers culinary delights prepared with the fresh local ingredients by celebrated chef Jean-Georges Vongerichten. Located on the second floor of the grand Plantation House, Fern offers intimate, candlelit indoor and outdoor dining with uninterrupted views of the resort's beach. The menu showcases a blend of Jean-Georges' distinctive repertoire with Puerto Rican traditional ingredients. Fern serves breakfast and dinner.

The restaurant's design presents a fusion of Latin and Afro-Caribbean materials and textures interpreted in a contemporary manner within the Spanish colonial building. The rich brown floor is a nod to the early coconut plantation in texture and feel and is matched against modern silver-leafed cork walls accented with handcrafted modern African light fixtures. In addition to the St. Regis Bar, the resort has two other dining venue: Molasses, an oceanfront restaurant and bar serving American cuisine with Puerto Rican accents; and the casual Seagrape, featuring Italian and Mediterranean cuisine along with healthy pool fare.

The Remède Spa, which offers a comprehensive menu of treatments, has seven treatment rooms, including several with private outdoor terraces, relaxation areas, steam and sauna facilities, cold and hot plunge pools, an exercise area, and a fully equipped fitness center.

The resort's golf course is Robert Trent Jones Jr.'s first design project in Puerto Rico. Operated by Troon Golf, a leader in golf course management, the course embraces views of 2-miles of beach, a native maritime forest, and views of El Yunque's rain forest-clad slopes from almost every hole. Committed to preserving the natural integrity of the site in its design, course holes along the ocean and lakes are cooled by ocean breezes, challenging golfers of all skills. The clubhouse houses a golf shop, bar, men and ladies lounges.

The resort's meeting facilities cover nearly 27,000 square feet of functional space, including the elegant Astor Ballroom, the ocean-view Astor pavilion, and three outdoor lawn event spaces.

The Iguana Kids Club is housed in its own bright and airy pavilion within easy reach of nature walks, birdwatching, and turtle-feeding. The children's program incorporates a learning center and video games for older children while a separate area offers activities for younger ones. The club also has a well-designed playground.

The resort's Aquatics Center offers equipment and lessons for snorkeling, kayaking, sailing, windsurfing, and fishing in the surrounding rivers. The swimming pool overlooking the ocean has patio areas used for dining and entertaining.

To earn Gold Audubon certification, the resort implemented a Natural Resource Management Plan that encompassed wildlife conservation, water quality monitoring and conservation, and integrated pest management, energy efficiency, and waste management. The plan included transplanting over 4,500 native trees, planting more than 12,000

trees, planting 70,000 native and natu-
ralized plants, creating island preserves
and sumps to prevent drainage into
lagoons and the Atlantic Ocean, captur-
ing storm water runoff, then used for
irrigation,and limiting use of pesticides
and fertilizers, among other actions.

ST. REGIS BAHIA BEACH RESORT
SR 187 Kilometer 4.2, Rio Grande,
Puerto Rico 00745 US
Phone: (877) ST-REGIS, (787) 809-
8000; **e-mail:** reservations.bahiabeach@
stregis.com; www.stregisbahiabeach.com
Owner: Interlink Group
General Manager: Erik Berger
Open: Year-round
US Reservations: reservations.bahia
beach@stregis.com or (787) 809-8061

Arrival/Departure: Car transportation
arranged upon request for fee
Distance from Airport: 16 miles
from Luis Muñoz Marin International
Airport.
Distance from Capital: 20 miles from
San Juan
Children: All ages; Iguana Kids Club
for ages 5 to 12 years; cribs upon
request
Rates: Per room, per night, double, **EP:**
High Season (Jan 3–Feb 17; Feb 27–Apr
30): from $929. *Shoulder Season* (May–
Aug; Nov–mid-Dec): from $759. *Low
Season* (Aug 20–Oct 28): from $589.
Christmas/New Year's: from $1,199.
Service Charge: $60 per night
Government Tax: 9 percent

W RETREAT & SPA, VIEQUES ISLAND

Vieques, Puerto Rico

With award-winning architects and
designers, restaurants by a celebrity chef, and owners who are investors
in contemporary luxury, fashion, and
hospitality businesses, you could say
that combination surely knows a thing
or two about putting the "Wow!" in the
W of W Retreat & Spa, Vieques Island.
Along with that, they also chalked up a
bunch of "firsts."

Opened in 2010, the Vieques resort is
W Hotels' first property in the Caribbean,
its first Retreat in North America, and
only the second Retreat worldwide that's
slated for expansion. At the same time, it's
Vieques' first international brand hotel,
bringing a new standard to the island.

Set on 30 acres of verdant beachfront
8 miles off Puerto Rico's southeast coast,
W Retreat & Spa is sophisticated yet
fun. The "Wow!" factor starts with your
arrival at Vieques Airport where the contemporary decor of W Retreat's private
welcome lounge will be your introduction to the resort's style.

After a warm welcome and refreshments, you will be whisked off to the
hotel. Immediately you will meet the
retreat's rustic yet ultra-modern decor—
by Spanish-born/Milan-based Patricia
Urquiola—where the stylish oasis weaves
natural and local elements into the
contemporary style of W Hotels. The
porte cochere and entrance are wrapped

in beautifully patterned wood set off by colorful lights. They lead into the reception area and the W Living Room with an eclectic mix of chairs, sofas, oversized pillows, and murals from classic to unusual with bold interconnecting circles, stripes, and squares—often wild and flamboyant in color—and somehow, it works.

The Rockwell Group Europe, a Madrid-based architecture and design firm, collaborated with Urquiola in some public areas, while EDSA of Fort Lauderdale did the landscaping. You will also be impressed by the attention to detail and the craftsmanship displayed in the use of locally recycled materials, organic forms, and Urquiola's modern Italian furnishings—most created for W Retreat Vieques by B&B Italia.

W Retreat's 157 exuberantly colorful guest rooms and suites, ranging in size from a very spacious 560 square-feet to 1,440 square-feet, are housed in 2 and 3 story blocks with private patios or balconies and views of the sea and coast. The decor, inspired by the tropical setting, uses shades of tan and beige accented with vibrant colors and prints, especially huge original wall art against the dark wood trim and shiny dark grey tiled cement floors in an open-concept bathroom. One of Urquiola's unique pieces, showcasing her theme of rustic nature interwoven with contemporary design, is her oversized bathtub, made from painted steel and crowned by a rain shower.

All rooms are furnished with the W signature bed and bedding, a 42-inch LCD television, a "munchie box" (W Retreat's version of a mini bar) with

sweets and snacks; high-speed Internet access, and an oversized desk that converts into a dining table. The room has a round oversize barrel chair, dubbed a "Potato/Patata" seat, with brightly colored pillows of varying design, as well as a multi-colored hanging chair on the balcony. Six of the largest suites have direct access to the beach, along with other amenities.

W Vieques offers 5 dining options created by famous chef Alain Ducasse and his team from Alain Ducasse Enterprise. Some selections can be described as Caribbean with a French twist; others are inspired by Ducasse's passion for Mediterranean flavors, and all use the bounty of fresh local products from the island's farmers and fishermen.

Have breakfast and dinner at miX on the beach, the Retreat's signature ocean view restaurant open to the breezes. Enjoy ice cream, cocktails and smoothies, along with light snacks, Mediterranean-inspired specialties, and traditional American fare at WET. WET encompasses 2 secluded beaches: it's a long swimming pool split down the middle by a concrete island planted with palm trees, with spectacular views of the ocean and W's signature service, so you don't have to lift a finger as you relax.

La Pescadora on the beach is another dinner option, offering al fresco dining on a wooden deck surrounded by tiki torches. Fresh-catch seafood and grills are the highlights on a menu changed daily. For those guests on-the-go, W Cafe has light fare, that can be packed in picnic boxes.

The AWAY Spa, a W Hotels brand, offers an array of health and beauty therapies, as well as a selection of luxurious products featuring Sue Devitt's Microquatic range. Designed by the Rockwell Group Europe, the spa is a separate ocean-side hideaway. Inspired by the natural surroundings, it has rivulets and canals that flow through the space and to serenity. The spa, surrounded by gardens with seating areas and pools, has 8 vine-covered indoor/outdoor treatment rooms separated from the main pavilion by a reflecting pool. Seaside yoga and holistic treatments are also offered.

SWEAT, the fitness center open 24/7, is equipped with Technogym machines including treadmills, elliptical machines, stationary bikes and other cardio equipment with personal television, complimentary headphones, and personal training. Several private cabanas are position at one end. Behind the main hotel building are 2 tennis courts.

Among the Retreat's other facilities: The Paradise Edge, a grassy point with rocky shores on both side, is a popular venue for weddings; the Fire Pit, an outdoor lounge, has banquettes set around a fire in the center; Wired, the business center, is fitted with work stations, laptops, printers, scanners, fax machines, audio/visual and telecommunications equipment, high speed Internet access; and The Store is the W brand gift shop.

And not to be overlooked, W Hotels brings to this island Retreat, its signature Whatever/Whenever service, providing guests with whatever they want—from beachside yoga at sunrise to private jet service from Puerto Rico, whenever they want it—as long as it's legal.

W RETREAT & SPA, VIEQUES ISLAND
SR 200, KM 3.2; HCI Box 9368, Vieques, Puerto Rico 00765
Phone: (954) 624-1768, (787) 741-4100; www.wvieques.com
Owner: REIG Capital and Vieques Hotel Partners, LLC
General Manager: Greg White
Open: Year-round
US Reservations: (877) WHOTELS; wvieques.reservations@whotels.com
Distance from Airport: 1 mile from Antonio Rivera Rodríguez Airport
Distance from Capital: 2 miles from Isabel Segunda
Accommodations: 157 rooms and suites (136 rooms, 21 suites) with balcony/patio; connecting rooms
Children: All ages
Rates: Per room, per night, double: *High Season* (Jan–Apr): from $589. *Low Season* (May–mid-Dec): from $289.
Service Charge: $60 per night
Government Tax: 7 percent

St. Lucia
CALABASH COVE RESORT & SPA
Gros Islet, St. Lucia

Tucked into a hillside that falls to a reef-protected beach on the northwest coast of St. Lucia, the Calabash Cove Resort & Spa is a few minutes south of Rodney Bay and Pigeon Island, the main venue for the St. Lucia Jazz festival. Designed to harmonize with its beautiful natural surroundings, the boutique resort nestles in the sheltered bay of Bonaire Estate in an amphitheatre of the tropical vegetation.

The Manor House, the main building at the top of the hill, has the lobby, restaurant, bar, library, and boutique. Below is Sweetwaters, the large infinity-edge swimming pool with a swim-up bar at one end and a full-service spa and fitness center along side the other end.

Along the beach are the Waters Edge Cottages, all but hidden in the lush vegetation and perfectly situated to view the island's glorious sunsets. Natural elements used in the buildings are represented in the exotic wood, stone and natural materials. The tranquil gardens, cared for by a fine landscape architect, optimize the natural splendor of the area and attract a variety of birds.

Opened in late 2009, Calabash Cove has 26 spacious suites, all with a Jacuzzi and either a terrace or patio and views of the bay. All are air-conditioned and furnished with a king-size bed plus a daybed in most; large deluxe bathroom, some with marbletop counters, shower, mini bar, large flat screen television, high speed Internet access, DVD, telephone, coffee/tea makers, and private balcony or patio with teak tables and chairs. The cottages have a private pool, an outdoor rain shower, and a hammock.

Calabash Cove's distinctive accommodations of rustic elegance come in four categories and include the nine handcrafted teak and Balinese mahogany Waters Edge Cottages, all with a private plunge pool and a Jacuzzi. The Balinese-style cottages (1,000 square feet) have a bedroom and separate living room, large patio, and porch. These hideaways also have outdoor rain shower and hammock surrounded by tropical flora, frequently visited by hummingbirds.

Most of the 7 Sunset Junior suites are located on the first and second floors of the Manor House and a neighboring one on the hillside above the pool. Four Swim-Up Junior suites (620 square feet), so called because they are located alongside the infinity-edge swimming pool and have steps from their patios that descend directly into the pool. From your patio you can swim across to the bar to watch the sunset or take a romantic midnight swim. Six Ocean View Junior suites are situated next to the main building and overlook the beach. All the junior suites have a private balcony, spacious living area extending from the bedroom, and large deluxe bathrooms.

Set on a terrace of the Manor House and open to the breezes and panoramic views, the Windsong Restaurant serves international cuisine with an Asian influence and specializes in seasonally inspired dishes made from fresh local products. It is open for breakfast, lunch, and dinner. The C C Bar, a cozy cocktail bar overlooking Bonaire Bay, offers appetizers as well as fine wines from the Calabash Cove Cellars, along with lively island music and great vistas of the coast and sea.

The Ti Spa provides massages, body treatments, yoga, meditation, and Pilates by professionally trained therapists. A beautician and aesthetician for both men and women are available on request. Revitalizing treatments combine European technique with St. Lucia's rich tradition of plant- and fruit-based cures. For example, a coconut and sugar scrub, an exfoliating treatment, uses coconut milk and oil, and is based on a tradition St. Lucian mothers use to keep their babies' skin supple. Treatments can be enjoyed in the spa or in the privacy of your suite. The Fitness Center is outfitted with Cybex cardiovascular equipment, and a full beauty salon offers hair treatments and manicure/pedicure services.

Whispers, the library, is a peaceful retreat where guests can enjoy music and books. Next door is Memories of Calabash, the resort's signature shop offering its own designer wear, knick knacks, and quality St. Lucian handicrafts.

The Cove Gardens, a labyrinth of groves and terraces where quiet walkways ablaze in local flora lead to a miniature cane field, pineapple bed, banana patches, and the resort's herb garden that supplies the kitchen, also lead to the custom-designed boardwalk and gazebo. One walkway by the Manor House ends at a gazebo, a popular venue for weddings; another walkway goes down to the pier, another wedding venue.

In addition to the resort's swimming, snorkeling, and kayaking, guests can chose from the array of activities that St. Lucia offers: diving, golf, soaking in the hot springs, a cable ride over a rain forest canopy, turtle watching, rock climbing, and cooling off under a waterfall. Whatever you wish, resort's leisure concierge will make the arrangements.

Calabash Cove is big on weddings and has a Wedding Program that includes an outdoor ceremony at the location of your choice—the pier, the beach, the gazebo, or the Cove Gardens bridge; a marriage officer, your choice wedding cake, tropical bridal bouquet and boutonniere, reception table arrangements, wedding dinner for two, chilled French champagne, regular legal fees, marriage license, certificate and registrar fees, witness if required, and a romantic champagne breakfast served in your room the following morning—for $1,250. The resort also offers other services, such as photography and videography, reception, and live entertainment for an additional fee.

CALABASH COVE RESORT & SPA

Bonaire Estates, Marisule, St. Lucia, W.I.
Phone: (758) 456-3500; **Fax:** (758) 450-4603; e-mail info@calabashcove .com; www.calabashcove.com
Owner: Private European partnership
Managing Director: Konard Wagner
Open: Year-round
US Reservations: reservations@calabash cove.com or (847) 841-7860

Minimum Stay: 5 nights; some days are subject to availability
Arrival/Departure: One-way, air-conditioned car transfer to hotel from George FL Charles Airport (Castries) $35 one way, from Hewanorra International $85–$150 per couple; helicopter transfer from Hewanorra to GFL Charles plus car to resort $320 per couple
Distance from Airport: From Hewanorra International, 1-and-a-half to 2 hours by car; from GFL Charles Airport, 30 minutes by car (see above for prices)
Distance from capital: 8 miles; taxi one-way, $40
Accommodations: 26 villas (9 cottages with plunge pool, 7 junior, 4 swim-up junior, 6 oceanview) all with Jacuzzi
Children: Children age 6 years or younger stay free in their parents' room; ages 7 to 16 half price. Some room categories not suitable for children; maximum of 2 children per room
Meetings and Packages: Destination wedding, family or corporate affair for up to 52 guests on all-inclusive package, $21,500 winter 2012; $17,000 summer; $23,000 winter 2013. Rates are per day plus tax and service charge.
Rates: Per room, double, per night. *High Season* (Jan 3–Apr 15): $445–$795. *Low Season* (Apr 16–Dec 22): $385–$565. *Christmas* (Dec 22–Jan 6): $520–$875. Rates include island breakfast buffet. All-Inclusive and singles rates, inquire.
Service Charge: 10 percent
Government Tax: 8 percent

St. Vincent
BUCCAMENT BAY RESORT
Buccament Bay, St. Vincent

St. Vincent's first large, luxury hotel, Buccament Bay Resort, is a member of Harlequin Hotels & Resorts, based in the Cayman Islands, and the group's fifth development in the Caribbean.

Located about an hour's drive from Kingston, the island's capital, the resort fronts the beautiful white sand beach of Buccament Bay; in the background rise the island's magnificent rain forest-clad mountains; and in-between stretch green valleys profuse with banana, papaya, and other tropical fruit trees. Buccament Bay Resort is designed as an active family destination and offers an impressive variety of sports and activities for a range of ages and interests as well as some unusual facilities. Among them are the Liverpool Football Club Soccer School, Pat Cash Tennis Academy, and the Harlequin Performing Arts Academy.

Accommodations range from one- to four-bedroom suites in low rise villas, all with plunge pools. Each is fitted with a king-size bed, dressed in fine white cotton linens against dark wood frames and furniture with neutral tones and rich color accents. The master bedroom has a large bathroom with a power shower, quality towels, and bathrobes. All are air-conditioned and equipped with a 40-inch LCD television offering 65 digital channels and 12 music channels, iPod dock, hair dryer, iron/ironing board, safe, direct dial telephone with voice mail, fridge with bottles of water, espresso machine, tea maker, turndown service, and free Wi-Fi Internet access.

The one-bedroom villas (850 to 900 square feet) are situated in tropical gardens and have a spacious living room with a high vaulted wood ceiling and dark wooden shutters that open onto a deck and plunge pool. The two bedroom villas (1,388 to 1,672 square feet) are similar with a king-size bed in one bedroom and twin beds in the other; each bedroom has its own bathroom. They also have access for disabled persons. The Plantation Villas (2,448 square feet) are four-bedroom units, well-suited for families or a group of friends, and enjoy sea views. Two master bedrooms are furnished with king-size beds, while the other two bedrooms have twin beds; each bedroom has its own bathroom. The resort offers concierge service 24/7 where guests can pick up newspapers, DVD players, and game consoles and choose from a library of DVDs and video games; board games and books are also available.

The resort has seven restaurants and bars: Arlecchino, a sophisticated setting for fine dining overlooking the waterfront, serves Italian cuisine emphasizing fresh ingredients and complemented by a large selection of Italian wines. Bamboo, a barefoot chic bar and restaurant under the palms, offers al fresco dining along with ocean views and typical Caribbean concoctions, draft beer, and wine by the glass. Ginger & Co. specializes in Asian cuisine with Singaporean, Japanese, and Malaysian influences, prepared in its show kitchen. It also offers Oriental-inspired cocktails and a sake menu. The luxurious decor of natural colors has wasabi green and orange highlights, a tranquil water feature, and Thai Buddha statues.

Jack's features local seafood and prime steaks prepared on a wood-burning grill in an open kitchen. Guests can pair their entrée with a wine from the restaurant's international wine collection showcased in its wine cellar. HQ, Harlequin's signature coffee shop, offers espressos and lattes with beans roasted especially for HQ, and a selection of Harney & Sons fine teas. Freshly baked croissants and pastries and fruit and vegetable juices and smoothies are blended to order. And for an afternoon treat, there's ice cream and sorbets. More treats can be had at the Bay Beach Club and Trader Vic's.

Along the Caribbean-washed beach and waterfront terraces are two swimming pools with loungers, umbrellas, waiter service and a children's pool. Little Harlequins Kids provides day care for young children with supervised, age-appropriate activities, toys, and games.

The Spa at Buccament Bay Resort offers ESPA treatments in four treatment suites or outdoors in a Thai pavilion or under a gazebo on the beach. It also has a beauty salon for hair and nail care. The Harlequin Fitness Centre is equipped with cardiovascular and physical training equipment by Technogym. Personal trainers hold daily group sessions in yoga, Pilates, spinning, and other methods. Private instruction can be arranged. A two-hour Individual Fitness Assessment costs $95; a Personal Training package for long-term fitness runs $70 per hour.

The Harlequin Sports Academy offers expert soccer and tennis coaching for children and adults. A series of exercises and circuit training on the resort's professional soccer ground is designed to improve strength, agility, and skill while boosting cardiovascular fitness. Suitable for adults and children over 14 years old who are already in training, the fee is $70 per hour.

The Pat Cash Tennis Academy provides training and coaching programs for all levels of skill. Cash is expected to hold coaching clinics and play in exhibition matches at the resort throughout the year. When there is no instruction, the tennis courts and artificial football pitch are available for use by guests. Pat Cash, a tennis star in the 1980s, crowned his career in 1987 by defeating Number 1, Ivan Lendl, to become Wimbledon Champion. He is a five times Grand Slam finalist, twice Davis Cup winner, and a television commentator.

Indigo Dive, a PADI facility, offers courses and dive trips for all levels of experience. Snorkeling, kayaking, boating, deep-sea fishing, dolphin and whale-watching are also available.

The resort's business center can provide Internet access, printing, copying, scanning, facsimile. A selection of gifts, branded clothing for the resort, Pat Cash Tennis Academy, and Liverpool Football Club Soccer School, jewelry, and swimwear can be purchased in the boutiques of retail village.

Buccament Bay Resort's most unusual amenity for a Caribbean resort is the Harlequin Performing Arts Academy where children and adults are coached in voice, acting, and movement by professionals from London's West End and Broadway in master classes based on popular hit musicals.

BUCCAMENT BAY RESORT

Buccament Bay, St. Vincent and the Grenadines
Phone: US (877) 502-2022; U.K. 01-268-242-467; **e-mail:** contact@harlequinhotelsandresorts.com; www.buccamentbay.com
Owner: Harlequin Hotels & Resorts, Ltd.
General Manager: Mark Sawkins
Open: Year-round
US Reservations: reservations@buccamentbay.com
Deposit: 100 percent at time of booking
Minimum Stay: 3 nights
Arrival/Departure: Roundtrip airport transfers included in price
Distance from Airport: E. T. Joshua Airport, 1-hour drive
Distance from capital: 45-minute drive from Kingstown
Accommodations: 115 villas/suites, all with deck and plunge pools; another 200 to be completed in 2012
Children: All ages; Little Harlequin Kids provides supervised, age-appropriate activities
Day Visitors: $50 per child under 12; $150 per adult
Rates: Per room, per night, double: *High Season* (Jan–Apr): from $1,424. *Low Season:* from $1,365.
Service Charge: Included
Government Tax: Included

INDEX

THE BEST OF THE BEST

This chart is not intended to be a complete inventory of each resort's facilities. Instead, it indicates the especially strong features of each establishment. For example, most beachside resorts in this book offer scuba diving or can arrange it; however, the chart notes only those resorts focused primarily on diving or that have a particularly outstanding dive facility.

Resort	Beachside	Hillside	All-inclusive	Budget	Value	Honeymoon	Romantic	Wedding	Children's Program	Families	Singles	Sports/Active	Dive	Golf	Tennis	Marina	Spa/Fitness Center	Nature Lovers	Hiking	Birding	History	Cuisine	Entertainment	Casino
Almond Morgan Bay (St. Lucia)	•	•		•					•	•	•	•												
Altamer (Anguilla)	•	•				•											•							
Amanyara (Turks & Caicos Islands)	•					•						•						•						
Anacaona Boutique (Anguilla)	•						•			•														
Anse Chastanet (St. Lucia)	•	•				•	•	•					•	•				•	•	•				
Asa Wright (Trinidad)		•		•	•							•						•	•	•				
Bakoua (Martinique)	•					•	•					•												
Baoase Luxury Resort (Curaçao)	•						•																	
Biras Creek (British VI)	•	•				•	•	•		•				•	•		•	•	•	•				
Bitter End (British VI)	•	•			•	•		•	•	•	•	•	•			•								
Body Holiday, The (St. Lucia)	•	•	•									•	•	•	•		•		•					
Breezes Grand Negril (Jamaica)	•	•			•			•				•	•	•										
Breezes Runaway (Jamaica)	•		•	•	•							•			•	•		•						
British Colonial Hilton (Bahamas)	•						•					•	•								•			
Buccament Bay (St. Vincent)	•								•	•		•	•		•									
Buccaneer (USVI)	•					•	•	•	•	•		•			•						•			
Calabash (Grenada)	•						•											•						
Calabash Cove (St. Lucia)	•	•				•	•	•																
Caneel Bay (USVI)	•					•	•	•	•	•					•		•	•	•	•				
Cap Juluca (Anguilla)	•					•	•	•							•		•					•		
Cap Maison (St. Lucia)	•	•				•	•			•														
Capt. Don's Habitat (Bonaire)	•		•									•	•					•						
Carlisle Bay (Antigua)	•					•	•			•					•									
Casa Colonial (Dominican Republic)	•					•	•																	
Casa de Campo (Dominican Republic)	•					•	•		•	•		•		•	•	•	•	•					•	•
Cobblers Cove (Barbados)	•					•	•								•									
Coco Palm (St. Lucia)				•	•			•	•								•							
Coral Reef Club (Barbados)	•					•			•	•	•	•			•		•					•	•	•

376

	Beachside	Hillside	All-inclusive	Budget	Value	Honeymoon	Romantic	Wedding	Children's Program	Families	Singles	Sports/Active	Dive	Golf	Tennis	Marina	Spa/Fitness Center	Nature Lovers	Hiking	Birding	History	Cuisine	Entertainment	Casino
Cotton House (The Grenadines)	•					•	•					•			•		•		•			•		
Couples San Souci (Jamaica)	•	•	•			•	•					•			•		•							
Couples Swept Away (Jamaica)	•		•	•	•		•					•	•	•	•		•						•	
CuisinArt (Anguilla)	•				•		•					•			•		•					•		
Curaçao Marriott Luxury Resort (Curaçao)	•				•		•	•	•			•	•		•		•						•	•
Curtain Bluff (Antigua)	•	•	•			•		•				•			•		•		•	•				
Dunmore, The (Bahamas)	•									•														
Eden Rock (St. Barts)	•					•	•										•					•		
El Conquistador (Puerto Rico)	•	•				•		•	•	•	•	•	•	•	•	•	•						•	•
El Convento (Puerto Rico)				•	•		•			•											•			
El San Juan (Puerto Rico)	•					•		•	•	•		•			•		•					•	•	•
Fairmount Royal Pavilion (Barbados)	•					•	•	•				•			•		•							
Four Seasons Nevis (Nevis)	•	•				•			•	•		•	•	•	•		•		•					
Frangipani (The Grenadines)	•	•								•														
Gallery Inn (Puerto Rico)		•				•						•									•			
Galley Bay (Antigua)	•	•			•	•						•			•		•	•		•				
GoldenEye Hotel (Jamaica)	•				•	•	•										•			•				
Golden Rock (Nevis)		•	•			•	•		•	•								•	•					
Grace Bay Club (Turks & Caicos)	•				•	•		•	•			•	•	•			•					•		
Graycliff (Bahamas)		•			•	•	•			•				•						•	•			
Green Turtle (Bahamas)	•			•					•	•		•			•	•	•							
Guana Island (British VI)	•	•	•			•			•			•			•			•	•	•				
Half Moon (Jamaica)	•					•	•	•	•	•		•	•	•	•		•					•		
Hermitage Bay (Antigua)	•	•	•			•		•				•			•		•		•					
Hôtel Guanahani (St. Barts)	•	•				•	•					•			•		•				•			
Hyatt Regency Aruba (Aruba)	•					•			•	•		•	•	•	•		•						•	•
Isle de France (St. Barts)	•	•				•		•		•		•			•		•				•			
Jamaica Inn (Jamaica)	•	•				•	•			•		•			•		•				•			
Jumby Bay (Antigua)	•					•	•	•	•	•		•	•		•		•		•	•				
Kura Hulanda (Curaçao)				•	•		•			•		•					•				•			
La Concha (Puerto Rico)	•					•			•		•	•					•						•	•
Ladera (St. Lucia)		•				•	•	•									•	•	•	•				
La Samanna (St. Martin)	•	•				•	•	•		•			•		•		•					•		
La Source (Grenada)	•		•	•								•	•		•		•							
Le Cap Est Lagoon (Martinique)	•					•	•								•		•					•		
Le Sereno (St. Barts)	•					•	•	•			•						•					•		
Le Toiny (St. Barts)		•					•													•	•			
Le Village St. Jean (St. Barts)	•			•						•														
Lighthouse Bay (Barbuda)	•					•	•										•							

	Beachside	Hillside	All-inclusive	Budget	Value	Honeymoon	Romantic	Wedding	Children's Program	Families	Singles	Sports/Active	Dive	Golf	Tennis	Marina	Spa/Fitness Center	Nature Lovers	Hiking	Birding	History	Cuisine	Entertainment	Casino
Maho Bay (USVI)	•	•	•							•	•							•	•					
Malliouhana (Anguilla)	•	•				•	•		•	•		•			•		•							
Meridian Club (Turks & Caicos Islands)	•		•			•				•								•	•	•				
Montpelier Plantation (Nevis)		•				•						•						•	•	•				
Mount Cinnamon (Grenada)	•	•								•		•												
Nisbet Plantation (Nevis)	•					•	•	•							•					•				
One&Only Ocean Club (Bahamas)	•					•								•	•		•							
Ottley's Plantation (St. Kitts)		•				•											•	•	•					
Palm Island (The Grenadines)	•	•				•	•				•	•					•		•					
Parrot Cay (Turks & Caicos)	•					•	•										•	•						
Peter Island (British VI)	•	•				•	•				•		•	•		•	•	•	•	•				
Petit St. Vincent (The Grenadines)	•		•			•	•					•												
Pirates Point (Cayman Islands)	•	•								•	•						•		•					
Regent Palms, The (Turks & Caicos Islands)	•					•	•	•	•					•										
Renaissance Curaçao (Curaçao)	•									•							•							•
Renaissance Jaragua (Dominican Republic)						•	•			•	•				•							•	•	•
Ritz-Carlton Grand Cayman (Cayman Islands)	•									•	•	•	•									•		
Ritz-Carlton Rose Hall (Jamaica)	•							•	•	•		•	•	•	•		•					•		
Ritz-Carlton San Juan (Puerto Rico)	•					•					•			•		•	•					•	•	•
Ritz-Carlton St. Thomas (USVI)	•	•				•			•	•				•			•							
Rockhouse (Jamaica)		•		•	•	•						•						•						
Rosewood Little Dix (British VI)	•					•			•	•	•				•	•	•	•	•					
Round Hill (Jamaica)	•	•				•	•	•		•		•			•		•							
St. Regis Bahia Beach (Puerto Rico)	•					•			•	•	•			•			•		•	•				
Sandals Grande Emerald Bay (Bahamas)	•					•			•	•	•	•		•	•									
Sandals Royal Plantation (Jamaica)	•		•			•		•							•		•							
Sandcastle (British VI)	•		•			•						•						•						
Scrub Island (British VI)	•									•	•					•	•							
Small Hope Bay (Bahamas)	•		•	•		•	•	•					•					•	•					
Spice Island (Grenada)	•	•			•	•					•	•						•						
Strawberry Hill (Jamaica)		•				•												•	•	•		•		
Sugar Mill (British VI)	•	•				•																•		
Sugar Ridge (Antigua)		•								•							•							
Tensing Pen (Jamaica)				•	•	•	•					•						•						
Tortuga Bay (Dominican Republic)	•						•	•						•										
Tryall Club (Jamaica)	•	•						•				•	•	•	•	•					•			
Twelve Degrees North (Grenada)	•	•		•						•								•						
W Retreat & Spa (Vieques)	•					•	•				•			•			•							
Young Island (St. Vincent)	•	•				•	•							•				•	•	•				

PHOTO CREDITS

Altamer (p. 2) Courtesy of Altamer Resort, Anguilla

Anacoana Boutique Hotel (p. 6) Courtesy of Susan Croft

Cap Juluca (p. 9) Courtesy of Cap Juluca, Anguilla

CuisinArt Resort & Spa (p. 12) Courtesy of CuisinArt Golf Resort & Spa, Anguilla

Malliouhana (p. 15) Courtesy of Malliouhana Hotel and Spa, Anguilla

Carlisle Bay (p. 20) Courtesy of Carlisle Bay, Antigua

Curtain Bluff (p. 23) Courtesy of James Callaghan and Curtain Bluff Resort, Antigua

Hermitage Bay (p. 30) Courtesy of Hermitage Bay, Antigua

Jumby Bay (p. 32) Courtesy of Jumby Bay, A Rosewood Resort

Lighthouse Bay (p. 36) Courtesy of Lighthouse Bay, Barbuda

Green Turtle Club Resort (p. 44) Courtesy of Green Turtle Club Resort, Abacos

Small Hope Bay Lodge (p. 47) Courtesy of Small Hope Bay Lodge, Andros

Sandals Grande Emerald Bay (p. 50) Courtesy of Sandals Resorts

The Dunmore (p. 53) Courtesy of The Dunmore, Harbour Island

British Colonial Hilton (p. 56) Courtesy of VRX Studios

One&Only (p. 61) Courtesy of One&Only Ocean Club, Nassau

Cobblers Cove (p. 67) Courtesy of Cobblers Cove, Barbados

Coral Reef Club (p. 69) Courtesy of Coral Reef Club, Barbados

Fairmont Royal Pavilion (p. 73) Courtesy of Fairmont Hotels & Resorts, Barbados

Captain Don's Habitat (p. 77) Courtesy of Captain Don's Habitat, Bonaire

Guana Island (p. 84) Courtesy of Guana Island, Tortola, B.V.I.

Peter Island (p. 88) Courtesy of Peter Island Resort & Spa, Tortola

Sugar Mill Hotel (p. 92) Courtesy of Sugar Mill Hotel, Tortola

Biras Creek Resort (p. 95) Courtesy of Biras Creek Resort, Virgin Gorda

Bitter End Yacht Club (p. 98) Courtesy of The Bitter End Yacht Club, Virgin Gorda

Rosewood Little Dix Bay (p. 102) Courtesy of Rosewood Little Dix Bay, Virgin Gorda

The Ritz-Carlton, Grand Cayman (p. 106) Courtesy of The Ritz-Carlton

Pirates Point Resort (p. 109) Courtesy of Pirate's Point Resort, Little Cayman

Curaçao Marriott Beach Resort & Emerald Casino (p. 113) Courtesy of Marriott

Hotel Kura Hulanda (p. 116) Courtesy of Hotel Kura Hulanda, Curaçao

Renaissance Curaçao (p. 120) Courtesy of Renaissance Curaçao Resort & Casino

Casa de Campo (p. 124) Courtesy of Casa de Campo, La Romana, Dominican Republic

Casa Colonial Beach & Spa (p. 129) Courtesy of Casa Colonial Beach & Spa, Puerto Plata

Tortuga Bay (p. 132) Courtesy of Tortuga Bay at PUNTACANA Resort & Club

The Calabash Hotel (p. 139) Courtesy of The Calabash Hotel, Grenada

Mount Cinnamon (p. 144) Courtesy of Mount Cinnamon Resort, Grenada

Spice Island (p. 147) Courtesy of Spice Island Beach Resort, Grenada

Twelve Degrees North (p. 150) Courtesy of Joseph Gaylord

Strawberry Hill (p. 154) Courtesy of Island Outpost

The Ritz-Carlton Rose Hall (p. 160) Courtesy of The Ritz-Carlton

Round Hill Hotel and Villas (p. 163) Courtesy of Round Hill, Montego Bay

Tryall Club (p. 167) Courtesy of Robert Manella

Breezes Grand Negril Resort & Spa (p. 170) Courtesy of Breezes Grand Negril

Couples Swept Away (p. 179) Courtesy of Couples Resorts

Rockhouse Hotel and Restaurant (p. 177) Courtesy of Rockhouse Hotel and Restaurant

Couples Sans Souci (p. 182) Courtesy of
Couples Resorts

GoldenEye (p. 185) Courtesy of Island
Outpost

Jamaica Inn (p. 189) Courtesy of Jamaica Inn,
Ochos Rios

Sandals Royal Plantation (p. 192) Courtesy of
Sandals Resorts

Breezes Runaway Bay Resort, Spa, &
Golf Club (p. 195) Courtesy of Breezes
Runaway Bay

Le Cap Est Lagoon Resort and Spa (p. 202)
Courtesy of Le Cap Est Lagoon Resort and
Spa, Martinique

Montpelier Plantation (p. 212) Courtesy of
Natalie Tkachuk

Nisbet Plantation Beach Club (p. 216)
Courtesy of David Massey Photography

El Conquistador Resort & Golden Door Spa
(p. 220) Courtesy of El Conquistador, A
Waldorf-Astoria Resort

The Gallery Inn (Galeria San Juan) (p. 226)
Courtesy of The Gallery Inn, Old San Juan

La Concha (p. 232) Courtesy of La Concha,
A Renaissance Resort

El San Juan Hotel & Casino (p. 235)
Courtesy of El San Juan Hotel & Casino, A
Waldorf-Astoria Resort

The Ritz-Carlton San Juan (p. 239) Courtesy
of The Ritz-Carlton

Eden Rock (p. 243) Courtesy of Eden Rock,
St. Barts

Hôtel Guanahani (p. 246) Courtesy of
Laurent Benoit

Hotel Saint-Barth Isle de France (p. 250)
Courtesy of Jean-Philippe Piter

Le Serano (p. 253) Courtesy of Le Serano, St.
Barts

Le Toiny (p. 255) Courtesy of Le Toiny, St.
Barts

Le Village St. Jean Hotel (p. 257) Courtesy of
Olivier Leroi

Ottley's Plantation Inn (p. 262) Courtesy of
Ottley's Plantation Inn, St. Kitts

Almond Morgan Bay (p. 266) Courtesy of
Almond Resorts, St. Lucia

Anse Chastanet Resort and Jade Mountain (p.
268) Courtesy of Jade Mountain Resort,
St. Lucia

The Body Holiday at LeSport (p. 273)
Courtesy of The Body Holiday, St. Lucia

Cap Maison (p. 277) Courtesy of Cap
Maison, St. Lucia

Coco Palm (p. 280) Courtesy of Micah Spears

Ladera (p. 283) Courtesy of Ladera

La Samanna (p. 288) Courtesy of Orient-
Express Hotels

Young Island (p. 293) Courtesy of Willie
Alleyne Photography

The Frangipani Hotel (p. 296) Courtesy
Wilfred Dederer

The Cotton House (p. 299) Courtesy of The
Mustique Company

Palm Island Beach Club (p. 302) Courtesy of
Palm Island Beach Club, Palm Island

Petit St. Vincent Resort (p. 305) Courtesy of
Neil Selkirk Photography

Asa Wright Nature Centre (p. 310) Courtesy
of Jerry Lower & Mary Kate Leming,
Caligo Ventures

Amanyara (p. 314) Courtesy of Amanresorts

Grace Bay Club (p. 318) Courtesy of Grace
Bay Resorts

The Meridian Club on Pine Cay (p. 322)
Courtesy of Christine Morden

Parrot Cay (p. 326) Courtesy of COMO
Hotels and Resorts

The Regent Palms (p. 330) Courtesy of
Regent Hotels & Resorts

The Buccaneer (p. 335) Courtesy of The
Buccaneer Hotel, St. Croix

Caneel Bay (p. 338) Courtesy of Caneel Bay,
A Rosewood Resort

Frenchman's Reef and Morning Star Marriott
(p. 346) Courtesy of Frenchman's Reef and
Morning Star Marriott Resort, St. Thomas

The Ritz-Carlton St. Thomas (p. 349)
Courtesy of The Ritz-Carlton

Sugar Ridge (p. 353) Courtesy of Alexis
Andrews

Scrub Island (p. 356) Courtesy of Scrub
Island Resort, Spa, & Marina, BVI

Baoase (p. 359) Courtesy of Baoase, Curaçao

Calabash Cove (p. 367) Courtesy of Mikael
Lamber

Buccament Bay (p. 370) Courtesy of
Buccament Bay Resort, St. Vincent

ABOUT THE AUTHOR

Kay Showker is a veteran writer, photographer, and lecturer on travel. Her assignments have taken her to more than 100 countries in the Caribbean and around the world. She has appeared as a travel expert on CNN, ABC, CBS, and NBC, and radio stations across the country, as well as guest host on America Online and the Travel Channel.

She has authored 14 travel guides, including *Caribbean Ports of Call* (winner of the Best Guidebook Award by the Caribbean Tourism Organization); and the *Unofficial Guide to Cruises* (named "The Best Guidebook of the Year" by the Lowell Thomas Travel Awards when it was first published in 1996); *The Outdoor Travelers Guide to the Caribbean* (Lowell Thomas Travel Awards, silver). She served as a senior editor at *Travel Weekly* and has written for such leading travel publications as *National Geographic Traveler, Travel and Leisure,* and *Caribbean Travel and Life,* among others. She was a member of America Online's creative team for *Cruise Critic,* for which she wrote the "Ports of Call" segment.

A native of Kingsport, Tennessee, Ms. Showker received a master's degree in international affairs from the School of Advanced International Studies of Johns Hopkins University in Washington, D.C., and a B.A. from Mary Washington University; she also studied at the American University at Cairo, Cairo University, and Georgetown University. She is the recipient of numerous awards for her travel writing and was the first recipient of the Caribbean Tourism Organization's Journalism Award; the first journalist to receive the Sucrier d'Or—a professional achievement award given by the government of Martinique. She is a member of the Society of American Travel Writers, the American Society of Journalists and Authors, and the New York Travel Writers Association. She has served as a consultant to government and private organizations on travel and tourism.

Ms. Showker lives in New York City and St. Petersburg, Florida.

A Word of Thanks

When a book covers 100 resorts on 40 islands, it goes almost without saying that the author needs the help of many people to complete the task. I am certainly no exception. This book has required an incredible amount of research, discussions with knowledgeable people, and follow-up. Dozens of people were tireless in their efforts to help me. I only wish I could name them all, but I would be remiss not to mention some.

First, I would like to express my everlasting gratitude to the late Marcella Martinez of Marcella Martinez Associates, New York, and her staff, who helped me every step of the way.

The questionnaire for the Green Leaf Awards was based on months of discussions with environmentalists, experienced hotel managers, architects, and others working in the conservation field. But none of it would have been possible without the help of Stan Selengut, the proprietor of Maho Bay Camp and a recognized authority and adviser to governments and tourism officials around the world on ecotourism, and Peggy Bendel of Development Counsellors International, whose work for the US Virgin Islands formed the basis of my questionnaire.

Others who made generous efforts on my behalf are Kim Duvall-Hutchinson, Premier World Marketing, Miami; Mary Brennan and Roberta Garzaroli, The Atrebor Group, New York; staffs of Adams Unlimited, New York; Laura Davidson Public Relations, New York; Cheryl Andrews Marketing, Coral Gables, Florida, and most of the general managers and their resort staffs included in the book.

Suzanne McManus, Jamaica, advised and helped me with the research on all the resorts in Jamaica. Katharine Gordon Dyson not only helped me edit much of the material in the book but also contributed Sandcastle (Jost Van Dyke, B.V.I.) and Mount Cinnamon (Grenada). Because the time constraints of writing and updating this book made it impossible for me to revisit every resort prior to my deadline, as I had wanted to do, I called on my writing colleagues for help. Some contributed specific material written for this book; others allowed me to use material from articles published elsewhere recently. In every case they are writers who specialize in the Caribbean and are as qualified as I am to write this book.